Constructionism in Practice
Designing, Thinking, and Learning in a Digital World

Constructionism in Practice
Designing, Thinking, and Learning in a Digital World

Edited by

Yasmin Kafai
University of California, Los Angeles

Mitchel Resnick
Massachusetts Institute of Technology

Routledge
Taylor & Francis Group
New York   London

First published by Lawrence Erlbaum Associates, Inc., Publishers
10 Industrial Avenue
Mahwah, New Jersey 07430

Reprinted 2008 by Routledge
Routledge
Taylor & Francis Group
270 Madison Avenue
New York, NY 10016

Routledge
Taylor & Francis Group
2 Park Square
Milton Park, Abingdon
Oxon OX14 4RN

Library of Congress Cataloging-in-Publication Data
Constructionism in practice : designing, thinking, and learning in a
   digital world / edited by Yasmin Kafai and Mitchel Resnick.
        p.   cm.
    Includes bibliographical references and indexes.
    ISBN 0-8058-1984-3 (cloth).—ISBN 0-8058-1985-1 (pbk.)
    1. Constructivism (Education) 2. Learning, Psychology of.
3. Social learning. 4. Instructional systems—Design. 5. Computer-
assisted instruction. 6. System theory. I. Kafai, Yasmin
Bettina. II. Resnick, Mitchel.
LB1590.3.C666   1996
370.15'23—dc20   95-44813
                                                        CIP

Publisher's Note
The publisher has gone to great lengths to ensure the quality of this
reprint but points out that some imperfections in the original
may be apparent.

In memory of Greg Gargarian, whose ideas and playful spirit enriched our work and lives for many years.
We miss you, Greg.

Contents

List of Contributors

Edith Ackermann
Laboratoire de Psychologie du
  Développement
Université de Provence
29, Avenue Robert Schuman
13621 Aix-en-Provence, Cedex 1
France

Aaron Brandes
The Media Laboratory
Massachusetts Institute of Technology
20 Ames Street E15-315
Cambridge, Massachusetts 02139-4307

Amy Bruckman
The Media Laboratory
Massachusetts Institute of Technology
20 Ames Street E15-315
Cambridge, Massachusetts 02139-4307

Michele Evard
The Media Laboratory
Massachusetts Institute of Technology
20 Ames Street E15-315
Cambridge, Massachusetts 02139-4307

Gregory Gargarian
The Media Laboratory
Massachusetts Institute of Technology
20 Ames Street E15-315
Cambridge, Massachusetts 02139-4307

Paula Hooper
The Media Laboratory
Massachusetts Institute of Technology
20 Ames Street E15-315
Cambridge, Massachusetts 02139-4307

Yasmin B. Kafai
University of California, Los Angeles
Graduate School of Education
2331 Moore Hall
405 Hilgard Avenue
Los Angeles, California 90024-1521

Fred Martin
The Media Laboratory
Massachusetts Institute of Technology
20 Ames Street E15-315
Cambridge, Massachusetts 02139-4307

Seymour Papert
The Media Laboratory
Massachusetts Institute of Technology
20 Ames Street E15-315
Cambridge, Massachusetts 02139-4307

Mitchel Resnick
The Media Laboratory
Massachusetts Institute of Technology
20 Ames Street E15-315
Cambridge, Massachusetts 02139-4307

Randy Sargent
The Media Laboratory
Massachusetts Institute of Technology
20 Ames Street E15-315
Cambridge, Massachusetts 02139-4307

Alan Shaw
The Media Laboratory
Massachusetts Institute of Technology
20 Ames Street E15-315
Cambridge, Massachusetts 02139-4307

Brian Silverman
Logo Computer Systems, Inc.
3300 Cote Vertu, Suite 201
Montreal, Quebec H4R 2B7
Canada

Uri Wilensky
Tufts University
Lincoln Filene 107
Medford, Massachusetts 02155

Introduction

Yasmin B. Kafai
Mitchel Resnick

In the 1960s, Seymour Papert and colleagues initiated a research project at Massachusetts Institute of Technology (MIT), dedicated to the study of how children think and learn, and to the development of novel educational approaches and technological tools to help children learn new things in new ways.

During the three decades since, that research effort has evolved and grown. One of its technological offspring, the programming language Logo, has been used by tens of millions of schoolchildren all over the world. At the same time, its theoretical foundation, which has become known as *constructionism*, has deeply influenced how educators and researchers think about directions for educational reform—and, within that context, about the roles for technology in learning.

Constructionism is both a theory of learning and a strategy for education. It builds on the "constructivist" theories of Jean Piaget, asserting that knowledge is not simply transmitted from teacher to student, but actively constructed by the mind of the learner. Children don't *get* ideas; they *make* ideas. Moreover, constructionism suggests that learners are particularly likely to make new ideas when they are actively engaged in making some type of external artifact—be it a robot, a poem, a sand castle, or a computer program—which they can reflect upon and share with others. Thus, constructionism involves two intertwined types of construction: the construction of knowledge in the context of building personally meaningful artifacts.

In 1991, Papert's research group at the MIT Media Lab published a collection of papers under the title *Constructionism*, edited by Idit Harel and Seymour Papert.[1] This current collection is, in some ways, a follow-up to the *Construc-*

---

[1]Harel, I., & Papert, S. (1991). *Constructionism.* Norwood, NJ: Ablex.

tionism book. Many of the ideas and projects presented here grew out of research described in *Constructionism*, but this collection also addresses new issues and steers into new directions. Constructionism is not a static set of ideas. Consistent with the theory we are writing about, we as researchers are continually reconstructing and elaborating what we mean by constructionism, and continually constructing new educational activities and tools to help us in that effort. For example, readers will notice a greater emphasis on ideas related to "community" in this volume. Of course, those ideas have always been a part of the Logo research effort, as evidenced by Papert's discussion of samba schools in *Mindstorms*.[2] But they play a more prominent role in many of the chapters herein.

In some ways, constructionist research is challenged by its success. In the 1980s, many constructionist ideas were viewed as radical and out of the mainstream. But today, at educational research conferences, the idea that children actively construct new knowledge is taken almost as gospel, and a growing number of research efforts are studying how children learn through design and invention activities. The challenge is to continue to refine constructionist ideas, and to make sure that these ideas spread not only to members of the educational research community, but also to the classrooms, homes, and community centers where children work, play, and learn.

This volume includes 14 chapters, divided into four sections: Perspectives in Constructionism; Learning Through Design; Learning in Communities; and Learning About Systems. These sections are somewhat arbitrary and possibly misleading, because many of the chapters cut across the boundaries. The section themes, however, provide a general framework for understanding some of the core issues in constructionist research today.

PERSPECTIVES IN CONSTRUCTIONISM

One of the main tenets of constructionism is that learners actively construct and reconstruct knowledge out of their experiences in the world. It places special emphasis on the knowledge construction that takes place when learners are engaged in building objects. Constructionism differs from other learning theories along several dimensions. Whereas most theories describe knowledge acquisition in purely cognitive terms, constructionism sees an important role for affect. It argues that learners are most likely to become intellectually engaged when they are working on *personally meaningful* activities and projects. In constructionist learning, forming new relationships with knowledge is as important as forming new representations of knowledge. Constructionism also emphasizes diversity: It recognizes that learners can make connections with knowledge in many different

---

[2]Papert, S. (1980). *Mindstorms*. New York: Basic Books.

ways. Constructionist learning environments encourage multiple learning styles and multiple representations of knowledge. The chapters in this section explore these core constructionist ideas, further developing the intellectual underpinnings of what we mean by constructionism.

In the first chapter, "A Word for Learning," Seymour Papert wonders why theories of teaching have received far more attention than theories of learning, and he addresses the fundamental issues of what we mean by the word "learning." He invites us to revisit our notions of learning through examining a personal experience. Using the example of learning flower names, Papert illustrates two important aspects of learning: "The simple moral is that learning explodes when you stay with it: A full year had passed before the effect in my mind reached a critical level for an exponential explosion of growth. The more complex moral is that some domains of knowledge, such as plants, are especially rich in connections and particularly prone to give rise to explosions of knowledge" (p. 23). The time to build personal connections is an essential ingredient strikingly absent from most school learning situations.

The next chapter, "Perspective-Taking and Object Construction" by Edith Ackermann, also addresses the issue of relationships with knowledge. Ackermann brings together Piagetian and situated-cognition approaches, illustrating how the alternation between assimilative and accommodative attitudes punctuates an individual's interactions with the world. Drawing on results from the study of perspective-taking, Ackermann argues that the ability to decenter from one's own standpoint and to take another person's point of view requires the construction of cognitive invariants: a recasting of the world's stabilities that transcends any given viewpoint. According to Ackermann, this separation is a necessary step toward the construction of a deeper understanding; adopting a god's eye view is by no means contrary to situating one's own stance in the world. Ackermann notes that the process of learning includes opposites: forging relationships and creating separations at the same time. One cannot relate without, at times, separating.

In chapter 3, "Elementary School Children's Images of Science," Aaron Brandes introduces the framework of *image of science* as a tool for understanding and enhancing children's science learning. Science education research has established that children's science learning depends critically on their ideas about science, scientists, and experimentation. Brandes extends this research to include affective components such as the child's identification with science or alienation from it. He describes three studies with elementary school students, designed to probe children's images of science. The studies show that children's excitement about science decreases with age, even as their ideas about science become, in many ways, more sophisticated. Furthermore, the process by which new knowledge is generated remains mysterious, leaving most children on the "outside" of science. In his conclusions, Brandes proposes criteria for evaluating science activities, based on his images-of-science framework.

LEARNING THROUGH DESIGN

Constructionist theory suggests a strong connection between design and learning: It asserts that activities involving making, building, or programming—in short, designing—provide a rich context for learning. But design and learning have not always been viewed as so closely connected. Theories of design and learning have very different origins. Traditionally, design theorists have been interested primarily in the final product, and in the ways that constraints influence the design of the product. By contrast, learning theorists were interested primarily in process, not product.

Recently, however, theories of learning and design have begun to move toward one another. Both design theorists and learning theorists now view "construction of meaning" as a core process. In this view, design involves building a relationship between designer and object. Designers sort out what objects mean to them or others; then they selectively connect features of an object and features of a context into a coherent unity. The relationships that designers build with objects or situations constitute the core focus of design theory; the final artifact itself is secondary. Design is now viewed as the process through which a designer comes to understand not only objective constraints, but also subjective meanings.

In this way, design theories overlap with constructivist learning theories: Both focus on the construction of meaning. At the same time, learning theorists have begun to pay more attention to the role of product and artifact. Constructionist theory goes beyond Piaget's constructivism in its emphasis on artifacts, asserting that meaning-construction happens particularly well when learners are engaged in building external and sharable artifacts.

Thus, there is a convergence in the fields of design and learning, with a natural intersection in the study of learning-through-design. The chapters in this section aim to contribute to the study of design and learning, exploring the nature of learning through design, its cultural contexts, activities, and tools.

In the first chapter in this section, "Learning Design by Making Games" (chapter 4), Yasmin Kafai examines learning through design in a rather unusual context: video games. These games are a central part of late 20th-century children's culture. In the playing of video games, children mobilize energies that many educators, parents, and researchers wish would be dedicated to learning. Whereas most conventional efforts have sought to harness these energies in the form of playing educational games, Kafai presents a different perspective: in children *making* their own video games instead of *playing* games made by others. In a 6-month project, a class of fourth graders was asked to design computer games for teaching fractions to younger students. In analyzing the students' learning experiences, Kafai focuses on their development of project management skills—how they approached and managed this complex task. The chapter analyzes the students' first steps in beginning the project and framing the design task, then examines their development of programming strategies. The results provide insights into the project's evolution, the different approaches chosen by students, and the potential of support structures for young designers.

In chapter 5, "Electronic Play Worlds," Kafai takes a close look at the video game artifacts designed by children to address the issue of gender differences. In studying the popularity of video games among children, many researchers have focused on explaining why boys, in particular, love playing these games. In this study, Kafai used the process of game design to elicit children's ideas and interests in video games. The students' choices are analyzed and discussed in regard to their game themes, worlds, characters, interactions, feedback, and narrative. The designs of the games reveal clear gender-related differences and provide strong support for design activities as a way for children to express their personal preferences. Conclusions address the potential of game-making environments.

In chapter 6, "The Art of Design," Greg Gargarian examines relationships between design and interpretation, reasoning in dynamic problem contexts, and the role of concept design in artifact design. He sees design (and learning) as a process in which designers customize their working environment around the artifact under design. Furthermore, designers are engaged in the process of situated planning as a means of reducing design problems to conventional ones. To illustrate the intertwined nature of designing and learning, Gargarian presents the *Textile Designer*, a computer-based environment that preserves the qualities found in design environments predating computers. In his final section, Gargarian reflects on the nature of future learning environments that allow for the creation of a commonwealth of skills. The discovery villages, as he calls these design-based learning environments, bring together the arts and the sciences, school and play, and work and life.

In the last chapter of this section, "Building and Learning With Programmable Bricks" (chapter 7), Randy Sargent, Mitchel Resnick, Fred Martin, and Brian Silverman discuss the applications and implications of the Programmable Brick, a tiny, portable computer embedded inside a LEGO brick that is capable of interacting with the physical world in a large variety of ways. Programmable Bricks make possible a wide range of new design activities for students in robotics and ubiquitous computing, a new research field that aims to spread computation throughout the environment by embedding computation in all types of objects and artifacts. The authors describe initial results from three types of applications: building active environments in which children use Programmable Bricks as sensors and regulators, making autonomous creatures that display various behaviors; and doing personal science experiments to monitor and control everyday phenomena. The authors conclude with a list of 20 things to do with Programmable Bricks.

LEARNING IN COMMUNITIES

In the minds of many, Rodin's famous sculpture *The Thinker* provides the proto-typical image of thinking: It shows a person, alone, in deep concentration. This image of the "individual thinker" plays a strong role in our culture. In most school classrooms, children must do worksheets and tests on their own. In the scientific world, Nobel prizes are given to individuals, not teams.

It is not surprising, then, that computers, when they first entered school classrooms, were used primarily for individualized learning. There were debates about "computer as tutor" versus "computer as tool"; but the unspoken consensus was that the computer was a tutor or a tool for an *individual* learner.

In recent years, there has been a surge of interest in the social nature of learning. There is a growing appreciation for the role that communities play in the learning process: Community members act as collaborators, coaches, audience, and co-constructors of knowledge. In current educational research literature, new attention is given to communities of practice, knowledge-building communities, and computer support for collaborative learning.

The idea of community has always been present in the constructionist vision. In *Mindstorms*, written in 1980, Papert discussed the Brazilian samba school as an example of a community of learners. But many of the early constructionist studies focused primarily on the development of the individual learner. It is only in recent years that idea of community has emerged as a major theme in constructionist research. The chapters in this section examine the nature of learning in many types of communities: classroom communities, urban communities, and virtual communities.

In chapter 8, "Social Constructionism and the Inner City," Alan Shaw focuses on the challenges facing underprivileged urban communities. He describes a set of new tools and activities that he has created to support growth and development in a Boston inner-city neighborhood known as Four Corners. Shaw developed a computer networking system called MUSIC (Multi-User Sessions in Community) that neighborhood residents used to discuss community issues and organize community activities. Using a theoretical framework that he calls "social constructionism," Shaw examines how such tools and activities support not only the development of individuals within the community, but the development of the community itself.

Whereas Shaw explores constructionist ideas in the context of a *proximal* (geographically connected) community, Amy Bruckman and Mitchel Resnick explore them in the context of a *virtual* community on the Internet. In "The MediaMOO Project: Constructionism and Professional Community" (chapter 9), Bruckman and Resnick describe a networked virtual-reality environment known as MediaMOO, designed to enhance community among media researchers. In MediaMOO participants not only interact in a virtual world; they help construct (and continually reconstruct) the world in which they interact. Bruckman and

Resnick explore how this combination of construction and community could lead to new possibilities for learning.

Michele Evard examines a different type of network-based community in chapter 10, "A Community of Designers: Learning Through Exchanging Questions and Answers." Evard examines how a computer-based network allowed elementary school children to share ideas with one another during an extended design project. Her study focuses on two classes. In one class, children were designing their own video games. Another class of children, who had already designed games, acted as consultants on the network. The children exchanged questions and answers with one another through a Usenet-style "newsgroup." Evard analyzes usage patterns of the network, examines the nature of interactions among children on the network, and discusses the evolving sense of community among the participants.

Finally, chapter 11, "They Have Their Own Thoughts," Paula Hooper describes her research at an African-centered community school. The school, Paige Academy, aims to create a community and culture rooted in African-American ways of knowing, values, and interactions. Hooper presents a "learning story" of an eight-year-old girl working on a Logo project. The story examines how children, in the process of making new computational artifacts, can take control of their own learning, developing and extending their own ideas. It also highlights the need for school environments to support and legitimize children's own personal ways of thinking with unique mental and physical constructs.

LEARNING ABOUT SYSTEMS

In discussions about computers in education, the focus is usually on *how* children learn. Indeed, some uses of computers can bring about profound changes in how children learn. But often overlooked are the parallel opportunities for transforming *what* children learn. Current school curricula were created in the era of paper and pencil. The current mathematics curriculum, for example, is not necessarily the best nor the most appropriate mathematics for children to learn. Rather, it is the mathematics most accessible with paper and pencil. As new tools and media become available, we must rethink the content of mathematics and other subject domains.

One area ripe for rethinking is the study of *systems*. The world is full of systems (biological, technological, and social) consisting of many interacting parts. Such systems are very difficult to understand, and often impossible to analyze with traditional precollege mathematics. But new computational tools can open up fresh approaches for studying and understanding the behaviors of systems. The chapters in this section expose the barriers to understanding systems concepts (such as feedback and self-organization) and describe computational tools and activities designed to support new ways of thinking about such concepts.

In chapter 12, "New Paradigms for Computing, New Paradigms for Thinking," Mitchel Resnick argues that new computational paradigms (such as object-oriented programming and parallelism) can significantly influence not only how people use computers, but how they make sense of the world. In particular, he describes a parallel-programming language called StarLogo that he designed to help students explore decentralized systems such as bird flocks, traffic jams, and market economies. By building models with StarLogo, students can move beyond the "centralized mindset" and develop a deeper understanding of decentralized systems.

Uri Wilensky (chapter 13) directs StarLogo toward a different goal: to help learners develop their intuitive conceptions of probabilistic ideas. In the chapter, "Making Sense of Probability Through Paradox and Programming," Wilensky presents a case study of a learner who uses programming to help resolve a probability paradox, and in the process develops stronger intuitions about randomness and distribution—and the connections between them. Wilensky's study illustrates that the primary obstacles to learning probability are conceptual and epistemological, and it shows how programming can play a powerful role in learning mathematics by making hidden assumptions explicit and concrete.

In the final chapter, "Ideal and Real Systems," Fred Martin probes students' thinking about systems in the context of a robot-design competition that he helped to design for MIT undergraduates. Martin analyzes how and why undergraduates have trouble developing effective strategies for controlling their robots. He shows that students tend to build robots that perform properly only under ideal conditions, not in the "messiness" of the real world. Martin calls for a change in undergraduate engineering education, arguing that the standard curriculum encourages design strategies that are not appropriate for many real-world technological systems.

ACKNOWLEDGMENTS

This book would not have been possible without the help of many people. All of the authors made major contributions of time, thought, and energy. Our current work benefits from the past and continuing contributions of the extended Logo community, including many former members of the Epistemology and Learning Group at the MIT Media Lab. We are grateful to Wanda Gleason and Florence D. Williams for helping with many organizational and editing tasks, and to Jacqueline Karaaslanian and Mai Cleary for providing general administrative support. The National Science Foundation (Grants 9153719-MDR and 9358519-RED), the LEGO Group, IBM, Nintendo Inc., and the Media Lab's News in the Future consortium have generously supported this research. Finally, we thank Seymour Papert for inspiring all of us to think in new ways about learning, children, minds, and computers.

PART I

PERSPECTIVES IN CONSTRUCTIONISM

1

A Word for Learning

Seymour Papert

Why is there no word in English for the art of learning? Webster says that the word *pedagogy* means the art of teaching. What is missing is the parallel word for learning. In schools of education, courses on the art of teaching are often listed simply as "methods." Everyone understands that the methods of importance in education are those of teaching—these courses supply what is thought to be needed to become a skilled teacher. But what about methods of learning? What courses are offered for those who want to become skilled learners?

The same imbalance can be found in words for the theories behind these two arts. "Theory of Instruction" and "Instructional Design" are among many ways of designating an academic area of study and research in support of the art of teaching. There are no similar designations for academic areas in support of the art of learning. Understandably: The need for such names has not been felt because there is so little to which they would apply. Pedagogy, the art of teaching, under its various names, has been adopted by the academic world as a respectable and important field. The art of learning is an academic orphan.

One should not be misled by the fact that libraries of academic departments of psychology often have a section marked "learning theory." The older books under this heading deal with the activity that is sometimes caricatured by the image of a white-coated scientist watching a rat run through a maze; newer volumes are more likely to base their theories on the performance of computer programs than on the behavior of animals. I do not mean to denigrate such books—I am myself the co-author of one and proud of it—but only to observe that they are not about the art of learning. They do not, for instance, offer advice to the rat (or the computer) about how to learn, although they have much to say to the psychologist about how to train a rat. Sometimes they are taken as a basis for training children, but I have not been able to find in them any useful advice about how to improve my own learning.

The unequal treatment by our language of the arts of learning and of teaching is visible in grammar as well as in vocabulary. Think, for example, of parsing the sentence, "The teacher teaches a child." *Teacher* is the active subject of the sentence; *child* is the passive object. The teacher does something to the learner. This grammatical form bears the stamp of school's hierarchical ideology in representing teaching as the active process. The teacher is in control and is therefore the one who needs skill; the learner simply has to obey instructions. This asymmetry is so deeply rooted that even the advocates of "active" or "constructivist" education find it hard to escape. There are many books and courses on the art of constructivist teaching, that talk about the art of setting up situations in which the learner will "construct knowledge"; but I do not know of any books on what I would assume to be the more difficult art of actually constructing the knowledge. The how-to-do-it literature in the constructivist subculture is almost as strongly biased to the teacher side as it is in the instructionist subculture.

A first step toward remedying these deficiencies is to give the missing area of study a name so that we can talk about it. Besides, it is only respectful to do this: Any culture that shows proper respect to the art of learning would have a name for it. In *Mindstorms* I proposed a word that did not catch on, but since I believe that there is more cultural readiness for such a word today, I shall try again— always bearing in mind that my principal goal is less to advocate this particular word than to emphasize the need for one. If the culture is really ripe for such a word, many people will throw in their own words (perhaps simply by quietly using them), and eventually one will take root in the soil of the language. Linnaeus, the father of botanical terminology, could decide to call a familiar white flower *Bellis perennis*, but the common language calls it a daisy, ignoring the Latin name just as it ignores the botanist's insistence that a daisy is an "inflorescence" and not a flower at all. A person can propose; "the culture" or "the language" disposes.

In any case, to illustrate the gap in our language and my proposal for filling it, consider the following sentence: "When I learned French I acquired _____ knowledge about the language, _____ knowledge about the people, and _____ knowledge about learning." *Linguistic* and *cultural* would fill in the first two blanks with no problems, but the reader will be hard put to think up a word to fill in the third blank. My candidate is *mathetic*, and I thereby make restitution for a semantic theft perpetrated by my professional ancestors, who stole the word *mathematics* from a family of Greek words related to learning. *Mathmatikos* meant "disposed to learn"; *mathema* was "a lesson," and *manthanein* was the verb "to learn." Mathematicians were so convinced that theirs was the only true learning that they felt justified in appropriating the word, and succeeded so well that the dominant connotation of the stem *math-* is now that stuff about numbers they teach in school. One of the few traces of the original sense of the root retained by current English is "polymath." This is not a person who knows many kinds of mathematics, but one who has learned broadly. Following my proposal, I would use the noun *mathetics* for a course on the art of learning, as in: "Mathetics (by whatever name it will come to be known) is even more important than mathematics as an area of study for children."

A comparison with another Greek term borrowed for talking about mental process will clarify the intended meaning of "mathetics" and perhaps support its "sound" and "feel." *Heuristics*—from the same stem as Archimedes' cry "Eureka!"—means the art of intellectual discovery. In recent times it has been applied specifically to discovering solutions of problems. Thus mathetics is to learning what heuristics is to problem solving.

Although the idea of heuristics is old—it goes back at least to Descartes and, if one stretches it a little, to the Greeks—its influence on contemporary educational thinking is mainly due to mathematician George Polya, who is best known through his book, *How to Solve It*. His theme runs parallel to my complaint that school gives more importance to knowledge about numbers and grammar than to knowledge about learning, except that in place of the word *learning*, Polya says "principles of solving problems." I would echo this wholeheartedly: In school, children are taught more about numbers and grammar than about thinking. In an early paper that supported and extended Polya's ideas, I even formulated this as a challenging paradox:

> It is usually considered good practice to give people instruction in their occupational activities. Now, the occupational activities of children are learning, thinking, playing, and the like. Yet, we tell them nothing about those things. Instead, we tell them about numbers, grammar, and the French Revolution; somehow hoping that from this disorder the really important things will emerge all by themselves. And they sometimes do. But the alienation-dropout-drug complex is certainly not less frequent. . . . The paradox remains: why don't we teach them to think, to learn, to play? (Papert, 1971, chap. 2, p. 1)

Traditional education sees intelligence as inherent in the human mind and therefore in no need of being learned. This would mean that it is proper for school to teach facts, ideas, and values on the assumption that human beings (of any age) are endowed by nature with the ability to use them. Polya's challenge started with the simple observation that students' ability to solve problems improved when he instructed them to follow such simple rules as, "Before doing anything else, spend a little time trying to think of other problems that are similar to the one in hand." He went on to develop a collection of other heuristic rules in the same spirit, some of which, like this one, apply to all kinds of problems and some to specific areas of knowledge, among which Polya himself paid the most attention to mathematics.

Another typical example of Polya's type of rule adapts the principle of "divide and conquer." Students often fail to solve a problem because they insist on trying to solve the whole problem all at once; in many cases they would have an easier time of it if they were to recognize that parts of the problem can be solved separately and later be put together to deal with the whole. Thus the Wright Brothers had the intention from the beginning of building a powered airplane that could take off from a field, but had they tried to build such a thing for their first experiments, they would very likely have come to the same gory end as many of their predecessors. Instead, they solved the problem of wing design by inventing and building a wind tunnel in which they tested wing sections. Then they built a glider that would take off from a track lined up with the wind in a place where winds were ideal. Independently of all this they also worked on an engine. In this way they gradually conquered all the problems.

Polya wished to introduce into education a more explicit treatment of the principles of what is often called "problem solving." In the same way, I want to introduce a more explicit treatment of the principles of learning. But thinking about heuristics helps to explain the idea of mathetics in another way as well. By offering my own unorthodox explanation of why heuristic principles help students, I shall try to bring out a contrast between *heuristics* and *mathetics*.

I believe that problem solving uses processes far more subtle than those captured in Polya's rules. This is not to say that the rules are not valuable as aids to solving problems, but I do think that their most important role is less direct and much simpler than their literal meaning. Attempting to apply heuristic rules checks students in the rush to get done with a problem and get on with the next. It has them spend more time with the problem, and my mathetic point is simply that spending relaxed time with a problem leads to getting to know it, and through this, to improving one's ability to deal with other problems like it. It is not using the rule that solves the problem; it is thinking about the problem that fosters learning. So does talking about the problems or showing them to someone else. What is mathetic here is the shift of focus from thinking about whether the rules themselves are effective in the immediate application to looking for multiple explanations of how working with the rules can contribute in the longer run to learning. To make the point in a possibly exaggerated form, I suggest that any kind of "playing with problems" will enhance the abilities that lie behind their solution.

This interpretation of why heuristic methods work highlights several mathetically important themes, each of which points to a way in which school impedes learning and to some good advice about how to do it better.

To begin with, the theme of "taking time," just mentioned in connection with Polya, is well illustrated by a passage from a book whose name has more than once raised eyebrows when I quoted it in academic circles: the best-selling, *The Road Less Traveled*, by psychiatrist M. Scott Peck (1980). I read the book in the first place for the same reason that I have made alliances with LEGO and

Nintendo, which has also caused some academically pure and politically correct eyebrows to rise at the idea of having any connection with people who make money. Anyone who can draw as many people into situations related to learning as Peck, LEGO, or Nintendo knows something that educators who have trouble holding the attention of 30 children for 40 minutes should want to learn.

Here is what Peck (1980) had to say about taking time:

> At the age of thirty-seven I learned how to fix things. Prior to that time almost all my attempts to make minor plumbing repairs, mend toys or assemble boxed furniture according to the accompanying hieroglyphical instruction sheet ended in confusion, failure and frustration. Despite having managed to make it through medical school and support a family as a more or less successful executive and psychiatrist, I considered myself to be a mechanical idiot. I was convinced I was deficient in some gene, or by curse of nature lacking some mystical quality responsible for mechanical ability. Then one day at the end of my thirty-seventh year, while taking a spring Sunday walk, I happened upon a neighbor in the process of repairing a lawn mower. After greeting him I remarked, "Boy, I sure admire you. I've never been able to fix those kind of things or do anything like that." My neighbor, without a moment's hesitation, shot back, "That's because you don't take the time." I resumed my walk, somehow disquieted by the gurulike simplicity, spontaneity and definitiveness of his response. "You don't suppose he could be right, do you?" I asked myself. Somehow it registered, and the next time the opportunity presented itself to make a minor repair I was able to remind myself to take my time. The parking brake was stuck on a patient's car, and she knew that there was something one could do under the dashboard to release it, but she didn't know what. I lay down on the floor below the front seat of her car. Then I took the time to make myself comfortable. Once I was comfortable, I then took the time to look at the situation. I looked for several minutes. At first all I saw was a confusing jumble of wires and tubes and rods, whose meaning I did not know. But gradually, in no hurry, I was able to focus my sight on the brake apparatus and trace its course. And then it became clear to me that there was a little latch preventing the brake from being released. I slowly studied this latch until it became clear to me that if I were to push it upward with the tip of my finger it would move easily and would release the brake. And so I did this. One single motion, one ounce of pressure from a fingertip, and the problem was solved. I was a master mechanic!
>
> Actually, I don't begin to have the knowledge or the time to gain that knowledge to be able to fix most mechanical failures, given the fact that I choose to concentrate my time on nonmechanical matters. So I still usually go running to the nearest repairman. But I now know that this is a choice I make, and I am not cursed or genetically defective or otherwise incapacitated or impotent. And I know that I and anyone else who is not mentally defective can solve any problem if we are willing to take the time. (pp. 27–28)

Give yourself time is an absurdly obvious principle that falls equally under heuristics and mathetics. Yet school flagrantly contravenes it by its ways of chopping time: "Get out your books . . . do 10 problems at the end of chapter

18 . . . DONG . . . there's the bell, close the books." Imagine a business executive, or a brain surgeon, or a scientist who had to work to such a fragmented schedule.

This story speaks as poignantly about a second theme—talking—as about time. Peck does not say this explicitly, but one can guess that he would have had the epiphany about taking his time at an earlier age than 37 had he talked more often to more people about his and their experiences with mechanical problems. A central tenet of mathetics is that good discussion promotes learning, and one of its central research goals is to elucidate the kinds of discussion that do the most good and the kinds of circumstances that favor such discussions. Yet in most circles talking about what really goes on in our minds is blocked by taboos as firm as those that inhibited Victorians from expressing their sexual fantasies. These taboos are encouraged by school, but go far beyond it, and point to ways in which our general culture is profoundly "antimathetic."

An extreme example will vividly illustrate the antimathetic process that exists in many more subtle, but destructive, forms in school. The incident took place in a "resource room," where children diagnosed as having a learning disability spend part of their day. Third grader Frank was one of them.

An aide gave Frank a set of sums to do on a piece of paper. I knew the child bitterly hated doing sums on paper, although under other conditions he could work quite successfully with numbers. For example, I had seen him do quite impressive calculations of how many and what shapes of LEGO pieces he needed for a job he wanted to do. To deal with the school demand to calculate with numbers in isolation from real needs, he had a number of techniques. One was to use his fingers, but his teacher had observed this and ruled that it was not allowed. As he sat in the resource room, I could see him itching to do finger manipulations. But he knew better. Then I saw him look around for something else to count with. Nothing was at hand. I could see his frustration grow. What could I do? I could pull rank and persuade the aide to give him something else to do or allow finger counting. But this wouldn't solve any real problems: Tomorrow he would be back in the same situation. Educate the aide? This was not the time or place. Inspiration came! I walked casually up to the boy and said out loud: "Did you think about your teeth?" I knew instantly from his face that he got the point, and from the aide's face that she did not. "Learning disability indeed!" I said to myself. He did his sums with a half-concealed smile, obviously delighted with the subversive idea.

In a classic joke, a child stays behind after school to ask a personal question. "Teacher, what did I learn today?" The surprised teacher asks, "Why do you ask that?" and the child replies, "Daddy always asks me and I never know what to say."

What did Frank learn at school that day? If asked, the aide might have said that he did 10 addition problems and so learned about adding. What would Frank say? One thing that is certain is that he would be very unlikely to speak to his teacher about his newly found trick for turning tongue and teeth into an abacus.

Despite his learning disability, he had long before learned not to talk too much about what was really happening in his head. He has already encountered too many teachers who demanded not only that he get the right answer, but also that he get it in the way they have decreed. Learning to let them think that he was doing it their way was part of belonging to the culture of school.

Frank's might be an extreme case, but most people share a similar fear of being made vulnerable by exposing themselves as having an inferior or messy mind. From this fear grows a habit that almost has the force of a taboo against talking freely about how we think and most especially about how we learn. If so, my joke with Frank fits very well with Freud's theory that jokes are funny precisely because they are not—they express repressed feelings that are not funny at all, in this case an undertone of something wrong with school's way of talking (and especially its way of not talking) about learning. Freud was thinking of jokes relieving tensions that come from hiding aggression and living with taboos on sexual instincts. I believe there is a similar situation in relation to learning.

This mathetic taboo has much in common with the taboos that existed until recently against talking about sexual matters. In Victorian days, or even when I was a child, sexual fantasies fell under the concept of "dirty thoughts," and although it was acceptable to recognize that other people had them, respectable people did not speak aloud about their own. It is relevant here to speculate about what lay behind this reluctance to talk. Imagine that you are a Victorian. Now, while you might be pretty sure that you are not the only one who has dirty thoughts, you would not know just how common it is, or whether people would assume you do. So better keep your mouth shut.

Whether or not this is an accurate account of Victorian sex taboos, I am sure that something analogous happens nowadays. Today, few people worry about letting on that their minds are full of sexual thoughts; many even feel a taboo against *not* talking in public about this topic. Contemporary taboos bear on different aspects of the mind. The most relevant here of many such restraints on intimacy shows itself as a widespread reluctance to allow others to see how much confusion pervades our thinking.

We do not like to appear "ignorant" or "stupid" or just plain wrong. Of course, we all know that our own minds are full of messy confusion, and that many others are in the same plight, but we imagine that some minds are tidy and neat and sharp. We see no reason to advertise not being in this class, especially in the presence of people such as bosses and teachers who have power over us. So voices within caution us to be careful of what we say: Talking too much might reveal what kind of mind we have and make us vulnerable. Eventually this caution becomes a habit.

The analogy with sexual taboos may seem to exaggerate our reluctance to talk freely about personal learning. I doubt it. My own struggle to achieve what degree of liberation I have in this respect has given me a sense of a very strong taboo. Even now, although I have a relatively good base of intellectual security, I often catch myself in the act of covering over the confusion in my mind. I cannot seem to help wanting to give certain people an impression of greater clarity than I have and, indeed, than I think anyone really has. I have developed—and I cannot believe that I am alone in this—a whole battery of defense mechanisms, as will shortly be seen.

Exaggerated or not, the suggestion of a taboo is intended to state emphatically that getting people to talk about learning is not simply a matter of providing the subject matter and the language. The lack of language is important. But there is also an active resistance of some kind. Thus, advancing toward the goal of mathetics requires more than technical aids to discussion. It also requires developing a system of psychological support.

The simplest form of support system I can imagine is to adopt the practice of opening oneself by freely talking about learning experiences. The rest of this chapter presents an example by describing how I myself emerged from what I believe it is appropriate to call a learning disability, which afflicted me for nearly twice as long as Peck's sense of himself as a mechanical idiot.

A child at school who fails to read or do arithmetic at the appropriate age is likely to be diagnosed as suffering from a learning disability and placed in special classes. I was able to read and add at the usual age, but there were other areas where my learning fell far behind what some other children did at my age. Peck reports that he discovered when he was 37 that he could, after all, deal with mechanical problems. It took me a longer time to recover from a learning disability that had plagued me as long as I can remember: I could not remember the names of flowers. Admittedly, my agnosia in this domain was not complete. For as long as I can remember I could correctly apply the words *rose*, *tulip*, and *daffodil* to the common varieties of these plants. But I cannot really say that I knew what a rose was. I was repeatedly in embarrassing situations; when I admired roses in a garden, they would turn out to be camellias or even tulips. I certainly did not recognize wild species as roses. The names *chrysanthemum*, *dahlia*, *marigold*, and *carnation* formed a blurry cloud in my mind. The extent of my not knowing is illustrated by an incident that happened when I was well into the transition to "flower literacy."

A pot of plants with rather showy blooms appeared in a common space in the building where I have my office. At the time I was beginning to pay attention to flowers and was delighted by what appeared to me to be a very exotic specimen. When I tried to remember whether I had seen one before, the only thought that came to mind was that it was not a morning glory (a species I had "discovered" in the previous weeks). As often happens to people with learning disabilities, a strong feeling of discomfort inhibited me from simply asking the name of the plant. Instead, I tried to strike up conversations about the plant's beauty, hoping that someone would mention the name in passing.

By the time I had failed four or five times, I was engrossed in the game of finding the name without actually asking. At this point I stopped to think, and came up with a better ploy than undirected conversation. Addressing someone who struck me as the kind of person who would know about flowers, I said, "Isn't that an unusual variety?" and success came in the form of "Oh, I don't really know one variety of petunia from another." Petunia! In the next few weeks I noticed petunias 20 times before I stopped counting. I don't imagine that some person or destiny was planting them in my path. In summer in New England, petunias are everywhere. The real puzzle is how I could have been blind to them all those years. How was it possible that so many people around me had always known what a petunia looked like while I did not? What was wrong with me?

I do not think anything is "wrong with me," but even with all the intellectual security I have been able to build on the basis of academic successes, I am still vulnerable to doubts about myself. The pain occasioned by my doubts makes me wonder about the feelings of children who find it so much more difficult than their comrades to learn to read or to add. Although the consequences of my disability were so much milder than theirs that any comparison risks being condescending, I do think there are enough common elements to make the comparison valuable. At the very least, my failure to benefit from schoolish remedies gives reason to think more carefully about standard approaches to "special education."

In school's discourse, the idea of motivation plays a primary role. "If kids won't learn they must be unmotivated, so let's motivate them." The advice certainly has no direct application to my case, for in every simple sense of the word I was already highly motivated. I often made resolutions to conquer my flower disability, and these would lead to a spurt of intense flower name-learning activity. For the same reason, laziness is no explanation either. We have to look more deeply for much more subtle and textured notions for thinking about these disabilities and strategies to overcome them. For example, in the place of the one-dimensional concept of "being motivated," I shall develop a concept of relation-ship with areas of knowledge having all the complexity and nuance of relation-ships with people.

I find it significant that despite all my fancy ideas about learning, I would fall back on schoolish modes of learning flower names. Looking for a teacher, I'd go into a flower shop and ask, "What are those? And those? And those?" Looking for a textbook, I bought a book from which I tried to associate photographs of flowers with their names. I even went on field trips to the botanical gardens where I would peer at the name tags of all the flowers. But to no avail. The frontal attack by rote learning did not work any better for me than the same schoolish methods do for children who have trouble learning school's subjects. It was like learning for a school test. I would remember the names of a few flowers for a while, but they would soon sink back into the familiar confusion. After a while the paroxysm of flower learning would pass, and I would resign myself for another year or two to being someone who "isn't good at" flower names.

One day a break came serendipitously. I was in the country in the late spring among people who were talking about how wonderful the lupines were doing. Feeling excluded and not wanting to admit in that particular company that I had no idea what a lupine was, I used the trick that later served me well in the petunia situation. I said, "Isn't *Loo Pin* a strange name? I wonder what its origin could possibly be?" (Getting a conversation going is a good ploy used cunningly by many "learning-disabled" children.) Someone speculated intelligently: "Sounds like Wolf—lupus the wolf. But I don't see the connection." After a few rounds of comment in scattered directions (which would have died out if I had not kept stoking the conversational fire), someone said, "It looks like a wolf's tail." Someone grumbled that it didn't really. That was a relative judgment, for what mattered to me was that of all the plants in sight, only one could possibly be perceived as being in the slightest like a wolf's tail. So I concluded, correctly, that those colorful masses of what I have since learned to describe as "tall spikes" were lupines.

The aspect of the serendipity that played a key role in my development was not discovering what those flowers were called; it wasn't making a connection between a flower and a name. It was making a connection between two areas of knowledge: flower names and a particular kind of interest I happen to have in etymology. Previous experience leads me to expect that I would soon have forgotten the name *lupine*, but this time I was so delighted at my cleverness and intrigued by the etymological puzzle that the incident was still buzzing in my head when I got back to my books and could explore the word. I read that *lupine* does indeed derive from the Latin word for "wolf," but not because of the tail-like appearance of its spike. The word is traced to a belief that lupines were bad for the soil because they "wolfed" all the nutrients. Enjoyment of the wolf-theory's ambiguous status between true and false led me to pursue the research and run into a twist in the story that made it still more evocative for me.

As long as I can remember, I have been excited by paradoxical aspects of words, so my level of excitement rose when I found a paradoxical slant to the etymology of *lupine*. One no longer thinks of the lupine as wolfing nutrients. On the contrary, the lupine, as a member of the pea family, is able to capture nitrogen from the atmosphere and add value to the soil. Seeing lupines in poor soil is cause for praise rather than blame. But the name has outlived the theory on which it was based, and so became one of many examples of old ideas that are preserved in our language and maintain connections of which we are only marginally aware. My relationship with flower names was taking on a new tone as they made contact with areas I found personally interesting.

This twist also touched on another personally evocative issue. One reason for my fondness for etymology is that it provides good examples for a vendetta against the idea of any single explanation for mental phenomena. They are *all* multiply determined—and this is the essence of the way the mind works. Now the origins of flower names began to show promise as an area in which I could find strong but very simple support for this way of thinking. At first blush etymology may seem to run counter to my preference for multiple explanations, because it so often seems to pinpoint a single historical source for a word. But finding a source is not a psychological or cultural explanation for the way the word is used. The wolfing-of-goodness theory may be at the root of a full explanation for old popular forms that seem to have been followed by Linnaeus when he called this genus of plants *Lupinus*, but it scarcely begins to be an explanation of why the name has stuck in our culture. Explaining why botanists call a plant what they do does not explain why plain folk do so—in most cases the popular language scorns the botanical name and develops its own. We say *lilac* rather than *syringa* and wear a *carnation* rather than a *dianthus* in a buttonhole. It seems plausible that a folk etymology such as the looks-like-a-wolf's-tail theory could have contributed together with the wolfing-the-goodness theory to making the name *lupine* stick in popular usage. After all, if the association occurred to one person, it is reasonable to assume that it occurred to others, and that it hovers near the threshold of consciousness of many more.

My mathetic theory does not depend on the truth of my amateur etymologizing. What matters here is that it was connected with regions of knowledge that were strongly evocative for me. The real moral of the story is how a certain engaging quality spread from words to flowers, and later from flowers to other mental domains. If I had to sum it up in a single metaphor, I would say it is about how "cold" mental regions were heated up through contact with "hot" regions.

One contact was not enough to heat up the previously chilly region of flower names. By now, as I write 2 years after the lupine incident, there has been dramatic change in my memory for flower names. It is as if they now find a place to stick. But this did not happen all at once, and by the time it did, much more than the ability to remember their names had changed in my relationship with plants.

For most of a year there was not much change, although I did not forget the word *lupine*, and I did notice myself paying attention to oddities in flower names. For example, I caught myself playing with the minor contradictions suggested by an etymologically literal-minded hearing of "white lilac" or "yellow rose." *Lilac* derives from a Persian word for the color lilac, and rosy cheeks never suggest jaundice or pallor. One can tune one's ear to sense the same kind of oddness in hearing that water lilies and arum lilies are not (in a botanical sense) lilies at all. Sometimes I felt impatient with myself for paying attention to such trivial thoughts, but they kept making small ripples in my mind, and in retrospect I am glad, because these ripples put me in a state of readiness for the grand whammer. One night (reading at about 2:00 in the morning) I ran headlong into the fact that for a botanist, a daisy is not a flower. I cannot tell whether I was more shocked at this being so or at my having lived so long without knowing it. A daisy not a flower? Come on! It's the prototypical flower—if you had asked me last year to draw a flower, I'm sure I'd have produced something more like a daisy than like anything else. Though it seems silly now, and rather ignorant, I really was upset

FIG. 1.1 The family of flowers that includes daisies, asters, sunflowers, and coneflowers are called inflorescences because what we usually call a flower is seen by the botanist as a mass of tiny flowers.

and excited. I ran from book to book in the small hours, trying to learn more. The news was bad: The putsch against standard nomenclature went beyond daisies to include sunflowers and black-eyed susans and chrysanthemums and dahlias. They were denigrated with names like "false flower" or elevated with fancy names like "inflorescence," but it appeared that in many circles it is a definite gaffe to call them flowers. How can this be? A sunflower isn't a flower? Even arum lilies, which had already been slighted in my mind by not being lilies, were now excluded from being flowers. (See Fig. 1.1.)

The most powerful moment came in the morning when I could at last get hold of some flowers. I found myself in a situation that would be repeated several times in the following year: I was looking at a familiar object with a sense of looking at it for the first time. Compare a buttercup with a daisy and you may begin to understand how the botanist sees them as fundamentally different things. For the botanist a flower is structured around its sex organs: The stamens and anthers, the pistils, stigmas, and ovaries are the essence of the flower. The petals and sepals that make such a spectacularly colorful impression on us and on the birds and insects are secondary features. In the buttercup, the tulip, and the lily you can see all these parts—but not in the daisy. Or rather, in the daisy you see the parts repeated many times, for those white slivers you may have pulled off one by one while reciting "loves me . . . loves me not . . ." are not petals surrounding sex organs but entire flowers. If you pull one out very carefully, you will see that it is like a miniature, lopsided, and elongated petunia. And what they surround, the central yellow disk, is itself a mass of even tinier complete flowers. So botanically speaking, the daisy is not a flower but a tight bunch of flowers of two kinds, ray flowers on the outside surrounding disk flowers on the inside. The botanist will call it a head or an inflorescence, though I suppose and hope that children will always call it a flower.

Up to this point my new involvement with flowers was confined to their names and belonged squarely in my established area of hot interest in etymology. With the daisy incident it broke out from words to things. I began to look at flowers and think about their structure. The concept of flower was changing, and new conceptual entities began to grow in my mind: The unit of thought shifted from the flower to the whole plant, and, by degrees, previously nebulous entities

FIG. 1.2. The disk or mass at the center of many inflorescences is made up of many tiny flowers like this one. What seem to be petals are also complete flowers in themselves.

such as "the rose family" (which includes cherries, apples, and strawberries as well as roses) acquired firmer reality. I also began to think about botanists. It was easy to see that their definition of flower excluded daisies; this was a simple matter of logic. But coming to appreciate the reasons for adopting such a definition was an essentially different and more complex process, better characterized as entering a culture than as understanding a concept. (See Fig. 1.2.)

Naming remained an important theme in an increasingly complex set of relationships in my mind. A simple example started with the name of the daisy. Now that the humble flower had become such a center of interest, I naturally poked around the origins and meanings of its name. I could hardly believe my luck: *Daisy* is "day's eye"! What a find, accompanied again by my amazement at not having known this and even some shamefaced puzzling about why it had not been obvious. The find got extra spice from the fact that different books gave different explanations. One theory had the daisy looking like the sun, which is the "eye of the day"; another associated it with the tendency of daisies to open in the day and close at night. Another started with a speculation. I had run into the fact that daisies were thought to have good medicinal properties for afflictions of the eye. A first guess that this might be related to its name seemed to me too implausible to be worth checking. Doing so, all the same, led to another curious find: the doctrine of signatures, which held that plants show by their visible properties their medicinal virtues. The self-heal, a wildflower, shows its value for treating throat ailments by the fact that its flower has a throat, and this is reflected in the derivation of its botanical name, *Prunella vulgaris*, from "Breune," the German word for "quinsy" (an old-fashioned name, as I learned through the same investigation, for tonsillitis). The coloration patterns of hepatica leaves are said to suggest the appearance of the liver, thus explaining both the name *hepatica*— from the Latin word meaning "having to do with the liver"—and the belief that it is good for liver ailments. Certain features of plants became more salient, for example, that some have throats and some do not. The interest in names was bringing me into the real world of flowers.

Other connections with names and naming led into new relationships with nature. The window of the room where most of this book was written looks out on a field where I see wildflowers of several colors, particularly yellows and purples. Among the yellows I can see tall, bushy Saint-John's-worts and even taller evening primroses, little cinquefoils, and some early goldenrod. Among the purples I see fireweed, loosestrife, and asters. I also see some that are question marks in my head: I have noted their existence but do not know what they are. Two years ago I saw an undifferentiated display of pretty flowers. It was beautiful. I loved it. But it was not at all what I am seeing now. Try as I might, I cannot make my eye go back to seeing it as I did before. I cannot imagine what it would be like to see those yellow flowers as a mass of yellow flowers without individual identity.

I want to pursue a detail in this development as a model for the process of learning. Two years ago I knew the name *buttercup* and correctly applied it to common buttercups. I cannot recall how widely I would have used this name to apply to other species, but I am sure that I had no other words for small yellow flowers. Early in the first summer I became aware of two other kinds of yellow wildflowers: cinquefoils and Saint-John's-worts. But my degree of flower dyslexia showed itself in the fact that I had to reidentify these flowers many times—like someone who cannot hold a tune, I could not hold the distinction from one day to the next. All the same, something had happened: It was as if I had made pegs in my head for three things—buttercups, cinquefoils, and Saint-John's-worts—but did not yet know what to hang on each peg, or that I had met three people and had been told their names, but knew nothing else about them. I often find myself in this situation and am struck by how I get new entities mixed up until a gradually growing sense of individuality becomes strong enough to keep them separate. The sense of individuality grew slowly and unevenly for the three kinds of plant.

I do not pretend to know exactly how this process of growth happened. But I do know how it did *not* happen: I tried to memorize the characteristics of each group taken from a book, but this simply did not work. Perhaps if I had been interested only in these three flowers, I would have been able to memorize their formal characterizations. But if I turned to other plants and came back to the three yellow ones, I would get them wrong again. Slowly something different from the rote memory of botanists' defining characteristics developed; I began to build up a more personal kind of connection.

I associate buttercups with folklore that tells about the appearance of a person's chin when a buttercup is held up to it. If the chin takes on the yellow color by reflection, this is interpreted in America as a sign of liking butter and in France, naturally, as a sign of being in love. Through these stories I associate the buttercup with shiny petals, one of the characteristics that in fact distinguishes it from the other two. Other associations were less direct. One of the three flowers has especially bushy stamens. I could not remember which. In fact, it is the Saint-John's-wort, but when I read that this plant is also known as Aaron's beard, I associated this name with its bushy stamens because these are like a beard, and with the name Saint-John's-wort because Aaron and St. John both have a biblical connection. So the name Aaron's beard acted as a kind of glue to stick the bushy stamen property to the name *Saint-John's-wort.* During the same period I found my visual attention shifting from the flower to the plant, and this brought new kinds of association. And so it went.

The deeper I got into my "affair" with flowers, the more connections were made; and more connections meant that I was drawn in all the more strongly, that the new connections supported one another more effectively, and that they were more and more likely to be long-lasting. Moreover, the content of my learning spread in many directions: I was learning Latin words, I was picking up insights into the history of folk-medicine, and I was gaining or renewing geographic and historical knowledge. The Renaissance in its artistic and scientific aspects came into new focus through the role of flowers in the new relationship with nature that developed at that time.

My learning had hit a critical level in the sense of the "critical mass" phenomenon of a nuclear reaction or the explosion of a population when conditions favor both birthrate and survival. The simple moral is that learning explodes when you stay with it: A full year had passed before the effect in my mind reached a critical level for an exponential explosion of growth. The more complex moral is that some domains of knowledge, such as plants, are especially rich in connections and particularly prone to give rise to explosions of learning.

My learning experience with flowers began with a very narrow "curriculum": learning to name them. In the end the experience widened and left me a different person in more dimensions of life than anything that is measured by the standardized behavioristic tests with which the conservatives judge school learning. It affected my stream of consciousness as I moved about the world: I see more as I walk in the street or in a field. The world is more beautiful. My sense of oneness with nature is stronger. My caring about environmental issues is deep and more personal. And recently I have surprised myself by enjoying systematic books on botany and having no trouble remembering what I read. It is as if I have made my transition in this domain from a concrete to a formal stage.

Early in this chapter I mentioned a mathetic weakness in the literature on constructivism. The metaphor of learning by constructing one's own knowledge has great rhetorical power against the image of knowledge transmitted though a pipeline from teacher to student. But it is only a metaphor, and reflection on my flower story consolidates my sense that other images are just as useful for understanding learning, and are more useful as sources of practical mathetic guidance. One of these is *cultivation:* Developing my knowledge of plants felt more like the work of a horticulturalist designing, planting, and tending a garden than the work of a construction crew putting up a house. I have no doubt that my knowledge developed even when I was not paying attention! Another image is the geographic metaphor of regions and the idea of connections between them. Indeed, the description "connectionism" fits my story better than "constructivism."

On a pragmatic level, "Look for connections!" is sound mathetic advice, and on a theoretical level, the metaphor leads to a range of interesting questions about the connectivity of knowledge. It even suggests that the deliberate part of learning consists of making connections between mental entities that already exist; new mental entities seem to come into existence in more subtle ways that escape conscious control. However that may be, thinking about the interconnectivity of knowledge suggests a theory of why some knowledge is so easily acquired without deliberate teaching. In the sense in which it is said that no two Americans are separated by more than five handshakes, this cultural knowledge is so interconnected that learning will spread by free migration to all its regions. This suggests a strategy to facilitate learning by improving the connectivity in the learning environment by actions on cultures rather than on individuals.

ACKNOWLEDGMENT

This chapter originally appeared (in a slightly modified version) in *The Children's Machine* by S. Papert, 1993 (pp. 82–105). Copyright 1993 by Harper-Collins Publishers.

REFERENCES

Papert, S. (1971, October). *Teaching children thinking* (Logo memo, unpublished).
Peck, M. S. (1980). *The road less traveled.* New York: Simon and Schuster.

Perspective-Taking and Object Construction
Two Keys to Learning

Edith Ackermann

KNOWING AS WAYS OF RELATING TO THE WORLD

In recent years, an increasing number of psychologists and cognitive scientists have adopted the view that knowledge is essentially situated, and thus should not be divorced from the contexts in which it is constructed and actualized (e.g., Brown, Collins & Duguid, 1989; Lave & Wenger, 1991; Rogoff & Lave, 1984). Lave & Wenger, 1991). This growing interest in knowledge as it lives and grows in context has led many researchers in developmental psychology and other disciplines to focus on people's interactions with, and descriptions of, specific situations. They look at how these interactions and descriptions evolve over time. Such an emphasis on the richness and diversity of individual paths-in-context provides a far less coherent picture of cognitive growth than is suggested by most stage theories. It challenges the prevalent view among developmentalists (such as Piaget and Kohlberg) that removed, analytical modes of thought are necessarily more advanced forms of cognitive functioning, and that cognitive growth consists of a unidirectional progression from concrete to abstract, from fusion to separation (Ackermann, 1991; Kegan, 1982; Turkle & Papert, 1991).

Several scholars further elaborate on the idea that divorcing knowledge from experience by adopting a "God's eye view"—an all-encompassing perspective that transcends any given viewpoint—is by no means a higher form of knowing, and that it certainly is not the most appropriate mode of functioning in all situations (e.g., Gilligan, 1987; Haraway, 1991; Harding, 1991; Keller, 1985). They argue that *to know is to relate* and that *to know better*, or gain deeper understanding, is to *grow-in-connection* (Jordan, Kaplan, Miller, Silver, & Surrey, 1991). Lave went so far as to suggest that learning should be distinguished from knowledge acquisition. Learning, to Lave, is the ability to function *in situ*, that is, to become an active participant within a multiplicity of communities of practices (Lave, 1992).

What is common to all these approaches is that they bring back *subjectivity*, *standpoint*, and *context* to the center of discussions about knowledge, science, and learning. They also remind us that, indeed, people can develop different ways of knowing while remaining excellent at what they do.

PIAGET AND SITUATED KNOWLEDGE: SITUATING STANDPOINTS

One could argue that situated cognition has been with us for a long time. Piaget has taught us that *knowledge is not a commodity to be transmitted*. Nor is it information to be delivered from one end, encoded, stored and reapplied at the other end. Instead, *knowledge is experience*, in the sense that it is actively constructed and reconstructed through direct interaction with the environment. This idea is similar, in many ways, to the ideas expressed by various "situated cognition" scholars: *To know is to relate*.

However, recent claims emphasize that people's ability to make sense of their world and themselves, and to construct progressively deeper understandings, cannot be portrayed as Piaget has done. A person's development is not a smooth, incremental progression from concrete to abstract, from fusion to separation, from connectedness to autonomy. A closer look into the meanderings of individual minds in context reveals a far more complex picture, which calls for a redefinition of Piaget's general stages of cognitive development (Ackermann, 1991; Carey, 1987; Karmiloff-Smith, 1992).

Stage theory emphasizes how the average child, or epistemic subject, becomes detached from the world of concrete objects and local contingencies and increasingly able to internalize action and to mentally manipulate symbolic objects within the realm of hypothetical worlds. Although this is an important aspect of cognitive development, it does not account for the processes by which knowledge is formed and transformed within specific contexts, nor does it describe how knowledge is cultivated by individual minds or shaped by the very media used to make it tangible. In Céllérier's words, Piaget has given less thought to "reflective concretization" than to "reflexive abstraction" (Céllérier, 1992). The situated knowledge approach invites us to pay closer attention to the ways in which individuals *give form to their ideas*, and *how these forms*, once built, *inform back their ideas* (Ackermann, 1994). Both personal expressions and cultural artifacts become objects-to-think-with (Papert, 1980), or mediational means (Wertsch, 1991). People build them to make ideas tangible, and they share them to negotiate meanings, or communicate. Such an emphasis on the processes by which people shape and sharpen their ideas in context provides a rich counter-point to Piaget's stage theory.

In paying closer attention to the ways in which people rely on their objects-to-think with, authors in the situated knowledge movement propose a conception of "self" that is distributed and decentralized (Haraway, 1991). If it is true that knowledge cannot be divorced from the contexts in which it is built and from the media that allow its expression, then we cannot think of the knower as an autonomous entity. If our minds, senses, and bodies are expanded through the use of personal and cultural tools, then these tools become incorporated, an integral part of ourselves. The boundaries of our mental, sensorial, and corporal enve-lopes are thus expanded in the same way that a blind man's cane is an extension of his sensory system. Authors in the situated knowledge movement allow us to rethink the notion of identity as well as the nature of the division between "self" and "not self."

COGNITIVE ADAPTATION OR REGULATING BOUNDARIES BETWEEN SELF AND WORLD

Although knowledge is necessarily situated, we should not lose sight of the fact that people's ability to be connected and develop deeper relationships also re-quires moments of separation and autonomy. This is where Piaget's "other" contribution is very relevant. Piaget has dealt not only with stages. He has also defined intelligence as *adaptation*, or the ability to maintain a balance between stability and change, closure and openness, or, in his own words, between *assimi-lation* and *accommodation*. Piaget's *functional theory* of intelligence provides a solid ground for understanding how people *regulate their boundaries* with the world.

Assimilation or Imposing One's Order Upon the World

Piaget's stage theory stresses children's growing ability to extract rules from empirical regularities and build cognitive invariants. The functional model em-phasizes the importance of these constructs—rules and invariants—for interpret-ing and organizing the world. Once built, they become the lenses, or assimilation frame, through which people attribute meaning to others and things. Piaget's interest, I suggest, was mainly in the assimilatory pole of adaptation, that is, the processes by which the cognitive system as a whole maintains its internal struc-ture and equilibrium. Moreover, what Piaget describes particularly well is the nature of this internal structure, or equilibrium, and its "complexification" and reorganizations over time.

Accommodation or Listening to the World

In accommodation, the subject is connected and sensitive to variations in the environment. Through accommodation, people "dive into" situations. Rather than looking at situations from a distance, they "become one" with the phenomenon that captures their attention. The cost of accommodation is momentary loss of control, or disequilibrium, but listening to the world allows for change through adjusting one's current views in the light of perceived mismatches. If Piaget himself has paid less attention to the accommodative pole of adaptation, he has nonetheless laid the ground for others to further explore its role in achieving a viable adaptive balance.

COGNITIVE GROWTH AS A DANCE BETWEEN DIVING-IN AND STEPPING-OUT

Along with Kegan (1982), I believe that both "diving in" and "stepping out" are equally important in reaching deeper understanding. I argue that separateness resulting from momentary withdrawal does not necessarily entail disengagement. It may well constitute a step toward relating even more closely to people and things. As the Chinese saying goes: "The fish is the only one who does not know that he swims" (anonymous). People cannot learn from their experience as long as they are entirely immersed in it. There comes a time when they need to step back, and from a distance reconsider what has happened to them. They must take on the role of an external observer, or critic, and they must revisit their experience "as if" it were not theirs. They need to describe it to themselves and others, and in doing so, they will make it tangible.

Once projected out and "objectified," personal experience can be newly reengaged. People can dive back into the situation of interest to them and get immersed at the cost of losing themselves one more time, until they eventually reemerge and, once more, look at things from a distance. It is this dance between diving-in and stepping-out that keeps us connected, while at the same time, enables us to grant the world an existence that goes beyond momentary relation with it.

PERSPECTIVE-TAKING AND THE CONSTRUCTION OF INVARIANTS

To illustrate my argument, I discuss research on *perspective-taking* and *the construction of cognitive invariants*. By *perspective-taking*, I mean the ability to experience and describe the presentation of an object or display from different vantage points. This ability involves objectifying one's own view of the object and anticipating that moving to another station point will result in specific changes in the object's presentation. In other words, perspective-taking involves both differentiation and coordination of viewpoints. By *construction of cognitive invariants*, I mean the ability to mentally hold onto some features of an object, to stabilize or "conserve" them in spite of modifications in other features. The building of invariants or stable referents is a central piece in what Nelson Goodman calls "world making" (Goodman, 1978).

Object permanency and *conservation of object size* are examples of invariants constructed in early childhood. At 6 months of age, babies learn to attribute "objectness" to events that occur in stable, reliable ways. An "object" may well evaporate as soon the baby turns away—out of sight means out of mind, out of existence—but since it reappears whenever s/he turns back, the baby starts attributing permanence or "objectness," to it. In conservation of object size, the child grants size identity to an object even though its projection becomes smaller or larger when displaced from the child. Again, it is the reliability of the object's behavior—the correlation between distance and projective size—that triggers the attribution of invariance or "sameness," despite obvious changes in appearance.

Perspective-taking is similar to the conservation of object size except that, in this case, it is the child who moves around the object, and not the object that goes away from the child. The invariance of an object's shape is constructed by detecting a stable correlation between movement around the object and changes in its presentation. From any particular vantage point, the object's presentation is always the same. Yet, as one moves around, its presentation changes. As long as the object behaves consistently with relation to the child's movement, the child will eventually ascribe permanence or "objectness" to it, in spite of its ever-changing and necessarily partial presentations.

Perspective-taking provides a good example of how people drift in and out of their own viewpoint, and how this drifting leads to the building of a so-called "God's-eye-view" that transcends any particular vantage point, recreates hidden parts, and imposes stabilities. To anticipate how another person perceives a phenomenon, we need to reconstruct the phenomenon for ourselves. Only then can we guess what others may perceive from their own standpoint. In discussing some classical experiments on perspective-taking, I wish to show that perspective-taking and object construction go hand in hand. The ability to decenter by taking on another person's view coexists with the construction of a God's-eye-view. It is the dance between the two that spurs growth. *Playing other* and *playing God* are equally useful to deepen our own connection with the world.

PERSPECTIVE-TAKING EXPERIMENTS

The experiment that laid the ground for further studies on perspective-taking involved a situation in which the perspectives of two or more protagonists were at odds with one another (Piaget, Inhelder, 1967). Subjects had to anticipate how a given object would appear from different viewpoints. By contrasting the classical three-mountain task (Piaget & Inhelder, 1967) with more recent *spatial perceptual* perspective-taking experiments (Flavell, 1990; Huttenlocher & Presson, 1973), I show that young children are not merely egocentric, as suggested by Piaget and Inhelder. Instead, they cannot build a God's-eye-view, stable enough to recreate the hidden faces of an object and to guess how it presents itself to others.

More intricate *psychological* perspective-taking experiments involve situations in which a child knows something—and knows that another does not know. The child's task is to guess what the other may believe. Psychological perspective-taking tasks include so-called "false belief" experiments (Flavell, 1988; Wimmer & Perner, 1983), research on youngsters' ability to adjust speech when talking to younger siblings, and research on their ability to modify instructions to match a recipient's perceived abilities (Astington, Harris, & Olson, 1988). These situations differ from spatial perceptual perspective-taking tasks in that they involve people's beliefs and knowledge about other people's beliefs and knowledge. Research on children's theories of mind shows that 4-year-olds understand very well that someone else can have a viewpoint different from their own. What is more difficult is the realization that viewpoints are lenses, and that different lenses transform reality in specific ways. Young children do not understand *how* a given lens informs the mind of the person who uses it (Perner, 1993). In what follows, I present some of the findings in spatial-perceptual research, leaving it up to the reader to discover their striking convergence with more recent findings on theories of children's minds (Wellman, 1990).

The Three-Mountain Task

Children from 4 to 12 years of age are presented with a miniature model of three mountains, different in shapes and colors. The model is placed in the middle of a table, and four characters (dolls or people) are seated around the table. The child, who figures among the characters, has to guess how the others will see the miniature landscape from their respective vantage points. Piaget and Inhelder found that children up to 11 years produce egocentric descriptions when asked to specify "what another person sees." The authors interpret young children's difficulties in terms of their inability to *decenter*, that is, to put themselves in other people's shoes. Piaget's notion of decentering, I argue, remains too undifferentiated. It involves (a) moving away from one's own viewpoint, (b) understanding *that* a person situated elsewhere will see things differently, and (c) figuring out *what* the other will see from his or her vantage point.

More recent studies (Flavell, 1990; Huttenlocher & Presson, 1973) showed that if young children fall back into "egocentric errors" in the three-mountain task, it is not because of their inability to decenter, as suggested by Piaget and

Inhelder. Instead, they are unable to keep hold of all the relative positions among elements within the 3-D scene (right/left, behind/in front, above/below, etc.), and cannot operate the transformations needed to infer the object's presentation to others (front becomes back, left becomes right, etc..). In other words, *certain displays are harder to reconstruct than others.*

The Cat–Dog Experiment

Instead of a 3-D miniature landscape, Flavell and his colleagues presented young children with a 2-D cardboard showing the image of a cat on one side, and the image of a dog on the other side. In this situation, children 3 to 4 years old can tell, without any hesitation, that if they see the cat, a person sitting in front of them will see the dog (Flavell, 1990). According to Flavell, the cat–dog experiment is easier precisely because the display is simpler. Children need only to keep hold of a single relation (cat on one side, dog on the other) and operate a single transformation (if I see the cat, the other will see the dog).

This simplified version of the classical experiment makes it clear that young children do not fail because they are egocentric. Children 3 to 4 years old are able to understand that another person's viewpoint is different from their own, and thus, that an object's presentation is different *from different station points.* What makes the classical experiment so difficult is the requirement to keep in mind all the relative positions among elements within the scene, and to figure out *how* these positions vary when seen from another vantage point. As Flavell put it, young children know very well *that* someone else will see things differently but they cannot specify *what it is* they will see (Flavell, 1990).

Mental Rotation and Perspective-Taking Experiments

Huttenlocher and Presson (1973) further demonstrated that if children are blindfolded and actually move around a 3-D miniature model, instead of just imagining what another person sees, they can more easily anticipate the other's viewpoint. The authors concluded that the actual displacement around the table facilitates the mental tracking of transformations in the display. As they move along, children progressively change their own relative position to the display. This physical repositioning enables them to locally readjust the changing relations among elements within the scene. Instead of having to compute whole transformations at once (inverting lefts and right, etc.), they can mentally unravel continuous changes, step by step, and in real time.

This experiment is relevant to the discussion on situated cognition in that it stresses the importance of actually being projected into a situation, and acting in it, instead of operating at a distance. "Diving into" a situation enables children to mobilize a wealth of knowledge-in-action from previous navigational experience, and even blindfolded, they can build on this sensori-motor wealth to mentally track progressive changes in the object's presentation as they move along.

The Shadow Box

Reith et al. (1989) have designed yet another variation of the classical perspective-taking experiment that is worth mentioning. In this case, none of the participants involved knows what the object actually looks like. Each has a partial view in the form of a shadow projection and needs to exchange information with others to figure out the shape of the "hidden object." The setting is a big box containing a 3-D object. The vertical sides of the box are semiopaque screens showing four shadow projections of the object. A person is seated in front of each window. No movement is allowed around the display. This experiment provides an excellent metaphor for what actually happens in any other perspective-taking situation. Objects are never visible. They are always "hidden" in the sense that they do not present all their faces at once. As in the shadow-box task, people necessarily reconstruct objects, for themselves and with others. They do so by keeping hold of partial presentations as seen from specific station points, and by imposing stabilities upon reliable changes in presentations, as noticed through moving around in consistent ways.

CONCLUSION

The most important contribution of the "situated cognition" approach is that it has brought back *subjectivity*, *standpoint*, and *context* to the center of discussions about knowledge and learning. In stressing the deeply personal and rooted nature of what we know and how we come to know, authors have challenged the view prevalent among developmentalists that removed analytical modes of thought are necessarily more advanced, and that cognitive growth is a smooth progression from concrete to abstract, from fusion to separation, from egocentrism to decentration.

On the other hand, we know from Piaget, Kegan, and others (Winnicott, 1971) that the ability to reach deeper understanding also requires moments of separation. As Kegan eloquently put it, cognitive growth emerges as a result of people's repeated attempts to solve the unresolvable tension between getting embedded and emerging from embeddedness (Kegan, 1982). Without connection people cannot grow, yet without separation they cannot relate. People need to get immersed in situations, but there also comes a time when they want to step out. They detach themselves by projecting their experience. They "objectify" it and they address it "as if" it were not theirs. They recast what has happened to them to make it more tangible. They become their own observers, narrators, and critics. Then, again, they newly reengage their previously "objectified" experience. They dive back into it and try once more to gain intimacy. Both "diving in" and "stepping out" are equally needed to reach deeper understanding.

Research on perspective-taking has illustrated how people drift in and out of their viewpoints, and how this drifting leads to the construction of a God's-eye-view which, in turn, is needed to understand another person's view. Such a God's-eye-view is obviously neither static nor permanent. It is bound to be constantly reshaped, but nonetheless plays a crucial role in the ability to adopt another person's viewpoint. Perspective-taking and object-construction, indeed, go hand in hand. In adopting too strong a view against the evil of God's-eye views, many scholars of the situated knowledge tradition lose sight of the fact that building stabilities, or invariants, is the flip side of our capacity to empathize. *Playing God* and *playing other* are equally important in keeping us connected while we, at the same time, are able to grant the world with an identity ("otherness") beyond our current interaction. Intelligence requires overgeneralizing. People can only understand novel situations in terms of what they already know—by imposing their order upon things. It is their ability to navigate between globalizing constructs and local stances that allows for a viable balance between closure and openness, stability and change or, in Piaget's words, between assimilation and accommodation.

Piaget's functional theory of intelligence provides a solid ground for understanding how people regulate their boundaries with the world. However, Piaget was mainly focused on the assimilative pole of adaptation, and has almost entirely overlooked the self-correcting function of accommodation. In paying closer attention to the ways in which people loosen their boundaries through accommodation, it becomes obvious that projections of self-in-context are a key to learning, and they can take various forms (Hatano & Inagaki, 1987).

In an article entitled, "Toward an Anthropomorphic Epistemology," Sayeki developed the idea that people often throw out pieces of themselves, which he calls "Kobitos" (little people), into the contexts that they try to understand (Sayeki, 1989). In doing so, they become able to feel situations "from within." They build an analog of the blind person's cane. This kind of "becoming other" is different from simply diving into a situation. It is a bit like remembering a sunny Sunday on the beach, picturing oneself running across the sand. Such a recast is obviously different from actually being on the beach. We cannot really see ourselves, so the actual experience is more like navigating in space. In contrast, the recast provides an airplane view of the scene that is populated, among other things, with a dispatched miniature "copy of self." A more intricate and humane God's-eye-view seems to emerge here. People are able reconstruct entire landscapes in their minds—as seen from nowhere—and then they throw little people ("kobitos") into these landscapes. Yet, as soon as their god-like creation is achieved, they turn around and project themselves into their previously built "kobitos." They dwell in the landscape with them; they accompany them everywhere, and they feel as they feel in any situation. It is not an overstatement to say that people end up inhabiting their own mental constructs.

Yet another form of becoming-other is illustrated by Woody Allen's movie, *Zelig*. The protagonist literally takes on the traits of other people. He becomes a chameleon. In this case, the fusion is total, the self has dissolved into the other.

A close examination of different forms of self-projection and self-diffusion is a necessary "fix" to Piaget's overemphasis on the assimilative pole of adaptation. It resets the balance by specifying the actual contribution of accommodation. It brings back to the center of discussion the too often minimized role of anthropomorphization in learning. It reopens the way to deepening our understanding of the productive tension between separation and fusion, closure and openness, stability and change.

ACKNOWLEDGMENTS

An early version of this chapter was presented at the 22nd annual symposium of the Jean Piaget Society on the theme, Development and Vulnerability in Close Relationships—Importance for Learning, Montréal, May 28, 1992. I thank Yasmin Kafai and Mitchel Resnick for editing this volume. Special thanks to my friends and colleagues, Wanda Gleason, Emiel Reith, Carol Strohecker, and Aaron Falbel for carefully reading and editing my first "Frenglish" draft. Thanks also to all the members of the Epistemology and Learning Group at the MIT Media Lab. The preparation of this chapter was supported by the National Science Foundation (Grant 9153719-MDR), the LEGO Group, and Nintendo Inc. The ideas expressed here do not necessarily reflect the positions of the supporting agencies.

REFERENCES

Ackermann, E. (1991). From decontextualized to situated knowledge: Revisiting Piaget's water-level experiment. In I. Harel & S. Papert (Eds.), *Constructionism* (pp. 269–295). Norwood, NJ: Ablex Publishing.

Ackermann, E. (1994). Construction and transference of meaning through form. In L. Steffe, & J. Gale (Eds.), *Constructivist education* (pp. 341–354). Hillsdale, NJ: Lawrence Erlbaum Associates.

Astington, J., Harris, P., & Olson, D. (Eds.). (1988). *Developing theories of mind.* Cambridge, MA: Cambridge University Press.

Brown, J. S., Collins, A., & Duguid, P. (1989). Situated knowledge and the culture of learning. *Educational Researcher, 18*(1), 32–42.

Carey, S. (1987). *Conceptual change in childhood.* Cambridge, MA: MIT Press.

Céllérier, G. (1992). Organisation et fonctionnement des schèmes. In B. Inhelder, G. Cellerier, E. Ackermann, A. Blanchet, A. Boder, D. Caprona, J. J. Ducret, & M. Saada-Robert (Eds.), *Le cheminement des découvertes chez l'enfant* (pp. 255–299). Nuchatel: Delachaux et Niestlé.

Carey, S. (1987). *Conceptual change in childhood.* Cambridge: MIT Press.

Flavell, J. (1988). The development of children's knowledge about the mind: from cognitive connections to mental representations. In J. Astington, P. Harris, & D. Olson (Eds.), *Developing theories of mind* (pp. 207–216). Cambridge University Press.

Flavell, J. (1990). *Perspectives on perspective-taking.* Paper presented at the 20th annual symposium of the Jean Piaget Society, Philadelphia.

Gilligan, C. (1987). *In a different voice: Psychological theory and women's development.* Cambridge, MA: Harvard University Press.

2. PERSPECTIVE-TAKING AND OBJECT CONSTRUCTION   35

Goodman, N. (1978). *Ways of world making*. Indianapolis: Hackett Publishing Co.

Haraway, D. (1991). *Simians, cyborgs, and women: The reinvention of nature*. New York: Routledge.

Harding, S. (1991). *Whose science? Whose knowledge?: Thinking from women's lives*. Ithaca: Cornell University Press.

Hatano, G., & Inagaki, K. (1987). Everyday biology and school biology: How do they Interact? *Quarterly Newsletter of the Laboratory of Comparative Human Cognition, 9*, 120–128.

Huttenlocher, J., & Presson, C. (1973). Mental rotation and the perspective problem. *Cognitive Psychology, 4*, 277–299.

Jordan, J., Kaplan, A., Miller, J., Silver, I., & Surrey, J. (1991). *Women's growth in connection. Writings from the Stone Center*. New York, NY: The Guilford Press.

Karmiloff-Smith, A. (1992). *Beyond modularity*. Cambridge, MA: MIT Press.

Kegan, R. (1982). *The evolving self*. Cambridge, MA: Harvard University Press.

Keller, E. (1985). *Reflections on gender and science*. New Haven, CT: Yale University Press.

Lave, J. (1992). *Legitimate peripheral participation*. Paper presented at the annual meeting of the American Educational Research Association, Chicago, IL.

Lave, J., & Wenger, E. (1991). *Situated learning: Legitimate peripheral participation*. Cambridge, MA: Cambridge University Press.

Papert, S. (1980). *Mindstorms*. New York: Basic Books.

Perner, J. (1993). *Understanding the representational mind*. Cambridge, MA: MIT Press.

Piaget, J., & Inhelder, B. (1967). The coordination of perspectives. In *The child's conception of space* (pp. 209–246). New York: Norton & Company.

Reith, E., et al. (1989). Social behavior and performance in a task of synthesis of points of view. *Archives de Psychologie, 57*, 289–301.

Rogoff, B. & Lave, L. (1984). *Everyday cognition: Its development in social context*. Cambridge, MA: Harvard University Press.

Sayeki, Y. (1989). *Anthropomorphic epistemology*. Unpublished manuscript, Laboratory of Comparative Human Cognition, University of California, San Diego.

Turkle, S., & Papert, S. (1991). Epistemological pluralism: Styles and voices within the computer culture. In I. Harel & S. Papert (Eds.), *Constructionism* (pp. 161–193). Norwood, NJ: Ablex.

Wellman, H. (1990). *The child's theory of mind*. Cambridge, MA: MIT Press.

Wertsch, J. (1991). *Voices if the mind: A sociocultural approach to mediated action*. Cambridge, MA: Harvard University Press.

Wimmer, H., & Perner, J. (1983). Beliefs about beliefs: Representation and constraining function of wrong beliefs in young children's understanding of deception. *Cognition, 13*, 103–128.

Winnicott, D. (1971). *Playing and reality*. London: Tavistock Publishers.

Elementary School Children's Images of Science

Aaron A. Brandes

INTRODUCTION

"If you need an apple seed to get a tree, and a tree to get an apple seed, where did the first tree come from?" This key question about the origins of life was posed to me by a bright, inner-city second-grade girl. Despite her curiosity about the natural world, her insightful contributions to class discussion, and her ready adoption of new concepts, this girl insisted that she was "not good at science." What is her image of science that she sees herself as "not good at it"? What can be done to help her construct an image that incorporates the questioning and curiosity that she, herself, has in such abundance? The underlying motivation of my research is to improve children's relationship to science by helping them construct a richer image of science, one that reflects the world and work of scientists and connects science to their own abilities and activities.

This research explores the ideas and feelings about science of an ethnically diverse group of children in Grades 2 through 6, using drawings, questionnaires, brainstorming sessions, ethnographic observation and clinical interviews. In this chapter I present some findings to date along with the framework and motivation for work in progress. This current effort involves working with children in science explorations. It is rooted in questions they generate and aimed at helping them understand in a deeper and more concrete (Turkle & Papert, 1991; Wilensky, 1991) way the process by which scientific understanding is generated.

FRAMEWORK

Children's Images of Science

A child's image of science incorporates both cognitive and affective components. Cognitive aspects include a child's beliefs about which topics are part of science, what activities scientists undertake, and the nature of the scientific enterprise. Important affective aspects include the child's feelings about science—the interest, dislike, indifference, and excitement they experience in relation to science. In addition, this affective dimension includes science-related self-esteem, which is reflected in statements such as "I want to be a scientist" and "I'm not good at science." The cognitive and affective elements within an image of science are inextricably interconnected. If an African-American girl's image of "what scientists do" is a White man working alone in a laboratory of shining glassware, this image may both create and reflect a feeling of distance and inadequacy regarding science.

Related Work

This research takes a constructivist approach that builds on Piaget's (1954, 1970) idea that our knowledge is constructed through an ongoing interaction between our environment and our current understanding of the world. It explores children's construction of their image of science. Because the image of science is comprised of children's ideas, epistemological beliefs, and attitudes towards science, this research uses and integrates ideas and methods used by researchers in these fields.

Research on "children's ideas" (Driver, Guesne, & Tiberghien, 1985; Osborne & Freyberg, 1985) and "conceptual change" (Carey, 1991; Posner, Strike, Hewson, & Gertzog, 1982) in specific domains in science such as living things (Carey, 1985) and mechanics (diSessa, 1982; McCloskey, 1982) has shown that although children's ideas may not be as explicit or coherent as formal theories, they are robust. Similarly, we can expect that children also construct an understanding of the nature of science. This has two important implications for science learning. First, if school science simply suggests that children's thinking is wrong, and fails to connect to or appreciate it, and furthermore presents ideas in an ineffective way, school may reinforce stereotyped ideas about the difficulty of science and leave many children feeling that they have no aptitude for it. Second, because research has shown that learning environments that do not engage children's prior understandings of a topic are likely to fail, we must take a deeper understanding of the nature of science as a goal for science learning and first understand the way children think about science.

Since thinking about the nature of science is "meta" to thinking about a specific topic in science, this research takes children's epistemological views, specifically their views about the nature and generation of scientific knowledge,

38

as important. Although epistemology might seem to be a topic of interest only to philosophers, Ackermann (1988) has shown ways that children, themselves, function as epistemologists. Some might doubt the importance of epistemological beliefs for learning, but Wilensky (1993, this volume) has shown how they are a critical factor in mathematics learning. Another source of complication is that because epistemological beliefs are on a "meta" level, one must also realize that behavior on the "lower level" may not be consistent with explicit epistemological beliefs. Hammer (1991) found that some college physics students believed that physics is a structured whole, but solved problems and prepared for tests in a manner more consistent with a belief that it consists of unconnected formulae.

Children's ideas about the nature of science have been explored by Carey, Evans, Honda, Jay, and Unger (1989) and Driver, Leach, Millar, and Scott (1993). They argue that a deeper understanding of science is an important goal of science education, and speculate that it may enhance science learning. I agree with this stand, but I additionally argue that children's beliefs about what science is also influence their interest in science.

Integrating the role of affect is an important aspect of my approach. If children do not see science as something "for them," they may not engage in potentially stimulating science activities. The increased attention being given to the role of affect in conceptual change was highlighted in a recent review article by Pintrich, Marx, and Boyle (1993). They cite research that supports the view that conceptual change should not be thought of as a process of "cold cognition." This research evaluates the impact of various factors that may enhance or retard children's attitudes and learning in science. These factors are primarily characteristics of the learning environment (e.g., teachers' roles, use of hands on materials, etc.). The goal of much of this research is to determine which factors are most strongly correlated with science learning and positive attitudes towards science. The methodologies used in this research could be used to study any domain of learning. No special attention is paid to specific characteristics of science. In contrast, my research is concerned with specific features of science and children's perception of science that may affect their attitude toward, and involvement in, science.

Two distinctive features of my approach are (a) a concern for the way children's assumptions and environment shape their construction of ideas and (b) the exploration of the interrelationship of children's ideas, epistemology and affect, which come together in a key concept for this study: image of science.

Cultural Stereotypes as a Source of Alienation

Children's images of science are influenced by societal images of science portrayed in books, movies, advertisements, and other media. For example, an advertisement for the Boston Museum of Science (see Fig. 3.1) portrays a wild-

FIG. 3.1. Advertisement for Museum of Science, exhibiting stereotypical characteristics of a scientist.

eyed boy with glasses and a pocket protector, and bears the subtitle, "If your little scientist misses this exhibit, he'll be really mad." The tag line reads, "After all, you never know who will be the next Einstein. Or Frankenstein." This ad compactly presents a stereotyped image of a scientist as a nerdy White male genius, perhaps a bit mad, to be handled with care. It suggests that even if you, as a parent, feel alienated from science, it is your duty to see if your child might be one of the few who have the ability to enter this odd elite and perhaps advance the cause of humankind. Despite the fact that the Boston Museum of Science is dedicated to the popularization and explication of science, the ad is a powerful exemplar of the mystification and alienation people feel in relation to science. This myth prevents many people from coming close enough to science to experience their own potential for enjoying and doing science.

School Science as a Source of Alienation

School science often fails to convey the wonder and excitement of doing science and thus leads to reduced student interest. Viewing science as a "storehouse of knowledge" ignores the process by which such knowledge is generated (Tinker, 1991). Approaches that emphasize science process skills often fail to convey the motivation for the use of such skills in an ongoing cycle of theory generation and verification (Duschl, 1990). The formally presented scientific method does not fully reflect the actual "messier" practice of scientists. Covering up the "messiness" of real science or mathematics can lead to brittle learning and damage learners' self-esteem (Wilensky, 1993). Furthermore, the learning and thinking activities of experts are more similar to those of everyday life than those employed in school (Brown, 1989). A goal of my research is to use such similarities to help children engage in science and construct richer, nonalienated images of science.

Real Science as a Potential Source of Connection

I believe that science need be neither as alien nor as mysterious as many people come to see it. A step in this direction is to help children build connections to aspects of science that are personally meaningful. Children may find resonances with their own interests and abilities in characteristics that they previously never linked to science. Aspects of science that are potential points of accessibility, but which are often absent from school science include (a) the importance of curiosity and a sense of wonder in motivating scientists' work (Nemirovsky, 1992); (b) the value of faith in one's scientific beliefs and agenda in sustaining protracted explorations (e.g., Kepler's search for a rational heliocentric model of the solar system that was consistent with the observational data [Gingerich, 1992; Toulmin & Goodfield, 1961]); (c) the role of creating physical and intellectual tools and instruments in scientific progress; (d) the significance of selecting and specifying which data to measure and collect; (e) the prevalence of team efforts and communities of research, which contrasts with the common image of the solitary scientist (Latour, 1987; Toulmin & Goodfield, 1961); (f) the ambiguities and debate surrounding scientific claims (Collins & Pinch, 1993); (g) the role of models and metaphors in building intuitions and fostering understanding; and (h) the importance of multiple ways of scientific "knowing" (Belenky, Clinchy, Goldberger, & Tarule, 1986; Turkle & Papert, 1991; Wilensky, 1991, 1993). Although science is often seen as distant and objective (Keller, 1985), a more subjective stance may help develop insight into a phenomenon. For example, Einstein's imagining what it would be like to travel on a wave of light was an early step in his development of the special theory of relativity. Similarly, Barbara McClintock was able to see and understand far more than other researchers about the development of the genetic material of corn by developing a "feeling for the organism" (Keller, 1983).

The aforementioned view of science as a collective effort to more deeply understand the workings of the world may prove more appealing to children than the stereotypic picture of the solitary scientist in the laboratory discovering eternal truths. Furthermore, children may see that they possess some of the wide variety of skills that are valuable for doing science (e.g., tinkering and building instruments, finding patterns in data, intuiting fruitful research directions, communicating one's findings in writing and face to face, and persistence in searching for elusive phenomena). Thus, in addition to giving children a deeper appreciation of the nature of science, this view may give them an inroad to participation in science, fostering the growth of both the cognitive and the affective sides of their images of science.

Summary

This research is guided by the belief that children construct images of science that are comprised of an interconnected complex of mental representations and feelings. This construction is influenced by cultural messages and school experience. Consequently, by the time they leave elementary school, many children believe that science is not for them. Yet it is possible for children to experience aspects of doing science that may lead them to a deeper understanding of the enterprise of science, and a greater feeling of identification as a person having abilities in science.

OVERVIEW

The ideas in this chapter have been developed during three studies conducted in public schools during the spring semesters of 1992, 1993, and 1994. The first two studies were conducted in the same inner-city school, employed many of the same research methods, and were guided by the same research questions. For this reason, both studies are presented and discussed in Part 4. The third study is more intensive and expands the focus from children's *ideas* about science to children's *images of science*, which includes the affective aspects. Therefore, results of the third study are presented in a separate section. The remainder of this overview presents the goals of the three studies.

Studies 1 and 2 were guided by two questions:

1. What ideas do elementary school children have about what science is and what scientists do?
2. What, in science, are children curious about?

The first study explored the ideas of second graders. The second study focused primarily on fourth graders, but also generated some data about second, third and fifth graders. Both studies involved brainstorming sessions with entire classes and individual interviews with children. They led to a preliminary understanding of the development of children's ideas about science.

These studies led to two refinements in my ideas and methodology. One involved an increased emphasis on the role of affect. I observed a decrease in overall excitement about science as children progressed from second to fifth grade. Furthermore, by the fourth grade, students seemed to be more labeled (both by teachers and by themselves) as good or not good in science. This change in affect and science self-concept led me to introduce the *image of science* concept in which children's feelings about science are affected by their ideas about what science is.

I also found that the science learning experiences in this school were not particularly rich. In order to study children's images of science in a setting that provided students with a better in-school science program, I chose a new site, a sixth-grade classroom known for its innovative science activities. The choice of a sixth-grade classroom was also motivated by my interest in features of children's epistemology of science that I did not find present in the fourth-grade students, but which some seventh graders exhibited in the study of Carey et al. (1989).[1] This third study continued the investigation of the first two questions and, in addition, asked the following question:

3. What is the relationship of children's feelings about science to their ideas about science and science learning?

STUDIES ONE AND TWO

Methods

Site: Studies One and Two.   The site was a predominately Hispanic and African-American inner city Boston public school. Although it was built as an open school in the 1970s, that model of education was never put into practice. Today the few rooms with four walls are prized by most teachers, who value insulation from the noise of adjacent classrooms. Most of the classroom teachers do little or no science teaching themselves. Students work with a science specialist about once a week. I chose the site because 2 years of previous support work (Brandes, 1992a) and research (Brandes, 1992b) in the school gave me connections and credibility with the teachers and principal.

Subjects: Study One.   During the first phase of the study I worked with a classroom of 28 second graders. Based on my classroom observations and the initial interview, I selected three children to interview in depth. One was a European-American boy, who was clearly seen by himself and others as gifted in science. Another was the African-American girl described in the introduction, who did not see herself as "good in science," despite her obvious talent. The third child was a Hispanic boy, who rarely contributed to regular classroom discussions but who participated in the brainstorming process with interest and enthusiasm. Over the course of the project, each of these children was interviewed four times in the second grade and twice during their third-grade year. In addition, nine other second graders were interviewed at least once.

Methods: Study One.   Three main methods were used during a 3-month period beginning in February 1992: classroom brainstorming sessions, clinical interviews, and ethnographic observation. The project began with a series of

---

[1]The first school only went up to fifth grade.

audiotaped brainstorming sessions, conducted to gain an overview of the children's ideas. The sessions varied in length from 40 to 60 minutes. Each session began with brief instructions (such as asking the children to say what they think science is, or what they are curious about); their ideas were listed on a large sheet of paper. At the end of each session, the children were asked to write briefly or draw a picture related to the discussion. These materials, and the transcribed notes, were used to guide subsequent sessions.

Clinical interviews have been an important tool in studying children's ideas about science (Carey et al., 1989; White & Gunstone, 1992). The interviews I conducted were shaped by a number of factors. Sometimes I followed up on topics that had been explored in the brainstorming sessions. The children's writing and drawing helped elicit responses. My analysis of the brainstorming sessions also led me to ask specific questions about such topics as potions and formulas. Often, however, a child and I discussed topics that evolved during the interview. For example, a discussion of a LEGO car competition led to the topic of gravity. A lengthy discussion of "zero g" ensued, which I pursued further in a subsequent interview. I also asked the children about their experiences with science classes. This included what they had done, what they had learned, and whether they had liked it. All interviews were audiotaped and transcribed.

I observed classes taught by the science teacher as well as sessions led by classroom teachers. I kept field notes describing activities in the classroom, as well as my own reactions and ideas. Ethnographic studies of children's science learning have focused on sociocultural analysis (Jackson, 1992) and patterns in student discourse (Theberge, 1994). My research combined detailed interest in children's thinking with a desire for a more situated (Lave & Wenger, 1991) understanding of the children and their environment.

Subjects: Study Two.   The subjects of my study were students in one classroom each from Grades 2 through 5. One purpose of these sessions was to look for developmental differences between the younger and older children. In addition, I was seeking a classroom for my more in-depth work. The second-grade teacher was the same for both studies.[2]

Methods: Study Two.   Classroom brainstorming sessions, clinical interviews, and small group projects were used over a 4-month period beginning February, 1993. I conducted brainstorming sessions about science with each class. Children were also asked to draw a picture of a scientist (Chambers, 1983). Fantasy experiments (which are described in more detail in a later section) were conducted with several children across the range of grades. Most of the effort in this study was directed toward the fourth-grade classroom. Further brainstorming sessions with these students explored their ideas about scientists and doing sci-

---

[2]A study of this teacher's approach to teaching is contained in Brandes, 1992a.

ence. Interviews were conducted with seven fourth-grade children. New questions focused on concepts such as "prediction" and "experiment," and on eliciting the children's attitudes towards science. I also conducted small group projects with the fourth graders.

Results

In this section I present selected findings from Studies 1 and 2. These findings include children's ideas about science, their criteria for deciding whether something is science, and their ideas about experimentation. The fantasy experiments and the group projects will be discussed in a later paper.

Ideas About Science.   The second graders' first responses to the brainstorming question "What is science?" reflected a number of themes that emerged more fully in further exploration. These themes included: a fascination with the potentialities of mixing and making things; the belief that science can be helpful, but also dangerous; the salience of high technology in science; and the belief that science involves learning and creating new things. The list generated by the children included "magicians who put things together and smoke comes out of it," "to learn stuff," "something like medicine," "electronics," "gasoline," "stuff to make things blow up," "combine medicines to make new medicine," "when you make machines and things," "scientists make stuff, it could taste bad," and "you could mix chemicals."

Third graders' initial responses to the same question were more connected to school: "when you do a project like make a volcano out of Play Doh," "a way of people coming up with new ideas like underwater golf," "make things, like a tornado in a bottle," "rocks," "put bottles together—soapy water," "studying volcanoes," "studying cliffs," "mess around with wires," "peanuts," "make volcano, lava comes out," "experiments," and "animals." From this point on, children focused on science topics (as opposed to activities), which included plants and flowers, electricity, pediatrics, and chemicals. Most of the activities the children mentioned were ones that they had done as part of school science. The children mentioned peanuts because growing and learning about peanuts had been part of a science curriculum developed by the teacher, which included learning about the life and work of George Washington Carver.

In mentioning science topics, children in all grades most frequently referred to subjects studied in school, such as plants, animals, planets, volcanoes, and other elements of the natural world. Technology was frequently mentioned, for example, disk brakes, robots, computers, and the computer language, Logo. These lists were mostly generated in brainstorms about "What is science?" and "I am curious about. . ." However, brainstorms about "science activities" and "what scientists do" also gave rise to lists of topics studied in science as well as references to "active" processes.

In talking about science activities, the second-grade children spoke a great deal about *mixing ingredients* (at least 10 items) *making things* (at least 8 items), *robots* (about 7 kinds), and *formulas* (about 10 kinds). Examples of the formulas were: "to make you sleepy," "to turn a house into gold," and "to make animals talk." The children mentioned robots "to make candy," "do homework," and "turn things into chocolate."[3] In contrast to these imaginative ideas, the mixtures they mentioned were more prosaic: "mix vinegar and baking soda;" also, "mix baking soda, alcohol, and other chemicals, and see what you get." Through interviews I found that these ingredients had been used recently by the school science teacher to make invisible ink.

In describing what scientists do, fourth graders said "experiment," "study lots of different things," "make other machines," "explore," "look at different things to see differences," "keep on trying things," "use microscopes," "go to different places to explore," "find new animals," and "make things to help people."

Fifth-graders' initial responses about what scientists do more closely resembled those typical of adults: "try to figure out things," "invent things," "experiment," "study animals," and "discover new stuff underwater."

Criteria for Science.   In the excitement of brainstorming, children mentioned items that to me appeared not to be science, but which had associations to items introduced by other children. Class discussions confirmed that some of these topics, such as super-heroes, were not seen as part of science. However, some of their judgments as to what does constitute science would not be shared by most adults.

Although they did not uniformly agree on what topics are part of science, second-grade children made distinctions between what was and what was not science. Some of these distinctions came from their school experience. Topics taught by the science teacher or explicitly labeled as science by classroom teachers were usually placed by children in the science category. High technology carried a strong association with science. The presence of electricity or electronics also made the children identify many items as part of science.[4] Some interesting criteria for deciding if something was part of science emerged when I had classes vote on whether different items were science topics or things studied by scientists. Each group had to give reasons for their choices. For example, second graders expressed very different opinions about whether or not sharks are part of science. One group said no—there was not much to learn about sharks. The other group said that there was a great deal to learn about them. Thus, the children saw

---

[3]In research on machines that I conducted with Edith Ackermann (Brandes, 1992b), children talked about robots of this kind, including robots to do homework.

[4]One surprising result of my machines study (Brandes, 1992b) was that many children did not think of mechanical clocks or watches as machines, either because they need to be rewound to keep going, or because they do not use electricity.

learning (echoing the item "to learn stuff" in the brainstorming session) as important for science.

For fifth graders, novelty—the discovery or construction of new things—was an important criterion for deciding if scientists would study something. Some said that scientists once studied shoes. Now that scientists understand shoes, they no longer have to study them. Others said that scientists *do* study shoes. They explained that this is necessary for making new kinds of shoes, such as the shoes you "pump up." Thus many children agreed that science was about studying and producing new things, although they disagreed as to which items qualified as novel.

Experimentation.   Children in all grades had two main points of view about experimentation. Some saw it as the exploratory testing of varying "ingredients," for example, "give stuff to lab rats and see what happens." Others saw experimentation as combining things with a goal in mind: "combine chemicals to make a new chemical to stop pollution."

Knowledge about how to do experiments was often seen as coming from an authoritative source. Many children saw the steps for doing an experiment as analogous to recipes for cooking; the source of recipes for experimentation is books or other scientists. The responses of two second-grade girls provide interesting variations on this theme. The first child talked about using an ingredients book to find out how to make a formula to "blow up the planet." She then went on to say how she would throw "library books, like math books and stuff like that" into a pot of boiling water:

> So the pot of hot water, and you have the soap in it, then the hot water can have a brain. It can know math, reading, and computer stuff. Then you don't have to know nothing else. And the pot of water does it all by itself. If the pot of water knows that it's right then it'll blow up. The pot will blow up.

With further questioning, the child said she "kind of" thought water could really learn from a book. Although this idea of learning is, perhaps, unusual, it reflects the fact that the children have little understanding of how new knowledge and experiments are generated. They therefore assimilate it to ideas that make sense to them.

The second girl spoke of how a man knew his great-great-grandson was going to be a scientist and wrote down the needed information to be passed down through the generations. Like the first child, she saw scientific knowledge as coming from an authoritative source. While one child made use of a more formal and public source of authority (i.e., library books), this girl personalized the authority by locating it in the African-American tradition of passing stories from one generation to another.

Children's drawings of scientists often revealed their ideas about experimentation. Although some second graders drew scientists with elaborate chemistry

FIG. 3.2.   A second-grade boy's picture of a "typical" laboratory scientist.

apparatus (see Fig. 3.2), in general, older children had more knowledge of equipment used in experimentation. They more frequently depicted the scientist handling the equipment, included protective equipment such as goggles, and gave the scientist a goal, such as "creating rubber," or "finding a cure for cancer." However, they overattributed the power of some equipment such as computers. One fourth-grade boy, explaining a picture he had drawn of a scientist trying to find a cure for cancer, said that the scientist gave the mixture he had made to the computer for evaluation: "Like, if it is, like if it cures cancer, it would say on the computer. If it doesn't it would say, like, try something else." He had, however, no idea how the computer could make this evaluation, just an irreducible belief that the computer had the knowledge.

Further Aspects of Children's Images of Science.   One positive aspect of science mentioned by children in all grades was the numerous ways in which science helps us. Second graders mentioned medicines and formulas to keep animals from dying. Older children talked about cures for diseases such as cancer and AIDS. They also linked science to the search for ways to stop pollution and improve recycling. For these largely inner-city children, helping others was the main goal cited by those interested in becoming scientists. In the context of the *image of science* concept, helping others is a perceived characteristic of science that resonates with some children's self-identity as helpers and healers. Learning experiences that connect to the helping potential of science may attract children more strongly than do the planets and other typical elementary school science topics.

Science was also seen to have a dangerous side. Children noted that scientists use and make chemicals that can help people but that can also be dangerous. One child's picture (see Fig. 3.3) portrays a scientist who, in the first panel, is testing a formula by drinking it; in the second panel, he is dead. Knowledge and caution

FIG. 3.3. A fourth-grade boy's picture of a scientist conducting a fatal experiment on himself.

are seen as important for avoiding danger.[5] Children spoke of the danger as arising primarily from accidents caused by careless or nonexpert practitioners of science. There is another side to danger: the excitement associated with explosions. For example, a simulated erupting volcano was one of the most memorable science activities for many children.

The impact of "science danger" on their images of science may vary from child to child. Taking care in doing experiments is certainly important. However, for some children the importance of expert practice may reinforce the idea that science is for a specialized elite, which may leave them feeling unqualified. In contrast, those who have positive self-images as learners may not see specialized training as a barrier. Furthermore, some of them may be motivated by the desire to master their environment and control powerful forces.

Discussion

Summary of Results. Children described science as involving certain activities, topics, materials, and characteristics. Younger children spoke of mixing and making things; conducting experiments figured prominently in the responses of the older elementary school children. Standard school science topics, such as plants, animals, volcanoes, planets, and chemistry were listed by children in all grades. High technology, which included electricity and computers, signified science for all children. Science was also characterized by novelty: Younger children talked about learning, whereas older children saw discovery and invention as key criteria for evaluating a topic as science.

---

[5]Children's science television shows such as *Beakman's World* and *Bill Nye, Science Guy* feature demonstrations and experiments accompanied by warnings for children not try them without adult supervision.

Experimentation was seen by many children, particularly the younger ones, as trying things out to see what happens. Older children more frequently mentioned testing things, typically as part of a goal-driven activity, such as finding the cure for a disease. Although producing novel results was seen as an important goal of experimentation, children did not have a sense of how that would come about except through the testing of new materials or combinations.

Differences Among Children.   Some differences between the younger and older children's responses were developmental. Seven-year-olds are more easily influenced than 10-year-olds. This was particularly noticeable during brainstorming sessions. Second-grade children frequently made responses that echoed the responses of their peers.

School activities were also a strong influence. For example, the children brainstormed many examples of "mixing" that involved ingredients used in a recent invisible ink science session. Because their responses are so easily influenced, it is important to use multiple approaches to probe for young children's ideas and feelings (White & Gunstone, 1992). Repeating questions on separate occasions may also be useful. For example, I found in follow-up interviews with three second-grade children that the distinctions they drew between "formulas" and "potions" had changed, but that both were still seen as types of mixtures (e.g., liquids and powders), created for a purpose (e.g., medicine or magic).

Some of the differences reflected learning accumulated from school, educational television, friends, family, and other sources. This included knowledge of more sophisticated topics as well as more knowledge of the activities engaged in by scientists. The older children usually had more science experience than the younger ones. However, children with close relatives who were scientists typically had more knowledge of science, and more positive attitudes toward science, than their peers. In contrast, some children with aptitude for science did not receive much support for their science interests. I illustrate these last two points in a later section of brief case studies.

There were also some gender differences among the children. Most of the children drew male scientists. The few exceptions were girls with interest in one of the life sciences. Girls were more interested in biological phenomena than were boys. Some of the girls who seemed the most gifted in science wanted to become doctors. The only children who wanted to be engineers were boys. However, when asked questions directly or with a "complete-the-sentence" probe, the children held that boys and girls were equally able to be scientists.

The school environment was not overtly gender-biased toward males in science. The children had both male and female science teachers. The teachers encouraged both boys and girls to participate in science activities and actually picked out more girls than boys as their best science students. However, the content of science lessons leaned more toward the physical sciences than the life sciences, which favored boys' interests.

Case Studies.   Mark was one of the few European-American children in his second-grade class. He was identified by himself, his classmates, and his teachers as someone with real talent in science. For example, when the teacher held a contest to build the LEGO car that would go the farthest, everyone expected Mark's group to win (they came in second). Mark cultivated this "scientist" image. When I asked the children what they were curious about in science, his first contribution had as many syllables as a second-grader could muster: "psycho-telekinetic powers." Beyond the level of appearances, though, Mark, was, indeed, very interested in science. He played with his older brother's chemistry kit (and was looking forward to getting his own), did experiments (such as investigating the effects of salt and pepper on worms), and watched many science and science fiction programs on television. When Mark had questions about science, he discussed them with his mother, who was a parent advisor on science curriculum in the school. Some of Mark's ideas about science laboratories came from visiting an uncle's laboratory. Thus, Mark immersed himself in the world of science and was familiar with a wide variety of science phenomena.

Mark illustrates the way children can become involved in a positive feedback loop with regard to science. He saw himself as a "science kid"; this supported his interest in science and enhanced his motivation to engage in science activities. These activities further promoted his enjoyment of science and his deeper understanding of science.

Ellen was the African-American second-grader who asked about the origin of apple trees. She was the only child in the class who spontaneously used the word "theory" in our discussions. "Theory," she said, when asked to define it, "it means that they [scientists] get ideas and they like to try them to the public. This thing I made, I had a theory." Ellen also spontaneously applied strong conceptual skills to science activities. For example, after the brainstorming sessions, most of the children found it difficult to find categories in which to group the things they were curious about. Ellen, however, raised her hand and said, "I already did that," and shared her groupings. Despite these intellectual abilities, Ellen believed she was good at math and reading but not science. This, she explained, was because she did not know many facts about science. Thus, Ellen's idea that science is an accumulation of facts resulted in a negative self-evaluation of her own ability in science. Furthermore, Ellen's challenging style did not earn her much approval from her teacher and classmates.

Interestingly, Ellen's expressed image of science changed between the beginning and end of the year. At the beginning of the year, she saw science as involving many specific facts that she did not know. By the end of the year, she saw invention as the key aspect of science, and then argued that everything is science: "See me talking and writing with a pencil? That's science because we had to invent how words were, how to talk." She also mentioned the science teacher: "She thinks we learn science by just her telling us. But it's wrong. We learn science by ourselves. We already know science."

Ellen's new construction of science was a more positive, and, in some ways, a deeper image of science. However, it was far too broad to promote a strong involvement in science. In contrast to her previous construct, which excluded her from science because she lacked a repertoire of "facts," this image did not promote her involvement because it failed to significantly differentiate science from any other endeavor. Given the opportunity to explore some of her many scientific questions, Ellen might have come to understand which kinds of thinking and activity are characteristic of science.

Jose, the third child I interviewed in depth, exemplifies the value of knowing a child before interpreting what he or she says. Jose participated actively in the brainstorming sessions, but was more tentative in expressing his ideas in our discussions. This may have been, in part, because he speaks Spanish at home, and our discussions were in English. The stimulation of other children's ideas may have been a supportive feature for Jose in the brainstorming sessions.

In our interviews, Jose brought the theme of danger up spontaneously at least six times. For example, he said that chemicals could be dangerous, and that if he went into a laboratory, he would not touch anything because of the potential danger. From this, one might conclude that danger is a significant part of his image of science. However, this theme was not limited to science. Half of Jose's danger references were to sports. He said that football was more dangerous than baseball, but that you could still be hit by a pitch in baseball. He wanted to meet Michael Jordan, but not Charles Barkley, who was too scary. It would thus appear that although danger is part of Jose's image of science, it is also characteristic of his overall relationship to the world.

One of the most striking differences between the younger and older elementary school children was their decreasing excitement about science as they progressed in school. Second-graders began with curiosity about the world and ideas about how science might empower them to do the things they care about (e.g., help animals and avoid homework). Yet as they progressed through elementary school, these critical aspects of the scientific enterprise faded from their image of science. I suspect that this is because they were not given the opportunity to connect science to their interests, and were not using science to explore the topics that excited them. In talking about what it takes to become a scientist, fourth graders focused a great deal on the importance of studying and hard work. Although these are necessary preparation for professional scientific work, they are not unique to science. To the extent that the children's view of science became more removed from their own goals and aspirations, their motivation to do this preparatory work declined.

The Role of Teachers in Shaping Children's Images of Science.   The teachers who participated in this study did not talk with children directly about the scope and goals of science. Nevertheless, their choice of topics and activities, and the way they presented these, had a powerful affect on the way the children thought and felt about science. For example, children frequently referred to classroom science topics and activities in discussing what is part of science. Furthermore, when asked to brainstorm science activities they would like, the younger children were more inventive than the older children. The older children seemed more constrained by the school science activities most familiar to them.

In most science sessions I observed, the teacher did not have a broad conceptual goal. In some class sessions, the goal was primarily task oriented (e.g., for the children to make a complete circuit using light bulbs, wires, and batteries). At other times the goal was a concept in a specific domain, such as "center of gravity." (This topic seemed beyond the grasp of the second graders to whom it was presented.) Sometimes, however, the teachers had an agenda that involved a more general scientific concept, creating a link between science lessons or conveying a message about science. I use three lessons to illustrate the teachers' mixed success, as measured by the children's learning.

The second-grade classroom teacher used the word and concept *prediction* as the focus of a class session. The children cut paper "whirlers" from a handout. There were four different types, with varying dimensions of wing length and breadth. When dropped, they spun around as they fell to the ground. Each child predicted which design would perform best, and the predictions were tabulated on the blackboard. The predictions were then put to the test as the children took turns dropping their four whirlers. Before a child pronounced one whirler the winner, there was much shouting as other children tried to influence the decision to favor their own prediction. This social pressure was part of the fun for the children, but because the evaluation was very influenced by the prediction, it obscured the role of prediction in scientific exploration.

Another difficulty was the absence of a clear criterion for deciding which whirler was best. Did "best" mean that the whirler fell faster? Slower? Straighter? Without explicit criteria, the children's evaluations were incommensurable. At the end of the activity I asked two children who made different evaluations to drop their whirlers and explain to me and each other their reasons for picking one as best. However, these second graders could not go beyond simply asserting that one was best. Not surprisingly, my follow-up questions indicated that most children did not understand the term to mean anything other than a guess. This was not a bilingual class, but some of the children lived in a primarily Spanish speaking environment. Many of these children could not use the word "prediction" in a sentence. Although the teacher had a clear goal for this lesson, the activity was too ambiguous for most of the children, who could not understand the meaning of the key concept and its importance for science. Furthermore, the teacher underestimated the language difficulty faced by some of the children.

The science teacher led a class that was ineffective for another reason: Her motivating context did not make sense to the children. Her topic was wind power. She intended to connect this lesson to other lessons about power. Unfortunately, her opening remarks about windmills and grinding flour for bread were strikingly unconnected to the children's understanding of the world. They had no experience of windmills, and I presume that most of them had only a limited understanding of how bread is produced.

The teacher's lecture certainly did not hold the children's attention. When she finished talking, she engaged the children in making pinwheels cut from ditto sheets. I saw it as an enjoyable arts and crafts experience. However, it did not appear to explain to them how wind could be made to do practical work, or why the activity should be seen as science. If the children had built a wind-driven device that actually lifted or turned something, they might have seen the activity as related to harnessing the power of a natural force. Given a chance to design their own variations of the design, they could have explored what factors were most important. The task as it was structured required no thinking on the children's part.

One third-grade teacher made it her goal to increase the involvement of her predominately African-American class in science. When I explained my ideas about children's images of science, she said they resonated with a curriculum she had developed to give her children an African-American scientist as a role model. She organized the lessons around George Washington Carver's life history and his inventive work with peanuts. The children grew peanuts and made things with them. The impact of this curriculum on the children's ideas about science was reflected in their inclusion of peanuts as a response to the question, "What is science?" Despite their study of Carver's inventions, however, the role of invention in science was not mentioned by any of the children during brainstorming sessions. Such metaconceptual points may need to be reinforced explicitly.

This third-grade teacher was unusual because she discussed Carver's motivation for his scientific work. In contrast, most of the other teachers I observed did not address why people do science, and what goals, activities and ways of thought are characteristic of science. A consequence of this approach was that although children were given a message that science is important, their school experience gave them no particular reason to value it. This may explain in part why fourth and fifth graders spoke less frequently than second graders about science producing things and the effects that they found personally exciting. School values became their model of science activity, and many of these children did not find science very appealing.

STUDY THREE: CURRENT RESEARCH

My current research explores children's images of science. In contrast to previous studies, I focus more on children's ideas about experimentation and the generation of scientific knowledge as well as on children's feelings about science and about their own potential for doing science.

Methods

Site. I am conducting my current research in a sixth-grade public school classroom in Cambridge, Massachusetts. The school is noted for its innovative curriculum and attracts students from varied socioeconomic backgrounds. The classroom teaching is shared by two teachers, each teaching 2 fixed days a week and alternating the remaining day. Each has nearly 20 years of teaching experience, and both have developed many learning activities, partly in conjunction with researchers from the local educational research community. Children are usually involved in individual activities, pair or group experiences, or teacher-facilitated whole-class discussions. Their work in science emphasizes the importance of "sense-making" (Rosebery, Warren, & Conant, 1992; Theberge, 1994) by the children. One teacher is leading activities that involve understanding connections between shadows, the position of the sun, length of day around the world, and the seasons. The other teacher is co-leading (with a science teacher from the school) activities that involve building structures and understanding what keeps them up (or makes them fall down). The "structures" activity covers a newly mandated city curriculum requirement for the sixth grade.

Subjects. The subjects of my study are the entire sixth-grade class, which is comprised of 25 students; 13 girls and 12 boys. Most of the 11 non-White students in the class immigrated from Haiti and were originally enrolled in the school's bilingual program.

Methods. I used drawings, questionnaires, clinical interviews, ethnographic observation, and small group work to explore and help develop the children's images of science. The first three methods were used over a 1-month period to develop an initial picture of each child's image of science. Before the children gained much knowledge of my agenda (which might have influenced their responses), I gave them a questionnaire about their general interests and abilities in and out of school (see Appendix A).

The drawing task was the Draw-a-Scientist Test (Chambers, 1983) in which the children drew a scientist at work. In addition, the children wrote on a separate paper the scientists' names, ages, where they live, what they are doing, and why they are doing it.

The study of children's attitudes toward science is replete with instruments (Moore & Sutman, 1970) and severe critiques of those instruments (Munby, 1983). These instruments are criticized for mixing dimensions of study, not measuring what they claim to, and not being adequately tested. In studies based primarily on correlations between attributes measured by such instruments, test scores, and quantifiable behaviors, this is a serious weakness. However, in research that relies primarily on qualitative data, such instruments may provide an additional quantitative "sketch" of the subject. I therefore used the following two instruments to supplement data gathered through observations and interviews with the children.

I chose the *Science Interest Scale* (Rennie & Parker, 1987) to measure interest in science. Children were asked to rate 16 specific items using a modified Likert-type scale in which they indicated whether they like the item content not at all, a little bit, a fair bit, or a lot. Rennie and Parker (1987) provided an analysis of issues concerning heterogeneity of populations and dimensionality of the instrument. This should be useful in the data interpretation process.

The children's attitude towards school science was measured with the *Attitude Toward Science in School Assessment*[6] (Germann, 1988). This instrument requires students to indicate their degree of agreement with a series of attitude statements about science or science in school. I developed an interview protocol to explore children's images of science (see Appendix B). This incorporated items from the nature of science interview protocol used by Carey et al. (1989), which probe children's ideas about what is meant by science and experimentation. Additional questions concerned their self-image regarding science, the science activities they are participating in, and their feelings about science activities. Earlier versions of the protocol were tried as follow-up interviews with fourth graders I had worked with last spring, and adjustments were made. All interviews were audiotaped and transcribed.

As part of my research I observed (and, at times, participated in) the science sessions of both teachers. These observations give me an understanding of the children's current school science experience as well as the participation of individual children. I keep field notes and audiotape or videotape sessions involving the whole class.

Working with small groups, I am using a method developed in my earlier work called the *fantasy experiment*. I chose this term because the experiments are not actually carried out, though they are imagined in detail.[7] The method was designed to help address the many questions children generate that cannot be answered by classroom experiments, such as "Is there intelligent life in the universe?" Before the fantasy experiment begins, the children brainstorm a list of topics they find interesting, as well as a list of questions they would like to answer. Then, the children and I construct an experiment to explore some of these questions together. For example, one child may begin with the question, "What is the temperature on Mars?" She then designs an experiment, with practical considerations reduced or eliminated. Because the experiment is a fantasy, the response, "First I would build a space ship" is a legitimate first move. Other participants, including the researcher, ask questions to help the experimenter

---

[6]I split one compound item into two in the version I administered.

[7]These differ from thought experiments because the results of a thought experiment are meant to be self-evident. The point of a "fantasy experiment" is to elaborate on the methods and issues. The results that would be found by carrying out the experiment are not self-evident.

sharpen her experiment. For example, if the final step proposed is "Then I would get the temperature," someone might ask, "How would you get the temperature?" Continued questioning promotes deeper thought about the role of measurement and the construction of special equipment in scientific research. In this case, it would probably be necessary to build a special thermometer to accommodate the extreme temperatures on Mars. Through my participation in the questioning process, I model concern for aspects of doing science that I find to be important and accessible to the children.

Results

Sixth Graders' Ideas About Science.   Some sixth graders' ideas regarding what science is about were very similar to those of younger elementary school children. Like the younger children, most sixth graders emphasized topics and activities; only a few explicitly spoke of science as a knowledge-generating enterprise. The topics they listed fell under the same general categories that younger children mention: biology, earth and space science, chemistry and medicine. However, the sixth graders mentioned more specialized topics, such as genetics. In addition, they were more likely to name disciplines of study, such as marine biology, instead of listing particular items such as sharks and whales.

The frequent mention of experiments as science activities showed a shift from the "mix things and see what happens" view of younger children toward a view of science as an enterprise focused on increasing our understanding of the world. In fact, six students explicitly described science as explaining things, finding out how things work or react, and finding out or using information. This aspect was also reflected in some children's view of the goal of science. Seven children saw the goal as expanding knowledge or discovering things; four saw it as explaining how things work; and two saw the goal as finding out new things. Helping people, animals, or the environment, an important aspect of science for the younger children, was given as a goal of science by six children.

Experiments and the Generation of Knowledge.   Sixth graders saw experiments as a more central to science than did many of the younger children. Nevertheless, many of them shared the younger children's "try something and see what happens" view of experimentation. For example, one boy defined *experiment* as "seeing the effects of radiation on people." Similarly, another child stated that an experiment is "finding out what happens to something when you do something to it." In contrast, some children expressed a more mature view of experimentation. One girl said she used to think, when she was "a kid," that experiments were about mixing things, but now she sees experiments as trying to answer questions. One of her peers saw experiments as trying to "prove something."

Several children mentioned ideas about experimentation that they had not fully assimilated. These included hypothesis, variables, and controls. For example, one girl said you always had to do an experiment three times, although she didn't know why. Another girl, who was interested in science and held more sophisticated views of science than most of her peers, spoke of the desirability of having only one independent variable when conducting an experiment. This, she explained, would make it easier to isolate which of many factors was responsible for the variability of an effect. Although she understood the logic behind this guideline, she did not fully understand what an independent variable was. In her mind, the independent variable was something the experimenter changed. The following example shows how she erroneously concluded that time was an independent variable in an experiment she designed to measure the effect of sugar on the body.

The girl correctly saw the amount of sugar (measured in brownies) as one independent variable. Yet she saw that it might be necessary to look at the effects of varying brownie doses over different time intervals to distinguish their effects. She decided, therefore, that time was also an independent variable. A more experienced experimenter might see time sampling intervals as something that might have to be adjusted, but would not see it as a variable affecting the sugar effect. Having two independent variables made the experimental design problematic for the student. In an attempt to help her clarify the role of time, I asked her to imagine an experiment in which the time for a ball to fall from varying heights was measured. In the context of this example, she was able to see the time the ball took to fall as a dependent variable. However, this did not help resolve her quandary about the brownie experiment.

Most children had heard of the word *theory*. They primarily thought theories were guesses, ideas, or thoughts about what might happen in a situation or why something would be true. A typical use of the word began, "My theory is that. . ." In this view, a theory is a prediction or an unsubstantiated explanation. For example, one of the more sophisticated thinkers believed that *theory* was just a less complex term for *hypothesis*. Similarly, six other children held that theories, once proven, undergo a change in status and become facts. In contrast, a number of children believed it was meaningful to speak of a "true theory," which they understood to be a correct explanation of a phenomenon. No children held the idea of theory as a conceptual framework, which is one of the most sophisticated views probed by Carey et al. (1989).

Some children were troubled by the apparent contradiction between the idea that theories are essentially unproven and the existence of theories, such as evolution, that are widely held to be true. One boy resolved the problem by explaining that although we may speak of a "theory of gravity," gravity is really a fact, and the phrase is probably a holdover from earlier times. A girl reconciled the contradiction by arguing that an explanation could be correct and still be called a theory because it is difficult to convince everyone that a theory is true.

For example, the idea that the earth is spherical can be called a theory because some people might cling to the belief that the earth is flat.

Half of the children thought that scientists make predictions at least some of the time. Some saw that predictions could have a guiding role. They said that if things did not work out as expected, the scientist would try to do something differently. Others held that the scientist would be upset or think he or she did not do the experiment correctly. Two children said that if a prediction was correct the scientist would do more experiments or make another prediction—and the result would generate new research. Others saw that a correct prediction would lead to knowledge—the scientist should write it down and perhaps use it to make further predictions. Generally, however, most of the children, even those most oriented toward science, found the process by which new information is generated to be quite mysterious. A conversation with one boy, Dan, illustrates this.

Dan is a bright sixth grader who wants to become a scientist so he can "expand human knowledge." He belongs to an astronomy club (with mostly adult members) and is grinding lenses for his own telescope. When I asked him how he thought scientists discover new things, he spoke rather vaguely at first, about "trying new things."[8] He seemed dissatisfied with his explanation, however, until he remarked, "You know, scientists often discover things by accident." He gave the example of Goodyear, who discovered that rubber, accidentally spilled on an oven, became hard. When asked, Dan took his line of reasoning a step further and stated that new discoveries are *usually* made by accident. "So," I asked him, "do you think that scientists go around trying to have accidents?" Together, as we explored what science would be like if one had to make accidents to generate new findings, and Dan suddenly shifted his view. "Really," he said, "why would anyone want to go to school and learn to be a scientist if it just involved accidents? Then anyone could do it." Finally, he proposed a new model in which the scientist starts with an idea, and then tries to work it out.

To summarize, in comparison to younger children, sixth graders showed a greater familiarity with the topics and activities of science. Some children showed awareness of science as an enterprise for answering questions about the world. They had some understanding of the logic of experimentation and saw it as more purposive than did many younger children. However, the process of generating new knowledge was still mysterious to them.

Children's Drawings.   In some ways the drawings of sixth-graders were similar to those of the younger children. Half of the pictures contained test tubes or beakers. The types of science most frequently portrayed were chemistry (8), biology (4), and medicine (4). Despite being part of a class in which effort was

---

[8]Some quotes given here are paraphrases based on notes immediately after the interview, during which the tape recorder failed.

FIG. 3.4. A sixth-grade girl's picture of a scientist, her dad.

made to involve boys and girls equally in science, only 5 (of 25) drawings (all five were made by girls) were of female scientists.

During the interview I sometimes elicited the personal significance of a drawing to a child. For example, one girl who is very interested in science drew a picture of her dad, who is a scientist (see Fig. 3.4). Another girl drew a picture representing a growth study in which she was participating (although she drew a male scientist measuring himself). Only one child drew a picture that was an explicit self-representation—one boy portrayed himself as a doctor.

Although many pictures fit the stereotype of the lab scientist with glassware, some sixth-grade children showed their awareness that such representations were stereotyped. One boy's picture was a classic "Eureka" moment of discovery in which the scientist says, "I've done it, I've almost completed the cloning system." Another boy mocked this idea by drawing a "dumb" scientist who announces, "I've done it, at least I think I've done it, what am I making?" One girl consciously went against the male nerd stereotype. She said she did not want to create a "lab coat scientist," but rather a "new kind of scientist." Her picture included a stylishly dressed female scientist with chemicals and a caged animal (see Fig. 3.5) working to make foods that are safe for the animals to eat.

Five children were reluctant to draw. All these children had negative attitudes toward science, as measured by their questionnaires and expressed in the interviews. Given encouragement, some of these children did produce pictures. However, three of these children drew pictures that evaded the task of showing a scientist at work. For example, one scientist was pictured taking a food break. Another boy's picture evolved to include more science. Initially, he drew his scientist watching television. Later, he decided to show the scientist at work. His solution was to give the scientist a screwdriver, explaining that the scientist was about to take the television apart to figure out how it works.

FIG. 3.5.   A sixth-grade girl's picture of a female scientist.

Interest in and Attitude Towards Science.   Through the interviews, question-naires, and drawings I have developed a preliminary sense of children's interests in and attitudes towards science. Science is, of course, multidimensional. There are many disciplines within science, and many activities within a discipline. A marine biologist might not be fascinated by ants. A theoretical physicist may have little desire to design the apparatus needed to test her theory. Furthermore, children experience science in a wide variety of formats and settings, including informal activities, class lectures, hands-on school activities, and science pro-grams on TV, and they need not have a uniform attitude toward or interest in all of them. Nevertheless, given these caveats, I feel that these affective constructs can be useful.

I would like to make a distinction between science and school science. In my view, it would be ideal if school science involved students in doing science explorations and developing an appreciation of what science is about.[9] One would then expect interest in science and school science to be highly correlated for the positive reason that the two appeared to be similar in essence. Unfor-tunately, I think the two are often highly correlated primarily because children identify science as school science.

The children in my studies often made statements that indicated a clear overall stance toward science. One girl said she was not a "science kid," but thought other children were. One girl warned, "You don't want to talk to me, because I hate science." Another girl indicated that she really liked science, but it was not her "top thing." This girl also showed that children are capable of discriminating subtle differences in attitude: "Other children may like Sundial (an activity that is

---

[9]For this reason I chose a research site offering children potentially rich science experiences.

part of the Shadows curriculum), but I'm probably the only one that looks forward to it."

CONCLUSIONS

This chapter has introduced the concept of *image of science* and reported the results of three studies of elementary school children's images of science. The results indicate that although science can be exciting and magical to many elementary school children (particularly in the younger grades), their school science experience does not necessarily foster a greater understanding of the nature of science. Rather, it seems to promote an image of science as a school-like enterprise, in which hard work and increasingly advanced courses are the key to success.[10] Furthermore, it may reinforce the belief that science is the realm for an elite few (a belief also promoted by popular media). By sixth grade, fewer students are excited by science or committed to learning about it. The *image of science* concept suggests that these cognitive and affective developments may go hand in hand.

To put this research in a broader context, I now discuss ways in which the *image of science* concept can be a useful tool in the realm of science learning and identify directions for future research.

Image of Science Uses

The concept of a child's image of science provides a potential ground for integrating findings from the now separate research programs of children's ideas about the nature of science and the role of affect in science learning. In exploring children's ideas about the nature of science, we can probe for aspects of science that are potentially accessible and inviting to children. Such aspects include the role of questions in science and the role of designing and building measuring devices. On the affective side, we can explore whether such aspects can be used to engage children in science and increase their self-perception of their science ability.

I would like to suggest a number of ways in which the image of science concept can provide a tool or language for analyzing the potential impact of a science learning activity (this list is not intended to be exhaustive, but rather to highlight some of the considerations brought to the foreground by the focus on children's images of science):

---

[10]I do not intend to suggest that hard work is not required, but rather that the sense of excitement is lost for many children. Children also see basketball as requiring a lot of practice and hard work. However, in playing the game, they get some immediate reward.

1. *Is the activity interesting, fun, and motivating? Is there a hook?*
Although some children are favorably disposed to activities labeled as science (i.e., they assume that they will be good at it, and that it will be interesting), many others are immediately wary of activities they suspect to be science. Activities with great potential for science learning will not be effective for children who do not choose to fully engage with them. If the activity is fun or taps into a deep interest or concern (e.g., helping animals), it is more likely to succeed.

2. *How does the activity portray science? As what kind of thing?*
Engaging children's interest is however, not enough. Does the activity portray science as a collection of facts? Does it emphasize the use of particular methods? Portraying science as an enterprise directed toward understanding the world may lead to a deeper and more satisfying understanding of science. Facts and processes both have a role in such an understanding and children are more motivated when given a context.

3. *What does the activity say about who can be a scientist?*
For example, pictures of "great men of science" may reinforce stereotypes of scientists being male (or White). On a more subtle level, teachers' interactions can easily privilege the views or participation of particular children or groups of children. Furthermore, subject matter may have a differential appeal to children along the lines of gender or socioeconomic background.

4. *Does the activity reinforce the idea of science as static and known?*
Even hands-on science explorations can reinforce the idea that doing science involves following recipes. If the only activities are those in which the answers are already known and the problems anticipated, students will expect that answers lie with the authority of others.

5. *Does the activity offer insight into how new knowledge is generated?*
Always concealing the messiness of the scientific process can make science unnecessarily mysterious and reinforce the notion that it is an activity only for geniuses and experts. Experiments that require students to generate ways of organizing, collecting, or interpreting data (or designing measurement devices) would be a step in the right direction.

6. *Does the provided experience connect children's strengths and abilities to science?*
What skills of the children are tapped and strengthened by the science experience? Are they rote skills, such as the ability to memorize facts or follow instructions, or do they tap children's other strengths, such as their ability to work with their hands or generate questions, ideas or solutions to problems? Science activities should provide children with a range of ways to succeed so that they can develop a realistic foundation for high self-esteem regarding science.

The image of science concept can also be used to understand and help individual children. For example, open-ended exploratory science activities may not make sense to children who conceive of science as a collection of facts to be learned. Helping children to broaden their understanding of science may help legitimize the activity. The activity may then help children construct a deeper understanding of science. Children who may automatically "tune out" during a science class because they are self-identified as not being "science kids" will benefit from experiences in which their abilities (e.g., to generate interesting questions or to make a measuring device) are valued.

Directions for Future Research

One direction of future research is to trace typical patterns of image of science development over a wider age span. In looking for such patterns it will be important to pay attention to issues of gender, race, socioeconomic class, and personal experience with science and scientists. I am particularly interested in the dynamics of the interaction between the cognitive and affective aspects of children's images of science. I have suggested elsewhere (Brandes, 1994) how feedback loops between these aspects may arise. A child's positive feelings about science may lead to involvement in science activities and to better understanding of what science is. More positive feelings about science and science self-concept then arise. Conversely, a child who dislikes science may avoid science activities, retain stereotyped views about science and become further alienated from science.

I am exploring the impact of children's science learning experiences on their images of science. I hope this research will lead to the generation of science learning environments and experiences that enrich the lives of children, enable them to build a better understanding of the world, and help them to form a lifelong connection to science.

ACKNOWLEDGMENTS

An earlier version of this chapter was presented at The American Educational Research Association meeting in New Orleans, April 1994. I would like to particularly thank my advisor, Edith Ackermann, for her support and suggestions. Many of my ideas emerged in rough form during our conversations and have gradually taken shape. Idit Harel has offered both enthusiasm for my work and practical advice. Uri Wilensky and I have had many stimulating conversations about science, math, and other learning, which have informed my work. I thank Amy Bruckman, Yasmin Kafai, Cynthia Krug, Mitchel Resnick, Carol Sperry, and Uri Wilensky for comments on a draft of this chapter. I thank the teachers who generously gave me both advice and access to their classrooms, then shared their thinking about what they do. I appreciate the challenges they face daily and respect the work they do. I am grateful to all the children who shared their time, ideas, and feelings with me. The preparation of this chapter was supported by the National Science Foundation (Grant 9153719-MDR), the LEGO Group, and Nintendo Inc. The ideas expressed here do not necessarily reflect the positions of the supporting agencies.

APPENDIX A: GENERAL BACKGROUND QUESTIONNAIRE

Name: Birthday (day, month, year):

What is your favorite thing to do outside of school?
What is your favorite thing to do in school?
What do you want to be when you grow up? Why?
What things are you best at outside of school?
What things are you best at in school?

What's hard for you outside of school?
What's hard for you in school?
What kind of thing do you dislike doing?
Is there anything else you would like me to know about you? (You can use the other side of this paper.)

APPENDIX B: IMAGE OF SCIENCE INTERVIEW GUIDELINE

Name: Date:

Ask a warm-up question based on children's personal information.

Ideas About Science
NOS[11] 1, 2, 3 (adapted)
1. What is science?

---

[11]NOS items are taken from the Nature of Science Interview protocol developed by Carey et al. (1989).

2. What is the goal of science?

3. What do you think scientists do? What are some other things that scientists do?

What kinds of things do scientists study?

What do you imagine scientists are like? What kind of people are they?

How do scientists compare to other people?

Ideas About Scientists:

Picture from Draw-A-Scientist Test (Administered in advance)

Clarify gender, if needed.

Clarify questions about picture (e.g., what scientist does in a work day).

Ask about any equipment scientist is using.

What other kinds of equipment do scientists use?

If more than one scientist is in the picture, ask about the relationship between them.

If one scientist is in the picture: I noticed that there is only one scientist in your picture. Does your scientist work alone?

Do scientists usually work alone or in a group?

What are advantages of working alone?

What are advantages of working in a group?

Nature of Science/How does the scientist proceed:

NOS 4–20 selected

NOS 4. Do you think scientists ask questions? What sorts of questions?

NOS 5. How do scientists answer their questions?

NOS 6. What is an experiment?

NOS 7. Do scientists do experiments?

IF NO, skip the next few questions.

8. Why do scientists do experiments?

IF "to test ideas," THEN: How does the test tell the scientist something about the idea?

When a scientist does an experiment, does the scientist expect it to come out a certain way?

IF YES: What do scientists think when their experiments come out the way they expected? What do they think when their experiments come out differently from what they expected?

NOS 18. When would a scientist change his or her ideas? Why?

NOS 13. Have you ever heard the word "theory"?

IF YES: What is a theory? Could you give an example of a theory?

Science Self-Image

Do you like science? How much?

Are you good at it?

What does that mean?

What abilities do you have that are important to be a scientist?

Are there any abilities you don't have that you would need to be a good scientist?

Attitudes Toward Science and School-Science

Do you ever do science activities for fun? Which ones?

If NO, ask about what they like which might be considered science (e.g., ask if they do nature activities—is that science?).

Do you ever read science books or articles for fun?

Do you watch programs on TV about science for fun?

What was your best science experience?

REFERENCES

Ackermann, E. (1988). Pathways into a child's mind: Helping children become epistemologists. In *Proceedings of the Symposium on Science learning in the informal setting* (pp. 7–18). Chicago, IL: The Chicago Academy of Sciences.

Belenky, M., Clinchy, B., Goldberger, N., & Tarule, J. (1986). *Women's ways of knowing.* New York: Basic Books.

Brandes, A. (1992a). *Constructivism goes to school.* Unpublished manuscript.

Brandes, A. (1992b). *Children's ideas about machines.* Paper presented at the annual meeting of the American Educational Research Association.

Brandes, A. (1994). *Children's images of science.* Unpublished manuscript.

Brown, J. S. (1989). Toward a new epistemology for learning. In C. Frasson & J. Gauthier (Eds.), *Intelligent tutoring systems at the crossroad of AI and education* (pp. 266–282). Norwood, NJ: Ablex.

Carey, S. (1985). *Conceptual change in childhood.* Cambridge, MA: MIT Press.

Carey, S. (1991). Knowledge acquisition: Enrichment or conceptual change? In S. Carey & R. Gelman (Eds.), *The epigenesis of mind* (pp. 257–291). Hillsdale, NJ: Lawrence Erlbaum Associates.

Carey, S., Evans, R., Honda, M., Jay, E., & Unger, C. (1989). "An experiment is when you try it and see if it works": A study of grade 7 students' understanding of the construction of scientific knowledge. *International Journal of Science Education, 11* (Special Issue), 514–529.

Chambers, D. W. (1983). Stereotypic images of the scientist: The draw-a-scientist test. *Science Education, 67*(2), 255–265.

Collins, H., & Pinch, T. (1993). *The golem of science.* Cambridge, England: Cambridge University Press.

diSessa, A. (1982). Unlearning Aristotelian physics: A study of knowledge-based learning. *Cognitive Science, 6*(1), 37–75.

Driver, R., Guesne, E., & Tiberghien, A. (Eds.) (1985). *Children's ideas in science*. Philadelphia: Open University Press.

Driver, R., Leach, J., Millar, R., & Scott, P. (1993). *Students; understanding of the nature of science: The curricular case for teaching about the nature of science*. (Working Paper 3). Leeds, UK: University of Leeds, and York, UK: University of York.

Duschl, R. (1990). *Restructuring science education: The importance of theories and their development*. New York: Teachers College Press.

Germann, P. (1988). Development of the attitude toward science in school assessment and its use to investigate the relationship between science acheivement and attitude toward science in school. *Journal of Research in Science Teaching, 25*(8), 689–703.

Gingerich, O. (1992). *The great Copernicus chase and other adventures in astronomical history*. Cambridge, MA: Sky Publishing.

Hammer, D. (1991). *Defying common sense: Epistemological beliefs in an introductory physics course*. Unpublished doctoral dissertation. Berkeley, CA: University of California.

Jackson, I. (1992). *Science literacy in theory and practice: A sociocultural analysis of teacher cognition in a multicultural setting*. Unpublished doctoral dissertation, Cambridge, MA: Media Laboratory, MIT.

Keller, E. F. (1983). *A feeling for the organism: The life and work of Barbara McClintock*. San Francisco, CA: W. H. Freeman.

Keller, E. F. (1985). *Reflections on gender and science*. New Haven, CT: Yale University Press.

Latour, B. (1987). *Science in action*. Cambridge, MA: Harvard University Press.

Lave, J., & Wenger, E. (1991). *Situated learning: Legitimate peripheral participation*. Cambridge and New York: Cambridge University Press.

McCloskey, M. (1982). Naive theories of motion. In D. Gentner & A. Stevens (Eds.), *Mental models* (pp. 299–324). Hillsdale, NJ: Lawrence Erlbaum Associates.

Moore, R. W., & Sutman, F. X. (1970). The development, field test and validation of an inventory of scientific attitudes. *Journal of Research in Science Teaching, 7*, 85–94.

Munby, H. (1983). Thirty studies involving the Scientific Attitude Inventory: What confidence can we have in this instrument? *Journal of Research in Science Teaching, 20*, 141–162.

Nemirovsky, R. (1992). Don't tell me how things are, tell me how you see them. In R. Ruopp, S. Gal, B. Drayton, & M. Pfister (Eds.), *LabNet: Toward a community of practice* (pp. 269–280). Hillsdale, NJ: Lawrence Erlbaum Associates.

Osborne, R., & Freyberg, P. (1985). *Learning in science: The implications of children's science*. Auckland, NZ: Heinemann.

Piaget, J. (1954). *The construction of reality in the child*. New York: Basic Books.

Piaget, J. (1970). *Genetic epistemology*. New York: Columbia University Press.

Pintrich, P., Marx, R., & Boyle, R. (1993). Beyond cold conceptual change: The role of motivational beliefs and classroom contextual factors in the process of conceptual change. *Review of Educational Research 63*(2), 167–199.

Posner, G., Strike, K., Hewson, P., & Gertzog, W. (1982). Accommodation of a scientific conception: Towards a theory of conceptual change. *Science Education, 66*, 211–227.

Rennie, L. J., & Parker, L. H. (1987). Scale dimensionality and population heterogeneity: Potential problems in the interpretation of attitude data. *Journal of Research in Science Teaching, 24*(6), 567–577.

Rosebery, A., Warren, B., & Conant, G. (1992). Appropriating scientific discourse: Findings from language minority classrooms. *Journal of the Learning Sciences, 2*(1), 61–94.

Theberge, C. (1994). *Participation in classroom science sessions: Issues of gender and explanatory style*. Unpublished doctoral dissertation, Cambridge, MA: Harvard University Graduate School of Education.

Tinker, R. (1991). Science for children: The promise of technology. In S. Sheingold, L. Roberts, &

S. Malcolm (Eds)., *This year in school science: Technology for teaching and learning* (pp. 11–30). Washington DC: American Association for the Advancement of Science.

Toulmin, S., & Goodfield, J. (1961). *The fabric of the heavens*. Middlesex: Penguin Books.

Turkle, S., & Papert, S. (1991). Epistemological pluralism and the revaluation of the concrete. In I. Harel & S. Papert (Eds.), *Constructionism* (pp. 161–191). Norwood, NJ: Ablex.

White, R., & Gunstone, R. (1992). *Probing understanding*. London: Falmer Press.

Wilensky, U. (1991). Abstract meditations on the concrete and concrete implications for mathematics education. In I. Harel & S. Papert (Eds.), *Constructionism* (pp. 193–203). Norwood, NJ: Ablex.

Wilensky, U. (1993). *Connected mathematics: Building concrete relationships with mathematical knowledge*. Unpublished doctoral dissertation, Media Laboratory, MIT, Cambridge, MA.

PART II ——————

LEARNING THROUGH DESIGN

4

Learning Design by Making Games
Children's Development of Design Strategies in the Creation of a Complex Computational Artifact

Yasmin B. Kafai

I made a game. It started out very slowly at first. It is very hard to put together your own game. You may think it is easy to do because of all the video games people play. They look so simple but try making your own game and it's a totally different story! Well, I started out with very high expectations thinking that I could make a great game in very short time. It turned out that I'm still not done with it even after about 4 or 5 months. (Rosemary, 10 years, toward the end of the project)

I really expected even though the teacher told me that it would take months and months and months to finish the game, I really did expect to do it, like start it, in one week and finish it up the next week. . . . I just went like: Oh, this will be easy. All it will be, is a little bit of this, a little bit of that, and a little research, and I'll be finished. But it didn't turn out that way because I had to spend a lot of days on research and programming. There were tons of problems, like one time my turtle was messed up. Plus I had to make all the graphics and everything. So it had problems, but it has been fun. (Jeremy, 11 years, at the end of the project)

As these quotes of two young game designers illustrate, there is something to be learned from making games that goes beyond learning programming and specific subject matter. The students' descriptions reflect their early expectations about making games, which were probably influenced by their experiences with regular classroom work and home assignments. Conventional school assignments rarely give students the opportunity to spend 6 months on a complex project such as making a game. Hence, most students have little experience in design (i.e., planning, problem solving, researching, dealing with time constraints, modifying expectations, and bringing everything together into one project). Previous research even suggests that young students may not be able to accomplish such projects because children have limited abilities in planning and dealing with complex tasks (e.g., Brown & DeLoache, 1978; Friedman, Scholnick, & Cocking, 1987).

Recent efforts in the educational research community, however, have stressed the importance of self-directed, personally meaningful, and cognitively complex projects for students' learning success (Blumenfeld et al., 1991; Collins, Brown & Newman, 1990; Harel & Papert, 1990). Design activities are one example of such project-based activities in which students are engaged in designing complex, interactive pieces of software to be used by other students for learning about a particular subject area (Harel, 1991). A variety of design activities have been proposed that range from creating interactive presentations to instructional software, simulations, and educational games (Carver, 1991; Guzdial, 1993; Kafai, 1993; Lehrer, 1991). A prominent feature of these activities is that students learn about design by managing the projects while, through design, they learn about academic subjects such as programming, history, mathematics, and physics.

One objective, then, of the research presented here was to examine the ways in which children approach a complex design task and identify the kinds of obstacles they face and overcome. A class of fourth-grade students became game designers and worked daily toward the goal of making the learning of fractions fun and easy for younger students. In this process they discussed issues related to fractions, teaching, programming, and games, meeting once a month with their prospective users. Students' design progress was observed and analyzed from the beginning of the product to its completion 6 months later. The following sections provide the theoretical background and describe in detail the nature of the design task and the methods used for gathering and analyzing the data. Selected results from analyzing the whole class of game designers and individual case studies have been included to provide support for reoccurring themes and trends.

REVIEW OF RESEARCH

In this research, design was an object of study as well as a context for a study of learning. Learning through design (Harel, 1988, 1991) is based on a constructionist theory that sees learners as builders of their own knowledge—a process that happens best when students are building external and shareable artifacts such as computer programs, machines, or games (Papert, 1980; 1993). When learners are asked to design something for the use of others, their learning becomes instrumental to a larger intellectual and social goal. In this context, students are in a continuous dialogue with their own ideas and with the ideas of intended users and co-designers. Student-designers assume control of their learning by asking questions, gathering information, and putting all this to work in creating an educational game.

Although learning and designing are closely intertwined in this process, it is important to point out a distinction between learning through design or through professional design. The learning through design is not exclusively represented in the final product, but also in the process of doing it. "Professional design" focuses on the product as the essential outcome, whereas "learning design" focuses on the students' process as the primary cause for learning (which is only partially reflected in the product). In learning through and about design, the process is more important than the product. This means that even though students may not achieve a well-rounded final product, learning can take place because of the involvement over time. Applied to the problem solving and planning abilities of younger children, this means that the context of design puts them in the mode of thinking like planners, problem solvers, and designers—all together—over and over again.

My particular focus is on how students as designers integrate planning and problem solving while building an artifact. Students act as problem solvers and planners in multiple ways, but in the design process they are the ones who identify the problems and plan how to solve them. Schauble (1991) spoke in this context of the student-designer's task to impose and manage the multiple constraints of complex situations in design. The extended time frame of the research project provides the opportunity for students to be engaged with different facets of the design process. For example, the designer begins by finding a problem, then discovers parts of the solution, tries to make sense out of it, considers how to reframe the situation, and continues with problem solving. In this process, the designer constructs a particular, personal relationship to the artifact that undergoes changes as the process continues. This process seems to stop when an artifact has been created, but, actually, it never ends because existing design solutions are used and reused in new design situations (Schön, 1983).

The traditions of school and academia have favored formal and abstract approaches to problem solving and design. Previous research on software design identified different approaches of handling complex design and used bipolar descriptions, such as "top-down" versus "bottom-up" (Jeffries, Turner, Polson, & Atwood, 1981; Newell & Simon, 1972) or "planning" versus "bricolage" (Turkle & Papert, 1991).

The bricoleur resembles the painter who stands back between the brush strokes, looks at the canvas, and only after this contemplation, decides what to do next. For planners, mistakes are missteps; for bricoleurs they are the essence of a navigation by mid-course corrections. For planners a program is an instrument of premeditated control; bricoleurs have goals, but set out to realize them in the spirit of a collaborative venture with the machine. For planners, getting a program to work is like "saying one's piece"; for bricoleurs it is more like a conversation than a monologue. In cooking, this would be the style of those who do not follow recipes, but instead make a series of decisions according to taste. While hierarchy and abstraction are

valued by the programmers' planner's aesthetic, bricoleur programmers prefer ne-
gotiation and rearrangement of their materials. (Turkle & Papert, 1991, p. 136)

The view that has been called planning, or top-down, tends to see the process
of problem solving as one of breaking down a problem into more meaningful
subproblems (Guindon, Krasner, & Curtis, 1987; Jeffries et al., 1981). Here, the
designer maps out the context, content, and structure of a design at the beginning.
The opposing view, called bricolage or bottom-up, describes problem solving as
a conversation with the situation, in which the design of the game emerges in the
process of implementing it. These two views suggest that students may approach
the design task from different ends, choose to emphasize different aspects of the
design, and think about it in different ways depending on their personal preferences. My intention in the game design project was to offer a design activity that
provided multiple avenues for students to approach a complex problem, build a
game around the idea of fractions, and find personal solutions. As Simon (1969)
pointed out, a unique feature of design problems is that they do not have a single
right solution; there are always alternatives.

Game design proposes a complex project that engages students over a long
period of time. The complexity of the task becomes clearer if one considers that
designing software involves more than the mere production of code: structuring
the control flow of the program, maintaining the connection between different
procedures and pages, designing the graphics, and providing the interface for the
prospective user. In addition, students must consider different ideas for fraction
representations, how the representations can be implemented in Logo, and pedagogical concerns, among many other issues. The actual challenge for the game
designers is to combine and integrate the instructional content and game context.
I hypothesize that these activities will place children in a situation that requires
them to design, plan, reflect, evaluate, and modify their programs on a constant
basis. The expected outcome is that these diverse activities will allow students to
acquire more sophisticated programming skills in conjunction with other subject
matter. Project management is one of the central issues: How do students deal
with the complexities of a design task? What kind of strategies do they use or
develop, if any, in the course of a long-term project?

The answer to these questions is of particular relevance because previous
research on the development of children's abilities to deal with complex tasks
suggests that children know how to plan, but are limited by their knowledge of
the situation (Bjorklund, 1991). In order to investigate these issues, I chose a
familiar, yet complex task: I investigated children's design approaches to programming a game. Unlike most research from the problem-solving domain, the
students were given neither a well-defined nor an ill-defined problem that could
be accomplished in a short amount of time (Dreher & Oerter, 1987; Kreitler &
Kreitler, 1987; Pea & Hawkins, 1987). Instead, they were given a space/context
in which they could construct their own problem—their own tasks, goals, activ-

ities, and rules that guided their game design activities. This situational approach created a microworld for children; students were autonomous in following their own paths of learning and activities. In doing so, however, they were also building microworlds of their own, game worlds for others to play and learn with. The goal of this investigation, then, was to analyze whether particular design approaches emerged over time, as has been described in the literature, and to what extent these approaches were consistent.

RESEARCH CONTEXT

In many ways, the project recreated the atmosphere of a professional design studio. A class of 16 fourth-grade students were engaged during an extended period of time (6 months) in the design and production of educational games that teach fractions. The students worked for 1 hour a day on their projects in class. In general, students first spent 5 minutes writing their plans and ideas in notebooks before they went to work on their computers for 45 minutes. As students worked on their games, they were allowed to walk around the room to see and discuss each others' projects. Students then returned to their own classrooms and wrote again about their experiences.

These daily sessions were complemented by several focus group sessions in which students discussed issues related to games, their projects, their ideas, or difficulties about fractions and how to represent them. The group sessions were designed for brainstorming and discussing issues of interest for all students. Every month younger students visited the classroom to evaluate and discuss the older students' game projects. Because the purpose of this project was to create a finished product, students worked concurrently in their art classes on cover designs for the packaging of their games and in their language arts classes on advertising for their products and the documentation for them. During the 6 months of the project, the students spent 92 hours programming and 20 hours on related activities and school materials.

The game design project took place at Project Headlight, located at an inner-city, public elementary school in one of Boston's low socioeconomic neighbor-hoods. The goal of Project Headlight, which started in 1985, is to explore the use of computers in classrooms as they might exist in the near future. Project Head-light operates as a school-within-a-school; the other two thirds of the school have traditional classroom and computer arrangements. One special feature of this elementary school is its open-architecture structure, which was not fully utilized before the project started. In two open areas, four clusters of computers are arranged, each with 16 computers in a circle, screens facing out. The clusters of computers are called "pods." As students come and go to their classrooms, they can walk among the computer pods and see other students' projects. Another feature of Project Headlight is that students are rarely using educational software; instead, they are working with LogoWriter to create their own software.

Approximately 250 students participated in this project, from first through fifth grade, including advanced, regular, bilingual, and special education classes. The participants were of diverse ethnic backgrounds, half boys and half girls. Most of the students had only joined the school in the fourth and fifth grades; hence, their beginning programming experience was not very extensive.

METHODS OF DATA COLLECTION AND ANALYSES

The game development of 16 student designers was observed every day over the course of 6 months. A combination of qualitative methods was used to document the students' ideas, thoughts, and progress in game development. Pre- and post-interviews were conducted to gather information on students' knowledge of programming, fractions, video games, and planning experiences. During the project, the students participated in research activities by keeping notebook entries and saving log files to provide additional information for the researcher. The data were examined in the following ways: (a) The students' projections of their game designs in the notebook and interviews were compared with their actual program implementations in Logo, (b) the development of the game theme and features over time; and (c) the development of the program code in regard to the use of modularization, that is, making procedures, which is described in the research literature as one important programming strategy (Carver, 1987; Pea & Kurland, 1984). Particular attention was paid to the beginning phase when students began formulating their first game ideas including expectations about upcoming difficulties, and to the period of first transition, 3 to 4 weeks into the study, when students had accomplished part of their implementations and had already handled design and programming problems.

RESULTS

During the 92 days of thinking, designing, programming, modifying, and playing their computer games, the students carried out many activities and touched on many issues.[1] The extended time frame allowed for a closer investigation of the

---

[1]Other parts of my investigation addressed the conceptual development of students' dealings with fractions, their understanding of the programming language Logo, their mastery of particular programming concepts, and their development of programming strategies. The results from these different investigations provided evidence that the students in the project were able to handle this complex and challenging task in a significant manner when compared to students instructed by other pedagogical means. I have reported elsewhere more extensively on this aspect of the students' learning experience (Kafai, 1993, 1995).

project trends and development. As the students started implementing their game ideas, they put their programming skills to the test and learned about the feasibility of their game ideas as well as different aspects of the design process. It is worthwhile to investigate transitions or shifts and whether they occurred throughout the class or were only experienced by individual students. Over time, two kinds of developments could be observed: One kind, of incremental nature, was reflected in the daily growth of the game designers' programs in terms of Logo code; the other kind represented shifts in the nature of the games as well as the approach chosen by the designers. Looking at the development of the students' games as a whole from beginning to end, seeing how students outlined features of their games and also set out to implement them, provides a first view on distinct design approaches.

In the following sections, design styles adopted by students and different phases of the design process are analyzed in more detail. Particular attention is given to the way students deal with the complex nature of game design by framing the task and imposing their own structures. In addition, students' development of programming strategies is examined using the cases of two young game designers, Amy and Albert.

Design Styles

One objective of this analysis was to investigate whether bipolar descriptions, such as "top-down" or "planner" versus "bottom-up" or "bricoleur," correctly assess children's approaches to a complex task such as designing a game. We could expect that "planners" would carefully lay out what they want to do in advance. We would expect "bricoleurs" to develop their games as they go along. To clarify this point, I chose the games of Barney and Gaby as two extreme examples of game development (see Fig. 4.1).

In her first interview, Gaby described the different parts that she would implement for her spider web game. She had already segmented her descriptions of the different game components into the blocks, the web, and the fractions. When Gaby started implementing her game, she focused first on the spider web, then the blocks on the screen, then colored blocks, before she started working on the fraction questions, one after the other. In her programming, each unit was assigned a procedure. For example, the five colored blocks all have the name BLOCK, but each color has a different prefix (LBLOCK, MBLOCK, and so on). One could say that from day one Gaby laid out the implementation of her game and followed through, even though she did not implement some aspects of her initial plans. In that respect, Gaby falls most clearly into the category of the planner. In the second part of the project (which is not represented in the diagram), Gaby wrote the introduction and directions, then programmed the spider's movements as it followed the fly.

In contrast, Barney described the idea of an adventure story in the interview and his notebook designs. He initially provided only one screen display: that of a

Gaby : I am going to make a **spider web**, right. I need to make some **blocks** up here, but I don't know how to make them . . . You see a square, like here, and it has a little space so the fly can get over here and then, you see, the spider, the web is going to be right over here and if it gets closer to the web, the spider is sitting there and it is going it eat. But if not, this is going to be the safe place and if it gets the right answer it's going to get a little bit closer and closer until it gets to the safe place and then like a smiling face.

Barney : Yeah I am just going to do like . . . you have to go on an adventure or something like this and people have to ask you all these fractions questions and if you get them right, you go on and if you get them wrong you . . . see it's going to be hard, if you get it wrong, once, then you are out . . . The questions will be pretty easy but it's just if you get it wrong once, you are out.

Spider Web

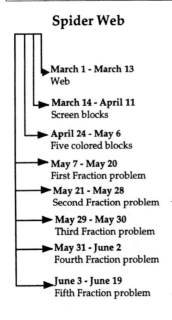

March 1 - March 13
Web

March 14 - April 11
Screen blocks

April 24 - May 6
Five colored blocks

May 7 - May 20
First Fraction problem

May 21 - May 28
Second Fraction problem

May 29 - May 30
Third Fraction problem

May 31 - June 2
Fourth Fraction problem

June 3 - June 19
Fifth Fraction problem

Jose in the Fraction World

March 4 - March 5
Welcome and Directions

March 6 - March 20
Meeting with Magician
First Fraction Question

March 22 - March 26
Hot air balloon
Second Fraction question

March 28 - April 6
Money robber
Kicking to the Moon
Third Fraction question

April 8 - May 2
Walking on the Beach
Swimming & Meeting
with the Shark
Fourth Fraction question

May 3 - May 21
At Home
Jungle & Talking Lion
Fifth Fraction question

May 22 - June
City & Airport

FIG. 4.1.   Comparison between the design approaches of Gaby and Barney from March to June.

fish speaking. As Barney set out to implement his game, he started with a welcome screen, introduction, and directions. From then on, he developed scene after scene. Even though most of his scene units, such as the magician or the money robber, are centered around a fraction quiz, they are composed of a series of connected animations that lead to the fraction question and then away from it to the next adventure. His game is a series of connected adventures created one after the other. In that sense, Barney is very much like a bricoleur.

I would categorize both Barney and Gaby as extreme cases for each approach. Other students (such as Darvin, Albert, Miriam, Trevor, Sina, Shanice, Amy, and Jero) also exhibited planning behavior, but to a lesser extent. Their planning seems to be more localized and deals with particular sequences. In particular, I refer the reader to Amy's blueprint for the instructional quiz that she clearly planned in advance (see the section, "Developing Programming Strategies"), or to Miriam's design of the ski slope, which was implemented to the smallest detail from her notebook design. Other students could also be described as working without a preformed plan. Sid, Juan, Tyree, and Rosy were engaged in a continuous dialogue with their game as they designed various scenes or fraction questions.

A combination of both planning and bricolage seems to be a more accurate way of describing the typical student's game design process. The results of my analyses indicate that most students chose to walk a middle line between bricolage and planning, and their approaches changed over time. Only 4 out of 16 students could be clearly classified as either planners or bricoleurs. At specific stages in the design process (for example, when programming the first fraction question), students tinkered around with different aspects: They designed different shapes and dialogues before deciding on a solution. In later stages, they switched over to reusing, in a purposeful way, program segments that they had written before (such as for the instructional dialogue). The clear distinction between planners and bricoleurs seems to fall apart during observations over a long period of time and over the construction of a complex product. This result speaks against bipolar descriptions. There is further evidence in the game design process that students did not adopt one particular strategy but rather negotiated the situation by imposing and coordinating multiple constraints with their personal interests in game design (Schauble, 1991). To provide better support for this statement, it is important to examine the beginning phase and the way the game design task was construed by students over time.

Defining Constraints of the Design Task

In the first days of the project, students formulated their game ideas and began to implement them. In the game programming process, children exhibited different design approaches. Many changes (game title, new introduction, main game idea) in the students' game design occurred either in the first days of the project or after 3 to 4 weeks into the project.

Game Design Approaches.   My observations of the students' work in this beginning phase captured a variety of activities, but two different approaches stood out. In the beginning phase, some students did not start working and implementing their game ideas right away; others started with one idea, abandoned it quickly, and moved on to a new one. Those who did not start programming immediately played with or explored areas seemingly unrelated to their assignment. For example, both Albert and Shanice experimented with some new Logo commands to which they had been introduced a few days earlier. Barney refused to start the project at all because, as he told me, he did not have any game ideas for fractions. Shanice, Sina, and Rosy wrote for several days in their notebooks, "I am going to start my fractions project."

A different approach was taken by several other students. They started with one idea, worked on it for a few days, and then moved on to a new game idea. In this category, we find Amy with her "fraction thing" that she later turned into a map design; Miriam with her "Mr. Fraction" that turned into the skiing game; Jero's magician that turned into a map with different levels; and Tyree's fraction screen that turned into a space game. In this approach, students outlined a few features of their first games in their notebooks or programmed a few lines before they came up with a new idea. This change in the beginning phase was rather abrupt, as most students did not indicate a lack of confidence in their first choices. Instead, their games seemed to take a new turn from one day to the next.

The students used both approaches to the design task to enter the new domain of game design. I do not interpret either approach as unproductive or inactive. Either one provided time for students to grapple with the issue of bringing together the two domains of fractions and game in one design. In Harel's (1991) instructional software design project (in which students designed educational software and not educational games), Debbie actually took several days before she started with the design of her instructional screens. In very much the same way that professional designers would start out, the students in the game design project either tried alternative ideas and designs or decided to postpone creating their game until they had formulated a more coherent game idea and knew what they wanted to do. A further look at the content of the students' first designs repeats this impression. Some students, such as Barney, Tyree, Shaun, Juan, and Rosy, started with their welcoming screen or introductions (the first screens usually seen by the player when starting the game). Other students immediately started working on their first game scene, designing shapes or the environment, and did not implement the welcoming screen and the introduction until midway through or toward the end of the project. The diversity of project themes, working styles, and entry paths in design activities has been described and discussed by Resnick (1991).

Definitions of the Game Design Task.   Very early in the project students developed game ideas that integrated fractions in different ways. Two distinct game formats were adopted by most students: extrinsic or intrinsic integration of fractions into the game (called Game Worlds or Fraction Worlds, respectively). The former is exemplified most simply in games or software where the player has to answer a question in order to proceed in the game. In contrast, intrinsic

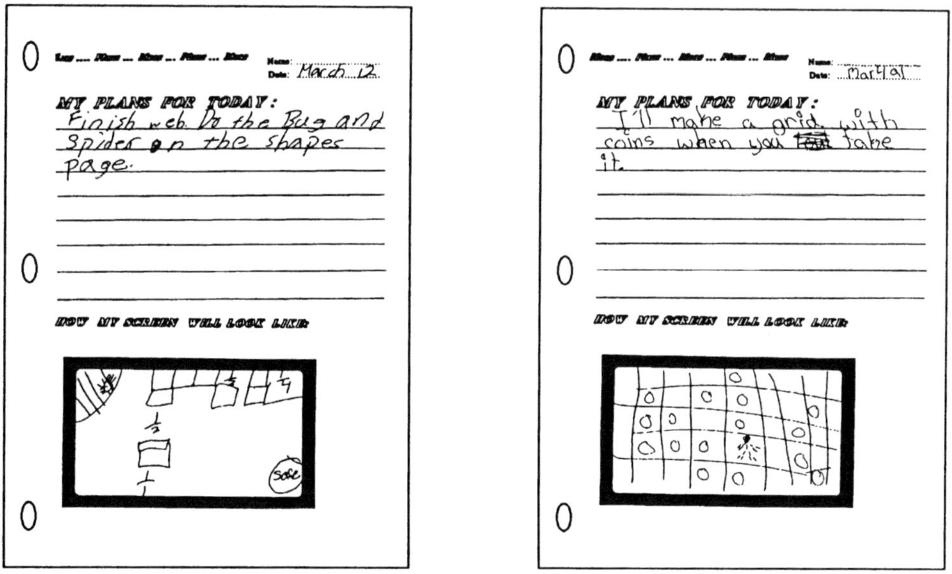

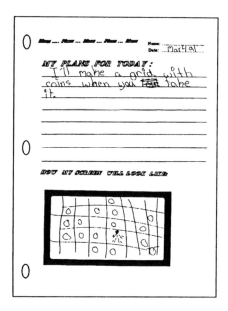

FIG. 4.2a. Examples of game worlds—Gaby's and Trevor's game designs. Gaby's game describes a spider web in which the player moves around as a fly, away from the spider, and turns on fraction blocks where questions are posed. Trevor shows the coin grid and a figure that represents the player.

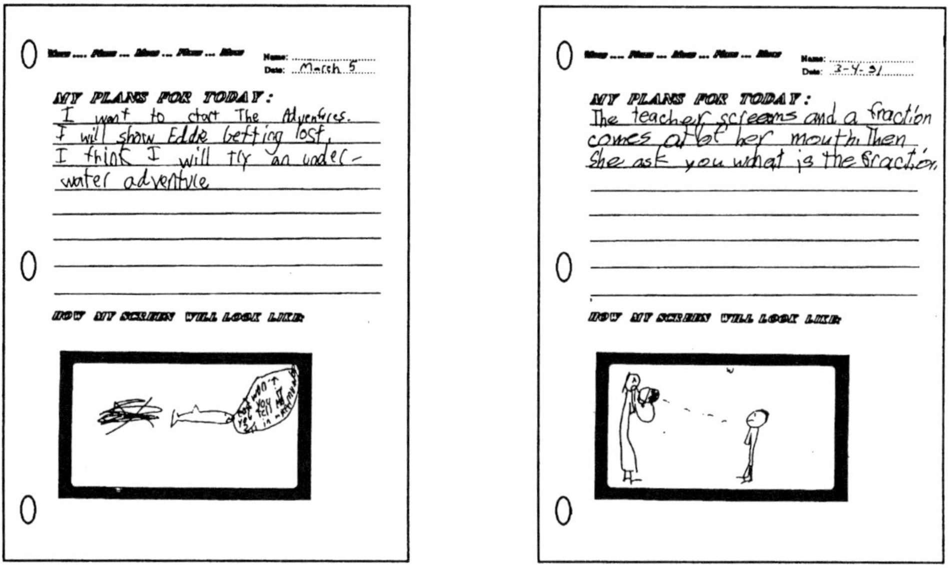

MY PLANS FOR TODAY: (Gaby, Date: March 12)
Finish web. Do the Bug and Spider on the shapes page.

HOW MY SCREEN WILL LOOK LIKE:

MY PLANS FOR TODAY: (Trevor, Date: March 21)
I'll make a grid with coins when you take it.

HOW MY SCREEN WILL LOOK LIKE:

MY PLANS FOR TODAY: (Date: March 5)
I want to start The Adventures. I will show Eddie getting lost. I think I will try an underwater adventure.

HOW MY SCREEN WILL LOOK LIKE:

MY PLANS FOR TODAY: (Date: 2-4-31)
The teacher screams and a fraction comes out of her mouth. Then she ask you what is the fraction.

HOW MY SCREEN WILL LOOK LIKE:

FIG. 4.2b. Examples of game worlds—Barney and Sina's game designs. Barney draws the underwater scene. Sina shows the two protagonists of the game, the teacher and the player.

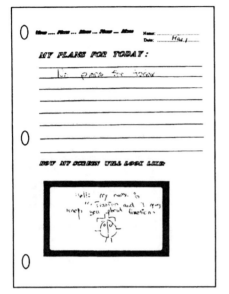 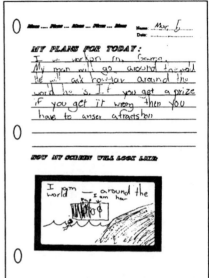

FIG. 4.3. Miriam and Rosy's fraction worlds. Miriam's text to the graphic of Mr. Fractions says: *Hello, my name is Mr. Fraction and I am going to teach you about fractions.* Rosy described her first game idea as: *I will work on my Game. My man will go around the world. He will ask how far around the world he is. If you get a prize if you get it wrong then you have to answer a fraction.*

integration is exemplified in a game where the designer integrates the subject matter with the game idea.

In Game Worlds, students developed different worlds in which the player interacts with fractions. What pertains to all the game worlds is that the rules are bound to the fraction questions, and the player's success depends on figuring out the correct answer in order to continue or finish the game. Many students' games make reference to those commercially available such as Nintendo. For example, Jero's different warp zones are reminiscent of Mario Brothers' tunnel system. Oscar made explicit reference to the Pacman game, but chose eating fractions instead of points. Sid's basketball game is available in various video game versions. Gaby took an educational game she had used in her previous school, the spider web, and adapted it to fractions. Some of the students used an educational situation when choosing a game theme. For example, Sina's outline of her teacher game shows a teacher asking, or rather, "screaming" a fraction. Gloria came up with a similar idea (see Figs. 4.2a and 4.2b).

Fraction Worlds, by contrast, described games in which the idea of fractions is inherent in the game concept. There were a few games in which the idea of fractions was central, such as Amy's "fraction thing," Miriam's "Mr. Fraction," or Rosy's "world map" (see Fig. 4.3).

Games with intrinsic integration could also be considered a form of micro-worlds in which fractions are situated. Papert has defined the microworld as "a computer-based interactive learning environment in which the prerequisites are built into the system and where learners can become the active, constructing architects of their own learning" (1980, p. 122). Initially, the term *microworld* was reserved for the creation of software tools that allow learners to explore their knowledge. Here the students became the designers of software tools for other children. They used Logo to design their games as microworlds for others to play and learn about fractions.

One issue of immediate concern is why so few students considered the design of fraction worlds. I have three possible explanations.

One explanation addresses the very nature of educational games: They lie somewhere between learning and playing. They are a specific breed because the rules necessary to play the educational games demand the use of valuable educational skills. The students obviously felt the tension between the demands of playing and those of learning. Darvin saw the two poles clearly, as he expressed in his notebook entries on March 1: "I want to make it [the game] as fun and educational as possible but especially fun."

My second explanation comes from observations of educational games designed by researchers and educators. For a long time, teachers have used educational games on and off the computer to keep students motivated (Avedon & Sutton-Smith, 1966; Block & King, 1987; Lepper & Malone, 1987). Teacher-designed games have shared an aspect common to most students' games: The game idea, content, or form was external to the game (Bride & Lamb, 1991; Fennell, Houser, McPartland, & Parker, 1984; Priester, 1984). In all cases, the game idea and format could also be used for other subject areas. By this I mean that the content—fractions—did not matter. The game context was used to keep the students' attention alive and to keep them motivated in accomplishing the tasks. Many of the student-designed games shared this quality.

Yet another explanation of why so few game designers made the ideas of fractions central to their games and why some of the good ideas were quickly abandoned is that fraction worlds or microworlds are harder to invent. A situation where answering fraction problems allows you to advance is conceptually simpler: The fraction challenges are fully factored out of the game context. This is a simpler, logical structure. Microworlds may also be harder to implement after one has the basic idea. The intertwining of fractions and the game context creates interactions between the two that may pose complex programming challenges. One can conclude that students defined the game design task in this fashion because it facilitated their entry into the design task, even though it happened to the detriment of fractions. They limited the range of options to consider. As in commercially made games, the greater number chose the easiest extrinsic integration by stopping the action at key places to ask the player a question. It is a strength and a weakness of the extrinsic integration that domains of knowledge become almost interchangeable. It is a strength because the integration is relatively easy: When answering a question correctly is what allows the next move in a game, the question can be on any topic. This is also a weakness, however, because it causes the designer to lose the incentive to think deeply about the particular piece of knowledge.

These observations of approach and content in the game design process indicate that there was no uniform way in which students handled the early days of creating their games. These observations, furthermore, reinforce the impression that there is no one "right way" to start a design task, and that many of the students' choices in approach and content were related to their personal preferences. The entrance point of forging a relationship with the task was not necessarily the same for everyone. A planner might consider it a bad strategy to start the game with the most important scene instead of designing the first screen. Yet for a bricoleur, this might be the only possible and reasonable way.

Negotiating Constraints of the Design Task

A further observation points out changes in students' own perceptions and expectations in the course of the game design process. In the beginning, students had varied expectations about upcoming difficulties. Some students were not concerned, whereas others considered the feasibility of their game ideas in the light of implementation difficulties.

Expected Difficulties. In interviews during the first days of the project (March 5), neither Amy nor Sid were concerned about any problems:

Interviewer:	What do you think is the biggest problem right now?
Sid:	I don't know. Actually I don't have a problem right now.
Interviewer:	What do you think could become a problem?
Sid:	Nothing.

Interviewer:	Let me ask you something. What do you think right now will be your biggest problem with this project?
Amy:	I have no idea right now [waves her hand], beats me.

In contrast, other students thought of some problems in relation to their game ideas or upcoming implementations:

Interviewer:	That sounds like a neat idea. The pacman who is eating fractions?
Oscar:	That's what I wanted to do.
Interviewer:	So work on that.
Oscar:	It's a little bit too hard.
Interviewer:	So can you think of a simpler version?
Oscar:	I am trying . . . but I am going to think of something different.

Interviewer: If you think about your project now, what do you think might be the biggest challenge for you?

Albert: Ahm, . . . right now, . . . I think the biggest challenge that I am gonna make here is making the robbers come at you or something. When you open a door, something, the guys come at you and making all that happen.

Interviewer: So, it has to do with Logo programming?

Albert: [nods yes] I can also have, once you type in you want to open the door, it shows you and the guy will step out with the knife and the guy will go like this [he indicates a cutting movement with his arms and he is laughing].

Interviewer: Are there any challenges related to fractions for you?

Albert: I don't think I will have any problems, but I might come across some of them that might be kind of difficult.

Oscar was concerned about the difficulties in his idea of adapting a Pacman game to eat fractions instead of points. Albert thinks about the difficulties related to programming future animations. In the following interview, Gaby discusses the number of different parts in her game, Spider Web, that she will have to implement:

Interviewer: OK, so you are going to make a spider web; there is going to be a safe place and some fractions? These are many things you are thinking about for your game. So what do you want to start with now?

Gaby: Well, I am starting a web because I am thinking it is going to be a little bit hard plus making the spider, and the fly, and the blocks and the fractions, and things and the smiling face, would be hard for me, you know, to get it all started. It will take me more than . . . it wouldn't take me less than a week. But it would take me more than a week trying to plan all these things. We have a short amount of time.

Reduced Expectations.   Students' reduced their expectations of how much they could accomplish in the project. One example of this is the number of fraction problems students intended to design. In the first days, Amy projected doing 21 fraction questions (taken from the parts of her map). Jero planned to do 20 questions on nine different levels, and Shaun was thinking about 100 fraction problems. The students' projections were probably influenced by worksheets, textbooks, or educational software that contain a large number of problems. These models might have influenced the students in their initial projections of how many questions they could or should incorporate in their games. This also replicates the experience of Debbie in the instructional software design project (Harel, 1988, p. 192), who wanted to show *all* the fractions in the world. In the course of the project, all of the students reduced their expectations, and the average number of instructional situations was approximately five.

The variations in expectations might be related to the students' lack of experience in working on such a complex and time-consuming project. The students' own evaluations written at the end of the project are a good indicator of this. For example, Gaby wrote: "I disliked it because sometimes I kept working on the same thing over and over again. I liked it because I finally finished it and I made everything move." Amy wrote: "I disliked working on the fractions software project because sometimes it got boring because you had to work on it day after day, week after week, month after month, but at the end I felt like I had accomplished something." In the past, students usually had worked 3 to 4 weeks on one assignment and then moved on to the next one. Their planning skills and estimations regarding the game design were based on their previous experiences. One should not forget that these issues are hard to express as students begin to formulate what their games will be about. Even if we expected students from the beginning to map out their plans and ideas for implementations, it would be unrealistic to think that they could take into consideration all of the aspects involved in planning and designing a game. Related to this, few students likely realized the complexities of the programming behind commercially available video and computer games. Many students might feel comfortable with the implementations of the graphical aspects, but the animations and interactions required a level of programming sophistication that most students had not achieved.

Dealing With Change.   To gain a better understanding of the dynamics in students' game development, I compiled information about major changes that students made during the project (see Fig. 4.4). In this figure, I have documented the changes of game ideas and titles or students' thoughts about starting a new game. The information is based on evidence from their notebook writings, program implementations, or interviews. Some students, such as Darvin, Gaby, Gloria, Miriam, Shanice, or Sina, implemented their projects and pursued their beginning ideas the whole way through. Other students changed some features of the game (what I called "surface changes"), such as the title or the introduction and directions, but did not require any new programming. This happened mostly in April, when many students changed the plot of their story. Amy, Albert, Juan, Rosy, Shaun, and Tyree fall into this category. A few students, such as Jero, Sid, and Trevor, started new games in the middle of the project. Most of the changes occurred either in the first days of the project or after 3 to 4 weeks into the project.

I see these changes (the real as well as the intended ones) as indicators of a critical phase in the project, even though they occurred at different times in the project for each student, depending on the individual's game design development. In this time period, the students were in close dialogue with the situation

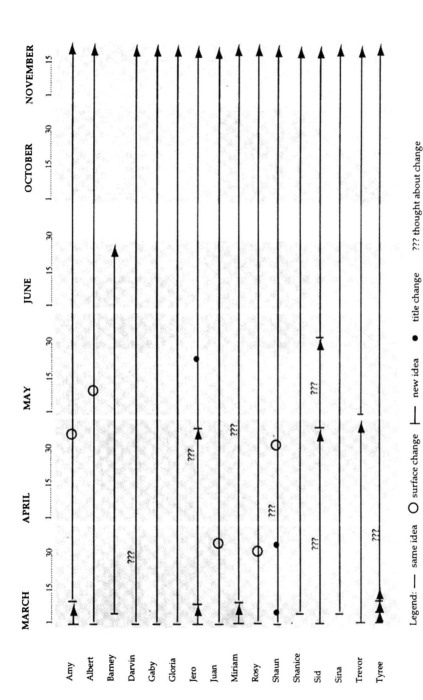

FIG. 4.4. Overview of changes anticipated and implemented by game designers.

Legend: — same idea   ○ surface change |— new idea   ● title change   ??? thought about change

87

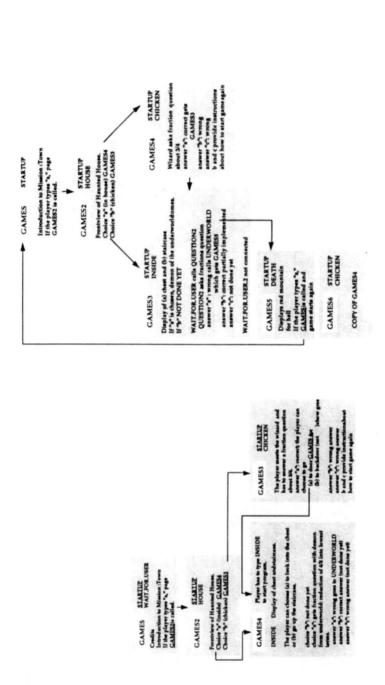

June 19 ----------------------------------->   September 25 ----------->

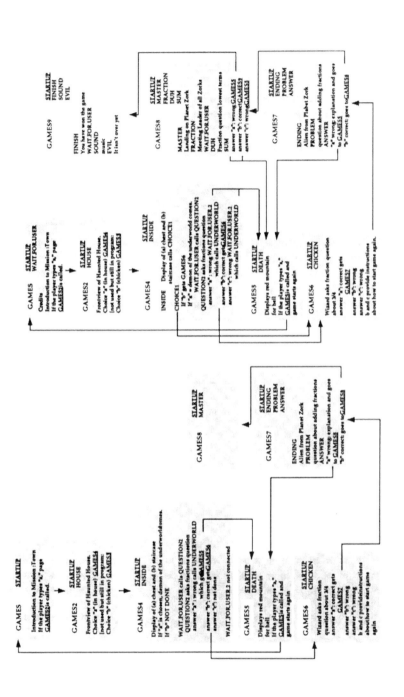

October 11-----------------------------> November 15

FIG. 4.5 Overview of Albert's program and procedure structure from June until November.

(Schön, 1983), or investigating whether their design was a structure adapted to the game's purpose of being fun and educational (Perkins, 1986) or whether their game ideas and implementations resonated with their personal interests (Papert, 1980). When students considered about these changes, they thought about what the project meant to them and whether or not they liked it.

Developing Programming Strategies

In the context of the game design process, it became apparent that students developed a wide range of strategies to deal with the complexities of the game design task. Most of these strategies developed in a later phase of the project. One strategy was the modularization of program code, in which students organized their game according to game scenes. To provide a better sense of the development, I use two cases, Albert and Amy, as examples.

Albert's use of procedures to control the growing complexity of his game program changed only in the last third of the project. All students had been introduced to the concept of procedures and super procedures before the project started. Yet in the first phase of the project, Albert preferred to place one big procedure on each page without segmenting the different parts of his code into individual procedures (June 19). When Albert came back after the summer and started working on his game again, his initial "one big procedure on one page" programming style changed into "several procedures organized in one super procedure on one page," with each page serving as the repository for an event consisting of several scenes (September 25 and October 11). In the same context, Albert also started using LogoWriter pages in a different way: to organize and structure his game, which, in the meantime, had grown to be dozens of different scenes distributed over eight pages (November 15). He used and manipulated the LogoWriter pages as procedures (see Fig. 4.5).

Albert's use of LogoWriter pages is quite unique, but it points out a general pattern observed in other students. All students used procedures in later parts of the project to organize their programs. This observation indicates that young students develop modularization strategies on their own, yet they need the demands of a complex programming project where it makes sense to do so.

Furthermore, students developed "blueprints" to deal with repetitive patterns in the program code. Amy's example is a good one for blueprint development. All of Amy's procedures for the fraction quizzes in her game have the same names; different problems are referenced through different numbers (see Fig.4.6).

Amy chose to create her modules around a set of procedures and to modify them accordingly. She recognized procedures as "entities, as things one could name, manipulate, or change" (Papert, 1980, p. 153). From a software design point of view, Amy adopted a structure that she knew to be efficient and bug-free. The reuse of procedures allowed Amy to be efficient in her programming produc-

PLAY	PLAY2	PLAY3	PLAY4	....
MOVING	MOVING2	MOVING3	....	
MOVE	MOVE2	MOVE3	....	
PROBLEM	PROBLEM2	PROBLEM3	....	
ANSWER	ANSWER2	ANSWER3	....	

FIG. 4.6. Overview of Amy's procedure structure.

tion. Amy finished her first fraction problem on March 24, her second on April 3, and her third on May 6. Through this approach, she produced and covered a large part of her game structure in a short amount of time. Amy was not the only one "reusing" already written procedure parts. Other classmates did the same for their fraction problems.

DISCUSSION

The investigation confirmed the diversity within students' approaches on many levels. From the very beginning, students developed different strategies for dealing with the demands of the design situation. Some students started quickly with one idea, then abandoned it and came up with a new one. Others preferred to explore new programming commands before beginning their games. In the course of the project, students learned about design principles, such as how to adjust their design expectations about what they wanted to accomplish in relation to their programming skills and time constraints. Students dealt with this particular situation in different ways: Some considered starting a new game but continued with their originals; some implemented several superficial changes, whereas others went about making a new game. Some students, like Gaby, approached the task of designing a computer game by deciding the content of their games at the beginning and implementing one feature after the other. Others, like Barney, designed their games as they went along. Based on these results, issues concerning the prevalence of design styles, the development of programming strategies, and the provision of design support are discussed in the following sections.

In my analysis of the students' games, I looked closely at their individual approaches in dealing with the game design task, addressing both programming and design issues. My starting assumption was that people tend to organize their work in different ways, labeled as *planning* and *bricolage* (Turkle & Papert, 1991). Analysis of the students' game development seems to confirm this distinction. There were clear differences, for example, in the way Gaby approached the design task compared to Barney's approach, to name the two extreme cases. Gaby, however, could not straightforwardly implement all the features she had planned. On many occasions she had to consider the situation in relation to her programming skills, game concept, and personal aesthetics to decide on the next step. Most students, in fact, choose to walk a middle line between bricolage and planning. At specific stages in their game design process, for example, when programming the first fraction questions, they tinkered around with different aspects: They designed different shapes and dialogues before deciding on one solution. In later stages, they switched over to reusing, in a purposeful way, program segments that they had written before (such as for the instructional dialogue). The point of this discussion is that *the clear distinction between planners and bricoleurs seems to fall apart when looking at the construction of a complex product over a long period of time.*

It is meaningful to ask in this context whether it would make sense for the students to outline all the features of their task. Several studies have asked programmers of varying degrees, from novices to experts, to solve a well-defined problem in a limited amount of time (several hours) (Guindon, Krasner, & Curtis, 1987; Jeffries et al., 1981). A general software design strategy used by most experts is to decompose a problem into smaller units. One result of these studies indicates that novices or inexperienced programmers do not have a model that guides their problem-solving process. One could then argue that the design and programming style chosen by the students reflected their lack of experience. In this particular task, however, the students' model or image of their game guided their programming. In Barney's case, it was a unspecified adventure scheme that was defined through the characteristics of the narrative. In Gaby's case, it was the model of a computer game that she had played previously and then planned to adapt to its new teaching purpose—fractions.

A further point could be made in regard to the students' use of modularization. Usually, the degree to which different scenes are decomposed is reflected in the use of procedures and super procedures. A planning style would make more use of procedures. However, analysis of the game designers' programs indicates that both planners and bricoleurs used super procedures or no procedures according to their personal preferences. The main problem encountered by the designers was the scarcity of their own design and programming experience. For example, when Sid was interviewed in October, he reflected on his own approaches to dealing with problems:

Interviewer: You got a good idea. What is the first thing you do?

Sid: First, I start from the hard thing; then I just go through the small ones so I can work my way down. Like if I want to have a major thing, I would do that right away, so I can get it out of my face. You know, just keep on doing it. So I feel that the game should end.

Interviewer: Also, if you have a good idea, you work on it immediately?

Sid: Also, I have different ideas. So I have to think for a while, then make my decision which I am going to do.

Interviewer: Where do you get most your idea?

Sid: I get my ideas like . . . first, when I started the game, well I am just typing that stuff. I get ideas. So I just keep on doing.

Sid made two points in his answers. The first point concerns his strategy for dealing with the different design components. He said about himself, "I start from the hard thing; then I just go through the small ones so I can work my way down." This more accurately describes the implementations of Sid's first two games in which he start programming the interactions and animations first. For his third and final game, however, Sid changed his strategy and designed his games as he went along. He said, "I get my ideas like . . . first, when I started the game, well I am just typing that stuff. I get ideas. So I just keep on doing." Sid's case emphasizes how both planning and bricolage can coexist in one person.

The size and complexity of the students' games by the end of the project raised the question of what kind of support for the process we can offer students. Albert's case provided one compelling example of how the growing complexity of his game created the need for structure in the form of LogoWriter page organization. A number of research efforts have been dedicated to helping software designers, especially beginners, deal with the complexity of their programs and to supporting them in their learning of proven design strategies (Guzdial, 1993; Soloway, 1988). What is pertinent to most of these approaches is that they include features in their programming environments that have been deduced from observing expert programmers at work. The reasoning behind this approach is that beginning programmers need to learn these strategies in order to become experts. Analysis of experts' work habits and processes has shown that they make extensive use of these tools to organize their work more efficiently. Although many experts share common strategies and knowledge, they do not necessarily achieve their expertise in the same fashion. This raises the substantial issue that the support structures or "training wheels" are built into a design environment (e.g., libraries, prompts, or multiple linked representations) might not have their complement in the designer's learning process.

The important point about Albert's case was that he created the organization of LogoWriter pages himself. If we had provided him with this tool in advance, I do not think that he would have taken advantage of it. This structure developed in Albert's understanding through his involvement in the long-term programming process. His recognition of its usefulness represented one of the crucial learning moments in his learning history. Now, after the Game Design Project, Albert might be ready to work with different structures to help him organize his next project. Of further importance is the observation that even beginning programmers use a variety of approaches in dealing with their problems. Hence, I leave the issue of design support structure open, but it is important that the designers of future environments take the various approaches into consideration.

CONCLUSION

To place students in the role of game designers is to confront them with a complex task. One of the insights gained from this analysis is that there are multiple ways of designing a game; there was no one "right way" to start, continue, and accomplish a design task. Students used approaches of both planning and bricolage in order to solve the task in a successful manner. Most importantly, students learned not only through design, but also about design, and reached a level of reflection that went beyond traditional school thinking and learning. They were able to see their design experience within a larger context. As Rosemary concluded at the end of her game description: "Truthfully, I hope next time you play a video or computer game, you think about its maker."

ACKNOWLEDGMENTS

This chapter is based on a presentation called "Children's Design Styles" given at the annual meeting of the American Educational Research Association in New Orleans in April 1994. The results presented here are based on my thesis research. I wish to thank my thesis committee members, David Perkins, Seymour Papert, Idit Harel, and Terry Tivnan, for their help and insightful comments. I also thank Joanne Ronkin and her students for their collaboration and great contribution to this work. Without them, this research would not have been possible. The research reported here was conducted at Project Headlight's Model School of the Future and was supported by the IBM Corporation (Grant OSP95952), the National Science Foundation (Grant 851031–0195), the MacArthur Foundation (Grant 874304), the LEGO Group, Fukutake, and Apple Computer, Inc. The preparation of this chapter was supported by the National Science Foundation (Grant 8751190-MDR) and Nintendo Inc. The ideas expressed here do not necessarily reflect the positions of the supporting agencies.

REFERENCES

Avedon, E. M., & Sutton-Smith, B. (Eds.). (1966). *The study of games.* New York: Wiley.

Bjorklund, D. F. (Ed.). (1991). *Children's strategies: Contemporary views of cognitive development.* Hillsdale, NJ: Lawrence Erlbaum Associates.

Block, J. H., & King, N. R. (Eds.). (1987). *School play.* New York: Garland.

Blumenfeld, P. C., Soloway, E., Marx, R. W., Krajcik, J. S., Guzdial, M., & Palincsar, A. (1991). Motivating project-based learning: Sustaining the doing, supporting the learning. *Educational Psychologist, 26*(3 & 4), 369–398.

Bride, J. W., & Lamb, C. E. (1991). Using commercial games to design teacher-made games for the mathematics classroom. *Arithmetic Teacher, 38,* 14–22.

Brown, A. L., & DeLoache, J. S. (1978). Skills, plans and self-regulations. In R. S. Siegler (Ed.), *Children's thinking: What develops?* (pp. 3–35). Hillsdale, NJ: Lawrence Erlbaum Associates.

Carver, S. (1991, April). *Interdisciplinary problem solving.* Paper presented at the American Educational Research Association, Chicago, IL.

Carver, S. M. (1987). *Transfer of LOGO debugging skills: Analysis, instruction and assessment.* Unpublished doctoral thesis. Pittsburgh, PA: Carnegie-Mellon University, Department of Psychology.

Collins, A. S., Brown, J. S., & Newman, S. (1990). Cognitive apprenticeship: Teaching the craft of reading, writing and mathematics. In L. B. Resnick (Ed.), *Cognition and instruction: Issues and agendas* (pp. 453–434). Hillsdale, NJ: Lawrence Erlbaum Associates.

Dreher, M., & Oerter, R. (1987). Action planning competencies during adolescence and early adulthood. In S. L. Friedman, E. K. Scholnick, & R. R. Cocking (Eds.), *Blueprints for thinking* (pp. 321–355). Cambridge, MA: Cambridge University Press.

Fennell, F., Houser, L. L., McPartland, D., & Parker, S. (1984, February). Ideas. *Arithmetic Teacher, 31*, 27–33.

Friedman, S., L., Scholnick, E. K., & Cocking, R. R. (Eds.). (1987). *Blueprints for thinking.* Cambridge: Cambridge University Press.

Guindon, R., Krasner, H., & Curtis, B. (1987). Breakdowns and processes during the early activities of software design by professionals. In G. M. Ohlson, S. Sheppard, & E. Soloway (Eds.), *Empirical studies of programmers: Second workshop* (pp. 65–82). Norwood, NJ: Ablex.

Guzdial, M. (1993). *Emile: Software-realized scaffolding for science learners programming in mixed media.* Unpublished doctoral dissertation, Ann Arbor, MI: University of Michigan.

Harel, I. (1988). *Software design for learning: Children's construction of meaning for fractions and logo programming.* Unpublished doctoral dissertation, Media Laboratory, Cambridge, MA: Massachusetts Institute of Technology.

Harel, I. (1991). *Children designers.* Norwood, NJ: Ablex.

Harel, I., & Papert, S. (1990). Software design as a learning environment. *Interactive Learning Environment, 1*(1), 1–32.

Jeffries, R., Turner, A. A., Polson, P. G., & Atwood, M. E. (1981). The processes involved in designing software. In J. R. Anderson (Ed.), *Cognitive skills and their acquistion* (pp. 225–283). Hillsdale NJ: Lawrence Erlbaum Associates.

Kafai, Y. B. (1993). *Minds in play: Computer game design as a context for children's learning.* Unpublished doctoral dissertation, Cambridge, MA: Harvard Graduate School of Education.

Kafai, Y. B. (1995). *Minds in play: Computer game design as a context for children's learning.* Hillsdale, NJ: Lawrence Erlbaum Associates

Kreitler, S., & Kreitler, H. (1987). Conceptions and processes of planning: the developmental perspective. In S. L. Friedman, E. K. Scholnick, & R. R. Cocking (Eds.), *Blueprints for thinking* (pp. 205–272). Cambridge: Cambridge University Press.

Lehrer, R. (1991). *Knowledge as design.* Paper presented at the American Educational Research Association, Chicago, IL.

Lepper, M. R., & Malone, T. W. (1987). Intrinsic Motivation and Instructional Effectiveness in Computer-Based Education. In R. E. Snow & M. J. Farr (Eds.), *Aptitude, learning and instruction. Volume 3: Conative and affective process analyses* (pp. 255–285). Hillsdale, NJ: Lawrence Erlbaum Associates.

Newell, A. & Simon, H. A. (1972). *Human problem solving.* Englewood Cliffs, NJ: Prentice-Hall.

Papert, S. (1993). *The children's machine.* New York: Basic Books.

Papert, S. (1980). *Mindstorms.* New York: Basic Books.

Pea, R., & Hawkins, J. (1987). Planning in a chore-scheduling task. In S. L. Friedman, E. K. Scholnick, & R. R. Cocking (Eds.), *Blueprints for thinking* (pp. 273–302). Cambridge: Cambridge University Press.

Pea, R. D., & Kurland, M. (1984). On the cognitive effects of learning computer programming. *New Ideas in Psychology, 2*(2), 137–168.

Perkins, D. N. (1986). *Knowledge as design.* Hillsdale, NJ: Lawrence Erlbaum Associates.

Priester, S. (1984, March). SUM 9.9: A game for decimals. *Arithmetic Teacher, 31*, 46–47.

Resnick, M. (1991). Xylophones, hamsters, and fireworks: The role of diversity in constructionist activities. In I. Harel & S. Papert (Eds.), *Constructionism.* Norwood, NJ: Ablex.

Schauble, L. (1991, April). *A developmental psychology of design: Generating and coordinating constraints.* A discussion for the symposium "Kids as Designers" at the American Educational Research Association, Chicago.

Schön, D. A. (1983). *The reflective practitioner.* New York: Basic Books.

Simon, H. A. (1969). *The sciences of the artificial.* Cambridge, MA: MIT Press.

Soloway, E. (1988). It's 2020: Do you know what your children are learning in programming class? In R. S. Nickerson & P. P. Zodhiates (Eds.), *Technology in education: Looking toward 2020* (pp. 121–130). Hillsdale, NJ: Lawrence Erlbaum Associates.

Turkle, S., & Papert, S. (1991). Epistemological pluralism: Styles and voices within the computer culture. In. I. Harel & S. Papert (Eds.), *Constructionism* (pp. 161–193). Norwood, NJ: Ablex.

Electronic Play Worlds
Gender Differences in Children's Construction of Video Games

Yasmin B. Kafai

Children's culture of the late 20th century—their toys, games and activities—has been marked by the advent of information technologies. Video games, more than any other medium, have brought interactive technologies into children's homes and hearts, and they have been received enthusiastically. In contrast to most adults, children usually do not feel threatened by computational media and other programmable devices. They seem to embrace the new media readily. With good reason, children have been dubbed media enthusiasts (Papert, 1991).

This increasing presence of computer and video games in homes has initiated many discussions in the media and educational circles about their value and influence on children's affective, social, and cognitive well-being (Baughman & Clagett, 1983; Provenzo, 1991). Most research efforts have focused on studying the effects on social behavior and cognitive skills of children playing video games (Greenfield & Cocking, 1994; Loftus & Loftus, 1983; Selnow, 1984). Discussions in cultural studies have centered around the issues of which particular messages are promoted in video games and in what ways they are received by children (Gailey, 1992; Kinder, 1991). As important as these findings are, researchers always look at children as consumers of games and try to deduce from children's game-playing interests and behaviors what impact and attractions video games hold.

In the present study, I address some of these issues from a different perspective by placing children in the role of producers rather than consumers of video games. In a 6-month-long project, called the Game Design Project (Kafai, 1993, 1995), sixteen 10-year-old children were in charge of creating imaginary worlds, characters, and stories in the context of video game design. My intention was to explore the extent to which the activity of making games revealed something about children's likes, dislikes, motivation, and interest in playing games. One question was whether children would import such features as the violence and male-oriented gender stereotyping that are embedded in commercially available video games into their own designs. A related issue concerned the relationship between girls and video games. Given the choice, what kind of video games would girls produce if the design of all the features—genre, place, characters, and interactions—were left to them? I used the process of video game design to allow children to visualize and implement their fantasies and ideas. A general goal of this study was to investigate whether constructive activities such as game making offer rich and playful opportunities for an ethnically diverse group of players.

In the following sections, I describe the research context and methodologies used to gather the data in the Game Design Project. I present the games developed by the children and analyze them in regard to their features, themes, and interactions. In the discussion, I raise issues concerning extent to which these choices were gender related and which particular cultural values they reflected, if any. Based on the results, the conclusions address the potential of different game-making activities, tools, and contexts with more powerful computational technologies. Before I enter the empirical arena, however, I briefly review what is known about video games in the research literature.

REVIEW OF RESEARCH

The prominence and social significance of video games in children's lives have not been matched by research efforts. Most of what we know about video games, which is little, comes from research on the effects of video game playing. Many research efforts have focused on identifying the psychological processes involved in the playing of video games (Dominick, 1984; Morlock, Yando, & Nigolean, 1985; Silvern & Williamson, 1987) and discussing the pros and cons of game playing (Harris & Williams, 1984; Selnow, 1984). Other research has focused on the development of children's spatial and attentional skills while or because of playing video games (Greenfield, Brannon & Lohr, 1994; Greenfield, deWinstanley, Kilpatrick, & Kaye, 1994; Okagaki & French, 1994; Subrahmanyam & Greenfield, 1994). Many of these studies point out gender differences in spatial skills, which sometimes disappear after extended exposure.

Other studies have investigated the relationships among video game playing, representational competence in various media, and the impact of cultural factors (Greenfield, 1993; Greenfield, Camaioni, Ercolani, Weiss, Lauber & Perrucchini, 1994). Still other research has addressed the gender differences found in game playing interests (Inkpen, Upitis, et al., 1993; Lawry et al., 1994) and the promotion of cultural values such as violence and sexism in video games (Gailey, 1992; Kinder, 1991). Researchers, such as Gailey, have questioned the extent to which these messages are received as transmitted. She analyzed what values video games convey, how children as players interpret the play process, and what children get out of the games. One of her findings was that children did not accept the universals provided in video games; they made up their own descriptions. Despite the considerable gender stereotyping found in many video games (portraying women as victims or prizes), girls seem to resolve the dilemma by redefining their roles, placing themselves in managerial roles. In contrast, Kinder (1991) argued that the values embedded in movies, toys, television, and video games provide powerful stereotypes for children's thinking.

Irrespective of the research focus, children's attraction to video and computer games has not changed. Children love playing these games as the multibillion-dollar game industry indicates. The reasons for the attractiveness of video games have been investigated from different perspectives such as those of psychoanalysis (Turkle, 1984) and cognitive psychology (Malone, 1981; Lepper & Malone, 1987; Malone & Lepper, 1987). Lepper and Malone investigated the intrinsic motivational value of computer games. They asked students to play a number of different computer games, then to rate the games according to attractiveness and name their outstanding features. In the presenting their results, these investigators distinguished between individual motivations (such as challenge, fantasy, curiosity, and control) and interpersonal motivations (such as cooperation, competition, and recognition) as the main attracting features of games.

A different view has been provided by Turkle (1984), who not only analyzed several video game players and their interests in games but also investigated the attractions of programming. Pertinent in her interpretations of the players' motivation is what she calls the "holding power" of video games. Part of the holding power comes from the role-playing and fantasy aspects included in video games. Turkle (1984) characterized video games as a

> . . . window onto a new kind of intimacy with machines that is characteristic of the nascent computer culture. The special relationship that players form with video games has elements that are common to interactions with other kinds of computers. The holding power of video games, their almost hypnotic fascination, is computer holding power and something else as well. At the heart of the computer culture is the idea of constructed, "rule-governed" worlds (p. 66).

This holding power is not the same for all players. One of Turkle's cases, Marty, played video games to enjoy control. In contrast, David liked to play video games because it allowed him to concentrate fully in a relaxed way and to be in the "perfect contest." One can conclude from these observations that playing video games resonated with different aspects of the players' personalities.

The research I report here does not investigate the effects of or reasons for game playing. It looks instead at the process of game *making* as a way of examining children's interest in games. My analysis must be preceded by the recognition that we do not know very much about children's making of games. A search through the psychological and educational databases of the last 10 years showed not one entry on making games. Incidentally, Turkle (1984) saw a parallel between the attractions of playing games and of programming computers:

> When you play a video game, you are a player in a game programmed by someone else. When children begin to do their own programming, they are not deciphering someone else's mystery. They become players in their own game, makers of their own mysteries, and enter in a new relationship with the computer, one in which they begin to experience it as a kind of second self (p. 92).

There seems to be a common denominator between why people love to play video games and what gets them involved in programming. Making games could combine attractions from both playing games and programming in that players not only explore worlds but also build them. The "holding power" of playing games, (i.e., moving in rule-governed worlds with determined boundaries) may also apply to the "holding power" of making games, in which the rules and boundaries governing the world are determined by the designer. This parallel provides the rationale for investigating game making as an avenue into children's minds to explore the features of game playing.

Of particular interest are gender differences as they might appear in the design of the video games. We know little about girls' interest and playing of video games because the majority of video game-players are boys. One obvious reason for this situation is that most commercial video games aim predominantly at the male player with their emphasis on fighting and sports. Furthermore, the principal game characters are almost always male; women are assigned the roles of victims and prizes (Gailey, 1992; Rushbrook, 1986). It seems worthwhile to ask how video games appealing to girls would look. Hence, the process of game making might give us a window into girls' likes and dislikes of particular video game features. Of interest are the design of the game worlds and the creation of characters as well as the interaction structure, the control and the feedback given into the hands of the player.

Research Context and Methodology

The Game Design Project provided the research context (Kafai, 1993, 1995). The project was conducted with a class of 16 fourth-grade students who were programming games in Logo to teach fractions to third-graders. The class was divided evenly between girls and boys from mixed ethnic backgrounds and ranging in age from 9 to 10. The children met every day and transformed their classroom into a game design studio for 6 months, learning programming, writing stories and dialogues, constructing representations of fractions, creating package designs and advertisements, considering interface design issues, and devising teaching strategies.[1]

The following scene captures the first 20 minutes of one day in the project and shows two students discussing their games, design ideas, and programming issues as they work at the computer:

> On a Wednesday morning, 10 weeks into the project, two students, Amy[2] and Trevor, sit next to each other at the computers while working on their games. The computers are arranged outside of their classroom in two circles, with 16 computers each. The notebooks in which the students write every day about their ideas, plans, and designs are stacked between their computers. Trevor sits with both his legs folded on the chair and types in the name of a Logo procedure to start his game. The introduction to his game, called "The Island of the Goon," reads: "You are a monkey. You are going to Island Snow. There are blue birds at a lake and a mountain. First go to the lake, then to the mountain, and last to the GOLDEN MOUNTAIN. You have to get the Golden Snow from the GOLDEN MOUNTAIN to cure the king monkey, Contrae, because he is sick. At the island, you will meet the monkey you just saw turned into a goon by the evil wizard. Use the arrow keys to move. He will ask you a fraction problem. If you get it wrong, you will become mentally deformed. Good Luck!!!"
>
> While the turtle begins drawing on the screen, Trevor looks over to Amy's computer screen, which displays a page full of turtle shapes. He points to one of her shapes and asks, "Why do you have a question mark?" then leans back waiting for Amy's answer.
>
> Amy replies, "It's for my game. What do you have done so far in your game?"
>
> On Trevor's screen, the turtle draws the outlines of a circle and fills the background with color. Trevor responds, "I have an island."
>
> Amy retorts: "That's it?! Why don't you tell what's going on?" She then comments on the player figure placed on the bottom of the Trevor's screen: "You can't see that's you."
>
> "How do you know?" Trevor asks.
>
> Amy replies, "Because I can read it, if I look very close. It just doesn't look good because it lies on top of the line." Pointing to Trevor's screen, she suggests a new place: "I'd just put YOU ARE here."
>
> Even though Trevor challenges Amy's observation—"So? It works for me"—he selects the page with all his shapes. He starts working on the player shape by

---

[1]One of the primary purposes of this project was to investigate game making as a context for learning Logo programming and fractions among other things (see also Harel, 1991). For that reason, the games designed by the students are a special breed of games called *educational games*. Yet, as my analyses will indicate, it was this particular constellation that emphasized game aspects because students had to think about how to create games that were educational and entertaining at the same time. In the following analysis, I focus more on the game aspects than on the learning aspects, which are discussed more extensively in other publications (e.g., Kafai, 1993).

[2]All student names are pseudonyms.

moving a cursor over a grid of squares. By deleting some of the squares, he changes the outline of his player's shape and explains: "I'm cleaning him up, so you can see the line."

When Trevor returns to his page with the island map, the new shape appears in the player's place. Amy congratulates Trevor on his improvement: "See, very good."

After Trevor has completed the revisions of his player figure, he looks again at Amy's screen and points to one of her shapes that shows six small squares, three of which are shaded in and comments, "This is one half."

Amy replies, "No, three sixths. I can't make them [the third graders] reduce. You know, I can't make them reduce it."

"Why can't you make them reduce it?"

"Because they don't know how to do it." Amy then starts playing her own game. She reads aloud the introduction: "You want to go to the home of Zeus but the map was ripped up by the Greek God Hades. All of the Greek Gods and Godesses have a fraction of the map. You are to go to the Gods and Godesses one at a time and they will ask you a fraction problem. If you get it right you will get a fraction of the map. When you get the whole map you will be at the gate of Zeus' home. The bull at the gate will ask you three hard fraction problems. If you get them right you will go inside Zeus' home and get to become the God or Godess of fractions and meet Zeus!"

As Amy continues to play her game, she answers one fraction question after the other and collects the different parts of the map. After she has correctly answered the third fraction question, she realizes that the third quarter of the map is not in the right place; it partially covers other parts. "This isn't right. This is messed up," she complains. She stops her program by pressing the control and S keys, then flips to the page where she can see all her procedures. She reads aloud the Logo code while scrolling down the page: "There is something wrong with SETSHAPE. SETPOSITION 60 50. It has to be 60 10."

Meanwhile, Trevor has been working on a new shape. Several times, he tries to get Amy's attention: "Now, does this look like a stick figure? Does this look like a stick figure? Answer me! Does this look like a stick figure?"

Amy briefly turns her head and says: "Yes. Shhh, I am trying to figure something out! SETSHAPE 11. SETPOSITION 75 10. Oh Oh." She slaps herself on the head: "75 10. I am on the wrong page! That's it! Heh, it worked." Amy and Trevor continue working on their games.

The previous description provides a snapshot of the actual game design process; in the context of their game design, students dealt on a daily basis with issues such as storytelling, character creation, and graphics during the 6-month-long project. The collaborative structure of the project provided opportunities for the game designers to discuss their project with their classmates, and to show it to their potential users and to a wider public. Several "focus sessions" presented opportunities for the teacher and researcher to initiate discussions around issues and ideas relevant to all game designers. For example, issues about games, students' experiences playing games, what they learned, and programming ideas were among the issues discussed on these occasions.

A combination of qualitative methods was used to document the students' ideas, thoughts, and progress in game development. Pre- and post-interviews were conducted to gather information on students' interest, knowledge, and evaluation of video games. During the project, the students participated in research activities by keeping notebook entries, saving log files, and interviewing to provide additional information for the researcher. In the interviews conducted individually with each student before the project began, I found that all students knew about and had played video games. However, the extent of the video game-playing experience varied considerably. The major difference was between girls and boys; most boys actively and consistently played video games, whereas only two girls said that they did so. In a few cases, the students also explained that their lack of video game-playing experience was due to their parents' resistance to purchasing a game system, so they were limited to playing at friends' or relatives' homes. Furthermore, most girls also stated that they had no particular interest in pursuing video game-playing because they did not like their themes and violence. To summarize, the girls' and boys' knowledge of video games was not comparable. This result, however, is not surprising considering that the majority of commercial video games are played by boys (e.g., Greenfield, Brannon, & Lohr, 1994; Provenzo, 1991).

RESULTS

Sixteen students were involved in designing and implementing a video game. Each of them completed at least one game in the course of the project; some students started or completed more than one game. The children's games were analyzed in terms of the following features: (a) the game genre, (b) the game worlds and places created, (c) the game characters and supporting cast of actors developed by students, (d) the interaction modes and feedback provided for the player, and (e) the narrative development in the game structure. To highlight potential gender differences in the design of the games, the results were arranged by gender groups: girls' and boys' games.

Game Genres

There are various kinds of video games, which can be divided into the following categories: adventure, sports-skills, teaching context, and simulation. This categorization is by no means exhaustive or exclusive, as many games actually fall into several categories at the same time. For example, an adventure game may also be a skill game because the player must overcome many obstacles, thus demonstrating considerable athletic skills. Or, a simulation game of city-building may as well have educational purposes because the player deals with the complexity of dynamic networked systems. Nevertheless, this general categorization may serve as a starting point. For analyzing the designed games, the category

Girls	Game Places &Worlds	Game Genre	Presence of Evil
Amy	fair, mount Olympus	adventure-mythology	no
Gaby	spider web	skill	no
Gloria	classroom	teaching	no
Miriam	ski slope	skill	no
Rosy	basement, castle	adventure-travel	no
Shanice	airport	skill	no
Sina	classroom	teaching	no
Tyree	space city	adventure-travel	no

Boys	Game Places &Worlds	Game Genre	Presence of Evil
Albert	haunted house	adventure-exploration	yes
Barney	city, ocean, forest, airport	adventure-travel	no
Darvin	surfing maze	skill	no
Jero	Hect Village	adventure-travel	yes
Juan	Funland	adventure	no
Shaun	space station	adventure	yes
Sid	basketball court/obstacle course/Peaceville	skill/skill/adventure	yes
Trevor	coin grid/island	adventure-exploration	yes

FIG. 5.1. Overview of game places and genres, and the presence of evil as they were designed and implemented by students. (The greater number of places and genres than actual students is due to some students who started and implemented more than one game. Some students used more than one world or place in their games; those places are separated by commas. The hyphen in game genre denotes the special nature of the game. The slash distinguishes between the different genres and places for students who created more than one game in the project.)

"adventure" was used when the player experienced extraordinary events or was sent to unknown places to be explored. The category "skill" was used for games of an atheltic nature, such as basketball or skiing. A third category described games that used the "teaching" context in an explicit fashion.

The majority of games used the adventure-travel-exploration genres (10 out of 18 games). Figure 5.1 provides an overview of all game genres and their distribution among boys and girls.

Almost all of the boys created adventure hunts and explorations, whereas the girls' games were more evenly divided among adventure, skill-sport, or teaching games. The sports theme was selected by a few students (two boys chose skating and basketball and one girl chose skiing) who focused on skill aspects such as navigating a maze or a spider web, or dunking basketballs. Only two students (girls) chose an educational format, a teaching game, to incorporate the content to be learned.

The sharpest thematic difference between boys and girls concerned the morality issue—the contest between good and evil where the player is on the good side fighting off the bad guys in order to achieve the goal. In the boys' games, the goal of the player was to recover a "stolen fraction wand" (Shaun) or "a stolen jewel" (Jero), to "defeat demons, evil fraction aliens, globe ghosts, or mash Martians" (Albert) in order to receive a "bucket full of gold, a trip to Orlandoville, a wedding to a princess" (Sid), or "tickets to a summer water park" (Shaun). In contrast, there are few evil characters in the girls' games (e.g., the sun in Miriam's skiing game or the spider in Gaby's spider game). In some of the girls' games, the player has to "go down the mountain without falling" (Miriam), "avoid a spider" (Gaby), "land a helicopter" (Shanice), or answer fraction questions (Gloria, Sina). Then the player can receive an unspecified "treasure" (Rosy) or "prize" (Gloria), "avoid French" (Sina), or "become the God or Goddess of fractions" (Amy). Not one girl incorporated the conquest for evil in her game, whereas five boys chose to do so.

In all of the games, the player's success depends on figuring out the correct answer to the fraction questions in order to continue or finish the game. Fractions are the obstacle to be overcome. This emphasizes an interesting relation with fractions. It might express the negative feelings many children have toward fractions, or it could just be that fractions are always positioned as "problems to be solved" in the classroom, and this carries over into the game. One could say that, at least in the beginning, the game designers were not able to decenter from and develop positive feelings about fractions.

Game Worlds

The diversity of genre and gender differences were also reflected in the design of the game world. All game designs centered around the construction of physical spaces. Many students had quite original ideas for their games: Gaby's spider

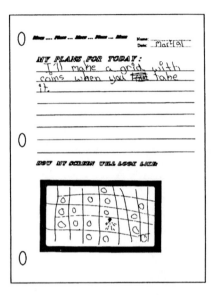

FIG. 5.2. Designer Notebook entries—Gaby's and Trevor's game designs. Gaby's game describes a spider web in which the player moves around as a fly away from the spider and turns on fraction blocks where questions are posed. Trevor shows the coin grid and a figure that represents the player.

web, Trevor's coin grid (Fig. 5.2), Jero's map game, and Shaun's street scene (Fig. 5.3) are just a few examples.

Yet there was an interesting difference in the "reality" aspect of the students' game worlds. In many instances, the game worlds could be described as fantasy places because they were imaginary worlds where the younger players could learn about fractions. The majority of students created fantasy places such as imaginary cities, islands, or countries (e.g., Funland and Peaceville). In contrast, a number of other games featured more well-known places such as the classroom, ski slope, airport, and spider web. Six out of eight girls confined their game places and worlds to real-life settings, whereas only one boy did so. In contrast, the games of seven out of eight boys included fantasy places. In a few situations, the players started out in familiar places such as the home, neighborhood, or street before venturing into more distant places such as schools, castles, mount Olympus, or encounters with spaceships. These were also counted as fantasy places if the major part of the game-playing took place in them.

Many games made reference to commercially available games from systems such as Nintendo. For example, Jero's different warp zones are reminiscent of Mario Brothers' tunnel system. Oscar made explicit reference to the PacMan game, but to eating fractions instead of dots. In Tyree's game the player could

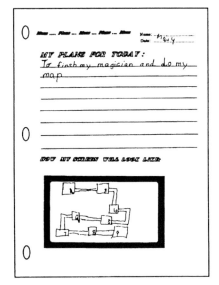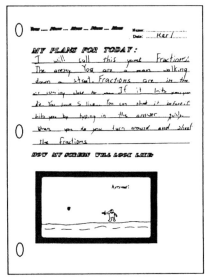

FIG. 5.3.   Designer Notebook entries—Jero and Shaun's game designs. Jero's map shows the different stations or levels of the world that the player has to pass. Shaun's street scene is the context in which the fraction questions will be posed.

earn fractions of a magic potion as a reward, and thus incorporate a feature found in the Nintendo game, Super Mario Brothers. Sid's basketball game is available in various video game versions. Gaby took an educational game she had used in her previous school, the spider web, and adapted it to fractions. Some of the students used the school situation when choosing a game theme. For example, Sina's outline of her teacher game shows a teacher asking, or more accurately, "screaming" a fraction. Gloria came up with a similar idea (see Fig. 5.4).

In the next section, I elaborate in more detail on the cast of characters and game figures that students designed for their games.

Development of Game Characters

The places or worlds in which the games were situated were populated with an interesting cast of characters. One group concerned the game character assigned to the player; the other described the supporting cast of game actors (see Fig. 5.5).

Apparent in the figures assigned to the game player is that all the boys (except for one) chose fantasy figures or assigned a specific gender to the player. In the case of fantasy figures, the students created an artificial game-player persona, such as a surfer (Darvin's game) or Gemini (Sid's game). Most of the boys also assumed that the player would be male as well. The fictive game player was

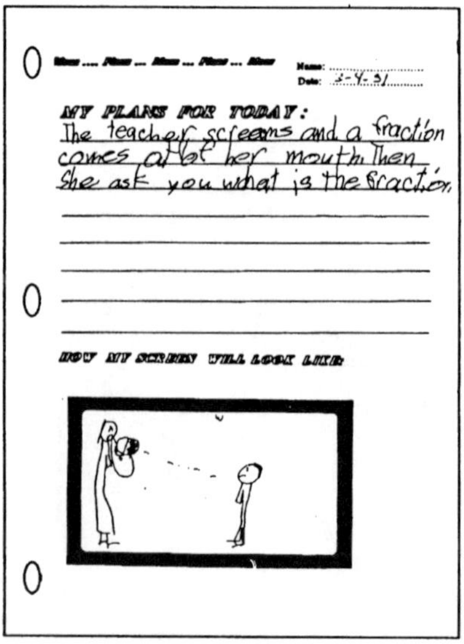

FIG. 5.4. Designer Notebook entry—Sina's game design. Sina shows the two protagonists of the game, the teacher and the player.

called Mike, Jose, Tommy, or Alex. Some game players had fantasy names with which the gender was more difficult to detect. Darvin was the only boy who addressed the player as both "dude" or "dudette." In contrast, most girls left the player's gender or age open: The player simply was addressed by a generic "you" without any further specifications. One might also interpret this choice as involving a more personal identification: The player and the character are one and the same. This analysis revealed a strong and significant gender difference: Whereas five girls chose a genderless or more personally identified player, only one boy adopted the same approach for his player choice.

The cast of supporting game actors emphasized this result even more: Most boys created several characters (e.g., demons, aliens from planet zork, magicians, dragons, soldiers from loft, or goons) with fantasy names (e.g., Zork, Zarcon, Garvin, Sparzi, or Marley) for the game world in which the player had to interact. Albert's thoughts are a good example of character development. In 4 weeks, he considered a whole cast before he settled on the demon figure. The excerpts in Fig. 5.6 are taken from his notebook entries and reflect his ongoing considerations.

In contrast, most girls chose one or two figures for their supporting cast (see Fig. 5.5). It is apparent in this comparison that the girls had a significantly different take on the role that player and actors have in the game. Whereas seven out of eight girls created between zero and two supporting characters, six out of the eight boys created three or more.

One could argue that commercial video game figures provided the inspiration for the game figures designed by the boys in the Game Design Project. This argument gains support if one considers the abundance of available video games

Girls	Player Character	Supporting Cast
Amy	you	Greek Gods and Godesses, snake, Zeus
Gaby	you	spider
Gloria	fly	teacher
Miriam	you	evil sun
Rosy	Plum, a cat	mouse, rich man
Shanice	you	-
Sina	Tom, a student	teacher
Tyree	you	martians

Boys	Player Character	Supporting Cast
Albert	you, a kid	demon from underworld, aliens from Planet Zork, leader of the Zorks
Barney	Jose, a third grader	Marley, the magician, man in balloon, shark, lion, man robbing money
Darvin	surfer	seven ghosts
Jero	Alex	King Martian
Juan	Tommy	Funland people
Shaun	Mike, a third grader	Zarcon
Sid	Gemini (with Swartz)	Garvin, the magician, Sparzi, dragon, soldier from loft
Trevor	monkey	evil wizard, goon, princess

FIG. 5.5.   Overview on students' choices for game players and game actors. For students who created more than one game, only the last game was included in the analyses because it was the most developed game.

and their focus on a male audience (Kinder, 1991; Provenzo, 1991). For the girls, on the other hand, there are fewer examples to draw from because of the lack of gender-appropriate video games.

The choice of familiar and personal figures provides room for the interpretation that girls grounded their designs in what they knew and liked. Rosy liked cats; hence a cat plays a major role in her game. Miriam used a skier because she liked skiing. Gloria and Sina used a teacher in their games. Another possibility is

On March 12, Albert wrote that "I made one change. I am going to make creatures ask you problems and if you don't solve them you die." He continued March 13 with "I will make a guy on shapes and make him do something." Then on March 26, he wrote, "I am going to make a bully and his gang on shapes and they'll ask you a fraction question and if you get it right, you quit or chicken out." He announced on March 27 that "I need to make a gang of punks and they will ask you a question and if the answer is wrong they kill you." At the end of that day, he wrote, "I need to finish the gang and make them ask you a question. I have to finish the outcome of what happens when you get the right answer and wrong answer."

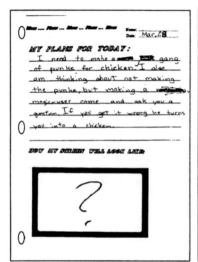
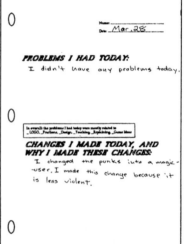

On March 28, he changed the characters of the game again: "I need to make a gang of punks for chicken. I also am thinking about not making the punks but making a magic user come and ask you a question. If you get it wrong he turns you into a chicken." At the end of the day, he decided that "I changed the punks into a magic-user. I made this change because it is less violent." His plans for the next day confirmed this decision: "I am planning to work on the question that the magic user asked. If you get it wrong he turns you into a chicken." After the month of March, Albert settled on the demon figure.

FIG. 5.6. Albert's game-character development during the month of March and notebook designs from March 28. Note that he did not actually implement any of these ideas except for the demon figure.

that the small number of supporting characters reflected preferred social group-ings: Girls are known to play in smaller groups than boys.

Design of Game Interactions and Feedback

Another difference became clear in the interactions that children designed for their players. One distinction can be drawn between the guided interaction mode and the manipulation mode. In the first mode, the player follows the game process as it has been determined by the designer. Most interactions between the player and the game consists of answering questions by pressing a key or typing an answer. Actions and animations of the game figures on the screen are pre-programmed by the designer; the player has no impact on their development. In contrast the player in the manipulation mode has to manipulate keys and move a figure around to certain designated places. The distinction between the two game interaction modes revealed no significant gender differences: Four girls adopted the guided interaction mode, whereas six boys choose this mode for their games. Two of those girls, Amy and Miriam, adopted the guided interaction mode only in the last scene of their games (see Fig. 5.7). For that reason, their interaction mode was counted as manipulation.

This trend in girls' preference for the manipulation mode has to be interpreted with care because the guided mode was much easier to implement than the manipulation mode. Yet, interestingly enough, most girls preferred to handle a more complicated programming task. It could be that the girls intended to give players more control by having them manipulate the principal game figure. This fits with the girls' construction of greater identification, noted earlier, between the player and game character. For the boys, in contrast, the programming of animations was more interesting (as documented by their interest in developing characters; see previous section), which forced them to keep more control over the game-playing process.

The feedback provided by the interaction between the player and the game differed as well: In case of a wrong answer, most boys choose to end the game in a violent fashion. "Game over," by itself, would not constitute a violent feedback if it were not in connection with loosing one's life or suffering harm. Game actors either lose their lives before the game is over or as a result of it. For example, game actors on the screen were "kicked to the moon" (Barney's game), "turned into an ice cube" (Shaun's game), "sent frying to the underworld" (Albert's game), or "mentally transformed" (Trevor's game). Darvin made his surfer char-acter insult the players' intelligence by saying, "Let me see how smart you are, Dude or Dudette" and "So you are telling me you're dumb" when they gave a wrong answer. The harm here is psychological rather than physical; but it is still a harm.

On the other hand, almost all of the girls (seven out of eight) programmed different kinds of feedback for a wrong answer most of the time. In the case of a

Girls	Interaction Mode	Feedback (in case of wrong answer)
Amy	manipulation mode (some guided interaction) player moves figure to Gods	non violent player does not get part of the map
Gaby	manipulation mode player moves fly around	non violent player gets correct answer
Gloria	guided interaction player answers questions	non violent no reward
Miriam	manipulation mode player moves skier down slope	non violent back to top of ski slope
Rosy	guided interaction (with some manipulation)	non violent doesn't get home
Shanice	manipulation mode player maneuvers helicopter	violent helicopter crashes
Sina	guided interaction player answers questions	non violent player has to take French
Tyree	guided interaction player answers question	non violent player can try again and does not get magic potion

Boys	Interaction Mode	Feedback (in case of wrong answer)
Albert	guided interaction player is given choices and answers questions	violent player is killed and sent to underworld
Barney	guided interaction playerpresses keys and answers questions	violent player disappears, gets kicked to moon, eaten by shark
Darvin	manipulation mode player moves figure around maze	non violent insults player verbally
Jero	guided interaction player answers questions to continue	violent game over
Juan	guided interaction player answers questions	violent game over
Shaun	guided interaction player presses keys and answers questions	violent freezes to ice cube; game over
Sid	guided interaction player answers questions	violent game over
Trevor	manipulation mode player moves figure on island to different places	violent player becomes mentally deformed

FIG. 5.7. Overview on game interaction modes and dominant type of feedback provided for the player.

wrong answer, the player continued but did not receive a piece of the map (Amy), had to start again from the top of the ski slope (Miriam), had to take French (Sina), or did not receive a fraction of the magic power (Tyree). One exception was Shanice, who ended her game with a helicopter crash if the player did not give the right answer. Miriam's game experienced a change in the course of its development. In the major part of her game, the skier went down a slope and was sent up back to the top in the case of a wrong answer. However, in last two scenes of her game, when the player is on the way back home, Miriam decided to end the game. I do not know the reason for her change of mind, but it is possible that she was influenced by the other games in her class. Furthermore, she might have tried to experiment with a new form of feedback as she also changed the narrative mode in her game structure (see the next section). To summarize, in feedback for the player, there were again significant gender differences: Boys' feedback modes were overwhelmingly violent, girls' feedback overwhelmingly non-violent.

Game Narrative

As students continued developing their games, defining their characters, and outlining their scenes in the subsequent weeks of the Game Design Project, they also created a story that situated the actors in a fantasy, yet meaningful, context. One of the most prominent examples for the development of the story or narrative in games can be found in Barney's game. I could see his impact on many other students as they were playing his game or talking about it. To emphasize the narrative stream in his game, I extracted the text from his Logo program code, excluding the fractions exchanges (see Fig. 5.8).

Barney's game starts with the story of Jose, who gets lost and experiences a series of adventures over several days and nights. His story is driven by the plot that Jose tries to find his way home. The story has several dialogues accompanying the graphics: Sometimes his text is direct speech; other times it gives information, and still other times, the text becomes the running inner thoughts of Jose or other actors in the game. The text essentially has an explanatory function because it sets the mood and annotates the events on the screen for the player.

The narrative format was not present from the beginning in many games. To document the shift toward the narrative in the students' game formats, I analyzed the game development of all 16 students and compiled the results (see Fig. 5.9). Some students, such as Barney, Albert, Gloria, Juan, Rosy, and Sina, started early to incorporate narrative elements into their game design. Several students stayed with their game format: Gaby's Spider web, Shaun's Fraction Killer, Darvin's Maze, Gloria's Teacher, Sina's Teacher, and Shanice's Helicopter Madness. However, the number of students who used the narrative format increased (from 6 to 12) in the course of the game development. Twice as many boys as girls made the shift from game to narrative format. No student moved from narrative to game format. By the end, 12 of the 16 children were using the narrative format.

This change took different forms. Some of the students changed their game on the surface without having to redo a lot of previous programming: Amy retained her map idea, but changed the content of the game to Greek myths; Albert's haunted house turned into a game called Mission Town; Rosy's game first took place around the world and then changed to a travel story.

You are Jose, a third qrade kid who gets lost and must find his way home. You will go on many different adventures. Along the way, people (or beasts, creatures, etc.) will ask you questions about fractions, (you will type A, B or C, remember to press enter.) If you get the question right, you will go on safely, but beware! Danger lurks if you get the question wrong. Have fun if you dare! Type play and press enter.
"Where am I?" "I have to get home!"
A mysterious man approaches you. "Hey kid, I'm Marley the Magician and I'm going to make you disappear if you don't tell me how much of this square is colored!, says the man.
A. THREE FOURTHS   B. TWO-FOURTHS   C. FOUR-TWELFTHS
    What is it?
NO! "Dumb Kid" GAME OVER
YES! Go free says the man.
A man comes out of a hot air balloon and approaches you. "I'm going to take you prisoner in my balloon if you don't tell me which one of these fractions is equal to two-thirds." says the man.
A. two-fourths   B. eighth-twelfths   C. one-third.
No! You idiot! let's go GAME OVER
Yes! See Ya'
I'm tired," you say. "I'll look for home in the morning."
While you are sleeping, a robber comes and takes the $33 dollars you have in your pocket.
"MONEY!"
Morning comes. You get up and realize you have no money in your pocket. "OH NO!" "I'll just have to do without it."
You see a man coming towards you. You need some money so you kindly say "Excuse me sir, could you please give me a few dollars, a robber robbed me broke!" It doesn't look hopeful. After a minute the man says "I'll give you $30 dollars if you tell me what one-half of $30 dollars is, otherwise I kick you to the moon!
A. $15   B. $ 20   C. $11   What is it?
NO! Whoa! THE MOON GAME OVER AND YOU WERE NEVER SEEN AGAIN
"Here kid, 30 dollars, don't spend it all in one place.
It gets a bit darker. You thought you would take a walk on the beach.
"I'll take a swim," you say.
Onder the water .....
A fish swims with you. You see a shark. You are too terrified to move but the fish swims away.
"You'll be makin' me a fine meal, lil' one."
Who said that?
It was you the shark! You can talk!
"Boy, kid, you're a regular Einstein!"
You are very scared.
"I'll just want to leave, please don't eat me!" you say.
"I'm hungry! But if you tell me what four-twenty-fourths is in lowest terms you can go."
A. one third   B. two sixths   C. one sixths   What is it?
SUPPER TIME CHOMP! MUNCH! MUNCH!.......... BURRRPPPPPPP! GAME OVER
I guess I'll go and eat that dumb old fish.
You get out.
Meanwhile at home ..... "Where's Jose, I'm so worried!"
It's getting late again. You walk around for a place to sleep. You walk into a jungle. You see a lion.
The lion is looking for supper when he comes upon you. Just as the lion is about to lunge forward and eat you, you dodge him. "You look like a nice little kid, I'll let you free if ....
A talking shark, a talking lion! This is getting wiered!
The lion says "As I was about to say, you can go free if you tell me which one of these decimals is equal to one-tenth."
A .1   B. 1.5   C. .7
Sorry kid! GAME OVER
Well, you're allright, see ya' later.
You go to sleep and when you wake up you walk back into the city.
AIRPORT
I don't even know where I am, I'll go into the airport to find out.
INSIDE THE AIRPORT TICKET BOOTH

FIG. 5.8. Barney's game Jose in the Fraction World. Barney's game was never finished because he left class after the summer and moved to another school. (Note that the spelling mistakes are Barney's.)

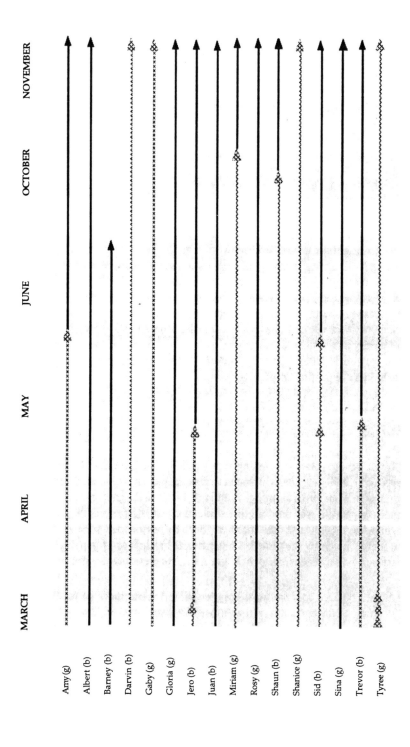

Legend: 〰 game format ▬ narrative format

FIG. 5.9.   Overview of changes in the games and narrative format. The arrows indicate the beginnings of a new game. Some students used the new game beginning also to change the format. [g = girl; b = boy]

115

In all of these cases, the change of the story plot, as some students called it, did not affect the programming done prior to the change, but for another group of students, it meant that they started a new game. For example, Sid's third game is a fractions journey of two characters, Gemini and Swartz. Trevor's second game, after he finished his first, involved adventures on the Island of the Goon. The characteristic of this conversion to narrative is that students designed scenes not solely for instructional purposes. They included additional scenes where different actors spoke to each other. The graphics were accompanied by text, and the fraction questions were asked in the context of dialogue. There is no logic for fractions learning to take place in the Greek myths, spaceships, and mazes that the students created, except, that it made sense to the students themselves.

A possible explanation for the popularity of the narrative game format is that it could be considered as a form of problem solving. It reconciled two seemingly adverse domains in a more coherent framework. Designing an educational game is a complex task. The programming of animations and concurrent actions—as they are found in many commercial video games—is difficult to accomplish in Logo, especially with the game designers' beginning programming skills. In the games, the narrative provides the glue or sugar coating that connects the different scenes or places *and* the instructional content. Furthermore, it allowed students to incorporate fantasy and to decorate their worlds in a more attractive way. Fantasy was also one of the features that the children in Malone and Lepper's study (1987) identified as appealing in playing games.

DISCUSSION

Sixteen children were involved in making video games, which resulted in sixteen different products. All the games included sophisticated graphics, animations, and interactions in their programming. Although boys' and girls' games were similar in many aspects, it was obvious that students chose themes that facilitated their entry into the design task and allowed them to personalize their games. Analyses of games made by the children regarding their choices of game genre, worlds, characters, interactions, feedback and narrative revealed the following:

- The adventure genre was the most popular game format, more so for boys than for girls. Some boys and girls chose skill game formats in which the player had to navigate an obstacle course such as a ski slope or basketball court. Girls were the only ones to create a teaching context.
- Games were organized around different spaces. Most of the girls chose familiar places such as classrooms, a fair, or a ski slope. The boys organized their games more around fantasy spaces such as imaginary islands and countries.

- Many students designed and developed fantasy game characters. Most boys preferred to assign the player a fantasy character persona, whereas most girls addressed the player with a generic and more personal "you."
- The players controlled the game in different ways. In some games, the players manipulated the game actors by pressing keys, whereas in other games the player was guided through the game by well-defined intervention opportunities. Girls preferred the manipulation mode in the design of their games.
- The feedback provided to the player was of a different nature for boys than for girls. In the games programmed by girls, this feedback was of a non-violent nature and allowed most players to continue the game. Violent feedback such as killing the player and terminating the game in case of a wrong answer was chosen mostly by boys.
- Narrative emerged as an increasingly popular element in both girls' and boys' games.

There is a clear trend in these results: The video games made by girls differ in several features from those made by boys. The most striking and significant differences could be observed in the character development and the design of the feedback, but even within the construction of their game worlds, places, and interaction modes, boys and girls choose different pathways. The prevalence of these gender differences begs for an explanation.

A simple answer would refer to the girls' lack of game-playing exposure and experience. It is well documented that the majority of video game players are boys (Provenzo, 1991). In the interviews of the game designers I found that the extent of the video game-playing experience varied considerably. Most boys actively and consistently played video games over the week, whereas only two girls said that they did so. One could argue then that the observed gender differences would disappear by simply providing more opportunities for girls to play video games.

This lack of game-playing experience also might be influenced by girls' less successful video game play. There is an abundance of research that documents gender differences in spatial skills that are crucial to successful video game play (e.g., Loftus & Loftus, 1983). This could lead to the argument that girls are not interested in playing video games because they are not successful, due to their lack of spatial skills. New research points out that these observed gender differences disappear after extended video game playing (Subrahmanyam & Greenfield, 1994). It seems, therefore, that girls could overcome their shortcomings in spatial skills if they only would play video games more often.

There is some appeal to these explanations, yet they all assume that the currently available commercial video games are models to emulate for all children, girls as well as boys. Popular media have a strong foothold in children's lives because they allow for the integration of the "affective, cognitive, and social" as Kinder (1991, p. 20) argued. The narrative of these different media formulates and highlights the children's understanding of their own position and place in the social context, and provides examples from which children can draw. Commercial video games make strong use of narrative. Many video games take the eternal conflict between evil and good from adventure and fairy tales. The main game figure usually is a male hero whose function it is to save the princess or to obtain a treasure. One could argue that the game designers transferred these narratives into their games because of the impact and presence of popular models.

The influence of commercially available games was especially strong in the case of boys' games. Many game designers started out with ideas taken from popular video games such as "Super Mario Brothers" or "PacMan." Many of the boys' game implementations included violent aspects as documented in the design of their feedback to player interactions. Violence is one of the most prominent features in commercial video games (Provenzo, 1991). Hence, popular media offered models on how to organize the game design (at least for the boys). This might offer an explanation of why more boys in the end chose the narrative form compared to the girls, even though in the beginning an equal number of boys and girls started using narrative.

Popular media, however, do not provide models for girls to emulate similar to those they project for boys. Female game figures rarely are cast in the main role. The thematic embedding of video games in hunts and adventures are not necessarily to girls' tastes. In the interviews, many girls also stated that they had no particular interest in pursuing video game-playing because they did not like the games, their content and their violent aspects. Because of this lack of popular models, girls chose as the starting point of their narrative a familiar and likeable figure (i.e., Rosy's cat) or a familiar place (i.e., Sina's classroom or Miriam's ski slope). In many ways, girls created their own worlds and characters while making their games, compensating for the sexism and violence found in many video games (Gailey, 1992).

Furthermore, in the design of their games girls renounced the use of violent feedback. Another feature, game player control, was more often included in girls' rather than in boys' games. Providing the player with control to manipulate the principal game actor allows the player also to control the pace of the game. A recent study conducted in a museum setting seems to confirm this interpretation (Inkpen Booth, & Klawe, 1993). Girls are most interested in playing those electronic games that do not favor quick-paced interactions.

These results allow some conjectures about why girls lack involvement in video game-play. It simply seems that most commercially available video games do not appeal to girls. In spite of gender differences, game design offered both girls and boys a framework in which to situate their preferred ideas and fantasies. In their choices of game themes and their programming of animations and interactions, the students offered a glimpse into what they found appealing and unappealing in the games and stories they experience through other media. Making a game and its rules allowed the game designers to be in charge and to determine the player's place and role in the world with all the consequences.

CONCLUSIONS

One of the conclusions to be drawn from these results is that most commercially available video games do not reflect the interests and tastes of half the game-playing population, namely girls. Many girls are not attracted to the "kill features" that dominate most video game interactions. Instead, they prefer less violent features to guide the game-play process as well as different kinds of game characters and worlds. One solution is for manufacturers to create video games that address these issues. Furthermore, one could suggest employing female game designers, because, in the past, this profession has been dominated by men.

A different solution is found in the activity of game making and suggests further constructive activities. The energy and motivation that the children dedicated to the task of game-making led me to believe that this is a promising avenue to pursue. In the following sections I briefly outline three different routes that children's game-making and game-playing can take into the future: tool kits for game construction, physical game construction with computational elements, and collaborative game construction. All of these approaches emphasize game-making and games to play.

Tool Kits for Video Game Construction

There have been some early attempts in the aforementioned direction, such as the Pinball Construction Set (Greenfield, 1984), which provides users with a blank board and all the necessary tools and parts to install flippers, backgrounds, and controllers for their own pinball game. The user can design innumerable versions of pinball games. Eventually, the user can play her or his own game alone or with others.[3] The present study suggests developing an environment that provides children with a video-game-design tool kit. With this, children could create their own characters, design their own environments or worlds, and determine the rules of their game. Children could be provided with primitives in terms of rules and actions, and could then adapt the parameters according to the game's needs and their desires. A first example of such a game construction tool kit is Live-World (Travers, 1994), in which the player can create so-called animate systems. The sharing of ideas and strategies that is already an essential part of the existing

---

[3]One of the drawbacks of designing pinball games is that certain feelings and sensations from the mechanical world (such as the tilting of the machine) cannot be replicated in the computational environment. A further limitation is that the designer must work with a given set of parts.

video game culture could continue in such an environment where children could invite each other to play their designed games (Gailey, 1992).

Physical Game Construction With Computational Elements

A different version of game making would move game design from the two-dimensional space of the computer screen back into the three-dimensional space of the real world while retaining the valuable connection to the computational domain. A first step in this direction is a construction kit that includes LEGO bricks as well as sensors and motors that can be connected via wires and controlled through programs written in Logo (Resnick, & Ocko, 1991). In this process, children would not only build mechanical objects, such as cars or robots, but also environments such as houses, gardens, or mazes. Children would then program the interactions between the environment and the mechanical objects. An extension of LEGO-Logo, called the programmable brick (see also Resnick & Sargent, 1994), allows one to control motors and sensors without being tethered to a personal computer and to construct objects that can interact independently with the world. One could then imagine a game world consisting of dozens of these bricks, each carrying their own programs and interacting with each other.

Collaborative Game Construction

Network developments can add collaborative dimensions to game playing and game making. Multiuser environments, also called MUDs (i.e., multiuser dungeons), and collaborative simulations take advantage of these features. MUDs are text-based virtual reality environments on the Internet that can be accessed by users from all over the world (Curtis, 1992). MUDs are organized around metaphors of physical spaces such as space stations, buildings, and so on. When users log into a MUD, they usually assume characters of their own choice and then explore the space by typing in commands and programming objects that can be used and manipulated by other users. One example of such a MUD is MOOSE (i.e., Multi Object Oriented Scripting Environment), a multiuser environment being developed for children (Bruckman & Resnick, 1994). In this environment, children can create their own worlds with different places, objects, features, and activities. The children use a specially developed language to describe and define their creations.

Whereas MUDs and MOOSE allow game-making in a text-based world, CitySpace (Conn, 1994) is an example for game-making with graphical features. Here children can build a virtual city with images, text, sounds, and models sent across the Internet using commercially available graphics software and real-time video conferencing for communication. In contrast to MUDs, objects built in CitySpace do not have behaviors. The goal of this environment is to have children construct collaboratively a living habitat and negotiate together its constraints and features. With reference to that goal, CitySpace picks up on existing simulation games, such as SimCity and SimEarth, that allow players to design and govern cities and ecological habitats according to their own choices.

Children making games provided us with a window into their minds. By placing children in the roles of producers rather than consumers of video games, we allowed them to express their ideas and fantasies. It was more than obvious that gender differences permeated all aspects of game designing. One conclusion is that today's commercial video games do not address girls' interests and concerns, if one takes the games girls construct as an expression of what they wish to see and play. Another important conclusion of this study is that making video games, as opposed to playing them, clearly engaged girls' and boys' minds and fantasies for a long period of time. When the tables are turned, video games become a medium for children's personal and creative expression.

ACKNOWLEDGMENTS

A similar version of this chapter was presented at the meeting of the Association for the Study of Play in Atlanta, April 1994. Many thanks to Patricia Greenfield, Mitchel Resnick, Uri Wilensky, and Greg Kimberly for their reviews. The results are based on my thesis research. I wish to thank my thesis committee members, David Perkins, Seymour Papert, Idit Harel and Terry Tivnan, for their help and insightful comments. I also thank Joanne Ronkin and her students for their collaboration and great contribution to this work. Without them, this research would not have been possible. The research reported here was conducted at Project Headlight's Model School of the Future and was supported by the IBM Corporation (Grant OSP95952), the National Science Foundation (Grant 851031–0195), the McArthur Foundation (Grant 874304), the LEGO Group, Fukatake, and the Apple Computer, Inc. The preparation of this chapter was supported by the National Science Foundation (Grant 8751190-MDR) and Nintendo Inc. The ideas expressed here do not necessarily reflect the positions of the supporting agencies. This chapter is a reprint (with slight modifications) from P. Greenfield and R. Cocking (Eds.), *Effects of Interactive Entertainment* (1996), with permission from Ablex Publishing Corporation.

REFERENCES

Baugham, S. S., & Clagett, P. D. (1983) (Eds.). *Video games & human development. Research agenda for the '80s.* Cambridge, MA: Harvard Graduate School of Education.

Bruckman, A., & Resnick, M. (1994). Virtual professional community. In Y. Kafai & M. Resnick, (Eds.), Constructionism in practice (pp. 133–146). Cambridge, MA: MIT Media Laboratory.

Conn, C. (1994). Coco's channel. *Wired, 2*(4), 58–60.

Curtis, P. (1992). *Mudding: Social phenomena in text-based virtual realities.* Proceedings of DIAC 1992.

Dominick, J. R. (1984). Videogames, television violence, and aggression in teenagers. *Journal of Communication, 34,* 136–147.

Gailey, C. (1992). Mediated messages: Gender, class, and cosmos in home video games. *Journal of Popular Culture, 15*(2), 5–25.

Greenfield, P. M. (1993). Respresentational competence in shared symbol systems: Electronic media from radio to video games. In R. R. Cocking & A. Renninger (Eds.), *The development and meaning of psychological distance* (pp. 161–183). Hillsdale, NJ: Lawrence Erlbaum Associates.

Greenfield, P. M. (1984). *Mind and media. The effects of television, video games, and computers.* Cambridge, MA: Harvard University Press.

Greenfield, P. M., Brannon, G., & Lohr, D. (1994). Two-dimensional representation of movement through three-dimensional space: The role of video game expertise. *Journal of Applied Developmental Psychology, 15*(1), 87–104.

Greenfield, P. M., Camaioni, L., Ercolani, P., Weiss, L., Lauber, B. A., & Perucchini, P. (1994). Cognitive socialization by computer games in two cultures: Inductive discovery or mastery of an iconic code? *Journal of Applied Developmental Psychology, 15*(1), 59–86.

Greenfield, P. M., & Cocking, R. R. (1994) (Eds.). Effects of interactive entertainment technology on development. *Journal of Applied Developmental Psychology, 15*(1), 1–2.

Greenfield, P. M., deWinstanley, P., Kilpatrick, H., & Kaye, D. (1994). Action video games and informal education: Effects on strategies for dividing visual attention. *Journal of Applied Developmental Psychology, 15*(1), 105–124.

Harel, I. (1991). *Children designers.* Norwood, NJ: Ablex.

Harris, M. B., & Williams, R. (1984). Video games and school performance. *Education, 105*(3), 306–309.

Inkpen, K. Booth, K., & Klawe, M. (1993). *Cooperative learning in the classroom: The importance of a collaborative environment for computer-based education* (Tech. Rep.). Vancouver, BC: University of British Columbia, Department of Computer Science.

Inkpen, K., Upitis, R., Klawe, M., Anderson, A, Ndunda, M., Sedighian, K., Leroux, S., & Hsu, D. (1993, December). *"We have never-forgetful flowers in our garden": Girl's responses to electronic games* (Tech. Rep. No. 93–47). Vancouver, BC: University of British Columbia, Dept. of Computer Science.

Kafai, Y. (1993). *Minds in play. Computer game design as a context for children's learning.* Unpublished doctoral dissertation, Harvard University Graduate School of Education, Cambridge, MA.

Kafai, Y. (1995). *Minds in play: Computer game design as a context for children's learning.* Hillsdale, NJ: Lawrence Erlbaum Associates.

Kinder, M. (1991). *Playing with power.* Berkeley: University of California Press.

Lawry, J., Upitis, R., Klawe, M., Anderson, A., Inkpen, K., Ndunda, M., Hsu, D., Leroux, S., & Sedighian, K. (1994, January). *Exploring common conceptions about boys and electronic games* (Tech. Rep. No. 94–1). Vancouver, BC: University of British Columbia, Department of Computer Science.

Lepper, M. R., & Malone, T. W. (1987). Intrinsic motivation and instructional effectiveness in computer-based education. In R. E. Snow & M. J. Farr (Eds.), *Aptitude, learning and instruction. Volume 3: Conative and affective process analyses* (pp. 255–285). Hillsdale, NJ: Lawrence Erlbaum Associates.

Loftus, G. R., & Loftus, E. F. (1983). *Minds at play.* New York: Basic Books.

Malone, T. W. (1981). What makes computer games fun? *BYTE, 6*(12), 258–277.

Malone, T. W., & Lepper, M. R. (1987). Making learning fun: A taxonomy of intrinsic motivations for learning. In R. E. Snow & M. J. Farr (Eds.), *Aptitude, learning and instruction. Volume 3: Conative and affective process analyses* (pp. 223–253). Hillsdale, NJ: Lawrence Erlbaum Associates.

Morlock, H., Yando, T., & Nigolean, K. (1985). Motivation of video game players. *Psychological Reports, 57,* 247–250.

Okagaki, L., & French, P. (1994). Effects of video game playing on measures of spatial performance: Gender effects in late adolescence. *Journal of Applied Developmental Psychology, 15*(1), 33–58.

Papert, S. (1980). *Mindstorms.* New York: Basic Books.

Papert, S. (1991). *New images of programming: In search of an educational powerful concept of technological fluency* (National Science Foundation Proposal). Cambridge, MA: MIT Media Laboratory.

Provenzo, E. F. (1991). *Video kids: Making sense of Nintendo.* Cambridge, MA: Harvard University Press.

Resnick, M., & Ocko, S. (1991). LEGO/Logo: Learning through and about design. In I. Harel & S. Papert (Eds.), *Constructionism* (pp. 141–150). Norwood, NJ: Ablex.

Resnick, M., & Sargent, R. (1994). Programmable bricks: Ubiquitous computing for kids. In Y. Kafai & M. Resnick, (Eds.), *Constructionism in practice* (pp. 101–108). Cambridge, MA: MIT Media Laboratory.

Rushbrook, S. (1986). *Messages of video games: Socialization implications.* Unpublished doctoral thesis, University of California, Los Angeles.

Selnow, G. W. (1984). Playing videogames: The electronic friend. *Journal of Communication, 34,* 148–156.

Silvern, S. B., & Williamson, P. A. (1987). The effects of videogame play on young children's aggression, fantasy and prosocial behavior. *Journal of Applied Developmental Psychology, 8,* 453–462.

Subrahmanyam, K., & Greenfield, P. M. (1994). Effects of video game practice on spatial skills in girls and boys. *Journal of Applied Developmental Psychology, 15*(1), 13–32.

Travers, M. (1994, April). LiveWorld. In *Proceedings of the Computer Human Interaction Conference* (pp. 341–350). Boston, MA: Addison-Wesley.

Turkle, S. (1984). *The second self: Computers and the human spirit.* New York: Simon & Schuster.

Wilensky, U. (1991). Abstract mediations on the concrete and concrete implications for mathematics education. In I. Harel & S. Papert (Eds.), *Constructionism* (pp. 193–204). Norwood, NJ: Ablex.

6
The Art of Design

Gregory Gargarian

FOREWORD BY EDITH ACKERMANN

Greg Gargarian has left us prematurely, only a few months after completing his PhD thesis. He has been robbed of the opportunity to collect the fruits of his own hard and promising work. In this chapter, we wish to bring to the reader a few excerpts of Greg's contribution to the fields of design, music, learning, and teaching.

Greg's intellectual trajectory within the Epistemology and Learning Group was unique. He was, all at once, a composer and a learning theorist, a tool builder, and a teacher. His careful analysis of the processes involved in music composition and interpretation, his case studies of expert composers and listeners, and his work with young children at Paige Academy in Boston allowed him to design some ingenious microworlds for exploring musical events. Greg offered children a construction kit for creating musical sequences, for playing around with musical objects, and for operating musical transformations for building variations around a theme. Children could design soundtracks to their own animations. They could put characters in motion and make them dance. They could record their own sounds and arrange them into a rhythmic or melodic sequence. As Greg's advisor, it was a joy for me to follow his work in progress, to share ideas with him, and to participate in the discussions with professional composers during our summer seminar at the NIED, Campinas, Brazil. Greg was a generous mind, a talented artist, and a sharp thinker. He was a generalist able to articulate his wide interests around a principled repertoire of concepts and tools for learning about music through design.

Although Greg himself has been taken away, his wife Jacqueline, his many close friends, and his colleagues from all over the world are currently joining forces to keep his contribution alive. The creation of the "Ateliers Gargarian" by Jacqueline Karaaslanian, with the help of Seymour Papert, Jose Valente, Chris Cleary, Howard Austin, and many others, is a step toward a truly pluridisciplinary and international learning center. The purpose of the learning center is to bring together thinkers and practitioners, decision makers and grass-root workers, artists and scientists, children and grown-ups from both "developing" and "developed" countries. Participants will meet regularly outside their institutions to collaborate on joint projects, to organize workshops, and to share experiences about learning in a convivial setting. The "Ateliers Gargarian" are our own way to give back to Greg and to the world some of the dreams he did not have the time to realize. His premature departure, as a friend and as a colleague, remains an intolerable loss.

The following sections are excerpts of Greg Gargarian's doctoral dissertation, which carries the same title as this book chapter. We include chapter 5, *Perspectives on Designing*, chapter 10, *The Textile Designer*, and the Afterword, *Creating a Commonwealth of Skills*. These chapters have been included just as they appeared in Greg's thesis, except for some minor editorial changes.

PERSPECTIVES ON DESIGNING

> I want to write about poetry not as a pedant, but as a practitioner. My article has no scholarly significance. I write about my work, which, by the light of my observations and convictions, I see as differing very little from the work of other professional poets.
>
> . . . I want to insist that I offer no rules to make anyone a poet, by following which he can write poetry. Such rules simply don't exist. A poet is a person who creates these very rules. (Vladimir Mayakovsky, 1974, *How Are Verses Made?*)

The preceding quote is from *How Are Verses Made?*, a beautiful little book published in 1926 by the Georgian poet Vladimir Mayakovsky.[1] Mayakovsky's motivation for writing *How Are Verses Made?* was to bridge the gap he observed between theory and practice. "Almost all editors complain to me that they don't know how to turn away a poetry manuscript, they don't know what to say about it" (Mayakovsky, 1974, p. 14).

Experts are often unaware of the skills they have learned; they simply use them. Consider the following rather recursive example from Cheney's book, *Getting the Words Right* (1983). In it he uses a sample of his own writing to demonstrate the "creative process":

---

[1]Mayakovsky was born in 1883. He was active in revolutionary politics, working on propaganda poems. He was also a leader of the Russian Futurist group.

Just as we are subconsciously satisfied by rhythm in what we read, we are additionally satisfied by sound.

Cheney says that the following progression of edits led to the previous sentence:

```
the following
   "rhythm satisfies our subconscious"
became
   "subconsciously satisfied by rhythm in what we read"
the following
   "we are moved by sound"
became
   "we are satisfied by sound"
became
   "we are also satisfied by sound"
became
   "we are additionally satisfied by sound"
```

Cheney says that he was unaware of the reasons for this progression of edits until he began to write about editing. Only then was he able to see that there is alliteration in the repetition of the initial consonant *s's*; assonance in the final vowel sounds *satisfied* and *by*; delayed alliteration in the *r* sounds of *rhythm* and *read*; alliteration in the string "what we read, we"; additional assonance in the long *e* in "we read, we"; "additionally" was added to "satisfied" to echo "subconsciously satisfied"; and the repetition of "we are" added coherence and rhythm (Cheney, 1983, pp. 166–167).

The question central to this chapter is: How can a designer know whether he is making progress? There are two kinds of answers, each reflecting a different perspective on designing.

- One kind of answer has to do with how the designer keeps design process complexity from getting out of hand. By *controlling process complexity*, the designer keeps the emerging artifact from requiring skills he does not have or cannot construct "on the fly."
- Another kind of answer has to do with how the designer evaluates the expressive utility of the artifact he is making.[2] By *promoting user utility* (or interpretability), the designer keeps the emerging artifact from becoming unusable.

---

[2]Most things are not like puzzles, discarded after the problems associated with them have been solved. Most designing involves the production of an artifact (a piece of music, a poem, a building, a computer chip, etc.) that is used by others. For example, a piece of music or poem is used by an interpreter to have an experience, people live and work in buildings, and programmers use computer chips as roads to traffic bits of information.

There is also the distinction between using a perspective and constructing it, a distinction that is important if one is concerned with the acquisition (as well as the use) of design skill.

- Sometimes the designer is engaged in *environment design*, constructing skills and organizing those he thinks he will need.
- Sometimes the designer is engaged in *artifact design*, using the skills he has already constructed.

What seems to distinguish the best designers from the rest of us is their ability to take charge of the skill construction and skill management processes. I argue that the perspectives on designing support these processes.

Controlling Design Complexity: Designing as Redesigning

Designing is in large part redesigning (editing, debugging, or refining). It is concerned with problems Anne von der Lieth Gardner (1987) describes as *open-textured*. In her study of legal reasoning, Gardner argues that lawyers are not governed but *guided* by rules. This is especially true in hard legal cases where a large part of the task is to determine the true state of the world (Gardner, 1987, p. 61).[3] The selection of facts is critical because it determines which legal *precedents*[4] might be applicable (Gardner, 1987, p. 56). Consider the following case:

> Let us suppose that in leafing through the statutes, we come upon the following enactment:
>
> IT SHALL BE A MISDEMEANOR, PUNISHABLE BY A FINE OF FIVE DOLLARS, TO SLEEP IN ANY RAILWAY STATION.
>
> Suppose I am a judge, and that two men are brought before me for violating this statute. The first is a passenger who was waiting at 3 A.M. for a delayed train. When he was arrested he was sitting upright in an orderly fashion, but was heard by the arresting officer to be gently snoring. The second is a man who had brought a blanket and pillow to the station and had obviously settled himself down for the night. He was arrested, however, before he had a chance to go to sleep.

In this case, what does *sleep* mean? It might mean "to spread oneself on a bench or floor, or as if to spend the night." Similarly, *person* might mean "someone who is not a passenger." These interpretations of *sleep* and *person* make certain facts relevant and others irrelevant, and will result in the passenger

---

[3]Presumably, lawyers would rule in the same way in clear cases.
[4]As an aside, for me, legal precedents play the same interpretive role in law as musical conventions do in music.

being innocent and the vagabond guilty. However, a different interpretation of *sleep* as "the physical state of sleep," and *person* as "any person," will result in the passenger being guilty and the vagabond innocent (Gardner, 1987, pp. 39–40).

Designing is open-textured because the way one interprets a problem (legal, musical, or otherwise) has implications for what facts are relevant or irrelevant, what previous experiences one uses to evaluate it, what new facts these previous experiences uncover, and so on. What is relevant about legal cases are those elements that have multiple legal indices. Hard legal cases are those that are so ambiguous, so richly indexed, that they allow lawyers the opportunity to evoke different kinds of precedents in the "design" of different, often opposing, arguments.

The highly successful money manager, George Soros, "plays the market," aware that markets are inherently reflexive. *Reflexivity* is present whenever interpretations of human action can change the course of subsequent action and interpretation. A market player can make money if he spots a reflexive cycle in which the perceived and real market values are different. Soros puts it this way in his book, *The Alchemy of Finance* (1987):

> The participants' perceptions [of the stock market] are inherently flawed, and there is a two-way connection between flawed perceptions and the actual course of events, which results in a lack of correspondence between the two. I call this two-way connection reflexivity (p. 14).

For example, stock prices are determined by both underlying trends and prevailing biases, and because both of them are influenced by stock prices, decisions are highly interactive. Reflexivity explains why there are disparities between the perceived and real values of a stock. It is for this reason that Soros is interested in *emergent* effects:

> I did not play the financial markets according to a particular set of rules; I was always more interested in understanding the changes that occur in the rules of the game (1987, p. 15).

Gardner's lawyers design legal arguments in a similar way. Lawyers apply a variety of precedents in an attempt to explore different patterns of facts which, in turn, provide new precedents and, reflexively, uncover new facts and precedents. Lawyers are often trained in legal reasoning by being given *issue spotters*, narratives so constructed that the facts embodied in them straddle the boundaries of several legal categories (Gardner, 1987, p. 7). By reinterpreting a case in several ways, lawyers gain skill in constructing durable legal arguments.

As a final example, the sociologist of music, Simon Frith (1987), describes how popular taste develops. His notion of beauty operates in ways similar to Soros' notion of value or Gardner's notion of truth. Frith argues that "popular music is popular . . . because it creates our understanding of what popularity means." Again, "What we should be examining is not how true a piece of music is to something else, but how it sets up the idea of 'truth' in the first place" (Frith, 1987, p. 137). Frith is not avoiding the issue with a tautology; rather, he is describing a dynamic process in which future judgments are progressively adjusted to accommodate the effects of past judgments.

These examples illustrate the reflexive nature of designing. A designer expects unanticipated problems and learns how to construct and use recovery strategies. This is why designing is always redesigning.

Creative Solutions: Strategies for Acquiring Strategies

In designing there is no way to plan a path toward a solution if what constitutes a solution is, itself, under debate. The solution to designing is *emergent* rather than planned because the designer is learning what a "problem" is about during the design process. Moreover, he is developing new skills for improving his design process as the following short study illustrates.

While in Brazil in the summer of 1990 I asked a young popular folk singer, who I will call Jose, whether I could observe him compose a folk song on his guitar. He agreed. Jose tried some things out on his guitar while I observed and asked questions. After about an hour and a half of this, I told him what I thought he was doing and corrected my description based on his response until he and I were both satisfied. The following is a schematic description of Jose's "compositional method" based upon this session. It serves as an illustration of creative solutions in music composition.

Jose said that he usually started with a poem that he liked (step 1). He then would try out a simple repeating rhythm on his guitar to accompany these words. This ostinato rhythm was for the guitar chords yet to be chosen (step 2). Next, Jose would try out different sequences of chords that could be used as the underlying harmony to mark each phrase of the poem and music. The combination of ostinato and chord patterns defined the duration of the phrase. He would either "borrow" chords from other Brazilian folk musicians—he favored the Brazilian folk musician Caetano Veloso—or use chord patterns that worked in his own previous songs (step 3).

```
Jose's songwriting steps:
1. Select text.
2. Decide on ostinato beat for chords.
3. Find pattern of chords.
4. Suppress chord rhythm; play with generic melody (i.e.,
   notes that fall within the notes of the current chord).
5. Use "syncopation" to fit text syllables to notes in the
   generic melody.
6. Put everything together.
```

After finding a pattern of chords, Jose would suppress the chord rhythms he had decided on earlier (i.e., the ostinato pattern) and concentrate on finding melody notes that fit each of the chords in the pattern (step 4).[5] These melody notes would not be the final melody but a *generic* melody having the minimum requirement that the notes fall within the current chordal context. With this generic melody Jose would explore possible rhythms for the text (step 5). Finally, Jose would reintroduce the ostinato pattern to complete the song (step 6).

Jose said that he especially liked the melody to be "syncopated." Sometimes what he meant was the conventional notion of syncopation: accented weak beats, deemphasized strong beats, or rests on strong beats. At other times what he meant by "syncopation" was a more elastic notion of time in which notes rushed ahead or lagged behind the clock-like meter underlying a phrase. The amount of rushing and lagging was substantially influenced by the number of syllables in the Portuguese text. Jose had to allocate text syllables to phrase elements. When a line of text was sparse he had to stretch syllables over the duration of the phrase; conversely, when a line of text was dense he had to shrink syllables into the duration of the phrase.

Only after the ostinato pattern and chord sequence had been decided did Jose specify the phrase lengths. Of course, it was still possible to revise the chord sequence but, at each revision, what resulted was something equally constraining.

According to Jose, the tricky part of the songwriter's craft was fitting text syllables to melodic elements (step 5). After some probing, Jose mentioned some isorhythmic exercises he was given by his composition teacher to deal with this problem. An *isorhythm* can be defined in the following procedural way: Given some collection of notes and some collection of rhythms, each with different numbers of elements, it is possible to construct a pattern of note-rhythms (i.e., a melody) using them in an ordered way. Fig. 6.1 illustrates isorhythm by using three notes and two rhythms to produce a six-note melody (2×3).

In fact, the assignment included an additional step. Each time the constructed pattern had been completed (i.e., when all orderings of both notes and rhythms had been made), Jose was asked to introduce either an additional note or rhythm. In this way, the component patterns and the resulting isorhythm would continuously expand. A side effect of these expansions would be the production of different metric frameworks.[6]

When I asked Jose how this activity became useful for text-fitting problems, he said that because all the patterns except the melody are rigid, the isorhythms helped him to "unlearn" his notion of meter. What he meant was that he learned

---

[5]To simplify a bit, a chord implies a musical scale of seven notes. To say that a melodic note "fits" a chord means that it is one of the scale notes implied by the chord.

[6]A similar method is used by the composer, Steve Reich, and described by him as the *process of gradual change.*

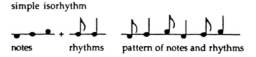

FIG. 6.1. Isorythm using three notes and two rhythms to produce a six-note melody.

to re-represent the music's meter in different ways. This gave him the mental elasticity he needed to explore different text-fitting solutions. He had acquired a new skill, a technique (e.g., metric re-representation), plus the kinds of cases in which it could be productively used (e.g., text-fitting).

Of course, the exercise Jose's teacher gave him, Jose might have constructed for himself. Composers do this all the time,[7] all the more reason to view environment design as an important aspect of artifact design.

Two Metaskills

Freedom in Restrictions.   Designing requires restricting design. Without restrictions, a designer would be unable to choose from the possible actions he could take; he would be paralyzed. Moreover, an action has little value if there is no way to evaluate the effect of the action. What I call *freedom in restrictions* is the counter-intuitive notion that restrictions provide the designer freedom rather than enslavement. Within a restricted collection of choices, a designer can explore possible choices using trial and error or algorithmic methods.

For example, Gross's Constraint Explorer (1978) was developed under the assumption that an architectural designer works with rules (e.g., beams should be no less than 12 times their depth), conventions (e.g., architectural style), laws (e.g., gravity), and principles (e.g., a room should have windows). The *design context* is the set of rules, conventions, laws, and principles that restrict current designing as well as relations among design parts and other requirements like materials and codes (Gross).[8]

Confidence Building.   Reflexivity explains why designing—in search of truth, value, or beauty—is a process in which provisional solutions serve as a means of further discovery. Still, designing imposes restrictions that become intractable. For this reason, designers are continually evaluating the restrictions they impose on their process. *Confidence building* is about how restrictions earn their credentials through use.

The psychologist, John Sloboda (1985), has observed that composers tighten

---

[7]Beethoven's sketch books are full of self-imposed "assignments." In his study of Beethoven's sketches for the *Diabelli Variations*, Kinderman remarks that "Most of the sketches, if they do not obviously relate to one of the finished variations, are related clearly enough to the development of ideas used in one, or, most often, several of the finished variations" (1987, p. 29).

[8]For Gross, designing does not happen without design rules; only "free expression" can happen in the absence of rules. I will argue that free expression is never "free" because of the need for methods to manage the complexity of decision making and because of external constraints like conventions, laws of perception, or user utility.

or loosen compositional constraints depending on the difficulties they encounter in their design problems (Sloboda, 1985, pp. 123–138). Sloboda's constraints are my restrictions. However, Sloboda keeps implicit the ranking of constraints/restrictions based on their productivity, my confidence building.

Once constraints are ranked, they offer different *degrees of freedom*. I think of the degrees of freedom found in the joints of the body. There are several ways one can reach for a glass: for example, by extending the arm using the elbow and shoulder joints, by walking forward while lifting the arm from the elbow, by leaning forward from the waist, by twisting from the waist, or by some combination of these movements. The movements chosen depend on physical restrictions created by the context. Whether one is sitting at a dinner table or standing among people crowded around a buffet table will determine the combination of movements one is free to use. In designing, there is also a context made up of a number of constraints. They are ranked according to their productivity, and this ranking restricts design choices.

Alexander's idea of design *fitness* is a similar idea (1964). Design fitness is the harmony created between an ensemble and any of its parts. He offers the simple case of a suit and tie. A suit is the ensemble in which a tie is a part. A different suit requires a different tie. If the suit and tie do not match, it is the tie, not the suit, that must be replaced. This is because the design investment is greater in the suit; it is ranked higher, less intractable, than the tie.

In complex ensembles there are many ways the ensemble can be broken into parts, and different ways to rank the parts. The designer may have nothing at the outset on which to substantiate a particular strategy for producing harmony. Fitness may be achieved indirectly, through a process of removing factors that lead to misfit (Alexander, 1964, pp. 15–27).

The designer needs strategies for identifying factors that restrict the degrees of design freedom. Sometimes the factor defining misfit is identified through a process of perspective taking. Through this process, a certain factor may emerge as particularly important because it is important from all perspectives. At other times the factor defining misfit may come with the design problem. Using the suit-tie example, one can imagine that the ensemble's most important element is a particular tie (perhaps, a gift which one wishes to wear on a special occasion to please a loved one). The tie must fit, and anything that does not match with it is a misfit.

In either case, growing confidence makes some restrictions rigid and certain solutions decreasingly provisional. Proof that artifacts become increasingly permanent is that they eventually get made.

User Utility (or Interpretability) Making Artifacts "User-Friendly"

The designer knows that he has privileged access to the thinking that gave rise to his designed artifact and takes this into account by considering its interpretive utility. This can be seen most clearly in artifacts that have day-to-day utility. Our success or failure to interact with doors, keys, VCR displays, washing machines, telephones, or watches depends upon how well the designers of these objects understand the way we interact with them. Everyday things are tools that we want to use, not contemplate. We do not want to think about doors, we want to go through them; we don't want to contemplate watches, we want to know the time.

According to the cognitive psychologist, Donald Norman (1988), our understanding of everyday objects requires either shallow or narrowly structured knowledge. Norman gives an ice cream menu as an example of *shallow knowledge*. "Difficulties arise from competing alternatives, not from any prolonged search, problem solving, or trial and error. In shallow structures, there's no problem of planning or depth of analysis" (Norman, 1988, p. 121). *Narrowly structured knowledge* does not require extensive planning either. Such knowledge is comprised of "a long series of steps, but at each point, there are few, if any, alternatives to consider" (Norman, 1988, p. 123). Norman gives a cookbook recipe as an example of narrowly structured knowledge. Shallow structures, like ice cream menus, are wide but not deep, whereas narrow structures, like recipes, are deep but not wide.

Because music is both deep and wide, it may not be subject to any of the design criteria mentioned by Norman (1988):

> In general, we find wide and deep structures in games and leisure activities, where the structure is devised so as to occupy the mind or to make the task deliberately difficult (p. 124).

Unlike Norman, I argue that many everyday objects (like software environments) are capable of supporting fairly complex activities. We judge the utility of these objects based on whether shallow or narrow initial access provides the means for deeper or wider subsequent access. In other words, the full utility of the artifact is something that is gradually discovered: Using it becomes a means of learning how to use it. One might say that a successful piece of software (or by analogy, a piece of music) is "user-friendly" when it is designed so that subsequent encounters (or rehearsals) build on previous encounters.

I have already argued that art objects have unanticipated interpretive utility. So also do software environments to some extent. To this extent, Norman's evaluative stance can serve as a bridge between these different kinds of designing.

Natural Mappings and Feedback

Norman (1988) argued that the primary source of problems with designed things is that there is a gap between the designer and the user of designed objects:

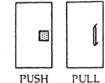

FIG. 6.2. Door designs illustrating the use of natural map-
pings.   PUSH   PULL

For a surprisingly large number of everyday tasks, the difficulty resides entirely
in deriving the relationships between the mental intentions and interpretations and
the physical actions and states (p. 50).

Norman attributes these difficulties to (a) unnatural mappings between mental
and physical states and (b) inadequate feedback of the effects of user actions.
Natural mappings take "advantage of physical analogies and cultural standards"
(Norman, 1988, p. 23). For example, it is clear from the design of some doors
what the user should do to open them. Fig. 6.2 shows that a small rectangular
plate invites the user to PUSH, whereas a narrow protruding bar invites the user
to PULL.

Even this simple case is problematic because there is more than one way to
open a door. For more complex objects the number of ways we might interact
with them can be quite large. "The difficulty of dealing with novel situations is
directly related to the number of possibilities" (Norman, 1988, p. 81). Finding
natural mappings helps to reduce the possibilities through design rather than by
taxing the user.

Natural mappings can rely on conventions. "Red means stop," or "walk on the
right side" are two examples. The backward clock in Fig. 6.3 (Quick? What's the
time?) is another vivid example. There is nothing about the world that demands
clock time to move in clockwise fashion. Nevertheless, making clock motion
standard reduces interpretive work and, thus, makes telling the time almost
effortless. "If you can't put the knowledge in the device, then develop a cultural
constraint: standardize what has to be kept in the head" (Norman, 1988, p. 170).

Feedback sends "back to the user information about what action has actually
been done" (Norman, 1988, p. 27). The "zzz" of a zipper, the whistle of a tea
kettle, and the increase in pitch when a vacuum cleaner gets clogged are all

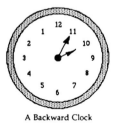

FIG. 6.3. The backward clock
goes against standard convention, taxing the viewer (from
Norman, 1988, p. 201).   A Backward Clock

examples of designed objects that provide immediate and obvious feedback (Norman, 1988, p. 102). We also get immediate feedback when doors we should have PUSHed rather than PULLed do not open.

Musical objects are like everyday objects in these respects. They, too, are more or less "user-friendly" depending on a composer's understanding of how listeners are likely to interact with them. Musical conventions, like our clockwise clock, standardize arbitrary pattern choices, and by doing so, reduce interpretive difficulty.

Interpretability

From a cognitive perspective, musical thinking is neither especially privileged nor are everyday concerns especially mundane. What is special about the musical experience is its interpretive potential. One understands how to open a door in order to open it. Musical objects, unlike everyday objects, are a source of virtual worlds in which observers live out an interpretive experience. The function of these interactions is to engage the observer in the process of interpretation itself, a process that is also crucial in everyday life. Norman ignores this valuable function of music. "Games and leisure activity" are difficult, not only because they "occupy the mind" of the observer as Norman says, but because they give us the opportunity to exercise and acquire interpretative skill. (Programming environments that are powerful give "designers" the ability to make tools for addressing unanticipated problems. Programming is also learning how to program, learning by designing.)

In music, interpretability is a necessary but not sufficient condition for "beauty." A piece of music is beautiful because it is interpretable and more (e.g., moving, involving, etc.). It is, like user-friendly itself, an elusive idea. The following ideas—of interpretive consistency and learnability—add more meat to interpretability, though even they are not sufficient for determining beauty.

Conventions and Interpretive Consistency

My notion of a musical convention is much like Norman's notion of a natural mapping. The clockwise clock is an example in everyday objects, and the traditional rules for chord progressions is an example of a convention in musical "objects."

What I call the principle of interpretive consistency is much like Norman's notion of feedback which, in turn, depends on natural mappings. Composers give interpreters the means to confirm or refute their interpretations by being consistent about the conventions they use in producing the artifact in the first place. Consistency restricts musical novelty and makes listening easier to do. A work that is difficult to interpret exercises interpretive skill. A work that is impossible to interpret discourages one from making an interpretation at all!

The Problem of Learnability

From a cognitive perspective, listening to a foreign score of music for the first time is like listening to an experimental piece for the first time. The problem in both cases is whether the unfamiliar is learnable. In general, *learnability* becomes an issue when something is too complex to grasp in one sitting. Here we move beyond Norman's prescriptions for the design of everyday objects. A listener will engage in repeated hearings of a piece of music because initial hearings are rewarding and subsequent hearings are likely to profit from them. During rehearings, the listener will take advantage of conventions of listening he or she has previously acquired in order to learn new ones.

Only when we are confronted with the unfamiliar do we begin to appreciate that our musical experience is informed by musical knowledge we have learned. When ethnomusicologists examine the music of an unfamiliar culture, one of their tasks is to identify the conventions of listening operating in that music. The same task is required of listeners of experimental music.[9]

Among musicologists, the idea that the interpretive process is a learning process is embedded in discussions about absolute music. *Absolute music* can be described as music defined in musical rather than extramusical terms (Apel, 1972, p. 2).[10] Even though the phrase absolute music is attributed to Wagner, according to the musicologist Ian Bent, the notion of absolute music was born in the 18th century, about the same time as phrase structure analysis and formal musical modeling began to develop within the western music community. These developments were important because they resulted in explicit statements about how musical elements are linked to each other through musical norms (Bent, 1987, pp. 12–16). It was no coincidence that the idea of absolute music and work in musical norms were codependent. With musical norms identified, it was no longer necessary for music to make reference to extramusical criteria. Music could now be *self-referencing*, evaluated exclusively in terms of musical norms.

In reading Carl Dahlhaus' account of the idea of absolute music (1989), one gets the impression that, at the birth of "pure" instrumental music, composers and theorists were truly puzzled by the fact that instrumental music was able to achieve its expressiveness without degenerating into noise. What could it mean for there to be a musical "idea" or "thinking with sounds"? How could one account for the affective side of music without a narrative reference?

According to Dahlhaus, there were two sorts of arguments. One argument, reflective of Rousseau's naturalism, was that music has its origins in the emotions produced by the "natural" inflections of passionate speech (i.e., music is a language). A second argument, reflective of Rameau's scientism, was that music

---

[9]Of course, the experimental composer can help the interpreter by providing him with interpretive aids. However, this assumes that the composer has some theory of interpretability.

[10]What we mean by *absolute music* is what some musicologists prefer to call *abstract music*.

had its origins in the Pythagorean proportions; (i.e., music is a mathematics). Both arguments assumed that in order for music to be absolute, it must be rooted in some universal principle (Dahlhaus, 1989, pp. 47–53).

A different idea began to emerge, the idea that one's experience of music is learned. This idea put in question the absoluteness of music. By admitting learning into the discussion, theorists had to give a higher intellectual status to the interpretive process. Dahlhaus (1989) placed the awareness of the role of interpretation in western musical experience in the romantic aesthetics of the late 18th century, which attempted to reconcile the particularity of art works with more universal criteria of beauty:

> For insofar as music does not exhaust itself in the acoustical substrate that underlies it, but only takes shape through categorical ordering of what has been perceived, a change in the system of categories of reception immediately affects the substance of the thing itself (p. 63).

The new challenge was to find a way to evaluate a "learned" music on absolute grounds. Music theorists became increasingly interested in principles of music organization, seeing in the fugue an illustration of "thinking with sounds," and in symphonic forms (e.g., concerto and sonata forms) a coherent system of harmonic control. What gradually became of evaluative interest was how the composer demonstrated near the beginning of a work the musical elements the listener should pay attention to while listening to the remainder of the work (e.g., themes, harmonic "plan," etc.).

> Language is the garment of thought, just as melody is the garment of harmony. In this respect, one may call harmony a logic of music, because it stands in approximately the same relationship to melody as logic in language stands to expression, namely, it corrects and determines melodic writing so that it seems to become a real truth to one's sensations (Johann Gottfried Herder, in Dahlhaus, 1989, p. 105).

The ideas of absolute music and interpretation continue to be debated until this day. One insightful critic of twelve-tone music, himself a twelve-tone composer and theorist, is Milton Babbitt (1987). He argues that one of the primary difficulties people have with twelve-tone music is that the music takes the ideas of absolute and interpretive music to an extreme. According to Babbitt, twelve-tone music establishes more than its "thematic" or "harmonic" premises within itself. What is normative is also a component of a music's premises. In the twelve-tone framework, listeners have to learn what is normative as they are listening—including what "theme" and "harmony" mean—and then continue to listen using these norms as interpretive instruments. (Babbitt reminds us that the interpretive process and the resulting musical experience suffers when too much has to be learned too quickly.)

Part of the composer's design problem is to make the music learnable by the listener. As I see it, the learnability of complex knowledge requires the satisfaction of at least two criteria.

1. *Learning is incremental.* Knowledge must be learnable in discrete steps; a little knowledge gets the learner to a little more knowledge, and so on.
2. *The pathways to knowledge are different for different people.* The steps in the learning progression must be rewarding in themselves. This criterion reminds us that the learner's receptivity to knowledge must be taken into account.

Criterion 1 asks the designer to deconstruct the knowledge into knowledge steps, each requiring the cognitive effort of Norman's everyday objects. Criterion 2 puts in question any pathway to knowledge that ignores the learner. In a sense, without criterion 2, any application of criterion 1 is arbitrary outside of a cultural context.

The Learnability of Music's Protean Forms

Good composers respect the criteria of learnability by providing listeners several rewarding pathways to knowledge. There is little else that composers usually do except modify previously stated material or introduce a little new material. Regardless of the stated form of a piece, most composers use either *theme-and-variations* or *theme-and-contrast* as a means for extending the musical material. These are the two protean musical forms (Reck, 1977; Rowell, 1983; Schoenberg, 1970).

In theme-and-variations, changing the harmonies associated with a melody results in *harmonic* variation; changing the details of a melody while preserving its overall contour results in *melodic* variations; and adjusting the rhythms of a melody so that it can fit in a different meter results in *rhythmic* variation. Listeners change their understanding of a piece of music through repeated hearings because repeated hearings offer the listener a chance to use previously identified elements to gain access to related and unidentified elements. In addition, listeners mentally construct different degrees of relatedness (Pollard-Gott, 1983, pp. 66–93).

Theme-and-contrast is a kind of *phantom*-form because whatever a composer needs to do in order to make the theme recognizable, he must also do to make contrasting material recognizable; namely apply variation methods to the contrasting material. For the listener, recognizing contrasting material is not unlike hearing a theme for the first time and requires the same pattern recognition strategies that were needed then.

Environment Design Versus Artifact Design

During the early phases of the design process there is no data on which to build confidence. Sometimes composers use strategies such as *composing by example,* a strategy that makes it possible for the composer to reappropriate elements from previously successful artifacts. At other times composers develop so-called precompositional methods to support compositional decision making. However, "precomposition" is also composition. For most composers, precomposition is the exploratory aspect of composition. Moreover, precomposition is ongoing and, therefore, inappropriately named.

My notion of environment design makes the distinction between composing and precomposition unnecessary. However, there is an important distinction to make, illustrated by Jose's reappropriation of isorhythmic thinking to address text-fitting problems: namely, a distinction between working on the design environment and working on the artifact.

Sometimes the designer is engaged in environment design, constructing skills and new organizations of them so that particular skills can be found. At other times, the designer is constructing the artifact itself, selecting the organizations of skills from which particular skills are then selected and applied. These two perspectives on designing need to be added to those already discussed.

Six Perspectives on Designing

In total, I have identified six broad perspectives on designing:

- In *managing design complexity* the designer constructs and ranks the restrictions he imposes on his process based on their past or anticipated productivity. Ultimately, this process leads to an emerging notion of design fitness for the design environment.
- In *promoting user utility* a designer reappropriates "user-tested" conventions or invents new ones that can be learned by the interpreter. An interpreter can learn that something is a convention because he has encountered many patterns that operate by it; he can recognize that a "law of invariance" (as Piagetians would say) applies for a number of pattern-cases. The notion of interpretive consistency says that a new convention can be learned if a composer applies it consistently. Ultimately, this process leads to an emerging notion of design fitness for the artifact.

While operating within the perspective of promoting user utility, the designer uses the interpretive perspectives presented next:

- User utility is promoted by making anticipatory listening easier to do.
- User utility is promoted by making anthropomorphic listening easier to do. Finally, the designer alternates between the perspectives of environment design and artifact design.
- Sometimes the designer is engaged in environment design, constructing skills and organizations of them so that they can be easily found.
- Sometimes the designer is engaged in artifact design, selecting the organizations of skills from which particular skills are then selected and applied.

THE TEXTILE DESIGNER

This section continues with the identification of criteria for constructionist interactivity, this time focusing on a textile pattern design microworld, what I call the *textile designer*. This microworld provides a context for discussing microworld design by novice programmers.

In the past, Logo researchers have discussed the power of "teaching the computer" as a way of learning. Microworld design by novice programmers has the potential of extending this idea in new and interesting ways. A learner can teach himself by designing his own environment of learning. He can also share this design environment with others. By sharing a design environment, a learner is not sharing experience directly; rather, he is sharing a particular collection of synthetic and analytic tools and commands for making new ones. In combination they reflect what I call a *design persona*.[11]

Because design tools are mind-stretching, sharing design tools promotes cooperative mindstretching. Microworld design and evaluation offers a context for cooperative learning and, thus, the potential benefits of making knowledge found within community available to each of its members.

Selecting a Domain

In the music microworld, the domain was a given, not chosen. I was a composer and wanted to find ways for using Logo to support composing by novices. In contrast, the textile designer was selected because I saw a human need and a way of giving domain knowledge operational content using Logo.

When I first began observing at Paige Academy, the art teacher described Logo graphics as "unmotivating." For her, the finished picture was not worth the work necessary to produce it. She was not interested in the kinds of patterns that were natural to proceduralize in Logo. In order to understand what she was interested in, I went to the Massachusetts College of Arts where she was taking a computer animation course. The software she was using (which I will leave unnamed) made it possible for her to use drawing tools to make color pictures of human figures the size of the computer screen. With a sequence of three or four figures she was able to produce crude screen-size animations of a person walking across the screen.

The animation tools that came with the software gave her the ability to cut and paste portions of drawings, and (with distortion) stretch, scale, or rotate images. The art teacher used these tools to take an existing drawing, modify it, then place the modified drawing in the next position in the animation sequence. "Programming" amounted to placing each of the animation frames in a visual sequence on

---

[11]Recall that a design persona *is* a "little designer" in the designer's mental society of designers. A design persona allows all of the perspectives on designing outlined in the previous section.

the screen. She could also loop a sequence so that it would run over and over again. More complex sequences were produced by editing video tapes of animated sequences. One might say that debugging happened at the video editing stage.

Logo is not designed to allow animated shapes to be computer screen size without erasing and then drawing each animation frame. This takes too much time for real-time animation effects. It also does not provide tools for animating drawings. On the other hand, the power of Logo is that production and debugging are closely connected. In Logo, one does not "debug pictures"; one debugs the programs that "draw" the pictures.

I had already committed myself to using Logo as the design environment. The challenge was to select a design domain that took advantage of it. I discovered that Paige's art teacher, the same one who was resistant to Logo, was a banner artist[12] and was planning to work on the design of banners and quilts with children at Paige. It seemed to me that Logo could facilitate these design interests. Logo shapes could be used as textile pattern elements that, in turn, could be organized into progressively more complex patterns using Logo procedures and superprocedures.

Constructing the Design "Language"

I began to work on the textile designer. In this world, Logo shapes are used as design elements. I call them *tiles*. One can "draw" a decoration (20 dots by 20 dots) using tiles, and stamp it on the computer screen, or one can stamp a color with these dimensions (see Fig. 6.4). In addition, one can superimpose color or decorative tiles to produce more complex tiles as shown in Figs. 6.5 and 6.6. This approach to using Logo shapes requires the following design commands (i.e., Logo procedures):

```
simple tile
   TILE [shape color]
superimposed tiles
   TILE [[shape color] [shape color] [shape color] [etc.]]
```

Naming

One can name a tile made up of a simple tile or superimposed tiles and use it as if it were a simple tile. Notice that shape and color numbers can be used, or names like *cross* or *blue* can be given to shape or color numbers (respectively).

---

[12]Many of her beautiful banners hang in the Roxbury Crossing subway station.

FIG. 6.4. Logo shapes used in 20-dot × 20-dot "tiles" to create textile pattern and color design elements.

color tile

simple decorative tiles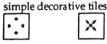

```
naming tile
    MAKE "EMBLEM [[19 4] [9 5]]
    MAKE "EMBLEM [[dots blue] [cross red]]
using it
    TILE:EMBLEM
```

Designing as Redesigning (Debugging)

I call a combination of tiles a *patch*. A patch can be made up of colored or decorative tiles. A patch 3 tiles high and 4 tiles wide is produced using the following a PATCH command (see Fig. 6.7).
There are several Patch commands.

```
patch commands
PATCH height width tile
BORDER height width tile
CORNERS height width tile
RANDOMPATCH height width list-of-tiles
CHECKERPATCH height width tile1 tile2
```

BORDER and CORNERS are illustrated in Fig. 6.8 with a 3 × 4 border patch and a 3 × 4 corner patch. RANDOMPATCH is the same as PATCH except that its third input is not one tile but a list of tiles used by the program to randomly populate the patch.

```
form
    RANDOMPATCH height width list-of-tiles
using it
    RANDOMPATCH 3 4 [star oriental emblem]
```

CHECKERPATCH makes a checkerboard pattern using two different tiles as shown in Fig. 6.9.

tile   tile   superimposed tiles (named *EMBLEM*)

FIG. 6.5. Superimposing the tiles creates more complex designs.

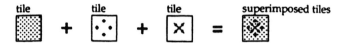

FIG. 6.6.   A combination of color and pattern tiles.

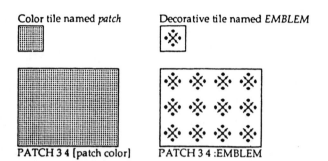

FIG. 6.7.   Tiles can be grouped to make a *patch*.

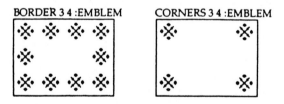

FIG. 6.8.   *Borders* and *corners*, two types of patch commands.

FIG. 6.9.   The *checkerpatch* combines two patches in a checkerboard design.

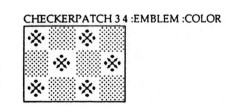

All of the patch commands leave the turtle at the upper left corner of a patch. This makes it possible for the user to overlay patches, either to add new pattern complexity or to cover over patterns that are unappealing. For example, the CORNERS command can be used to place a pattern in the corners of a patch or to cover over corners with the background color of the patch.

Objects-To-Think-With

A design microworld needs an *object-to-think-with*, Papert's idea of a turtle-like entity with which a user can relate. In the textile design microworld objects-to-think-with are tiles and patches.

Drawing Versus Programming

The textile designer uses the shape editor to draw tiles, microworld commands to superimpose them and make patches, and Logo procedures to make progressively complex textile designs.

In a thoughtful paper entitled *Programmable Applications: Interpreter Meets Interface*, Mike Eisenberg describes a research perspective that examines the creative tension between user-interface and language design. For him, a user-interface should allow users "to perform those tasks best suited to the human skills of hand–eye coordination," and "the programming language should provide a good match between language primitives and domain concepts" (Eisenberg, 1991, p. 3).

> The potential exists for a new class of applications software, more expressive, more extensible, and more respectful of the user's imagination than that which preceded it. Instead of dividing the world into computer gurus and computerphobes, these applications would welcome the spread of a programming culture. And because these applications would make maximum expressive power their fundamental goal, they would truly be user-friendly, rather than—as is often the case—user-condescending (Eisenberg, 1991, p. 2).

As Eisenberg sees it, direct manipulation user-interfaces offer certain advantages. He uses standard paint programs as an example. Because painting on the computer resembles painting on paper, these programs provide ease of initial access. Although Logo's shape editor provides a rather limited drawing environment, because it is used to draw simple tiles, it illustrates Eisenberg's point. Writing programs to draw simple tiles would be unnatural.

For Eisenberg, programs allow only direct manipulation are limited because they take little advantage of standard programming ideas like conditionals and recursion, the ability to create data objects like arrays and lists, or the ability to name procedures or build abstractions (Eisenberg, 1991, pp. 6–8). Although general purpose programming environments provide these features, they are seldom designed with users other than professional programmers in mind (Eisenberg, 1991, pp. 10–11). Domain experts should not be required to become professional programmers; rather, programming should amplify the "programming" that experts already do in their heads.

The textile designer provides many of these features. It provides commands for superimposing tiles, abstractions for making different kinds of patches, and user extensibility, the facility to construct new kinds of abstractions.

Design as Environment Design

There are five navigation commands for moving a tile in tile-size steps. Four of them were used to produce the design commands PATCH, BORDER, CORNERS and CHECKERPATCH, and RANDOMPATCH.

```
navigation commands
   MOVEUP number-of-tiles
   MOVEDN number-of-tiles
   MOVERT number-of-tiles
   MOVELT number-of-tiles
```

Because of user extensibility, a user can construct new patch commands using TILE and the navigation commands. In fact, CHECKERPATCH and RANDOMPATCH were added in later versions of the microworld once it became clear that more design tools were necessary. This is a clear example of design as environment design.

Feedback that Improves User Utility

The fifth navigation command, MANUALMOVE, makes it possible to move the turtle manually by using the arrow keys. Pressing the space bar stops MANUALMOVE, which then outputs the current position of the turtle in X–Y coordinate values. The X–Y value can be used to position the cursor at this location at a later time.

```
using it
   MANUALMOVE
   arrow keys
   PRESS space = [X Y]
```

The idea of providing the user with the turtle's position (the X–Y value) is simple enough, yet it illustrates how the designer can give an environment more user utility by offering additional forms of immediate feedback.

Design Persona **Formation**

The combination of commands in the textile designer reflects a particular *design persona*, designing through the successive addition of design layers, or *designing-by-layers*.[13] Within this design persona, a designer can take advantage of different perspectives on designing; he or she can work on the artifact to produce layered patterns, or work on the microworld to extend its power. Regarding the latter, the commands RANDOMPATCH and CHECKERPATCH were added after it appeared that users wanted pattern exploration tools.

After seeing the textile designer, one person wanted to design ceramic tiles for her swimming pool. Her particular application required *supertiles* (i.e., composite tiles of two sizes) and commands for making *superpatches* as shown in Figs. 6.10, 6.11, and 6.12.

Logo shapes could not be used for these tiles and patches because she wanted the outline of her tiles to represent the color of the "grout." This made most of the commands in the *designing-by-layers* persona irrelevant. It was necessary to construct a different design persona to satisfy her request: supertile and superpatch procedures. Whereas Logo made the construction of a new design persona possible, the textile microworld did not.

The Developer's Dilemma

At first, the woman's request for supertiles was somewhat surprising to me. What I thought (but did not say to her) was: "You shouldn't want to make such designs!" I do not believe that this problem is unique to the textile designer. It is quite consistent with the notion of learning by designing that a tool is mind-stretching. New tools make new kinds of designing thinkable and necessitate still newer tools. I call this unavoidable problem the *developer's dilemma*. The developer's dilemma reminds us that a design environment needs to support user-programming.

Design Conventions, Biased and Neutral

It is useful to establish conventions within the design environment to make actions easy for the user to remember. For example, the patch commands always leave the cursor in the upper left-hand corner of the designed textile. Leaving the cursor in the upper left-hand corner is useful because it facilitates designing and debugging by layers. However, because it facilitates designing by layers, it is not a neutral convention but biased by a design perspective.

---

[13]I use "design persona" instead of a "design perspective" for two reasons. One, "perspectives" is already taken by the "perspectives on designing." Having a different term for a different administrative level keeps discussions unambiguous. Two, a design persona can accommodate a variety of perspectives on designing as I have defined them.

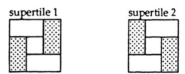

FIG. 6.10.   *Supertiles.*

In contrast, some conventions make the arbitrary predictable. I think of Donald Norman's example (1988) of the clockwise motion of clocks (see previous section, Perspectives on Designing). There is nothing that requires clockwise motion; it simply makes reading the time easier to those who are accustomed to it. The inputs to PATCH, *height* and *width*, follow a convention and illustrate this idea.

Producing an Operational Folklore

I use the phrase *operational folklore* to refer to the collection of practices that support tool use. Simple examples of operational folklore are also found in the STARTUP procedure for the textile designer. When a user loads the textile designer, STARTUP causes the following text to be printed on the screen:

```
Type TUTORIAL for a brief introduction or TEXTILEHELP for the
commands.
```

TUTORIAL is a procedure that shows the user what the cursor looks like and the list of textile design commands. TEXTILEHELP is for experienced users who have forgotten the names of some commands. TUTORIAL also prints the following text on the screen:

```
Type EXAMPLES for examples of textile patterns.
```

EXAMPLES is a procedure that displays on the screen two textile designs and their names, DESIGN1 and DESIGN2.

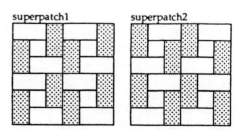

FIG. 6.11.   *Superpatches.*

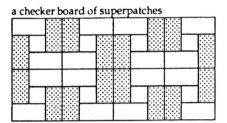

a checker board of superpatches

FIG. 6.12. A checkerboard of *superpatches*.

Instruction On Demand Versus On Schedule

In earlier versions of the textile designer, the introductory tutorial, the list of commands, and the examples were all presented together. In keeping this information under program control, instructions for the user were based on a schedule determined by the programmer, me. This became annoying for experienced users. By dividing this information into separate procedures (TUTORIAL, TEXTILEHELP, and EXAMPLES), I made it possible for new and experienced users to take different paths into the environment, by choosing a novice-track or an expert-track. Now, information was under the control of the user, solicited *on demand* rather than *on schedule*.

Whether instruction is obtained on demand or on schedule illustrates a piece of what Papert means when he contrasts the educational paradigms of instructionism and constructionism. In *instructionist education*, a learner is asked to learn what the instructor thinks he should learn. The problem with this approach to education is that the instructor cannot know what the learner is ready to learn. The instructor does not have perfect knowledge of the intellectual and emotional state of the learner and is likely to be blind to the barriers that make what the instructor wants to teach inaccessible to the learner.

Even a simple conversation is full of miscommunications that are rectified through continuous debugging. To facilitate debugging, *constructionist educators* try to give the learner the freedom to demand knowledge when he is most receptive to it.

Learning by Example

In an earlier version of the textile designer, there were no examples of how the commands work within the microworld. Because most people find it easier to learn from concrete examples rather than abstract principles, I improved the microworld by providing examples.

Notice that introducing design examples was a good idea, but making them available on demand rather than on schedule was an even better idea.

Minimizing Instruction to Serve Constructionist Goals

Radical constructionists are quite sensitive about the notion of instruction. They would argue that my improvements in the textile designer were revisionist.

By offering users more control over the kinds of instruction they could receive or by offering them design examples, I made a painful process less painful, not more constructionist.

Even though I accept this criticism, I operate with a pragmatic heuristic: If the interactions within a microworld require instruction, then the microworld needs to be improved. I may need to represent the domain knowledge differently; maybe the object-to-think-with does not offer the concreteness I had hoped it would. The point is that the presence of instruction serves as a source of feedback for the microworld designer rather than a cause for alarm. This pragmatic approach recognizes the unavoidable tension between short-term and long-term goals. Although I am doing something less than perfect today, I can develop strategies for doing something better tomorrow.

Microworld Design by Learning Communities

Many years ago, Papert described Logo as having "no floor and no ceiling" (1980). What he meant by "no floor" is that the Logo turtle was sufficiently natural to use and identify with that a user would require only a minimum of instruction before using it. What he meant by "no ceiling" is that Logo was sufficiently rich in possibilities that a user's previous experiences in Logo would provide a framework for acquiring new experiences in Logo.

A microworld like the textile designer is much more application-specific than the environment in which it was designed (i.e., Logo). This creates two problems. One, narrowing the kinds of tasks one can do in a design microworld increases the need for task-related knowledge, violating the principle of "no floor." This problem was reflected in the discussions about instruction versus construction. Two, task-specific microworlds reduce knowledge transfer to other tasks, violating the principle of "no ceiling." This problem was reflected in the discussion about learning by designing and the developer's dilemma.

These problems can go away only if users design their own microworlds, or their own design persona within them. This, however, makes some notion of "programming" desirable, all the more reason why an aesthetic is needed to support the process of environment design by novices as well as experts.

Supporting Social Constructionism

It has long been understood that a good way to learn is to teach. However, if everyone is teaching, who is learning? If the answer is "everyone who is teaching," we are caught in a viciously antisocial circle. One way to break this vicious circle is by using microworld evaluation as a tool to support cooperative action.

Papert invented the notion of microworlds to answer critics of Logo's discovery learning. The main argument of critics was this:

Discovery learning is fine; it may even be the best way to learn. However, it takes too much time. If it took the whole of human history to bring us to our present knowledge, how can we expect children to 'discover' this knowledge on their own?

Microworlds provide the means to control what is discoverable without giving up discovery learning. Moreover, powerful ideas—those that are useful in many kinds of situations—are what design microworlds make discoverable. For example, melodic development is a powerful idea in the music designer, and the layered approach to design is a powerful idea in the textile designer.

Social constructionism mobilizes the knowledge of the community to support learning among each of its members. The community is itself a microworld (or microculture). Using computer-based microworlds to facilitate the discovery of what the culture-based microworld knows is a Papertian answer to critics of discovery learning.

The basic idea of *social constuctionism* is that a community (e.g., school, classroom, friendship network, corporation, etc.) is more intelligent than any of its members, including its leaders. The problem is how to mobilize community knowledge so that its members benefit from it.

Perhaps an answer can be found in microworld design and evaluation, a process that necessitates cooperative learning. For example, my desire to satisfy the request for supertiles caused me to construct a design persona I did not anticipate. Through this process my ideas about "tiles" and "patches" were enriched.

One of the factors that limits discovery learning is inadequate design support tools. One reason for examining the design process is to understand how computer-based design environments could retain the quality of design environments that predate computers.

A second factor that limits discovery learning is inadequate support for cooperative action. Constructionist interactivity provides this support by identifying a number of ideas for engaging in microworld design and evaluation, and by providing a social framework in which the expertise of a community of designers is placed at the service of each of its members.

What follows is a condensed summary of the ideas and practices that have been presented:

Design Domain. A good match between human need and programming environment occurs when domain knowledge can be formulated so that it has operational content.

Design Content. Look for the powerful ideas within a domain and build the system around them.

Identification. Objects-to-think-with serve as a sources of feedback during the debugging process.

Transcend the learning paradox. Provide multiple pathways to the same knowledge. Look at the history of ideas within the domain for clues.

Respect learning styles. Provide different ways to represent the same data or solve the same design problem. Provide both synthetic and analytic tools to support different kinds of debugging.

Developer's dilemma. Learning by designing requires facilities for the development of new tools.

Establish conventions. Eliminate unnecessary decision making when choices are arbitrary.

Learnability. Provide incremental learning steps that are rewarding in themselves.

Constructionism. View the need for instruction as feedback for system redesign.

On-demand instruction. If instruction is unavoidable, increase user control by supporting access to instruction on demand rather than on schedule.

Operational folklore. In order to promote the formation of a design culture, construct a collection of practices around the use of a design tool.

CREATING A COMMONWEALTH OF SKILLS

Design is basic to all human activity. (Papanek, in *Design for the Real World*)

While in Brazil at the University of Campinas (1992), I made an important discovery. One day I caught two members of the administrative staff in front of the Macintosh using my textile designer. Unlike the researchers whose interest in the textile designer is academic, these administrators were making textiles for a hobby. For them, having a textile designer was a useful technology. With my encouragement they continued to design, often interrupting me (and others) in order to get assistance. After a couple of weeks they had the courage to express frustration in the fact that it was not possible to get a life-size color copy of their patterns so that they could use them to make real textiles.

The enthusiasm of these administrators gave me conviction that environments to support designing could provide links between crafts and information technologies. This is similar to D'Ambrosio's (1990) way of thinking about *ethnoscience*. Ubiratan D'Ambrosio is a Brazilian mathematician, who for many years has been concerned about the widening gap between the haves and have-nots in Brazil. By examining the coherence of craft practices, he has shown how these practices reflect the kind of thinking that is valuable in science. The textile designer is a simple example of a tool that could support D'Ambrosio's ethno-

FIG. 6.13. Artificial bugs.   Bug facing up   Color patch

science; it is a potential point of entry into the information age for those who already find meaning in textile design.

Seeing Science with a capital "S" as ethnoscience with a small "e" suggests how the computer can play a pivotal role in the formation of new kinds of cultures that are welcoming for all of the world's inhabitants. Collisions between culture and information have been a source of resistance to science and technology in the past. The computer can make future collisions between culture and information synergetic rather than catastrophic.

Designing can serve as a core element of a new curriculum that unites the sciences and the arts. Consider the "poetry" in "scientific" activities such as artificial life design. *Artificial life* can be described as the activity of making synthetic life forms as a means to understanding natural life forms.[14] The two artificial bugs in Figs. 6.13 and 6.14 illustrate this.[15] In this artificial world, a bug can move, recognize *scents*, or leave behind *scents* (represented as patches of color in the figure). Bugs on the screen move up, down, left, or right, depending on what they smell.

Imagine an invisible checker board whose squares are the size of the bugs. The shaded squares are the scents each bug leaves behind while it moves in bug-size steps.

While the bugs look alike, they do not "think" or "act" alike because their behaviors are not the same. Notice that bug 2 has a larger repertoire of behaviors than bug 1.

```
Bug 1
1. If it senses black, it leaves a red scent and goes one
   square to the left.
2. If it senses red, it leaves a black scent and goes one
   square to the right.
3. Otherwise, it moves forward one square
Bug 2
1. If it senses black, it leaves a red scent and move one
   square to the right.
2. If it senses red, it leaves a yellow scent and moves one
   square to the right.
```

---

[14]Also see Kevin Kelly's article (1988) "Designing Perpetual Novelty: Selected Notes from the Second Artificial Life Conference."

[15]This project was inspired by an article by A. K. Dewdney (1989) entitled, "Two-dimensional Turing machines and tur-mites make tracks on a plane."

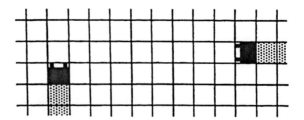

FIG. 6.14.   Artificial world with two bugs.

```
3. If it senses yellow, it leaves a green scent and moves one
   square to the left.
4. If it senses green, it leaves a black scent and moves one
   square to the left.
5. Otherwise, it moves forward one square.
```

Bug 2 is more "sensitive" than bug 1 who does not "know" what to do when encountering the yellow scent or the green scent. It even appears that bug 2 "helps" an immobile bug 1 when bug 2 replaces an unrecognizable scent with a scent bug 1 does recognize (black and red). I think of bug 1 as the child of bug 2.

Part of the fun for the human observer is to identify the rules that each bug follows. An observer can also experience differences between anthropomorphic and mechanistic descriptions. Sometimes creatures (natural or synthetic) appear more intelligent than they really are because the behaviors we observe tempt us to produce anthropomorphic descriptions. Although we cannot be easily taught when anthropomorphic thinking might be useful, we can use artificial life design to reflect on the strengths and weaknesses of such descriptions.

Some observers will ignore the "scientific" implications of artificial life design. Instead, they will enjoy the colors produced by the bugs or "humanize" the interactions between the bugs as I did.

Artificial life exists in a terrain where science and art overlap. As science it can be thought of as hypothesis exploring activity in which one comes in contact with the powerful ideas of mechanism and anthropomorphic descriptions. As art, artificial life design can be thought of as computer animation, painting, or as a vehicle for self-understanding much as fairy tales are: persona exploring, rather than hypothesis exploring. Artificial life design can be described in either way, depending on whether it speaks to the "little humanist" or the "little scientist" within us. In general, designing welcomes these various modes of human inquiry.

There is no need for everyone to become a scientist, nor is there a need for everyone to become an artist. However, there is an urgent need for everyone to develop design skill. Those who have been following the current revolution in industrial production method—the "Toyota way"—also described as *lean production* by Womack, Jones, and Roos—will have noticed the importance of educating the new work force. According to the authors of *The Machine that*

Changed the World, the three major paradigms of production are craft, mass and lean production. In *craft* production, producers use highly skilled workers and simple but flexible tools to make exactly what the consumer asks for—one item at a time. In *mass* production, producers use narrowly skilled professionals to design products made by unskilled or semiskilled workers who run expensive, single-purpose machines that churn out standardized ("good enough") products in very high volume. Finally, in *lean* production, producers combine variety and quality, the advantages of craft production, with high volume and low cost, the advantages of mass production (Womack, Jones, & Roos, 1990).

Unlike the transition from craft to mass production where worker skills were abundant, the transition from mass to lean production requires reskilling a deskilled labor force. Moreover, the kinds of skills required in lean production are learning skills; a worker not only needs to learn to perform complex operations; he must become a perpetual learner. Industrialists who wish to "go lean" are being forced to see learning as the new competitive advantage. Industrial settings of the future will need to become learning as well as producing environments.

At a NATO-sponsored conference in November of 1992, Martial Vivet reported on "project-based teaching,"[16] which he is using to educate blue-collar workers in France. The microworld he created was a table-size model of a running factory. Workers were asked to build micro-robots (similar to Lego-Logo robots) that could be used in this microworld. Through this process it was hoped that workers would begin to understand principles in robotics and the role of robots within an integrated system of manufacturing.

There was a sense of urgency in Vivet's work. His pedagogy had to work because the economic lives of workers were at stake. Vivet found that it motivated workers when he selected robot projects that appeared useful to them and that resembled robots they had seen on the factory floor. He organized workers into small teams, each working on the same kind of robot project. The best projects were those with no apparent solution, even to the instructor. This placed the instructor in the role of a researcher and established trust between him and the workers. In addition, projects that could be solved in many ways created opportunities for teams of robot designers to discuss robot similarities and differences.

Vivet asked work teams to debate the efficiency of their different robots and to identify factors of efficiency. For example, some teams were able to produce a robot more quickly than others, though robots produced by quick teams were sometimes not as efficient to use as the robots produced by slower teams. Some teams were very slow in designing a robot, but the superior design of their robot (e.g., the use of subassemblies) made it possible for the robot to be quickly reconfigured to perform a different function. Some robots were easier to integrate into the factory than others. These debates, often heated, were a testimony to Vivet's success; they demonstrated that the workers had not only begun to con-

---

[16] I think "project-based teaching" is more appropriately described as "design-based learning."

sider different kinds of robot constructions; they had begun to think about the integration of robots into a total production system (Vivet, 1992).

One might characterize Vivet's pedagogy in the following way. His first task was anthropological: Build on the daily experiences of the workers. A second task was contractual: Build trust among the workers and clarity about the pedagogical goals of the activity. A third task was managerial: Organize the teams, design types of projects, and manage the discourse around the project activity. A fourth task was advisory: Provide assistance when requested.

Contrast Vivet's approach with the rigid approach of conventional schooling. Vivet's anthropology replaced curriculum; his social contracts with the workers and his knowledge about robots replaced brute authority; and his management methods replaced assessment. I call conventional schooling, unlike Vivet's lean approach, mass education to emphasize that conventional schooling reflects a mind-set inherited from several decades of mass industrialization.

In mass education, teachers are like assembly-line workers, ordered to teach a standard curriculum over which they have no control. Mass education produces students unable to meet the minimum educational standards while fostering habits of mind appropriate for mass production workers: obedience, an ability to tolerate alienation, and blind adherence to routine (Gargarian & Cleary, 1992b). In short, mass education has deskilled society.

When mass education is used to support mass work, it is doubly deadly; an out-of-date pedagogy is used to instruct workers in an out-of-date form of production. It is no wonder that corporate training is usually given a low priority. It does not accomplish much in the way of "added value"—everyone knows training as it is commonly practiced does not really work (Gargarian & Cleary, 1992a).

Of course, lean production should not dictate a new system of pedagogy as mass production did; indeed, it seems vulgar to think of learners as items that are manufactured. However, even the most cynical among us, willing to completely embrace my analogy between school and work, will recognize the need for a revolution in education in which design is likely to play a central role.

What is a "revolution in education"? I think of Piaget's notions of assimilation and accommodation. A learner can *assimilate* new ideas that are only slightly different from his own, whereas a learner has to change his perspective to *accommodate* ideas that are very different from his own. Revolution requires support for accommodative thought. "Revolution" also makes me think of an important difference between Piaget-the-practitioner and Papert-the-practitioner. For Piagetians, "if you want to get ahead, get a theory." This phrase from Annette Karmiloff-Smith and Barbel Inhelder (1974/75) suggests that one way to make mental progress is to construct a model of the world and then test it against the real world. If it works, one gains additional confidence in one's model; if it does not, one has new data from which to construct a new model. In Piaget's hands, the scientific method is a learning method.

For Papertians, "if you want to get a theory, get ahead." This phrase from Edith Ackermann (1991) suggests that tools (e.g., telescopes, microscopes, and powerful ideas) give learners access to data previously unavailable to them. With this new data learners can construct new theories with which to get ahead. In Papert's hands, tools support new kinds of systematic inquiry and expression.[17]

Individuals are not only constrained by their own thoughts but by institutional constraints. When thinking about "revolution," I also think of Mary Douglas's analysis of the cognitive function of institutions in her book, *How Institutions Think* (1986). We need institutions for at least two reasons. First, we need them because we cannot think about the world without partitioning it into manageable parts. Second, we need them in order to sustain particular kinds of cooperative action. Both reasons lead directly to classification, no matter how primitive. "The more fully the institutions encode expectations, the more they put uncertainty under control. . . . An institution needs some stabilizing principle to stop its premature demise. That stabilizing principle is the naturalization of social classifications" (Douglas, 1986, p. 48).

The process of building institutions requires two sorts of cognitive acts, *systematic forgetting*—"what are the impossible thoughts?"—and *systematic remembering*—"what are the accredited ways of thinking?" (Douglas, 1986, p. 71). "For better or worse, individuals really do share their thoughts and they do to some extent harmonize their preferences, and they have no other way to make the big decisions except within the scope of the institutions they build" (Douglas, 1986, p. 128).

Because institutions are resistant to the kinds of inquiry and expression for which they were not designed, their strengths can also be their weaknesses. They can become disabling when the objectives they embody do not meet the objectives required by changed circumstances. I argue that it is not natural—indeed, it is epistemologically irrational—for most of our current institutions to assimilate constructionist tools and practices. We need a new kind of institution, one in which design is the core curriculum. I call it *Discovery Village*.

In a paper written by Cleary and myself, we describe Discovery Village as "a hybrid of learning laboratory and theme park whose themes are technology, media, and the arts." We imagine Discovery Village as a public access institution for use in developing countries to support the formation of a media-rich culture. We argue that most attempts at "technology transfer" have failed—indeed, usually have been experienced as "technology invasion"—because the implicit knowledge surrounding a technology's use is also not "transferred" (Gargarian & Cleary, 1992b).

I was recently at a party where I mentioned autonomous robots to a couple of

---

[17] One might say that Piaget-the-practitioner is an assimilator, whereas Papert-the-practitioner is an accommodator. One might also say that Papert-the-theorist assimilates Piaget-the-practitioner into his learning paradigm.

dancers. They were intrigued by the idea and asked for more detail. I must have gotten carried away because I could see a certain anxiousness in the dancers' eyes. It then occurred to me that these dancers had devoted many years of their lives to movement and, in their own way, understood these issues much better than I did. I remembered *contact improvisation*, a kind of dancing in which dancers interact physically through a process of give and take and, through these interactions, produce a spontaneously choreographed dance. I then mentioned to the dancers that when programming autonomous robots, it is necessary to make the rules of interaction more explicit than they are among the dancers during a contact improvisation. There are also far fewer rules and kinds of movement. I then asked whether the kinds of interaction among dancers change because each contact improvisation produces a different dance, a different emergent effect. This question led to a rich discussion in which the dancers felt perfectly comfortable talking about "mechanism," "parallelism" and "emergence," but in a culturally meaningful way. My error was in giving the impression that "robotics" is an idea that comes from outer space. In fact, "robotics" was a part of the daily experience of these dancers. If I had been Vivet the anthropologist, I would have avoided the technology transfer mind-set I had used at the start.

Discovery Village could be thought of in different ways depending on how it is used. After reading about the problems in reskilling labor, I imagined Discovery Village as an environment installed within factories. After talking with a media company about the "textbook of the future," I began to think of Discovery Village as a learning environment where publishers could explore design-based learning. In seeing the favelas in Brazil, I imagined Discovery Village as a community square maintained by teenagers. After the riots in Los Angeles (1992), I imagined Discovery Village as a new kind of hangout that combined both physical and cognitive aerobics.

For Discovery Village to be an experiment in institutional redesign, it needs subjects operating within a social context. This is why it is a "living laboratory" and not just a research laboratory. Discovery Village experiments could facilitate the development of a variety of installations populated with a variety of microworlds, each with designing as the core activity. Discovery Village could serve as a resocialization mechanism through which the artificial barriers that separate science from art, school from play, or work from life are gradually dismantled. In place of these barriers one would find the growth of a commonwealth of skills. This is constructive revolution.

REFERENCES

Ackermann, E. (1991). From decontextualized to situated knowledge: Revisiting Piaget's water-level experiment. In Idit Harel & Seymour Papert (Eds.) *Constructionism* (pp. 269–294). Norwood, NJ: Ablex.

Alexander, C. R. (1964). *Notes on the synthesis of form.* Cambridge, MA: Harvard University Press.

Apel, W. (1972). *Harvard dictionary of music.* Cambridge, MA: Belknap Press of Harvard University Press.

Babbitt, M. (1987). The unlikely survival of serious music. In D. Stephen & J. N. Straus (Eds.). *Words about music*. Madison, WI: University of Wisconsin Press.

Bent, I. (1987). *Analysis*. New York: Norton.

Cheney, T., Rees, A. (1983). *Getting the words right: How to revise, edit and rewrite*. Cincinnati, OH: Writer's Digest Books.

Dahlhaus, C. (1989). *The idea of absolute music* (R. Lustig, Trans.). Chicago, IL: University of Chicago Press. (Original version, 1978).

D'Ambrosio, U. (1990). *Ethnomatematica*. Campinas: Editorada Unicamp.

Dewdney, A. K. (1989). Two-dimensional Turing machines and tur-mites make tracks on a plane. *Scientific American, 261*(9).

Douglas, M. (1986). *How institutions think*. Syracuse University Press.

Eisenberg, M. (1991). *Programmable applications: Interpreter meets interface*. Unpublished manuscript, MIT Laboratory for Computer Science, Cambridge, MA.

Frith, S. (1987). Towards an aesthetics of popular music. In R. Leppert & S. McClary (Eds.), *Music and society: The politics of composition, performance and reception* (pp. 133–149). New York: Cambridge University Press.

Gardner, A. (1987). *An artificial intelligence approach to legal reasoning*. Cambridge, MA: MIT Press.

Gargarian, G., & Cleary, C. (1992a). *Enabling corporate learning*. Unpublished paper.

Gargarian, G., & Cleary, C. (1992b). *Discovery village: A new kind of institution for reskilling society*. Unpublished paper.

Gross, M. D. (1978). *Design as exploring constraints*. Doctoral thesis, MIT, Cambridge, MA.

Karmiloff-Smith, A. & Inhelder, B. (1974/75). If you want to get ahead, get a theory. *Cognition, 3*(2), 195–212.

Kelly, K. (1988). Designing perpetual novelty: Selected notes from the second artificial life conference. In J. Brockman (Ed.), *Doing science*. New York: Prentice-Hall.

Kinderman, W. (1987). *Beethoven's diabelli variations*. Oxford: Clarendon Press.

Mayakovsky, V. (1974). *How are verses made?* First published in 1926 in the USSR. Grossman Publishers (US). London: Cape Editions.

Norman, D. A. (1988). *The design of everyday things*. New York: Doubleday.

Papert, S. (1980). *Mindstorms: Children, computers and powerful ideas*. New York: Basic Books.

Poolard-Gott, L. (1983). Emergence of thematic concepts in repeated listening to music. *Cognitive Psychology, 15*, 66–94.

Reck, D. (1977). *Music of the whole earth*. New York: Charles Scribner & Sons.

Rowell, L. (1983). *Thinking about music: An introduction to the philosophy of music*. Boston, MA: University of Massachusetts Press.

Schoenberg, A. (1970). Fundamentals of music composition. In Gerhard Strang & Leonard Stein (Eds.), *Fundamentals of music composition*. New York: Faber.

Sloboda, J. (1985). *The musical mind: The cognitive psychology of music*. Oxford, England: Clarendon Press.

Soros, G. (1987). *The alchemy of finance: Reading the mind of the market*. New York: Simon & Schuster.

Vivet, M. (1992, November). Educational uses of control technology. Paper presented at NATO-sponsored conference at the University of Liege.

Womack, J. P., Jones, D. T., & Roos, D. (1990). *The machine that changed the world*. New York: Macmillan Publishing Company.

7
Building and Learning With Programmable Bricks

Randy Sargent
Mitchel Resnick
Fred Martin
Brian Silverman

INTRODUCTION

In many educational computer projects, children control and manipulate worlds in the computer. Using one program, children can control the movements of Newtonian "dynaturtles" in physics microworlds (Abelson & diSessa, 1980). Using a different program, children can create and manipulate simulated urban worlds, constructing houses, roads, and factories, and setting tax rates for the city (Wright, 1990).

But instead of controlling and manipulating *worlds in the computer*, what if children could control and manipulate *computers in the world*? That is, what if children could spread computation throughout their own personal worlds? For example, a child might attach a tiny computer to a door, then program the computer to make lights turn on automatically whenever anyone enters the room. The child might program the computer to greet people as they enter the room— or to sound an alarm if anyone enters the room at night.

In this chapter we describe a new technology, called the Programmable Brick, that makes such activities possible, and we explore how this new technology might open new learning opportunities for children. The Programmable Brick is a tiny, portable computer embedded inside a LEGO brick about the size of a deck of cards. The brick is capable of interacting with the physical world in a large variety of ways (including sensors and infrared communication). Our hope is that the Programmable Brick will make possible a wide range of new design activities for children, encouraging children to see themselves as designers and inventors. At the same time, we believe that these activities could fundamentally change how children think about computers and computational ideas.

UBIQUITOUS COMPUTING

Our work on the Programmable Brick fits within an area of research sometimes known as "ubiquitous computing." This research aims to change the nature of computing in very fundamental ways. As described in one research article: "We live in a complex world, filled with myriad objects, tools, toys, and people. Our lives are spent in diverse interaction with this environment. Yet, for the most part, our computing takes place sitting in front of, and staring at, a single glowing screen attached to an array of buttons and a mouse" (Wellner, Mackay, & Gold, 1993, p. 24). Ubiquitous computing, by contrast, aims at "integrating computers seamlessly into the world at large" (Weiser, 1991, p. 94). The goal is to spread computation throughout the environment, embedding computation in all types of objects and artifacts.

For example, at some laboratories, people are starting to wear "active badges" so that the building can "know" the location of all people in the building at all times. At other sites, researchers are using "smart whiteboards" that keep track of everything written on them. To some, ubiquitous computing means that computation "disappears," becoming totally integrated into everyday objects. We take a somewhat broader view of ubiquitous computing, including new artifacts like "personal digital assistants" and handheld computers that enable people to access and exchange information wherever they are.

Our work on the Programmable Brick is resonant with these efforts to distribute computational power, but it differs along several important dimensions:

- *The Programmable Brick is designed for children.* Most work on ubiquitous computing is aimed at adults, particularly adults in business settings. For example, most personal digital assistants are designed for tasks such as keeping track of appointments and downloading stock quotes. Those activities are not of great interest to children. In developing the Programmable Brick, we considered how we could make ubiquitous-computing activities meaningful to the lives of children.

- *The Programmable Brick gives users the power to create and control.* In many ubiquitous-computing activities, the roles of designers and users are separate and distinct. Designers create ubiquitous-computing devices (such as active badges and smart whiteboards), and users interact with them. Our goal is to blur this distinction, giving much greater control to users so that they can create their own ubiquitous-computing activities. The Programmable Brick is explicitly *programmable* so that users can continually modify and customize its behavior. In this way, the Programmable Brick fits clearly within a constructionist approach to learning (Papert, 1991).

- *The Programmable Brick provides rich connections to the world.* Many ubiquitous computing activities focus on transfer of information (such as downloading airline schedules). We are more interested in connecting computation to physical objects, enabling people to program computers to sense the world around them and perform actions in response. Toward that end, the Programmable Brick has a rich assortment of input–output capabilities, including a dozen ports for motors and sensors, and built-in speaker and microphone for sound interactions.

LEGO/LOGO

The Programmable Brick project extends our previous work with LEGO/Logo (Resnick, 1993; Resnick, Ocko, & Papert, 1988). LEGO/Logo links the popular LEGO construction kit with the Logo programming language. In using LEGO/Logo, children start by building machines out of LEGO pieces, using not only the traditional LEGO building bricks but newer pieces like gears, motors, and sensors. Then they connect their machines to a computer and write computer programs (using a modified version of Logo) to control the machines. For example, a child might build a LEGO house with lights and program the lights to turn on and off at particular times. Then the child might build a garage and program the garage door to open whenever a car approaches.

Logo itself was developed in the late 1960s as a programming language for children (Papert, 1980). In the early years, the most popular use of Logo involved a "floor turtle," a simple mechanical robot connected to the computer by a long "umbilical cord." With the proliferation of personal computers in the late 1970s, the Logo community shifted its focus to "screen turtles." Screen turtles are much faster and more accurate than floor turtles, and thus allow children to create and investigate more complex geometric effects.

In some ways, LEGO/Logo might seem like a throwback to the past, since it brings the turtle off the screen and back into the world. However, LEGO/Logo differs from the early Logo floor turtles in several important ways. First of all, LEGO/Logo users are not given ready-made mechanical objects; they build their own machines before programming them. Second, children are not restricted to turtles. Elementary-school students have used LEGO/Logo to build and program a wide assortment of creative machines, including a programmable pop-up toaster, a "chocolate-carob factory" (inspired by Roald Dahl's *Willy Wonka* children's stories), and a machine that sorts LEGO bricks according to their lengths. The LEGO company now sells a commercial version of LEGO/Logo. It is used in more than a dozen countries, including more than 15,000 elementary and middle schools in the United States.

LEGO/Logo has some limitations. For one thing, LEGO/Logo machines must be connected to a desktop computer with wires. Wires are a practical nuisance, particularly when children use LEGO/Logo to create mobile "creatures." Wires get tangled with other objects in the environment; they get twisted in knots as the creature rotates; and they restrict the overall range of the creature. Wires are also a conceptual nuisance. It is difficult to think of a LEGO/Logo machine as an autonomous creature as long as it is attached by umbilical cord to a computer.

Members of our research group have tried to solve these problems in several ways. We experimented with various technologies for wireless communication, to get around the problem of wires, but none of these approaches satisfied us. We therefore decided to make a more serious modification: We began to build electronics *inside* the LEGO bricks. We have taken several approaches. The "Braitenberg Brick" system, developed primarily by Fred Martin, with inspiration from the book *Vehicles* (Braitenberg, 1984), is based on a set of low-level "logic bricks" (such as and-gates, flip-flops, and timers). Students can create different behaviors by wiring these bricks together in different ways (Granott, 1991; Hogg, Martin, & Resnick, 1991).

PROGRAMMABLE BRICKS

The Braitenberg Bricks have dedicated functions. The flip-flop brick, for instance, has a very specialized function: It holds one bit of state, and it changes that state whenever it receives a sharp transition in its input. Why, however, should we be restricted to dedicated bricks? Why not put a full computer in a LEGO brick?

That is what we have done in the Programmable Brick project. In designing the Programmable Brick, we had several overarching goals. Each goal involved some type of "multiplicity":

• *Multiple activities.* We wanted the Programmable Brick to support a wide variety of different activities—so that it could connect to the interests and experiences of a wide variety of people. Whereas some people might use the Brick to create their own scientific instruments, others might use it to create their own musical instruments.

• *Multiple input-output modalities.* We wanted the Programmable Brick to connect to many things in the world. To do that, the Brick needed many different types of output devices (such as motors, lights, beepers, and infrared transmitters) and many different types of input devices (such as touch sensors, sound sensors, light sensors, temperature sensors, and infrared receivers). Indeed, the number of possible applications of the Brick expands greatly with each new input or output device, because each new device can be used in combination with all of the others.

• *Multiple processes.* Children working on LEGO/Logo projects often want to control two or more things at the same time. For example, they might want to make a Ferris wheel and merry-go-round turn in synchrony while a song plays in the background and an electric eye automatically counts the rotations of the rides. With standard programming languages, it is very difficult to achieve this effect: The user must explicitly interleave the multiple threads of control. In the Programmable Brick, we wanted to support parallel processing so that users could easily write programs to control multiple outputs and check multiple sensors all at the same time.

• *Multiple bricks.* We wanted Programmable Bricks not only to act on their own, but to interact with one another. In that way, children could program Bricks to share sensor data with each other, or they could create "colonies" of interacting creatures. These types of activities would enable children to explore the scientific ideas of emergence and self-organization (Resnick, 1994).

With these goals, we developed the Programmable Brick shown in Fig. 7.1. About the size of a deck of cards, the Programmable Brick is based on the Motorola 6811 processor with 256K of nonvolatile RAM memory and has a wide variety of input-output possibilities. The brick can control four motors or lights at a time, and it can receive inputs from eight sensors. A speaker and microphone are built into the brick for sampling and emitting sounds. Around the sides of the brick are six infrared transmitters and receivers, so that the brick can communicate with other Programmable Bricks (and other electronic devices). On top of the brick is a two-line liquid-crystal display, plus a knob and two buttons for direct interaction with the Brick. (An earlier version of the Brick had many fewer input-output features. See Bourgoin, 1990, and Martin, 1988, for more details.)

To program the Programmable Brick, you first write programs on a standard personal computer, then download the programs via a cable to the Programmable Brick. Then you can disconnect the cable, and take the brick with you. The programs remain stored on the brick. When you want to execute a program on the brick, you can scroll through a menu of programs on the two-line liquid crystal

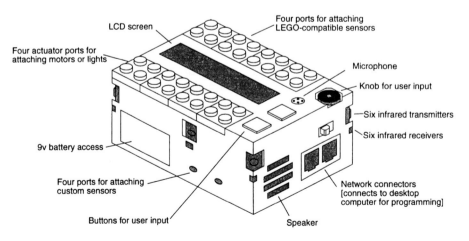

FIG. 7.1.   The Programmable Brick.

display screen (using the knob to scroll), then press a button to run the selected program.

EXPERIENCES WITH THE BRICK

In our early experiments with the Programmable Brick, we observed three broad categories of applications: active environments, autonomous creatures, and personal science experiments. In this section, we discuss one example project in each category.

Active Environments

One of the earliest projects with the Programmable Brick involved two kids named Andrew and Dennis. The kids, ages 11 and 12, were intrigued with the idea of making an "active environment"—making the environment "come alive" and react to people. After some consideration, they decided to make a device to flip on a room's light switch when people entered the room, and flip it off when people left.

At first, Andrew and Dennis studied the different possible sensors, trying to figure out which one could be connected to the door, and how. They decided to try a "bend" sensor to sense the opening of the door. (The bend sensor is a plastic whisker several inches long that gives a measure of how much it is bent.) They first tried to mount the sensor to the wall approximately where the doorstop was, but then decided that people would need to open the door very wide before the sensor detected anything. Then they tried mounting the sensor at the door hinge in such a way that the sensor was bent in proportion to how widely the door was opened.

Before programming, Andrew and Dennis tested the value of the bend sensor at different positions of the door to find out if they had mounted the sensor well and if the sensor would really give them the information they wanted. Then they built a LEGO mechanism to flip the light switch on the wall of the room. The mechanism connected a motor, through a gear train, to a lever that pushed against the light switch. They designed their mechanism so that spinning the motor one way would turn the light on, whereas the reverse direction would turn the light off.

At this point, Andrew and Dennis started focusing on the algorithm for flipping the light switch when the door opened. They realized that there was a problem: The door sensor indicated when the door was opened, but it did not tell whether people were entering or exiting the room. The kids wanted some sort of sensor to tell whether someone was entering the room (in which case their machine should turn on the light) or leaving the room (in which case the machine should turn off the light).

After a little thinking, Andrew and Dennis came up with a clever solution: They attached a LEGO bar to the door handle on one side of the door, and connected a LEGO touch sensor to this bar. In this way, the Programmable Brick could tell if people were leaving (in which case the door would be open while the touch sensor in the handle was pressed), or if people were entering (the door would be open with no signal from the touch switch).

Once the second sensor was in place and tested, they wanted to begin programming. Their program turned out to be pretty simple and worked without too many iterations. The finished program looked similar to the following:

```
to light
   if (sensor-a < 105) and touch-b [turn-off-light]
   if (sensor-a < 105) and not touch-b [turn-on-light]
end
to turn-off-light
   motor-a, this-way        ;;run motor forward for 3 seconds
   onfor 30
end
to turn-on-light
   motor-a, that-way        ;;run motor backward for 3 seconds
   onfor 30
end
```

Once Andrew and Dennis got the project working, they ran in and out of the room repeatedly, breaking into big smiles each time the lights switched on and off.

Autonomous Creatures

In a 4-day workshop at the Boston Museum of Science, five students used Programmable Bricks to create "artificial creatures." The participants, ages 12 to 16, had 3 hours of workshop time per day, for a total of a 12 hours. Although students had varying amounts of previous experience with LEGO and programming (three had not programmed before at all), all were able to make a working programmable "creature" by the end of the workshop.

One focus of this workshop was the use of multiple processes for multiple behaviors. With the Programmable Brick, different simple programs (such as "follow light" or "follow wall") can be run as separate processes. Users can turn these individual programs on and off using the brick's screen, knob, and buttons. The brick's software also includes primitives that allow students to turn the different processes on and off from program control. Thus, processes have the ability to start or stop other processes.

The three participants who had not programmed before wrote fairly simple programs for their creatures. One made a creature that followed a line (a piece of tape laid down on the floor). Another made a creature that simply backed up when it hit an obstacle. The third made a creature that backed away from bright light (this participant had lots of fun playing with his creature using a flashlight).

The other two participants, Darryl and Mark, who had both programmed before, used multiple, interacting behaviors in their programs. In his project, Darryl created two procedures, one to make the creature follow a light, the other to make the creature avoid obstacles. He made both procedures run at the same time. The parallelism of the Programmable Brick was very useful: The creature could check for obstacles even as it followed the light. When the creature detected an obstacle, however, there were problems. As the obstacle-avoidance behavior tried to guide the creature around the obstacle, the light-following behavior kept pointing the creature back toward the light. Darryl solved this problem by modifying the obstacle-avoidance behavior to temporarily turn off the light-following behavior while the creature was navigating around a detected obstacle.

Mark's project started with a single, simple behavior. The creature tried to navigate a path between several rooms using timing only (no sensor feedback): go forward for 20 seconds, turn left, go forward for 15 seconds, turn left, go forward for 20 seconds. This path was intended to make the creature leave the classroom, go down the hall, make a left into a different classroom, and turn left again to try to get out the other classroom's back door. This simple behavior, however, did not have a good chance of working: The second classroom was full of tables and chairs, and the creature invariably hit one or two and got stuck. Sometimes, also, the timing of the path was a little off, or the creature drifted off its planned path and ran into a wall. For this creature, running into a wall, chair, or table typically meant getting stuck and progressing no further.

In trying to deal with this problem, Mark added a second behavior: When the creature ran into an obstacle, it attempted to pilot around the obstacle and end up heading roughly in the same direction as before. The behavior looked something like this:

```
to avoid-obstacles
   if touch-a [spin-right
               wait 10
               go-forward
               wait 10
               spin-left
               wait 10
               go-forward]
end
```

The added behavior did not completely solve the navigation problem—the creature did not navigate its course reliably. However, the creature typically got much further with this new behavior than without it.

Personal Science Experiments

We believe that the Programmable Brick will open up new types of science experiments, in which students investigate everyday phenomena in their lives (both in and out of the classroom). For example, a student could attach a Programmable Brick (and related sensors) to her own body to monitor and analyze how her legs move while she is running. We believe that students are much more likely to make deep connections to scientific thinking and scientific ideas when they use computation in this new way, continually designing and redesigning their own personal investigations.

Brian Silverman, along with his son Eric, used a Programmable Brick to conduct one such investigation. Brian wished to graph the speed of his bicycle during his daily bike trips commuting to and from work. He attached a Programmable Brick to the handlebar of the bike and programmed it to collect data from a sensor on the front bicycle wheel. After trying various sensors to measure the rotation of the wheel, Brian and Eric settled on a magnet mounted to the wheel and a reed relay (mechanical magnetic sensor) mounted next to the wheel. Once in each rotation of the wheel the sensor would detect the magnet. The brick was programmed to record, every two seconds, both the speed of the wheel and the total number of wheel rotations.

In order to graph the results, Brian and Eric wrote a special-purpose program. Although the recorded data measured speed versus time, they decided to graph speed versus distance instead. With this graph, they could superimpose trips taken on different days. Events at the same location on each trip (such as traffic lights or stop signs) would be at the same place along the x axis of the graph. The graph is quite striking: It shows things like train tracks (where Brian had to slow down every day) and traffic lights (where he came to a stop only some of the time). See Fig. 7.2 for the graph of a single trip to work and back.

By plotting return trips in reverse and superimposing them, many of the features (such as slowing down for the train tracks) proved to be identical. However, consistent discrepancies (one stretch of the trip consistently being faster in one direction than the other) indicated something was different between the trips to and from: Consistent differences in speed indicated an uphill or downhill slope.

Twenty Things to Do With a Programmable Brick

Our work with Programmable Bricks is just beginning, but it is not too early to start speculating. More than 20 years ago, as researchers and educators were just beginning to explore the possibilities of computers in education, Seymour Papert and Cynthia Solomon wrote a memo called Twenty Things to Do With a Computer (Papert & Solomon, 1971). The memo described a wonderful collection of activities, pushing computers in directions that few other people had imagined. Some of the activities on their list eventually became commonplace;

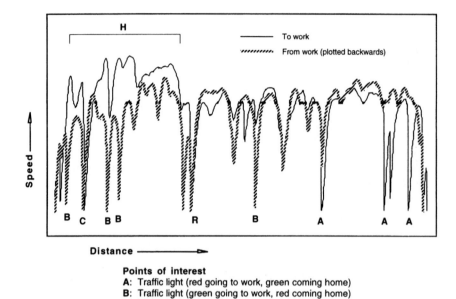

FIG. 7.2.   Speed versus distance riding bike to and from work.

others are still visionary. A few years later, Danny Hillis (then an undergraduate at MIT) wrote a memo entitled Ten Things to Do With a Better Computer (Hillis, 1975), describing a new set of activities that would be possible if computers could execute instructions in parallel. Hillis later realized some of these ideas in his massively parallel Connection Machine computer (Hillis, 1985).

In the same spirit, we have compiled a new list, entitled Twenty Things to Do With a Programmable Brick:

1.   Create a "haunted house." Attach a Programmable Brick to the door to make creaking sounds whenever the door is opened. Program another Brick to drop spiders on people when they walk through the door. Build a LEGO platform for a pumpkin and program a Brick to drive the pumpkin around the room.

2.   Connect sensors to various parts of your body. Then program a Programmable Brick to monitor your heartbeat and breathing as you walk and run, or program the Brick to play different sounds when you move different parts of your body.

3.   Take a Programmable Brick with you to measure the pH level of the water in local streams or the noise levels at a local construction site.

4. Create LEGO musical instruments. The instrument might have buttons like those on a flute, a sliding part as on a trombone, or a completely new interface that you invent. Start by writing a simple program so that the Programmable Brick plays different notes (or melodies) when you move different parts of the instrument. Then enhance the program so that the Brick improvises on your notes, or program the Brick to play rounds (by playing a second copy of your notes with a delay).

5. Put a Programmable Brick and light sensor on the door to keep track of the number of people that enter the room. Then program the Brick to greet people as they enter the room (with music or digitized speech).

6. Set up a weather station on the roof of the building.

7. Use a Programmable Brick to find out if the light really does go off when you shut the refrigerator door.

8. Attach a Programmable Brick to an ashtray and program it to play a coughing sound whenever anyone uses the ashtray.

9. Build a remote-control LEGO car. Use a standard TV remote control to communicate (via infrared) with a Programmable Brick in the car.

10. Create an "intelligent room" that automatically turns on the lights when someone walks into the room. (Here is one approach. Build a LEGO machine that turns on the light switch and connect it to a Programmable Brick. Use another Programmable Brick to detect when anyone enters the room. Use infrared to communicate between the two Bricks.)

11. Use a Programmable Brick to control a videocamera (via infrared). Program the Brick to make a time-lapse video of a plant growing (taking a few frames every hour or day).

12. Use a Programmable Brick to program your VCR.

13. Send secret messages across the room to someone else who also has a Programmable Brick.

14. Put a Brick on your dog's collar and collect data about your dog's behavior. How much time does your dog spend running around? Discuss whether experimenting on your dog is ethical.

15. Use a Brick to record your dog barking. Then put the Brick in a remote-control LEGO car. Play the barking sound when the LEGO car gets near a cat. How does the cat react?

16. Build a LEGO creature that you can interact with. Program the creature to act in different ways when you clap once, or clap twice, or shine a light in its "eyes."

17. Build a LEGO creature that explores its environment. Program the creature to find the part of the room with the most light or the highest temperature. Next, put a plant on your LEGO creature so that the plant will always move to the part of the room with the most light (or the

highest temperature). Use other sensors to monitor the growth of the plant.

18. Build a LEGO machine that can water your plants. Then program a Brick to make the machine water the plants every few days.

19. Create a game where each player carries a Programmable Brick. Program the Bricks so that they give instructions to the players and send messages from one player to another.

20. Think up twenty more things to do with a Programmable Brick.

ACKNOWLEDGMENTS

Seymour Papert, Steve Ocko, and Allan Toft have provided encouragement, inspiration, and ideas for the Programmable Brick project. Andrew Blumberg, Fei Hai Chua, Dennis Evangelista, Chris Gatta, Hanna Jang, Owen Johnson, Mark Neri, Darren Schmidt, Victor Tsou, and Elaine Yang all contributed to the development effort. The LEGO Group and the National Science Foundation (Grants 9153719-MDR and 9358519-RED) have provided financial support.

REFERENCES

Abelson, H., & diSessa, A. (1980). *Turtle geometry: The computer as a medium for exploring mathematics*. Cambridge, MA: MIT Press.

Bourgoin, M. (1990). Children using LEGO robots to explore dynamics. In I. Harel (Ed.), *Constructionist learning* (pp. 141–155). Cambridge, MA: MIT Media Laboratory.

Braitenberg, V. (1984). *Vehicles*. Cambridge, MA: MIT Press.

Granott, N. (1991). Puzzled minds and weird creatures: Spontaneous inquiry and phases in knowledge construction. In I. Harel & S. Papert (Eds.), *Constructionism* (pp. 295–310). Norwood, NJ: Ablex.

Harvey, B. (1985). *Computer science logo style*. Cambridge, MA: MIT Press.

Hillis, W. D. (1975). *Ten things to do with a better computer* (Unpublished memo.) Cambridge, MA: MIT Artificial Intelligence Lab.

Hillis, W. D. (1985). *The connection machine*. Cambridge, MA: MIT Press.

Hogg, D., Martin, F., & Resnick, M. (1991). *Braitenberg creatures* (Epistemology and Learning Memo No. 13). Cambridge, MA: MIT Media Laboratory.

Martin, F. (1988). *Children, cybernetics, and programmable turtles*. Unpublished master's thesis, MIT Media Laboratory, Cambridge, MA.

Papert, S. (1980). *Mindstorms: Children, computers, and powerful ideas*. New York: Basic Books.

Papert, S. (1991). Situating constructionism. In I. Harel & S. Papert (Eds.), *Constructionism* (pp. 1–11). Norwood, NJ: Ablex.

Papert, S., & Solomon, C. (1971). *Twenty things to do with a computer*. (Artificial Intelligence Memo No. 248.) Cambridge, MA: MIT AI Laboratory.

Resnick, M. (1993). Behavior construction kits. *Communications of the ACM, 36*(7):64–71.

Resnick, M. (1994). *Turtles, termites, and traffic jams*. Cambridge, MA: MIT Press.

Resnick, M., Ocko, S., & Papert, S. (1988). LEGO, Logo, and design. *Children's Environments Quarterly*, *5*(4), 14–18.

Weiser, M. (1991). The computer for the 21st century. *Scientific American*, *265*(3), 94–104.

Wellner, P., Mackay, W., & Gold, R., (Eds.). (1993). Computer augmented environments: Back to the real world. *Communications of the ACM*, *36*(7):24–26.

Wright, W. (1990). *SimCity*. Orinda, CA: Maxis.

PART III

LEARNING IN COMMUNITIES

Social Constructionism and the Inner City
Designing Environments for Social Development and Urban Renewal

Alan Shaw

INTRODUCTION

> Not very long ago, and in many parts of the world even today, young people would
> learn skills they could use in their work throughout life. Today, in industrial coun-
> tries, most people are doing jobs that did not exist when they were born. The most
> important skill determining a person's life pattern has already become the ability to
> learn new skills, to take in new concepts, to assess new situations, to deal with the
> unexpected. This will be increasingly true in the future: The competitive ability is
> the ability to learn. (Papert, 1993, p. vii)

As the rapid pace of change has become a common denominator in industrial
countries, it has become increasingly difficult for many people to adjust to the
new pressures they face. Consequently, there are those who are left with a
growing sense of alienation in modern settings, especially in big cities and
among the poor. In particular, for the underprivileged, the urban setting has
become less of a tight-knit community as neighbors have begun to distrust one
another as much as they have historically distrusted outsiders. As a larger proportion of our society has moved to the city, cities have become increasingly more
difficult places in which to live (Heilbrun, 1981, pp. 1, 6, 269).

> No one can doubt that most American cities these days are deeply troubled places.
> At the root of the problems are the massive economic shifts that have marked the
> last two decades. Hundreds of thousands of industrial jobs have either disappeared
> or moved away from the central city and its neighborhoods. And while many
> downtown areas have experienced a "renaissance," the jobs created there are differ-
> ent from those that once sustained neighborhoods. Either these new jobs are highly
> professionalized, and require elaborate education and credentials for entry, or they
> are routine, low-paying service jobs without much of a future. In effect, these shifts

in the economy, and particularly the disappearance of decent employment possibilities from low-income neighborhoods, have removed the bottom rung from the fabled American "ladder of opportunity." For many people in older city neighborhoods, new approaches to rebuilding their lives and communities, new openings toward opportunity, are a vital necessity. (Kretzmann & McKnight, 1993, p. 1)

In their introduction to *Building Communities From the Inside Out*, John Kretzmann and John McKnight (1993) argued that these are troubling times for our cities. Urban environments are experiencing economic shifts that are resulting in social upheaval. These unforeseen consequences are forcing many to rebuild the premises, the assumptions, and the institutions that serve as the organizational foundations for their lives and their communities.

Schools in urban America are experiencing enormous difficulties adjusting to the changes in the surrounding social setting. As issues concerning crime, violence, drug use, and teen sexuality become more prevalent, we are seeing record high drop-out rates and declining academic performance. In practically all big cities public schools are struggling with the attrition of a large percentage of their teenage student body. Many social theorists view the situation as one that will continue to worsen with no end in sight, especially in light of political realities that include shrinking budgets and declining commitment to public education (National Commission on Excellence in Education, 1983).

Without better methods for understanding the difficulties involved in urban experiences, much of the public debate is centered around how to *force* schools and students to perform, often by threatening to purge schools and students who fail. School departments are being blamed, teachers are being blamed, parents are being blamed, and the children themselves are being blamed. Assigning this blame, however, has done little to change the situation. This scenario is one of social retrenchment and retreat, but I believe that constructionist paradigms can help.

In this chapter I describe a theoretical framework for the concept of social constructionism, and within that framework I explore certain developmental ramifications faced within inner-city social settings. I attempt to demonstrate that by using constructionistic principles in the design and implementation of social activities and technologies, one can help to promote neighborhood environments that support profound examples of social development and urban renewal. I also describe a particular set of these activities and technologies that I have put to use in my research. In particular, I describe a telecommunications system designed according to these principles and producing concrete examples of this theory's urban potential.

CONSTRUCTIVISM, CONSTRUCTIONISM, AND THEIR SOCIAL EXTENSION

To understand the utility of constructionist theories in urban settings, it is important to understand the usage and efficacy of the concept in other settings. The academic usage of the word *constructionism*, which I am appropriating, expands on the concept known as *constructivism*. In social and developmental psychology, constructivist models view the subject as a builder of knowledge—not a passive receptor, but an active constructor. Theorists such as Jean Piaget attempt to describe how this building process takes place in order to better understand childhood learning and development (Piaget, 1954).

Constructionist thinking adds to the constructivist viewpoint. Where constructivism casts the subject as an active builder of knowledge, constructionism places a critical emphasis on particular constructions of the subject that are external and shared.

> We understand 'constructionism' as including, but going beyond, what Piaget would call 'constructivism.' The word with the v expresses the theory that knowledge is built by the learner, not supplied by the teacher. The word with the n expresses the further idea that this happens especially felicitously when the learner is engaged in the construction of something external or at least shareable . . . a sand castle, a machine, a computer program, a book. This leads us to a model using a cycle of internalization of what is outside, then externalization of what is inside and so on. (Papert, 1990, p. 3)

Constructionism highlights the notion that through the construction of shared outcomes and artifacts, a subject engages in a developmental cycle in the social setting. This focus on the shared nature of certain constructions opens the door to understanding how these ideas are linked to theories in the social and anthropological sciences that focus on processes that enable outcomes and artifacts to be actively constructed by groups of people, instead of simply by individuals. These outcomes and artifacts are social and cultural constructs. To Thomas Kuhn, for example, the constructs produced by the community of researchers who focus on "normal science" can be described as "shared paradigms" (Kuhn, 1970, pp. 10–11). Similarly, Michael Cole looks at cultural traditions and norms among the Kpelle tribe in Liberia as constructs serving as "functional cognitive systems" (Cole & Scribner, 1974, p. 194; Gay & Cole, 1967). In either case, the constructs are defined through the activities and characteristics of a particular social group that has functional objectives and needs.

Social constructionism extends the constructionist view by explicitly including as constructions the social relations and social activities that become shared outcomes and artifacts at work in the developmental cycle. To social constructionism, the social setting itself is an evolving construction. When the members of a social setting develop external and shared social constructs, they engage the setting in a cycle of development that is critical to determining the setting's ultimate form, as I examine in more detail later.

Constructivist notions have provided breakthroughs in outlining some of the hidden mechanisms that produce constructive and evolutionary individual developmental stages. Constructionist notions shed light on how internalized and externalized expressions of a subject's constructs interrelate and spur further development. Social constructionism focuses upon the developmental ramifications inherent in the social nature of certain constructions. There is a complementary nature to the interplay between these various areas of focus that can be fleshed out by examining certain aspects of the research of Lev Vygotsky.

Duality in Sociocultural and Cognitive Processes

Vygotsky pioneered a sociocultural approach to understanding cognitive processes in childhood development. Rather than focusing his research on uncovering the dynamics of mental activity in an isolated individual, he sought to reveal how social and cultural interactions were critical to the genesis of cognitive functions. In fact, he believed that it is our need to interact and communicate in the sociocultural context that makes human cognitive development intellectual and distinct from animal cognition (Vygotsky, 1978, pp. 28–29, 57).

By highlighting the effects of social interactions on cognitive development, Vygotsky reveals a critical role that external activities play in sparking internal mental constructions. Understanding this interplay, as Papert stated, is at the heart of constructionism's paradigm. Although these internal and external dynamics are cyclic, Vygotsky clearly views the external component (the shared and communicated experiences) as being primary in many key instances, such as when children develop the pointing gesture in a social context that later forms an internalized concept (Vygotsky, 1978, pp. 56–57). The communicative use of a sign by the child requires some type of internalized intellectual order, which can allow it to become meaningful and reusable to the child, and Vygotsky demonstrates that this internal order can be initiated by the external context of social relations. This primary role played by external relations suggests that profound implications are involved in the effects that social and cultural settings have on individuals during developmental stages. In fact, Vygotsky (1978) went so far as to claim that *all* higher mental functions evolve from social relations:

> Every function in the child's cultural development appears twice: first, on the social level, and later, on the individual level; first *between* people (*interpsychological*), and then *inside* the child (*intrapsychological*). This applies equally to voluntary attention, to logical memory, and to the formation of concepts. All the higher functions originate as actual relations between human individuals. (p. 57)

Vygotsky's emphasis on the priority of the social level in all higher mental functions has drawn considerable fire from constructivist critiques arguing that many internalized mental structures evolve before being exposed to the sociocultural milieu (Bereiter 1994; Carey & Gelman, 1991). However, it is essential not to let this important critique detract from the idea that the social and the individual areas of intellectual development are both critical planes to consider. Vygotsky's sociocultural focus and the more classical constructivist's individualized focus can find harmony, as Paul Cobb recently argued from a constructivist viewpoint when he stated, "Each of the two perspectives, the sociocultural and the constructivist, tells half of a good story, and each can be used to complement the other" (Cobb, 1994, p. 17). He developed this point further when comparing Barbara Rogoff's (1990) sociocultural viewpoint to Ernst von Glasersfeld's (1995) Piagetian perspective:

> In comparing Rogoff's and von Glasersfeld's work, it can be noted that Rogoff's view of learning as acculturation via guided participation implicitly assumes an actively constructing child. Conversely, von Glasersfeld's view of learning as cognitive self-organization implicitly assumes that the child is participating in cultural practices. In effect, active individual construction constitutes the background against which guided participation in cultural practices comes to the fore for Rogoff, and this participation is the background against which self-organization comes to the fore for von Glasersfeld. (Cobb, 1994, p. 17)

From the viewpoint of urban social anthropology, Elizabeth Bott (1971) came to a similar conclusion. She argued that the sociological concept of internalization of sociocultural experiences needs to be balanced with the psychological concept of internal cognitive reorganization:

> The basic argument of both chapters is that people do not acquire their ideology, norms, and values solely by internalizing them from outside. They also re-work the standards they have internalized, conceptualize them in a new form, and project them back on to the external situation. The more varied their social experience and the more unconnected the standards they internalize, the more internal rearrangement they must make. (Bott, 1971, p. 223)

> In brief, I had to give up the attempt to interpret norms and roles as social and entirely externally determined and role performance as internal and psychologically determined. Sociological and psychological concepts were now used simultaneously at every stage of the analysis. (p. 229)

Constructionism offers an important bridge for the sociocultural and constructivist viewpoints by arguing that individual developmental cycles are enhanced by shared constructive activity in the social setting. *Social* constructionism adds further harmony to sociocultural and constructivist views by revealing that the social setting is also enhanced by the developmental activity of the individual. The duality of this interplay has important ramifications for urban social conditions. If the constructionist notion that shared constructions and social relations are key to individual development, then social settings marked by fractured and limited social activity and less cohesive social relations—as is the case in many urban settings—may present troubling developmental barriers. However, because the social setting is not immutable, introducing socially constructive activities may provide rectifying responses. Indeed, this possibility speaks to the need for better insight into the nature of the developmental processes involved in social settings. This insight is the goal of social constructionism's inquiry.

The Paradigm of Social Constructionism

From the mindset of social constructionism, social settings are not viewed as simply neutral grounds in which developmental activities take place, but they are seen instead as intimately involved with the process and outcome of that development.

> All builders need materials to build with. Where I am at variance with Piaget is in the role I attribute to the surrounding cultures as a source of these materials. In some cases the culture supplies them in abundance, thus facilitating constructive Piagetian learning. For example, the fact that so many important things (knives and forks, mothers and fathers, shoes and socks) come in pairs is a 'material' for the construction of an intuitive sense of number. But in many cases where Piaget would explain the slower development of a particular concept by its greater complexity or formality, I see the critical factor as the relative poverty of the culture in those materials that would make the concept simple and concrete. In yet other cases the culture may provide materials but block their use. (Papert, 1980, pp. 7–8)

Here, Papert points out that the sociocultural context may be providing materials necessary for the building of particular internal cognitive structures. He makes the point that cultural materials can even form concrete bases for certain conceptual underpinnings. Uri Wilensky (1991) took this point further when he argued that making a concept concrete is not always an act of merely simplifying the idea, but it is also one of creating new well-defined relationships to the idea:

> The above discussion leads us to see that concreteness is not a property of an object but rather a *property of a person's relationship to an object*. Concepts that were hopelessly abstract at one time can become concrete for us if we get in the 'right relationship' with them. (Wilensky, 1991, p. 198)

He then compared these relationships in the cognitive domain to social relations between people:

> It is through people's own idiosyncratically personal ways of connecting to other people that meaningful relationships are established. In a similar way, when learners are in an environment in which they construct their own relationships with the objects of knowledge, these relationships can become deeply meaningful and profound. (Wilensky, 1991, p. 202)

In this view, developing personal cognitive constructs and shared social constructs are both a function of building relationships. One is internal, the other is external. In one case "objects of knowledge" are involved, and in the other case additional subjects are involved. However, both cases involve profoundly meaningful experiences, so the mechanisms through which such experiences happen within any given environment are very consequential. These mechanisms are involved with the sociocultural activities and processes that the members of a setting engage in, and they can be seen as functions of a three-part social constructionist paradigm.

To understand this paradigm, it is important to understand that in any given social setting, certain social relationships and relationships to cultural materials already exist. When sociocultural activities and social and cognitive processes act in the context of those preexisting relations, outcomes are formed that make up new internalized and externalized constructs. These constructs can bring about development in the internal cognitive order and in the external social order. This suggests a three-part synergy. The social setting presents a context of *social relations and cultural materials* that sets the stage for *sociocultural activities and processes* through which developmental *internalized and externalized constructs* can be formed. These constructs can further influence the setting and cause it to evolve by changing existent relationships; adding or altering cultural materials, activities, and processes; and fostering new cognitive and social developments. Each of these components—social relations and cultural materials, sociocultural activities and processes, and internalized and externalized constructs—are influenced by one another. Nothing is static here. As individuals in the social setting develop, constructs are produced, relationships and activities are affected, and the setting evolves.

Another way to understand this three-part breakdown is to see the processes and sociocultural activities referred to as Piagetian and Vygotskian developmental processes and mechanisms (i.e., schools are a sociocultural activity where Piagetian and Vygotskian learning processes occur). The internal and external constructs are Papert's constructionist artifacts, and the social relations and cultural materials are the social context for developing social constructions. There are five types of social constructions that I focused on during the field work for my research:

1. *Social relationships.*   The social relationships in question are the friendships, the familial relationships, the partnerships, and the varied associations that people actively develop and maintain in their social setting.

2. *Social events.*   The social events are the potlucks, the block parties, the Easter egg hunts, and the other activities that will not happen unless people come together and organize them.

3. *Shared physical artifacts.*   The shared physical artifacts are things like wall murals, community gardens, a public well, a swing or a basketball hoop, or any shared space that neighbors build or maintain through their own efforts or expense.

4. *Shared social goals and projects.*   The shared social goals are the impetus for things such as keeping the streets clean; donating food or clothing to those in need; helping the very young and the elderly; or participating in shared economic activity, crime watches, and democratic processes such as voting.

The shared social projects are the activities involved in accomplishing the social goals, but these goals and projects are only social constructions if the primary active proponents for them come from within the social setting.

5. *Shared cultural norms and traditions.*   The cultural norms and traditions are things such as shared dialects, music, styles of interacting and dressing, an accepted neighborhood identity, and the organizational processes that people are comfortable with, including town hall meetings, neighborhood workshops, and church participation.

This paradigm applies for all social settings whether it is a grade school classroom, a scientific research community, or an urban neighborhood. When social relations are fractured and social interactions and communications are strained, the social setting is affected and the developmental and evolutionary processes are disrupted. Conversely, when social relations are not damaged, the interactions and processes in the setting spur individual and social development, which has an evolutionary effect on the setting. Social constructionism makes the claim that the individual and the social planes are intrinsically linked, that developmental activity is a matter of both internalized construction and externalized constructive interaction. Understanding the issues that make for a positive or negative outcome provides insights into finding adaptive responses to one's social setting, even when that social setting is unstable and unpromising.

The Praxis of Social Constructionism

Before examining what a paradigm like social constructionism implies about certain urban conditions, it can be helpful to use the following model to think about a remote social setting, thus weighing the paradigm's utility. In *Mindstorms*, Papert (1980) described a Brazilian social setting developed around the context of the carnival in Rio de Janeiro; this is a description of the samba school, which has become a classic example of a social setting with important learning and developmental experiences:

> For example, at the core of the famous carnival in Rio de Janeiro is a twelve-hour-long procession of song, dance, and street theater. . . . The processions are not spontaneous. Preparing them as well as performing in them are important parts of Brazilian life. Each group prepares separately—and competitively—in its own learning environment, which is called a samba school. These are not schools as we know them; they are social clubs with memberships that may range from a few hundred to many thousands. . . . Members of the school range in age from children to grandparents and in ability from novice to professional. But they dance together and as they dance everyone is learning and teaching as well as dancing. . . . Every American disco is a place for learning as well as for dancing. But the samba schools are very different. There is greater social cohesion, a sense of belonging to a group, and a sense of common purpose.

In this book we have considered how mathematics might be learned in settings that resemble the Brazilian samba school, in settings that are real, socially cohesive, and where experts and novices are all learning. The samba school, although not 'exportable' to an alien culture, represents a set of attributes a learning environment should and could have. Learning is not separate from reality. The samba school has a purpose, and learning is integrated in the school for this purpose. Novice is not separated from expert, and the experts are also learning (pp. 178–179).

Within this informal social setting people come together to work on something that is very much a part of their relationships and commonalities. It involves "social cohesion, a sense of belonging to a group, and a sense of common purpose," It also involves learning and development at some profound levels. Indeed, the samba school is what the concept of social constructionism is all about. Everyone is being developed: "Novice is not separated from expert, and the experts are also learning." Here is a practical example of social constructionism's three-part paradigm. The samba school itself—with its traditional routines and learning environment—represents the *sociocultural activities and processes* that bring people together. Coming together establishes or reinforces certain *social relations* between the participants, which—along with the music, the instruments, the costumes, and the activities themselves—provide the *cultural materials* used to construct in this setting. Finally, the constructive acts lead to *internalized* learning and development with the *externalized* constructs being the new and old dances and routines, which act to define and redefine the school itself. This is a social setting representing a learning environment that is always alive and evolving.

UNDERSTANDING THE URBAN SETTING

Unfortunately, urban conditions often make it difficult for these types of environments to exist. To understand why, I think it is necessary to intimately understand the urban setting. In fact, I have spent the past 6 years researching these questions in the inner city community where I live, a neighborhood in the Dorchester area of Boston. This community is struggling with many of the troubling concerns that worry big city residents. It is a predominantly black and Hispanic urban community known as Four Corners. Primarily a low-income community, it is marked by especially fragmented and alienated relationships among neighbors, making it very difficult for residents to pull together as concerned parties to address common issues. In Appendix A, I document some disturbing personal and statistical information about the economic and social realities confronted by this community.

Why did so many relationships break down in the first place in urban communities? It could have to do with the requirements of the new modes of production in our rapidly changing world, such as the need for increased mobility in the work force and the growing population in urban centers. For the underprivileged, the economy has not provided stable living patterns, and perhaps this is also a factor. Incidents of crime, violence, and drug addiction are generally on the rise. Whatever the causes, the breakdown in relations among the young and the old and between one neighbor and the next has had devastating effects on social environments. In turn, these environments are robbing young people of rich developmental opportunities and activities. How can this be changed?

Social Constructionism and the Urban Setting

There are at least two types of approaches that can be taken when attempting to address the difficulties faced by those who live in the inner city. One focuses on what institutions and individuals outside the inner city can do, whereas the other focuses on what can be done by those within that setting. Both are important to consider, but it often seems that we lack theories and models that focus on internal development, so the approach most commonly adopted concerns what outside forces can and should do to *fix* the inner city, rather than how internal forces can make an impact. Although outside support is valuable, it cannot fix the inner city any more than a teacher can fix a student. If the teacher is doing the fixing, then the student is passively being fixed. Constructivist development, however, requires an active learner. A relevant comparison can be drawn between the fact that children caught in certain passive educational models often lose developmental opportunities, whereas members of social settings can similarly lose developmental opportunities when they are caught in passive roles in those environments.

Social constructionism stresses an active model of the subjects who make up the social setting. Yet in urban settings, passive models often dominate the social agenda. Rather than settings where members see themselves as agents of change, urban residents often feel that there is nothing that they can do to bring about much change in their communities. As in the constructivist critique of corresponding educational settings, the subject is a passive receptor rather than an active constructor, which disrupts both the development of the individual and the setting.

Focusing on efforts that stress social constructionist models can help to provide new options for urban communities. Developing research projects in this area is therefore an important issue to consider, and I believe that such projects are not very difficult to conceive. Because creating shared externalized constructs is important to constructionist theories, this is one concrete area where investigations can focus. Thought must be given to ways that neighbors can take advantage of some methods for developing social constructions. A social construction is simply a shared artifact, which can be either an object or an activity. A social construction might be anything from a wall mural to a summer festival to a food coop. Projects that change some qualitative or quantitative aspect of community life represent important areas of relevant constructions, so investigating different types of activities and tools that might become catalysts for the development of such constructions has become a clear point of my research.

Social Constructionism and Appropriate Tools

Long ago, urban residents were more actively involved in creating social constructions. However, the rapid pace of change in modern cities has left many without a clear sense of what can be done in their current context. This lack of vision is related to a lack of appropriate tools for social constructions. The need for appropriate tools in the social settings is not a peripheral issue. In fact, it is central. Tools represent the opportunities and artifacts in the social setting necessary to mediate developmental activities. Indeed, the very term *instrumental* points to this. Instruments are always critical. An active builder will naturally develop tools that serve as instruments in the building process. Tools can be empowering, because without effective tools, a task may be too difficult to be viable. This issue was of critical importance to Vygotsky:

> The third theme in Vygotsky's writings is the claim that higher mental functioning is mediated by tools and signs. . . . The fundamental claim here is that human activity (on both the interpsychological and the intrapsychological plane) can be understood only if we take into consideration the 'technical tools' and 'psychological tools' or 'signs' that mediate this activity. These forms of mediation, which are products of the sociocultural milieu in which they exist, are not viewed as simply facilitating activity that would otherwise take place. Instead, they are viewed as fundamentally shaping and defining it. (Wertsch, 1990, p. 114)

A social setting can become impoverished in certain areas of activity due to a lack of appropriate tools. Therefore, it is important to examine various tools that are available and relevant in urban settings. In my research, I have found that some extremely useful tools to consider are certain telecommunications systems. One of the most difficult problems that I encountered in my work in Four Corners was the lack of organizational infrastructure in the neighborhood. From my experience I knew how difficult it was to develop the types of social connections and networks necessary to establish well-coordinated social activities in an urban community. However, neighborhood computer networks and communal databases are demonstrating that large numbers of people can contribute to the organization and development of very complicated systems of information while remaining informal and social. Whether it is a gaming environment, as in the case of various computer networks known as MUDs (Multi-User Dungeons), or whether it is a BBS (Bulletin Board System) developed around special interests, networking is a tool opening the door to new organizational potential in various social settings.

This issue touches on a concept adopted by the Clinton Administration in its push to develop the National Information Infrastructure (NII). The concept is called the "information commons" (U.S. Department of Commerce, 1993). It calls for establishing local computer networks that can provide the infrastructure for on-line neighborhood services and electronic forums. Lee Felsenstein (1993) argued that this use of computer networks can reestablish the communal atmosphere of the village commons or the "agora" (a Greek word for the city-state's place of assembly) in urban communities. In fact, he believes that the loss of these types of spaces has contributed to the deteriorating conditions in urban settings.

> The degree to which such a 'village square' is unavailable to people is, I maintain, the degree to which people are strangers to each other, and this situation is directly related to the development of social pathologies such as criminality, alcoholism, brutality, and the like. I claim that we all have an inherent need for the function of the village square, which I call the 'function of the agora.' (Felsenstein, 1993, p. 18)

> As urbanization proceeded, a somewhat similar process of privatization of the commons of information took place. The place where people could gather and exchange information began to lose its function to the gradually centralizing mass media. . . . I remember the moment in 1969 when I looked out my window down the street and saw all the living room windows glowing with the blue light of TV. I realized that they were all getting their information from Walter Cronkite in New York, but that we had no ready way to get information from each other. (p. 19)

Working in Four Corners I learned that neighborhood-based electronic networks can indeed provide viable organizational infrastructures for communities that are having a difficult time pulling together. However, before I learned this, I made an effort at organizing activities for social constructionism without this type of tool. In the next section, I discuss a set of initial activities that I organized in Four Corners that aimed to create active social networks in the community without explicitly incorporating computer networks. Following that, I discuss a more recent project of mine, which did make use of a computer network to accomplish the same goal.

SUMMER PROJECTS: 1990–1994

I do not believe there are any magical cures to problems facing inner-city communities, but in my work over the past four summers, I have seen some very encouraging results that I believe present important signs of hope. Each of these summers I organized a group of teenagers—many were former gang members—to work and learn together with me as we sought to figure out ways that they could develop meaningful projects and find employment in their own neighborhood during the months while school was out. There were 15 boys and girls the first summer, about 25 in each of the next two summers, 38 after that, and 30 during this past summer.

There is nothing new in the fact that most of these youth usually could not find jobs during the summer and that many of them had previously become involved in illegal activities to raise money during those months of the year. Each year over half of the teenage participants we worked with had extensive court records and seemed to be in a persistent cycle of dangerous activity. In fact, most of their parents were adamant about the need for them to find summer jobs to keep them off the streets, and the results seem to bear out their parents' concerns. During our first summer together, none of the youth were arrested until 2 weeks after the program ended, when three of the boys were locked up. The next year, none of the youth were arrested again, although one was committed to the Department of Youth Services (DYS) by his mother because he had become too difficult for her to handle. During the third summer, one young man was arrested midway through the program, but again no one was arrested during our fourth and fifth summers when we had our largest groups of teenagers.

Because getting a job was so important to the teenagers and their parents, we focused each summer on projects addressing that issue. We tried to come up with activities that people would pay youth to do in their own neighborhoods. This meant, though, that the young people had to learn skills that were valued by their neighbors. To learn these skills, the youth had to find someone who was willing to apprentice them, so during the first two summers, a few assistants and I taught them how to fix basic appliances. The young people used this skill to run a business fixing appliances for their neighbors for a fee [see the next section]. We experienced both successes and failures during these projects, but we were encouraged enough to try the third summer to expand the type of services the youth offered to their neighbors. We surveyed the neighborhood to determine what things the neighbors might be interested in having the youth do. We also wanted to see if other neighbors might be interested in developing apprenticeships with some of the youth to teach them additional skills relevant to the services.

As time went on, we worked to build a database chronicling the talents, resources, and assets among the neighbors in the local community that might be available to the kids as they sought to offer their services [see the section on Project II]. In the end, the job became too big for us to complete, although the issues we addressed were a necessary first step, and the database project continued into the fourth summer. Finally, a neighborhood computer network began to take shape from all of this work, as we attempted to find a better way for accessing and communicating the information that we were attempting to compile in the database.

In the following sections, I detail these activities and examine their implications through the lens of social constructionism. I divide the activities into two main projects, one centered around an environment for urban apprenticeships, and the other focusing on a neighborhood computer database and network.

Project I: Urban Apprenticeships

During the first summer, the initial plan was to set up a program to help the participants develop skills in appliance repair, but that was not all. My fellow trainers and I also wanted to engage young people in the development of their own social setting as they resolved certain economic issues that they faced. We designed the project with the model of the samba school in mind: young and old working and learning together with a common goal while remaining informal and social, and yet producing many individual outcomes and social constructions. A few other neighbors and I apprenticed the young people during the first two summer. As we taught and learned about the basics of electrical appliances with the kids, we discovered many other things as well, as the following quote from one of the participants reveals:

> well since i have been in this program i have learned alot about computers and circuits boards. for example on the computer, i learn about the mouse and how it is run. i also learnet how to move the mouse and how it is run and how it enables me to get access to certain things on the computer. i learned how to drag point and click wile using the mouse and that was kind of fun . . . wile on the circuit board i learnet about wires and how to connect wires to the connectors also switches. anyway i think this program is very educational interesting and enjoying. on yesterday i learnet how to use the sourdering iron by connecting the lights and joining them together with other wires then to the battery . . . (From the journal of Keneon Isaac, July, 1990)

We worked in the basement of a local church during the first two summers. The program lasted 8 weeks each summer. There were 15 participants the first year, and 25 participants the second, with ages ranging from 15 to 18. During the first 4 weeks of the summer we focused on training in appliance repair, and during the second 4 weeks we focused on organizing the neighborhood repair service. We developed a loosely structured curriculum for the training phase of the project that focused on learning about electricity (current flow, voltage, etc.), circuitry (wiring, soldering, etc.), and the mechanical components in appliances (motors, gears, etc.). In the second half of the summer, the youth made fliers and business cards to advertise their services. Then they hit the streets in an effort to find customers.

Appliance Repair Training: Samba School Style

> On the computers me and my paartner were with the mouse to try to find out how it works, and i found it to be very easy, and very suitable. The same day we worked on the board, at first i tought it was hard, but soon as we got to the board i found out that it was very easy, if you [know] what you were doing, if you don't i feel very soory for you.
>
>   Last week we also learned a little about word processing which i already know about from school, and i really like typing and i love to work on the computer. This

july fourth i went to the brockton fair it was nice, but i lost my wallet i had no money in it, but I lost my liscence in my wallet. know i have to pay thirty five dollars to get it back. (From the journal of Jean Auguste, July, 1990)

To come up with activities to help us teach about electricity and circuitry, we used materials known as the "Mystery Boards" project, developed by Tim Barclay of the Technical Education Research Center in Cambridge (TERC), and we used a *Time-Life* home repair manual and a *Reader's Digest* fix-it-yourself manual. Barclay's Mystery Board project is a simple exercise designed to provide students with a tool to investigate electrical connections and simple circuits. The students built the boards in Fig. 8.1 out of a cardboard, batteries, lights, switches, and wires. Any number and configuration of batteries, lights, and switches can be used. Once the students have designed their boards, they soider the components onto them. Then they attach wires from one end of the power sources to the lights and from the other end of the power sources to the switches. Next, they decide on light patterns they would like to achieve and determine what type of wiring from the switches to the lights can create that pattern. The students then challenge other participants to duplicate their patterns on different boards.

When we started to do the board construction, first we cut the connectors, and the lights. Then we hook up the wires with the batteries and the lights. When we finished all that, we took a long black wire and connect it to the power source and the other end to each of the four parts of the connectors and the lights come on each and every time we try it. After that we knew that our connections was alright and everything was in the right place. So our next step is to connect some more wires with the switches. (From the journal of Max Bresca, July, 1990)

By having each student create these simple circuit boards from start to finish, we were able to make transparent the principles involved in each of the components. After a time, the basic ideas behind the flow of current through the wiring on their mystery boards were clear enough for each student to apply to the ideas behind the flow of current through circuits and electrical wiring in home appliances. This made the *Time-Life* and *Reader's Digest* manuals easier to understand, because the most common issue that needs to be addressed in appliance

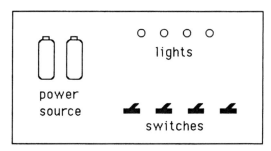

FIG. 8.1.   Mystery board.

repair concerns rewiring. We looked at broken flashlights, lamps, toasters, and fans and, with the diagrams and step-by-step instructions in our manuals, we treated them like extensions of our mystery boards and learned to rewire them. As in the samba school example, each of the participants developed their own constructions (the mystery boards) and were able to play with them, change them, and add their own design and innovations to them as they saw fit. This produced an environment for learning things that could be applied to other problems that this group had come together to address, namely figuring out how to repair appliances.

Developing a Neighborhood Service.   The second half of the summer project focused on developing a neighborhood appliance repair service. The young people developed fliers and business cards announcing their services to their neighbors. They walked around their neighborhood, going door-to-door some-times to get the word out. These efforts met with mixed results. One reason for this was that some of the youth were good at representing themselves to the adults in the community, whereas others were not. Figures 8.2a and 8.2b show two of the more successful business cards that certain kids created; Figs. 8.2c and 8.2d are examples of the less successful ones.

a.   b.

c.   d.

FIG. 8.2. Young people's business cards.

Some of the participants, particularly those who seemed to have some level of involvement with local gangs, clearly needed to represent some of their desire for a sinister reputation in their business cards. However, even with the cards that were not especially useful in attracting customers, the experience of developing the cards seemed to make the whole idea of running a neighbor appliance repair service more real and achievable to the participants.

Another reason that attracting customers seemed difficult at times was that the group worked from 9:00 a.m. to 3:00 p.m. on the weekdays when most of their neighbors were not at home. During that first summer, therefore, the young people only received about 25 appliances from their neighbors. They were able to fix 15 of them. Those 15 successes over a 4-week period provided great moments of satisfaction, but they did not prove the enterprise to be viable, because on average there was only one successful repair per participant. The next summer, when we had 10 more participants, we actually ended up with even fewer appliances to repair because I had a difficult time finding assistants that summer, and coordinating the project for 25 teenagers proved to be too much for me.

Understanding the Lessons Learned.   During the first summer, we celebrated our modest successes on the last night of the program. We had an awards ceremony to which parents and community members were invited. Each of the participants received an award identifying their particular contribution to the program, and each participant was given a trophy. It was a very emotional night. Many of the neighbors who came did not know the kids personally, but some said they were very impressed by what they saw.

> The awards ceremony was a good community building event. It gave a chance for neighbors to see some young people who have done something positive with their summer. And I really like that it was all home-grown. The kids were neighbors, the ones who gave out the awards were neighbors and just about everybody who came that night were neighbors. This is the type of local initiative that helps build up neighborhood pride. (Mark Scott, a neighbor in Four Corners)

However, as we discovered the second summer, there simply were not enough adults involved in this project to give the teenagers adequate support in creating local services. Furthermore, we decided we should try to do other services in addition to appliance repair to better represent the range of interests and talents among the youth involved. We came up with a number of potential services, such as videotaping, landscaping, baking, and word processing. Yet this only increased our need for greater involvement by other adults who could take on some of the apprenticeships. We needed to get a better sense of how many people in our neighborhood would be interested in this kind of activity, and we wanted a better idea of the talents and resources in the neighborhood to help us better conceive what services were possible. Accordingly, during the third summer, we decided to try to build a directory and database of the local personalities, skills, talents and resources that existed in our neighborhood.

Project II: Neighborhood Networking and Community Building

The appliance repair service was a social construction that the youth worked on in order to improve their economic plight. Yet by working on this project, the young people began to see the need for greater cooperation and support from their neighbors. As neighbors acted to apprentice the youth, and others made use of their services, the neighbors began to create a type of interdependence with them that could lead to the social cohesion Papert pointed to in the example of the samba schools. This is a model of approaches encouraging members in an urban social setting to invest in the relationships that can bring about the developmental synergy of the social constructionist paradigm.

However, as one of those neighbors, I found it difficult to help the young people organize an effective outreach to their neighborhood, given the size of the population and the complexity in peoples' lives that makes them too busy, too distrustful, or too disorganized to get involved. Some type of local infrastructure was sorely needed to assist the kids in their outreach efforts and make it easier for the neighbors to connect with what was going on. During the third summer, my wife and I attempted to help the participants pull together the information they might need to establish a more structured approach at outreach. To this end, we surveyed the neighborhood and put the information into a directory and database.

During this same summer, my wife began teaching word processing to the youth as a potential service, and I worked on teaching videotaping and computer maintenance. By the end of the summer, our surveys had not been very successful, and our new services had not gotten off the ground. Once again, it was clear, we needed to get more of the adult neighbors involved. Throughout the next year, this began to happen, and we found ourselves in need of better ways to coordinate neighborhood activities and share critical information. We found that by networking computers placed in the homes of the most involved neighbors and youth, we were able to create a type of organizational infrastructure that we have just recently begun to make use of and evaluate. Many new projects and relationships have formed because of the opportunities this network has provided.

MUSIC.   The neighborhood computer network I created is called MUSIC (Multi-User Sessions In Community). It is a BBS application that I designed, wrote, and developed at the MIT Media Laboratory to facilitate sharing information and organizing programs run by neighborhood residents. The server for the network is in my home, connected to six phone lines—which limits the number of people who can have simultaneous access. We put the client software on 18 computers in specific homes in the community. Eight people already had

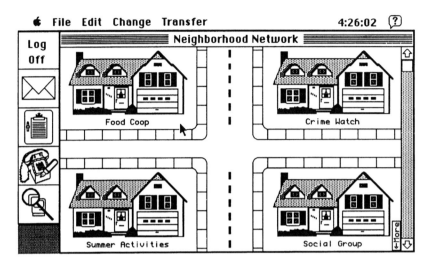

FIG. 8.3.   MUSIC's graphical user interface.

computers in their homes, and others were given computers so that they could participate in my research. I had 10 computers to give out, and I gave them to neighbors of mine who had already been involved in some local organizing efforts. I was interested in seeing whether those who had already shown interest in neighborhood activism could be more effective working with the network.

MUSIC has been designed in the spirit of the public market-place of ideas. There are various documents and information on the system that anyone can access, modify, remove, or add. However, there is also support for private communications and information storage. Each account has its own private electronic mailbox, and there is one set of documents put on by members of a local church that can be accessed only by members of that church. There are also news stories put on by the Boston Globe that anyone on the network can read, but only the Globe can modify.

In keeping with current user-interface trends for this type of system, the database in MUSIC has been developed around certain spatial and visual metaphors. The system is designed with a graphical user interface (GUI) modeled after a neighborhood with streets and buildings (see Fig. 8.3). The buildings represent the neighborhood programs being organized on the system, and data is stored in the "rooms" of the various buildings.

Rooms are organized around different topics and discussions. Users can enter a room and add information to its "objects" (e.g., text, pictures or recordings), or they can engage in real-time text and voice communications in the "chat" mode (see Fig. 8.4). When a user enters a room, his or her icon shows up in the "Insiders:" column along with the icon of anyone else who is currently in that room. By clicking on a user's icon, another user can enter a chat with that user.

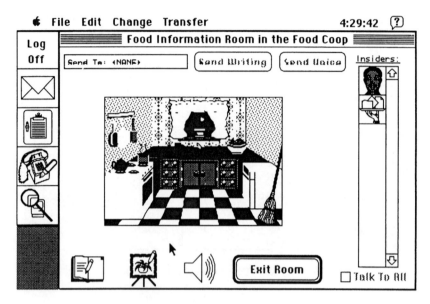

FIG. 8.4.   A room in MUSIC.

Most people on the system have Macintosh computers with microphones built right into their monitors. Thus, users can just talk into their screen and have their voice messages sent over to another user's computer and played on that computer's speaker. The more traditional text chatting mode is also support.

Electronic mail and bulletin board facilities are also included. You can send text, graphics, or recordings as mail. Each user has both a name and a person

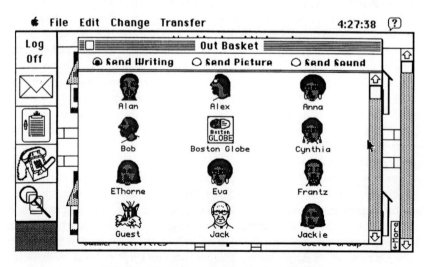

FIG. 8.5.   Icons for outgoing mail on MUSIC.

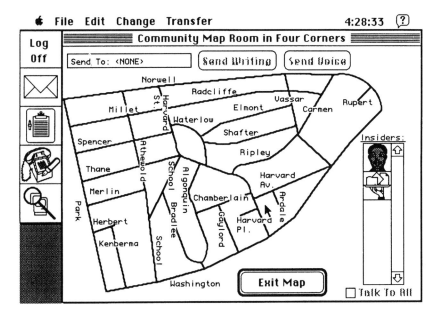

FIG. 8.6.   The map room in MUSIC.

alized icon identifying them on the system. To send mail to someone, you just click on that person's icon (see Fig. 8.5). By recording a sound message with the computer's microphone, a user can send and receive voice-mail on the MUSIC system.

A special map room also exists, which allows users to get information about a resident in the neighborhood by simply clicking on that person's street—which brings up a list of names of the residents who live on that street—and then clicking on that person's name (Fig. 8.6).

Using MUSIC.   Thirty-nine adults and young people are currently connected to MUSIC, which means, on average, more than two people per household has an account. Because the neighbors have the computers in their own homes, they can log on at any time of the day or night. Some have used the network to discuss and debate community issues. Others have placed drawings and poetry on the network. Still others have organized potlucks, group trips, and various social gatherings on the network. The network is also being used to organize the neighborhood apprenticeships, as well as other community projects, including a food co-op and crime watch. A few outside groups are also involved with the network. As I mentioned earlier, the Boston Globe daily downloads to the network stories related to topics of special interest that concern the neighbors. Moreover, individuals from a nearby health center and members from other community agencies and churches log on regularly to promote various projects in which they are involved. During the summer of 1994, a public school in the Four Corners neighborhood opened itself to the community during the day, which allowed public access to a few additional computers during this period. Twenty more people started accounts during that summer for a total of about 60 accounts. However, when the summer ended, these accounts generally could not be used because the computers were no longer available.

It is difficult to determine all of the activity that occurs on the network. A record is kept of when people log on and log off and whether or not they send mail, check the bulletin board, read news articles, modify or read documents, enter a chat with someone, or check the directory or other on-line information. However, no record is kept of the content of any user's mail, chats, or documents. A user must give me explicit permission to see or use any of this content. Therefore, there are probably many things which happened on-line with MUSIC about which I do not know. I did, however, ask people to let me know whenever something they thought significant occurred if they did not mind me publishing it. These are the things that I discuss here, along with some raw data about generic usage patterns.

Over a period of a year, many projects were organized on-line, most of them either directly or indirectly related to a few core projects. The core projects were the summer youth programs, the crime watch, the social activities, and the church neighborhood outreach activities. About 90% of the log-ins to the system occurred when people were participating in one of these projects. About 95% of the text documents placed on the system were created by users involved in running one of these neighborhood projects. What these two statistics told me was that most users did not log in much unless they were actively involved in an on-line project, and the more critical their role in a project, the more likely they were to develop on-line documentation concerning the project.

However, there were some exceptions to this rule. Some users put some pieces of their own original artwork on the system; two users put several pieces of poetry on-line; and one user published a paper on-line that he had written on Black theology. A number of other users posted interesting bulletin topics, one third of which were job notices. The total number of users involved in this type of publishing activity came to about 10, or one fourth of the total number of users. For these users, publishing information on-line did not require having some explicit connection to the ongoing projects.

The most common usage of the system has been for electronic mail (E-mail)—about 78% of the time that users were on-line. About 16% of the time was spent browsing documents, reading news, and checking the bulletin board, whereas only about 6% of the time was spent adding new documents, editing old documents on the system, or doing other things. Three of the 39 users consistently sent more mail out to groups (which can be done through a "CC" facility) than to individuals. Everyone else sent mail most frequently to individuals. This particular statistic shows that just under one tenth of the users seem to have taken on the role of "information providers" for some subgroup of the other users.

The system was designed to help residents organize and manage neighborhood programs, and I believe that it was successful in this. Eleven projects that I know of were organized and run with the help of the network during the last year, and two of the projects—the first two listed below—had very large budgets. Eleven projects supported by 39 people is a high level of activity, and it is quite possible that other projects may have happened that escaped my notice. The 11 projects organized or supported by the network were these:

1. A summer jobs program for neighborhood teenagers.
2. A group trip to Jamaica.
3. A group letter to a woman in Brazil.
4. A poetry collection.
5. A discussion about Black religious issues.
6. Discussions about the Black community.
7. Discussions about local neighborhood development.
8. Some potlucks and parties.
9. Crime watch information updates.
10. A neighborhood food cooperative project.
11. An on-line newsgroup with the help of the Boston Globe.

Of course, user activity was not uniformly distributed. In fact, five of the people with accounts never logged on even once. Another six logged on only two or three times. Just under half of the users logged on a little over twice a week on the average, and another 10 users logged on more frequently than that. Two of the users, who were "information providers," logged on almost every night during certain weeks.

These usage patterns reveal that the users of MUSIC were involved in many different levels and types of activity. Some were very seriously involved, whereas others were relatively serious. Still others were not at all serious about using the system. Natural roles developed within the system based on the interest level of the various users. A good percentage appreciated and applied MUSIC's organizational potential, whereas others did not. Yet just about everyone enjoyed using it as a medium for such interpersonal communications as the following:

```
From: Tiffany
Date: 12-01-93, 10:07:40 PM
Title: Network ?
Sent to: <Server>
```

Hi, Alan, Michelle and Chinua!

My first full-time MUSIC experience! I love it. Thanks so much, Alan, this is such a wonderful way to communicate with everyone.

I have a small technical question, Alan (or Michelle - my dea-
conness is BAD). How do I change my icon (Tara and I look like
twins)?
No rush, get back to me when you can. God bless.

Tiffany

From: Mark
Date: 02-24-94, 5:45:58 PM
Title: MUSIC IS GOOD
Sent to: Alan

Alan,

I was just thinking about what makes MUSIC so great! It is
better than other networking schemes (like the Internet and
CompuServe) because it is actually based in a real community,
neighborhood, and village. The virtual network is just that—
virtual, not real. Then the faces, homes, and maps brings you
closer to the people you are talking to.

When I am sending stuff to Azusa folks it just like a fellow-
ship gathering. Sending this note to you is like talking to
you. I would say this system makes a major contribution to
building community.

Mark

Making Beautiful MUSIC.   On the average day throughout the year that I
monitored the network, nothing remarkable happened. However, every now and
then there were some especially exciting experiences that I could never have
predicted. In one instance, within weeks of setting up the network, the 4-year-old
son of a woman on the system learned how to log on and began sending E-mail to
various people at random. He could hardly read, and he did not even know most
of the people to whom he sent his E-mail. In light of social constructionism
theory, this activity helped him to develop new internalized conceptual relationships and new externalized social relationships. MUSIC was an appropriate tool
sitting on his mother's desk in the right place at the right time.

From: Cynthia
Date: 10-01-93, 1:54:41 PM
Title: hi al
Sent to: Alan

Hi Alan,

We are having fun already. Omari has sent out about 6 messages
and helped me to give my icon a hair cut. We also introduced
ourselves to Bob Thornell and told him about the paintings we

made with ink berries from the edge of his yard-sticking out
of the fence.

Omari already can recognize two new words "send" and "log
on". This is going to be helpful for his reading skills as he
sends his messages and dictates messages for me to send.
Thanks again!

Cynthia and Omari

On another occasion, a group of neighbors discussed starting a crime watch
and using the network to promote discussions about the issue and to keep each
other informed. Within days after this conversation began, one of the people
discussing the idea was robbed. One of his neighbors saw the thieves breaking
into his home and knew whom to call because of the recent discussions about the
crime watch. The thieves attempted to steal one of the computers connected to
the MUSIC network, but they were caught and the equipment was returned
within an hour of their departure from the scene of the crime. This was an
amazing example of how effective the social construction of a crime watch could
be, and how useful on-line discussions were concerning this topic. In the following example, 5 days after Mark asked people to start thinking about a date for a
crime watch meeting, he reported on a successful outcome of the project.

From: Mark
Date: 10-06-93, 10:50:46 PM
Title: Crime Watch
Sent to: Alan
CC: Michelle, Mike, Anna, Valerie, Frantz, Michael, Bob,
Tiffany, Theresa, Rocklyn, Eva, Jay, Gene, Cynthia

Crime Watch

When and where do we want to have our next crime watch meeting?

Mark

From: Mark
Date: 10-11-93, 7:55:13 PM
Title: Crime Watch Working
Sent to: Alan

CC: Michelle, Jack, Anna, Valerie, Veronica, Frantz, Michael, Bob, Tiffany, Theresa, Rocklyn, Eva, Jay, Rivers,
Cynthia

Neighborhood Notes

An example of a crime watch working!

My apartment was burgulized!!!! Three men went into the window at about 1:00 PM during a week day. My neighbor saw was

```
standing on the porch and saw them go through the window. She
called me at work and sent someone around the corner to a local
Minister. I called the police and headed home. By the time I
arrived the Minister and the police were on the scene. We got a
describtion from the witness. And we found out they went
"that-a-way".

The Minister went with the police in the direction of the sus-
pects. One of them and the stolen goods were found around the
corner. The police helped me carry the goods back home. I was
back at work within the hour. Home secure and one suspect un-
der arrest.

That is only half of the story!!!! To finish the job you have
to work with the court. Last week this young man case came
before Dorchester District Court. The Minister, the wit-
ness, and I were there to make sure the suspect received jus-
tice. Justice in this case is get the young man attention and
push him into taking responsiblity for his life.

Stay tuned for more information on the other two suspects.

Mark
```

Another interesting activity came about when 10 users organized a set of group letters that they sent to a woman in Brazil once a month for 5 months. The woman was only in Brazil temporarily, but she said she was extremely homesick for her family and friends. A group letter was therefore organized to maximize the amount of people that would keep in touch with her. Anyone in the group could add to the letter any time, day or night, during the period before the letter was sent, and only one person was needed to mail out the correspondence at the end of the month. This was a convenient usage of the system since the woman did not have access to E-mail herself. The shared document was actually sent to her by "snail mail" (ordinary transport mail). This seemed to be a novel idea, and the woman was extremely appreciative when she got returned. She said that she believes she would not have heard from so many people so regularly without the MUSIC network.

Other Bulletin Board Systems.   There are literally thousands of other BBSs. In 1993, one estimate put the number at 45,000—and growing—that are accessible to the public through dial-up connections (Lambert & Howe, 1993, p. 23). This estimate also states that there are over 10,000,000 active users on these BBSs, with the number growing at a rate of over 9,000 per day. Most of these systems focus on servicing users from a local telephone area code that incorporates many municipalities, but a large number of BBSs also provide services to users at the national and international levels, usually via Internet-access. The vast majority of these systems are designed for people who have a particular shared interest or association, but do not live in close proximity to one another. These types of users make up "virtual" communities. A limited number of other networks are designed to address the needs of a constituency in a particular city, but rarely do they focus exclusively on a particular neighborhood. It is even more rare when the neighborhood of focus is economically disadvantaged, as is the case in MUSIC's target group.

MUSIC is a type of network best described as a "neighborhood network." Anne Beamish (1995) recently described this type of network this way:

> A second model for community networks, of which there are few examples, is the small-scale bulletin board which usually focuses on a particular neighborhood rather than a city. These bulletin board systems (BBSs) are frequently scaled-down versions of city networks and can either be stand-alone systems or parts of larger city-wide networks. They are usually established by an individual who runs the system from their home with a modest investment in hardware and software, or they can be run by a small group of community activists. Neighborhood BBSs focus on an even more local level of information and discussion and emphasize community development; they have the advantage that participants often know each other personally. Their disadvantage is that the system's existence often depends on a single individual. (p. 75)

Even though an enormous number of BBSs are in existence, there are few that focus on the type of neighborhood approach that typifies MUSIC. As Beamish pointed out, because these types of systems usually depend on a single individual or a small number of individuals, their existence is usually tenuous. However, neighborhood networks also have important advantages.

When a network's existence is dependent on the support of individuals at the neighborhood level, it can become more connected to the neighborhood's personality and internal dynamics. This can foster more neighborhood ownership over the network, which is an important part of the "information commons" ideal. In fact, this is what connects the MUSIC network to the model of social constructionism. The social relations and cultural materials in a particular neighborhood must be rallied through various sociocultural activities and processes to keep the network alive.

Almost all BBSs provide a method for people to communicate via E-mail and discussion groups, and they usually provide these people some type of access to a database or some other store of information. As long as these types of networks are seen as valuable services, people will continue to use them. However, this type of usage is not necessarily functioning to improve the social setting in which the users live. For that to happen, the networks must take an approach that supports their users in developing active social constructions in their neighborhood setting. The commonly used networking paradigms of "information highways" and information "surfing" or "browsing" do not necessarily support this type of focus. Riding the highway, surfing, and browsing all emphasize taking advantage of information content produced by other sources, so such modes are more focused on consumption than on production. By definition this is not constructionistic unless and until a user produces his or her own content with resources within this medium.

When a BBS is run by a large organization or by a group of professionals who can better guarantee its continued existence, the BBS starts to acquire the status of an institutional entity supplying something to the constituents who take advantage of it. Unlike the information commons model, this institutional model of network providers does not encourage those who use these BBSs to see themselves as the defining entity and driving force behind the network's existence. This raises the problem of the network providers becoming outside forces in the lives of the people who use the systems. These outside forces become the expert fixers or the active producers on the system, while the users become the passive recipients or consumers of a product. This is not a model that can foster active and engaging urban communities. In a recent article advocating the involvement of underprivileged communities in the benefits of information technology, I wrote:

> Proponents of electronic networking have been focusing almost exclusively on how these networks will make it easier for people to get access to the broader national and international scene. But for fragmented and alienated communities, local issues are often the most essential for pulling together. If networks focus the attention of the poor outside their community, then the networks will provide just one more obstacle to addressing local concerns.
>
> To make the information "superhighways" of the future more democratic . . . we need to look for ways to make networks helpful in promoting local issues and local leadership. We need to try to discover ways that this technology can help neighbors work on projects that affect their lives together. Networking should help people tell their own stories and develop their own programs, not simply help them to consume more of the stories and programs that come from the experts. In this way, networking can help people recapture the magic of a community where everyone is important and each has something to offer. (Shaw, 1994, p. 136)

FINAL THOUGHTS

As computer networks continue to grow and multiply, and individuals from vastly different geographical regions begin to form virtual communities, much attention has focused upon the benefits to users interacting in cyberspace. Little attention has been paid to how these networks can be useful to the members of proximal communities—those communities made up of individuals who live in the same neighborhood. In proximal communities the relatively small distance between neighbors can often mask a lack of connectedness that can be far more consequential than the distance separating members of virtual communities.

Many common concerns with devastating impact can plague the members of a proximal community, and yet it is often very difficult for local residents to pull together and address them. Low-income communities have an especially difficult time organizing forums and programs that speak to their concerns, leaving many to suffer through critical issues in silence.

To break the silence, we must seek to develop communities whose residents are active in shaping their own social setting. This means that we need to think about how to encourage active social models within urban communities rather than passive ones. Social constructionism provides one such model, and the MUSIC system is an example of a social tool consistent with the model. The MUSIC network provides an electronic infrastructure that is locally situated. When people in the neighborhood put it to use as an organizational tool, they demonstrate ownership over their own social setting in a way that can serve as a catalyst for new, neighborhood-based leadership and development. This project has attempted to address specific difficulties faced by urban residents as they relate to their own community and as they deal with information technologies. The project is also raising important questions concerning how the same computers that enhance the independence of the individual might also be used to help the local community stay interdependent.

In this project, I have seen many disappointments outweighed by many signs of hope. The most important signs were the beginnings of better relationships forming between the youth and some of their adult neighbors. As these relationships formed, I saw more trust and hope awaken in both parties. From the perspective of a social constructionist, these relationships are clearly a key part of any solution to the problems that exist in urban social settings. As stated earlier, social relations are critical to the development of both the individuals in the social setting and the setting itself.

This research project has gone through a developmental cycle of its own. The early work centered around apprenticeships, and I structured my work around the model of the samba school. The successes and failures of this project led to new initiatives among the kids, which we found difficult to manage without more support from the neighbors. It became clear that to reach out to the neighborhood more effectively and to support the kids' initiatives, we needed better tools for building social constructions. Tools for constructionism are simply the technology used to organize activities and create the constructs that involve the subjects of a social setting. Thus, developing new tools—such as neighborhood-based telecommunications systems—is a key to opening the door to new potential.

In conclusion, social constructionism can help bring to light some of the factors involved in deteriorating conditions in many urban settings. With a better sense of the critical role that social relations and cultural materials play, and with models of sociocultural activities such as the samba school where cohesive interactions and activism can exist, it is possible to begin to look at new approaches that support social development in the urban settings. Finally, it is essential that these approaches come with appropriate tools that allow both young and old in these settings to be as constructive and as creative as possible.

ACKNOWLEDGMENTS

This chapter is based on research I am currently working on for my doctoral thesis. I would like to thank Seymour Papert, Mitchel Resnick, Ceasar McDowell, and Anthony Maddox, the members of my thesis committee, for all of their help and support in this effort. The work described in the chapter was performed at the MIT Media Laboratory and was supported by grants from the National Science Foundation (Grant 9153719-MDR), Nintendo Inc., the LEGO Group, and the Wood Foundation. The ideas presented in this chapter do not necessarily represent the views of these funding agencies.

APPENDIX: STATISTICAL DATA ABOUT THE FOUR CORNERS NEIGHBORHOOD

An article in the *Boston Sunday Globe* (Luz Delgado, 1993, September 26, "Restoring Neighborhood Pride in Four Corners," *City Weekly Section*, pp. 1, 8) revealed the following statistical data about my neighborhood:

- Nearly 20% of Four Corners' 6,000 residents live in poverty.
- 37.5% of the neighborhood's families with children under age 5 live below the poverty line.
- Nearly one third of families with children under age 17 live below the poverty line.
- At 12.4%, the unemployment rate is double that of the city of Boston (6.1%) and 25% higher than that of Dorchester (8.2%).
- Nearly 2,000 residents, 40% of adults in the area, do not have a high school diploma.
- Statistics from Boston police Area C-11 showed that from December 1992 to July 1993 there were 15 aggravated assaults, 35 auto thefts, 15 robberies, 13 burglaries, 10 larcenies, and 2 rapes in the portion of Four Corners that C-11 patrols. (Parts of Four Corners are covered by Area B patrols. Data on Area B were not included in the article.)

A resource assessment by the Codman Square Healthy Boston Coalition entitled "Neighborhood Resource Assessment," dated June 1993, revealed the following about Four Corners and the larger Codman Square community that surrounds it:

- The median age of the population is 29.6 years, suggesting a high concentration of young people. In fact, 30% of residents are under the age of 18. A full 42% are under the age of 25.
- 34% of households are headed by single parents.
- Whereas the mean household income is $35,000, some 48% of households have incomes of less than $20,000.

Furthermore, this neighborhood has seen an increase in violence that has resulted in killings over the last few years. In fact, in 1994, one of the young people in Four Corners who was a good friend of mine was shot to death.

During the 6 years that I have lived in Four Corners, I have seen these problems from the position of one of the neighbors. The devastation I have witnessed is appalling. I personally know eight teenage boys who were shot but survived since I have lived there. Three others were shot and killed in my neighborhood during the same time. One adult male was stabbed to death during that period. The rapes and domestic violence are less openly discussed, so I do not know much about those occurrences, but most statistical reports suggest that such instances are growing. Two years ago a bullet was shot into my car, and one year ago bullets were fired into the home of a local church pastor. I know some of the boys who sell drugs, and I have come to know many of the addicts. Two women, who are good friends of mine, have had their children taken away by the Department of Social Services (DSS) because they were involved in prostitution and led drug-addicted lifestyles that actually endangered their children on occasion. Two other women I knew died of alcoholism—cirrhosis of the liver. One man I knew well and another who was the father of a friend of mine died of AIDS. Another friend and former neighbor of mine is currently HIV positive. I know countless young boys and a few young girls who have been frequently arrested, and I know many who are in jail at the time of this writing. Of course, I also know many who have dropped out of high school and seem to have nowhere to go.

REFERENCES

Beamish, A. (1995). *Communities on-line: Community-based computer networks.* Unpublished masters thesis, Massachusetts Institute of Technology, Cambridge, MA.

Bereiter, C. (1994). Constructivism, socioculturalism, and Popper's World 3. *Educational Researcher, 23*(7), 21–23.

Bott, E. (1971). *Family and social network: Roles, norms, and external relationships in ordinary urban families.* New York: The Free Press.

Carey, S., & Gelman, R. (1991). *The epigenesis of mind: Essays on biology and cognition.* Hillsdale, NJ: Lawrence Erlbaum Associates.

Cobb, P. (1994). Where is the mind? Constructivist and sociocultural perspectives on mathematical development. *Educational Researcher, 23*(7) 13–20.

Cole, M., & Scribner, S. (1974). *Culture and thought: A psychological introduction.* New York: Wiley.

Felsenstein, L. (1993). The commons of information: A computer pioneer looks at where we've been and where we might be going. *Dr. Dobb's Journal.* Redwood City, CA: M&T Books.

Gay, J., & Cole, M. (1967). *The new mathematics and an old culture: A study of learning among the Kpelle of Liberia.* New York: Holt, Rinehart and Winston.

Heilbrun, J. (1981). *Urban economics and public policy.* New York: St. Martin's Press.

Kretzmann, J., & McKnight, J. (1993). *Building communities from the inside out.* Evanston, IL: Center for Urban Affairs and Policy Research, Neighborhood Innovations Network. Northwestern University.

Kuhn, T. S. (1970). *The structure of scientific revolutions.* Chicago, IL: University of Chicago Press.

Lambert, S., & Howe, W. (1993). *Internet basics: Your online access to the global electronic superhighway.* New York: Random House.

National Commission on Excellence in Education. (1983). *A nation at risk.* Washington, DC: Author.

Papert, S. A. (1980). *Mindstorms.* New York: Basic Books.

Papert, S. A. (1990). *Constructionist learning.* In Idit Harel (Ed.), Cambridge, MA: MIT Media Laboratory.

Papert, S. A. (1993). *The children's machine: Rethinking school in the age of the computer.* New York: Basic Books.

Piaget, J. (1954). *The construction of reality in the child.* New York: Ballantine Books.

Rogoff, B. (1990). *Apprenticeship in thinking: Cognitive development in social context.* Oxford: Oxford University Press.

Shaw, A. (1994). Neighborhood networking and community building. S. Cisler (Ed.), *Ties that bind: Building community networks* (pp. 134–137). May 4–6, Cuppertino, CA: Apple Computer.

U.S. Department of Commerce. (1993 September 15). *National information infrastructure: Agenda for action.* Washington, DC: Author.

von Glasersfeld, E. (1995). Sensory experience, abstraction, and teaching. In L. P. Steffe (Ed.). *Constructivism in education* (pp. 369–383). Hillsdale, NJ: Lawrence Erlbaum Associates.

Vygotsky, L. S. (1978). *Mind in society: The development off higher psychological processes.* Cambridge, MA: Harvard University Press.

Vygotsky, L. S. (1986). *Thought and language.* Cambridge, MA: The MIT Press.

Wertsch, J. V. (1990). The voice of rationality in a sociocultural approach to mind. In L. C. Moll (Ed.), *Vygotsky and education: Instructional implications and applications of sociohistorical psychology* (pp. 111–126). Cambridge: Cambridge University Press.

Wilensky, U. (1991). Abstract meditations on the concrete and concrete implications for mathematics education. In I. Harel & S. Papert (Eds.). *Constructionism* (pp. 193–203). Norwood, NJ: Ablex Publishing Corporation.

The MediaMOO Project
Constructionism and Professional Community

Amy Bruckman
Mitchel Resnick

VIRTUAL PROFESSIONAL COMMUNITY

Once or twice a year we stand with name badges on, sipping coffee in a corridor, exchange ideas over expense-accounted lunches, and maybe attend a few talks. Friendships are made and projects hatched. Then it is back home to file for expenses, perhaps write a trip report, and get back to "real work" and relative isolation.

MediaMOO is a text-based, networked, virtual reality environment designed to extend to a daily activity the type of casual collaboration that occurs at conferences. Visitors to a conference share not just a set of interests, but also a place and a set of activities. Interaction is generated as much by the latter two as the former:

```
Person A: Can you tell me how to get to Ballroom A?
Person B: I'm headed that way now. It's up this way.
Person A: Thanks!
Person B: I see you're at Company X. . . .
Person C: Is this seat taken?
Person D: No, it isn't.
Person C: I'm surprised the room is so packed.
Person D: Well, Y is a really good speaker. . . .
```

A text-based virtual environment can provide both a shared place (the virtual world) and a shared set of activities (exploring and extending the virtual world). As at a conference coffee break, there is a social convention that it is appropriate to strike up a conversation with strangers simply based on their name tags. On

MediaMOO, you can read descriptions of people's research interests as well as their names, and this can form a basis for striking up a substantive conversation.

However, name tags alone are not enough. The best sorts of interactions occur when people participate in a shared activity and not just a shared context. On MediaMOO, this takes the form of constructing and interacting with the virtual world. The constructionist theory of learning emphasizes the value of constructing personally meaningful artifacts (Papert, 1980, 1991). This theory has guided design decisions made in MediaMOO. For example, in most text-based virtual reality environments, the privilege to extend the virtual world is restricted to a small number of users. However, in MediaMOO everyone is automatically a programmer with full privileges to create new objects and places in the virtual world.

The philosophy of constructionism argues that people learn with particular effectiveness when they are engaged in constructing personally meaningful projects; learning by doing is better than learning by being told. This approach is most often applied to children's learning. We believe that not enough attention is paid to its broader applicability. We have found that letting the users build a virtual world rather than merely interact with a predesigned world gives them an opportunity for self expression, encourages diversity, and leads to a meaningful engagement of participants and enhanced sense of community.

This paper has two main goals. First, it documents experience with the MediaMOO project to date and evaluates its success as a virtual professional community. Second, it explores the importance of constructionist principles in virtual reality design.

WHAT IS MEDIAMOO?

MediaMOO is a text-based, networked virtual reality environment or "MUD" (Bruckman, 1992; Curtis, 1992, 1993) running on the Internet. Its basic structure is a representation of the MIT Media Lab. Users connect in the LEGO Closet, then step out into the E&L (Epistemology and Learning research group) Garden:

```
> connect guest
*** Connected ***
The LEGO Closet
It's dark in here, and there are little crunchy plastic
things under your feet! Groping around, you discover what
feels like a doorknob on one wall.
Obvious exits: out to The E&L Garden
> out
The E&L Garden
The E&L Garden is a happy jumble of little and big computers,
papers, coffee cups, and stray pieces of LEGO.
```

```
Obvious exits: hallway to E&L Hallway, closet to The LEGO
Closet, and sts to STS Centre Lounge
You see a newspaper, a Warhol print, a Sun SPARCstation IPC,
Projects Chalkboard, and Research Directory here. Amy is
here.
> say hi
You say, "hi"
Amy says, "Hi Guest! Welcome!"
```

Users from around the world connect to this virtual place to socialize, talk about their research projects, interact with the virtual world, and create new objects and places. People from the Media Lab are encouraged to build their own offices; users from other places can build their offices as well and connect them via a "virtual Internet." The system developers constructed basic infrastructure and a few interesting and evocative objects and places, but almost all the building was left to the users. This was not a result of time constraints, but is a central principle of the project that is elaborated throughout this paper.

The first Multi-User Dungeon (MUD) was developed in 1979 as a multiplayer Dungeons and Dragons game. In 1989 James Aspnes, a graduate student at Carnegie Mellon University, decided to see what would happen if the monsters and magic swords were removed and each user was allowed instead to help extend the virtual world. Aspnes' project, which he called TinyMUD, became less like a game and more like a community. There was no longer a score or goal, but instead a gathering of people who enjoyed one another's virtual company and worked together to extend the virtual world.

At the MIT Media Lab, we decided to see whether this technology, which began as a game, could be adapted to a more serious purpose: enhancing professional community among media researchers. We chose to build on top of the MUD Object Oriented (MOO) software developed by Pavel Curtis at Xerox PARC (Curtis, 1994). System development began on October 28th, 1992, and MediaMOO was opened to the public on January 20th, 1993, with an opening celebration called the MediaMOO Inaugural Ball, scheduled to coincide with Bill Clinton's inauguration as President of the United States. As of December 1994, MediaMOO had over 1,000 active participants from 29 countries. (see Table 9.1.) An average of 18 people are connected at the peak hour of the day (4 p.m. EST); 7 people at the quietest hour (5 a.m. EST). MediaMOO runs on a Sun SPARCstation IPC where it uses 50 Mb of memory. The database is currently 25 Mb on disk. MediaMOO can be accessed from any computer on the Internet at the address mediamoo.media.mit.edu, port 8888. (From UNIX workstations, type "telnet mediamoo.media.mit.edu 8888"; from computers running VMS, type "telnet mediamoo.media.mit.edu /port=8888".)

Some readers may be surprised that the virtual world of MediaMOO is built entirely in text. With current technology, graphical virtual worlds are awkward at best. For example, no graphical system developed to date can give users the

TABLE 9.1
An International Community

Domain	Name	Number of Users
edu	Educational (USA)	575
com	Commercial (USA)	182
ca	Canada	50
uk	United Kingdom	48
au	Australia	28
us	Misc (USA)	16
nl	The Netherlands	10
gov	Government (USA)	10
no	Norway	10
org	Nonprofit organization (USA)	10
se	Sweden	9
at	Austria	9
net	Network provider (USA)	9
de	Germany	8
jp	Japan	6
za	South Africa	6
mil	Military (USA)	5
il	Israel	5
nz	New Zealand	3
pl	Poland	3
br	Brazil	3
pt	Portugal	3
bitnet	Bitnet (USA)	3
si	Slovenia	2
ch	Switzerland	2
ie	Ireland	2
be	Belgium	2
it	Italy	2
fi	Finland	2
hu	Hungary	1
kw	Kuwait	1
hk	Hong Kong	1
pe	Peru	1
gr	Greece	1
sg	Singapore	1
fr	France	1

ability to express more than a minimal range of human emotions. However, the choice of text over graphics for MediaMOO is not based entirely on technical limitations. Text and graphical virtual worlds are different media forms, like radio and television. Television did not replace radio; it changed what radio is used for. Similarly, we believe graphical virtual worlds will change what text-based worlds are used for, but both forms will persist. Text-based worlds are particularly good for writing and foreign language education, giving students a fun and personally meaningful context to use their writing skills. Furthermore, the expressive power of text facilitates rapid creation—in just a moment one can write, "On top of the hill you see a gnarled peach tree." It would take most people much longer to convey the same concept in pictures. Additionally, the written word leaves more to the reader's imagination. For some applications, a text-based world may be preferred for the same reasons a book is preferred to a movie. Neither books nor movies, radio nor television, text-based nor graphical virtual worlds are inherently "better." They are different media forms, each of which may be better suited to certain applications.

A COMMUNITY OF RESEARCHERS

Whereas people of a wide variety of ages and backgrounds participate in MUDs, the majority of players on publicly announced Internet MUDs are college students. On MediaMOO, we wanted to attract media researchers, so we advertised selectively on electronic mailing lists devoted to media studies and required people to submit a description of their research interests to register. Initially, admissions were primarily a self-selection process. With time, word of mouth has spread the address of the system to a broader population, and we have needed to enforce admissions requirements more stringently. An elected committee of users advises the MediaMOO administration on admissions decisions.

MediaMOO participants represent a wide variety of disciplines: anthropologists, broadcasters, computer scientists, cultural studies researchers, historians, interface designers, journalists, librarians, linguists, network administrators, psychologists, sociologists of science, teachers, virtual reality researchers, and the like. Particularly strongly represented are writing teachers. A community of writing teachers organized by Tari Fanderclai and Greg Siering meets every Tuesday evening at 8 p.m. eastern time in The Tuesday Café to discuss how computer technology can be used to improve writing instruction. Fifteen to 30 people attend each week. A group organized by Marcus Speh meets regularly to discuss the Global Network Academy, an organization working to use the Internet for education. A group organized by Lee-Ellen Marvin has regular poetry readings.

In most MUDs, characters are anonymous. People who become friends can exchange real names and E-mail addresses, but many choose not to do so. Conventions about when it is acceptable to talk about "real life" vary between communities. In most MUDs, people begin to talk more about real life when they get to know someone better. However, in some communities, such as those based on the "Dragonriders of Pern" series of books by Anne McCaffrey, talking about real life is taboo.

On MediaMOO, we wanted to promote discussions of real life and real research interests. Consequently, we initially offered users the opportunity to get an anonymous or identified character, or both. With time, we realized that having identified participants was an important part of establishing a professional atmosphere. Since August 1993, all new members of MediaMOO have been identified with their real names and E-mail addresses. Real names and E-mail addresses are specified on a person's application and can be changed only by a system administrator or "janitor." (System administrators on most MUDs are called "wizards" or "gods." On MediaMOO, we chose to change the name to "janitor." The janitors are the people who clean up after others. They have the keys to the entire facility, but try not to get in the way of its inhabitants.) While it is possible for people to lie about their real names, it is not possible for them to lie about their E-mail addresses, because their initial password is delivered to the address they supply.

Each member also has a description of his or her research interests. One user of the system, Professor Ken Schweller (aka "cdr"), created a research directory to search through all members' research interests:

```
> examine directory
Research Directory (aka #1458, Research Directory, re-
search, directory, and dir)
Owned by cdr.
You see a musty, dusty, leatherbound book. You might try
something like 'find neural net in dir.'
Obvious verbs:
  find <anything> in directory
  g*et/t*ake directory
  d*rop/th*row directory
  gi*ve/ha*nd directory to <anything>
> find "narrative" in directory
Guest consults the Research Directory . . .
Vortex(#116)—Programming environments, animal behavior
simulation, sociology of virtual spaces, AI & Narrative
DougO(#1829)—Modeling narrative reality in an online real-
time multiuser environment.
Viridian(#7233)—I'm interested in writing and its many
forms (poetry, fiction, etc.), cyclic visual narratives,
and, among other things, dreams.
Gee(#7202)—Gee is currently researching multi-user envi-
ronments for a possible TV documentary in Australia. He is
interested in how MOO's may impact on visual artists and how
art might be created in virtual space. Video Art and digital
narrative.
```

The research directory facilitates users with common interests meeting one another. It was built soon after MediaMOO's official opening, not by the system administrators, but by an interested member. Encouraging users to build new things for the system lets them add value to it, and also strengthens their sense of connection to the community.

A "THIRD PLACE"

In *The Great Good Place*, Ray Oldenburg eloquently argued for the importance of "third places," places that are neither work nor home (Oldenburg, 1989). The book's subtitle is *Cafés, coffee shops, community centers, beauty parlors, general stores, bars, hangouts and how they get you through the day*. Oldenburg summarized:

> Third places exist on neutral ground and serve to level their guests to a condition of social equality. Within these places, conversation is the primary activity and the major vehicle for the display and appreciation of human personality and individuality. Third places are taken for granted and most have a low profile. Since the formal institutions of society make stronger claims on the individual, third places are normally open during the off hours, as well as other times. The character of a third place is determined most of all by its regular clientele and is marked by a playful mood, which contrasts with people's more serious involvement in other spheres. Though a radically different kind of setting from the home, the third place is remarkably similar to a good home in the psychological comfort and support that it extends. (p. 42)

The population of third places are self-selected—people go to a café because they choose to and not because they must. From this self-selection process emerges a group of people with some degree of common interests and values. Traditional third places draw people from the local geographic area. On the Internet, MUDs become third places that draw people with common interests from all around the world. People from the opposite hemisphere can become a part of your daily life. On MediaMOO, those people also share research interests. MediaMOO can be described as an endless conference reception. The conversation fluidly moves between personal and research issues.

As Oldenburg pointed out, conversation is the primary activity in third places, and MediaMOO is no exception. Most of those who chose to respond to an E-mail survey of randomly selected MediaMOO users stated that they had enjoyed interesting conversations and met new people in their field through Media-MOO. Paul Dourish of Xerox EuroPARC wrote:

> I've met a number of people whom I've talked to about my research and theirs, although I think there are fewer (probably just the one or two) whom I've actually talked to enough to refer to as "new professional contacts."
>
> One I met while he was a Guest; we started talking after he read my research description. The other I met early on when I was stumbling around asking all sorts of people for help on doing things just after I got my character.

The process of helping new players, often called "newbies," is an important part of MUD culture. For Paul, the process of being new and reaching out for help has led to his most meaningful professional contacts—once while he himself was new, and once while he was helping another new player. The context of the MUD in these instances provided a shared context and shared activity that promoted social interaction.

A number of users commented that their most meaningful interactions on the MUD were with the "regulars"—the people who use MediaMOO the most and are most likely to be logged on at any given time. Oldenburg emphasizes the importance of the regulars to a third place—they give a place its character.

Some question the value of the sort of interaction that takes place on Media-MOO. One user wrote that "frankly it strikes me for now as a schmooze place for people with nothing better to do, not a place where more productive things will happen than already happen in other communicative modes." It is worth noting that to determine whether an activity is "productive" requires a definition of what it means to be productive, and this quickly leads to questions of a philosophical nature. MediaMOO challenges the boundaries between work and play, forcing one to rethink what counts as productive. Most veteran conference-goers attest to the fact that the conversation at coffee breaks and receptions is usually more valuable than the sessions attended. We believe that the exchange of ideas and networking that take place on MediaMOO are similarly productive. Serious exchange of ideas often takes place because of, not in spite of, more informal social interaction.

CONSTRUCTIONISM

In an important sense, MediaMOO is more like a community center than a tavern or conference reception, because it serves as a context for member-organized events and projects. The center itself—its rooms and objects—are constantly being constructed and reconstructed by the participants. This is an example of the application of *constructionist* ideas to virtual reality design.

The term *constructionism*, first coined by Seymour Papert (Papert, 1991), involves two types of construction. First, it asserts that learning is an active process in which people actively construct knowledge from their experiences in the world. (This idea is based on the theories of Jean Piaget.) To this, construc-tionism adds the idea that people construct new knowledge with particular effec-tiveness when they are engaged in constructing personally meaningful products. They might be constructing sand castles, LEGO machines, computer programs, or virtual objects. The important thing is that they are actively engaged in creating something meaningful to themselves and to others around them.

This philosophy is central to the design of MediaMOO. The goal of Media-MOO's initial design was to create not a complete virtual world for users to enjoy, but the barest skeleton to inspire users to construct personally meaningful objects and places. The next three sections discuss users constructing places in the virtual world, taking an initial step toward programming through "contribu-tory objects," and programming new objects and places.

A WORLD BUILT BY ITS INHABITANTS

The center of MediaMOO is a virtual copy of the MIT Media Lab. There is a psychological power in the ability to construct a representation of a real place in the virtual world that is your own. The challenge was this: How do we let people build offices in California and Australia without trying to build everything in between? We developed a "virtual Internet" as a technique for spatial ellipsis. Users from other places can build their own offices by connecting them via the virtual Internet. You step inside a computer and dematerialize into a collection of packets. Then you can travel through a tree-like structure, going down to root and back up through the hierarchy (actually a much more orderly arrangement than the real Internet!). Each user can add his or her own Internet site if it is not already there.

Daniel (Daniel Rose) wrote of his first experience on MediaMOO:

> I logged in first as a Guest, and came out in the E&L Garden. I had never been to the Media Lab IRL [in real life], so I felt a bit lost. . . . Then I met Michele, and when she found out I was from Apple, she said that someone had constructed our building, and she'd take me there. . . . When we stepped out into the Apple R&D building atrium, I felt this incredible shock of recognition. . . . More than that, I felt a sense of relief that there were places here that were familiar and home to me just as the Media Lab was to you. And all of this was from a couple of lines of textual description.

The actual text a user sees when they arrive at apple.com in the virtual Internet and step out looks like this:

```
apple.com
You are in a maze of twisty little passages.
You see the back of a computer screen here.
Obvious exits: down to com and out to Apple Computer R&D
Atrium
> out
Your packets gather in a glob, and then flow into the screen!
You feel yourself rematerializing.
Apple Computer R&D Atrium
You are in a glass atrium, four stories tall. Offices look out
from the walls. Beyond the glass wall to the east, there is
some arcane construction taking place. A walkway exits the
atrium to the west.
```

To most people, this is a rather unremarkable description. The idea of re-materializing might appeal to *Star Trek* fans, but the room description itself is bland—it sounds like an office. However, to Daniel this provoked a "shock of recognition" and a sense of belonging. Representations of the real give users a sense of comfort and make the medium more appropriable: If your office is there, then you belong there.

The geography of MediaMOO has no real unity. A visitor once called it "a multicultural mess." We consider this to be a high compliment. Each person's virtual "home" is an expression of his or her personality. For example, consider the virtual homes of members of the MediaMOO elected Membership Advisory Committee at the time of this writing: Michael Day, a writing teacher, lives in "the panopticon"; Randy Farmer, a researcher in virtual communities, lives in his company headquarters, "Electric Communities"; Beth Kolko, a professor of cultural studies and rhetoric, lives in "in media res"; and Diane Maluso, a psychology professor, lives in "Quiet Light." The public areas of MediaMOO are neatly organized; however, they are a minimal part of the virtual world. The private areas are not coherent with one another, but express the rich diversity of the population.

CONTRIBUTORY OBJECTS

Objects in the virtual world serve many of the same functions as places; building amusing or useful MUD objects or both is a means of creative expression for the designer, and completed objects promote social interaction for the community. One design paradigm which has proved particularly successful is the idea of a contributory object. For example, in the dressing rooms of the MediaMOO Ballroom, it is possible to design new costumes for the clothing racks:

```
> northwest
You step through the velvet curtain into the women's dressing
room.
Women's Dressing Room
The dressing room is a clutter of gowns, hats, and gloves from
all different eras. Type 'examine rack' for more informa-
tion.
Obvious exits: east to Ballroom Foyer and south to The Ball-
room
You see women's clothing rack and a gold plaque here.
> list rack
Outfits on the rack:
[Space permits us to show only a few of the 89 costumes cur-
rently on the rack.]
1: a classic black cocktail dress and snakeskin pumps by Amy
(#75)
7: a halter wrap dress, cut to mid-thigh, colored in pastels
with a distinctly tie-died look to them by Lenny (#115)
14: black leather one-piece jumpsuit with glistening alloy
lapels by Guest (#113)
```

```
21: a shimmering jester's costume, in mauve and lavender,
with a headdress of orchids and dove-feathers, and turquoise
pendant earrings, set off by turquoise high-heels by Mauve
_Guest (#702)
58: An elegant white lace stretch blouse with tailored red
hunting jacket and black stretch pants. Tally ho! by rowena
(#8642)
> wear 1 from rack
You slip into a classic black cocktail dress and snakeskin
pumps.
```

At the MediaMOO Inaugural Ball, people spent as much time in the dressing rooms as in the ballroom itself. The costumes on the rack are effective conversational props. More important, however, is the ease of contributing a new costume to the rack. One can simply type "design Convergence T-Shirt and mirrorshades for rack," and it is added to the collection of available costumes with the designer's name attached. Contributory objects offer a lower threshold to participation than actually programming a new object. The user has a sense of having taken a first step toward mastering the computational environment, and a sense of having contributed something to the community.

Another example of a contributory object is Lucy, the ballroom's bartender. Lucy can be taught what to say when a drink is served. An anonymous guest with a philosophical bent taught Lucy how to serve a "metaphysical Pepsi":

```
> order metaphysical Pepsi from Lucy
Lucy says, "One Metaphysical Pepsi, coming your way . . . or
possibly it's heading in the opposite of your direction, but
still coming toward you through a time-space continuum."
Lucy says, "I'll have that for you in just a minute."
> say thanks
You say, "thanks"
Lucy pours your Metaphysical Pepsi. Or maybe she doesn't.
Maybe Lucy is just a product of your imagination. Maybe ev-
erything is just a product of your imagination. Your senses
tell you what is going on around you, but why should you trust
your senses? Just because they've always been there does not
by any means prove their reliability. Go ahead and 'drink'
your Pepsi, but next time maybe you'll give a little thought
to the fact that you may not actually be drinking any-
thing . . . in fact, you may not even be standing here. Lucy
hands you your Metaphysical Pepsi. "Here ya go."
> look at Pepsi
It's a Pepsi . . . or is it? How can you really be sure? Of
course, your senses tell you it is a Pepsi, but who's to say
your senses are not controlled by some external factor?
> drink Pepsi
You drink your Metaphysical Pepsi.
```

Ordering a metaphysical Pepsi can turn the conversation in a rather philosophical direction. However, even if the bartender is just serving a more mundane sort of beverage, it helps to create a context for social interaction. There are a variety of contributory objects around MediaMOO, including statues of famous sociologists and historians of science that you scribble on (designed to promote discussion of their work), and a projects chalkboard for ideas about new objects and places. Some have more "serious" purposes than others, but even the most playful serve a useful function—facilitating social interaction. Just as in real life, conversations often make an elegant transition from casual small talk to a serious exchange of professional ideas.

It is interesting to note that attributing the contribution to a person is an essential feature—it allows people to take pride in what they have done and discourages virtual vandalism. Even though guests are effectively anonymous, there have been few inappropriate contributions to the costume racks. However, at one point it was possible to add messages to the bartenders without any attribution. One might add something like "Lucy starts polishing glasses behind the bar" to the bartender's program. Unfortunately, people have added messages that were trivial or obscene and have even deleted other people's contributions because the program allowed it. The software was, therefore, rewritten to provide attributions for messages that are added just like the other contributory objects around MediaMOO.

PROGRAMMED OBJECTS

Contributory objects are just a first step; they facilitate users learning to build and program new objects in the virtual world. Another easy step into greater involvement with the computational world is the use of object-oriented programming (OOP). The virtual world is made up computational "objects," each of which has its own characteristic properties. When a "child" object inherits from a "parent" object, the child acquires the characteristics of the parent. For example, it is possible to create an object that moves around simply by creating something that inherits from "generic portable room." The child object can then be customized and new programs added to extend it. The generic portable room has been used to create a diverse collection of objects:

```
> @kids #445
generic portable room(#445) has 124 kids.
Yellow Cab(#296)
Generic Neo-Scrabble Board(#1439)
MediaMOO TV Helicopter(#1659)
The Bob Marley Community Media Bus(#3655)
Generic Train(#4559)
Sound Proof Room(#3136)
```

```
an emacs window(#4607)
'77 Jeep Cherokee(#5731)
goldfish bowl(#4761)
portable hole(#6165)
The Autonomous Drone(#7815)
StarkNet School Bus(#7930)
Box of Delights(#8233)
Bible Study Room(#4014)
Generic Cards Room(#8757)
Jack's Laboratory(#3401)
dictionary(#6303)
water(#9225)
tiny envelope(#9566)
An Igloo(#8999)
an aluminum mailbox(#5449)
[etc.]
```

These projects range in complexity from simple customization of the generic portable room to substantial projects using the generic as their starting point. For example, a user named Moose (Tom Meyer) used generic portable room as the first element of his train system. The train system gives new users a tour of interesting places in the virtual world. The object-oriented environment makes it easy to create something satisfying, then later refine it.

The combination of the ability to construct things and a community context for that construction is particularly powerful. In an informal ethnographic study (Bruckman, 1994) of twelve adults who learned to program for the first time on a MUD (eight on MediaMOO, four on other MUDs), we found that the community provides

- motivation for learning,
- emotional support to overcome technophobia,
- technical support, and
- an appreciative audience for work completed.

Regardless of whether users already have technical experience, the ability to extend the virtual world with new objects and places provides

- an opportunity for creative self-expression,
- a means to establish a personal identity within the community,
- a way for individuals to contribute something to the community,
- a context for social interaction (both in the process of creating the objects, and in their use when finished), and
- an enhanced sense of connection to the community.

FUTURE DIRECTIONS: A MUD FOR KIDS

The MediaMOO Project was conceived in part as preparation for a MUD for kids, "MOOSE Crossing," which is currently under development. We believe that this technology can provide an authentic context in which children can learn reading, writing, and programming. In these virtual worlds, writing and programming become means of self-expression to a community of peers. MUDs are a constructionist playground.

Developing good MUD objects reflects as much creative writing as programming. One hypothesis of this research is that divisions between the humanities and the sciences are often too sharply drawn and counterproductive, and a more integrative approach has advantages for many children. A second hypothesis is that the social and contextual nature of these worlds may help young girls to be more comfortable with computers and programming.

If kids are really to make good use of MUDs, however, it will be necessary to improve the programming language and the interface. We are currently developing a new programming language called MOOSE designed to make it easier for children to program new objects. (MOOSE stands for "MOO Scripting Environment." The MOOSE language is built on top of Pavel Curtis's MOO software.) We are also developing a multiple-window client program called MacMOOSE, which we hope will make the system more usable. We hope to apply lessons learned in the development and use of the Logo language to make a MUD language more accessible to kids.

At the conclusion of *Mindstorms*, Seymour Papert (1980) described his vision of a technological samba school. In samba schools in Brazil, members of a community gather to prepare a performance for Carnival. Everyone is learning and teaching—even the leads need to learn their parts. People of all ages learn and play together as a community. Papert believes that computers can create a kind of technological samba school, and we believe MUDs may begin to realize that vision.

CONCLUSION: CONSTRUCTIONISM AND VIRTUAL REALITY

Many current virtual reality projects, particularly those intended for entertainment, are like Disneyland: Artists and programmers design wondrous creations for users to experience. If this technology is "interactive," it is in the limited sense that most hypertext systems are interactive: There are multiple paths through the material, and the system has a limited ability to react to the user. However, the ways in which the system reacts are designed by the artists and engineers who constructed it and not by the users.

220

Virtual reality applications in the fields of scientific visualization and training simulation often promote more meaningful user interaction, but are typically not situated within a virtual community. The chemist's walk-through molecular model would be more useful if placed in his or her virtual office where colleagues could come to visit. Current research in text-based virtual communities points to the importance of developing tools to allow the chemist to build his or her own virtual office. The chemist could fill the office with objects that are both useful and an expression of personal taste, some personally designed and some designed by others, just like those in a real office.

If the power of this technology is to be unleashed, users need to be the creators and not merely the consumers of virtual worlds. We believe that constructionist principles are of central importance to the design of virtual reality systems. MediaMOO is an exploration of this idea.

ACKNOWLEDGMENTS

This chapter originally appeared in *Convergence, 1* (1). An earlier version of this chapter was presented at the third International Conference on Cyberspace in Austin, Texas, on May 15th, 1993. The authors would like to thank the National Science Foundation (Grants 9153719-MDR, 9358519-RED), the LEGO Group, Interval Research, and AT&T for their support of this research. Thanks also are due to Pavel Curtis for his wonderful software. The authors thank the janitors and membership advisory committee of MediaMOO for volunteering their time to help make the project a success. Most of all, we thank MediaMOO's members.

REFERENCES

Bruckman, A. (1992). *Identity workshop: Social and psychological phenomena in text-based virtual reality.* Cambridge, MA: MIT Press. (Available via anonymous ftp from media.mit.edu in pub/asb/papers/identity-workshop.{ps.Z,rtf.Z}.)

Bruckman, A. (1994). *Programming for fun: MUDs as a context for collaborative learning.* Boston, MA: International Society for Technology in Education. Available via anonymous ftp from media.mit.edu in pub/asb/papers/necc94.{ps.Z,rtf.Z,txt}.)

Curtis, P. (1993). *Mudding: Social phenomena in text-based virtual realities.* Paper presented at the Directions and Implications of Advanced Computing, Berkeley, CA. (Available via anonymous ftp from parcftp.xerox.com in pub/MOO/papers/DIAC92.{ps,txt}.)

Curtis, P., & Nichols, D. (1993). *MUDs grow up: Social virtual reality in the real world.* Paper presented at the third International Conference on Cyberspace, Austin, TX. (Available via anonymous ftp from parcftp.xerox.com in pub/MOO/papers/MUDsGrowUp.{ps,txt}.)

Curtis, P., & White, S. (1994). *MOO.* Palo Alto, CA: Xerox PARC. (Available via anonymous ftp from parcftp.xerox.com in pub/MOO/LambdaMOO1.7.8p4.tar.Z.)

Oldenburg, R. (1989). *The great good place.* New York: Paragon House.

Papert, S. (1980). *Mindstorms: Children, computers, and powerful ideas.* New York: Basic Books.

Papert, S. (1991). Situating constructionism. In I. Harel & S. Papert (Eds.), *Constructionism* (pp. 1–11). Norwood, NJ: Ablex.

A Community of Designers
Learning Through Exchanging Questions and Answers

Michele Evard

INTRODUCTION

One week into her design of an educational video game, 10-year-old Renee asked the following question:

> How do you make words appear on the screen when you reach a certain point of the screen or you reach a shape that is on the screen?

This query itself might be unsurprising, but the fact that this quiet girl addressed it to the combined populations of two classrooms, rather than to a teacher or one of her friends, is unusual. In the environment described in this chapter, however, it was welcome and became a frequent occurrence. Seven fifth graders answered this question, three from Renee's class and four from the other. Of these children, four were male and three were female, three were African-American, one was Hispanic, and three were Caucasian. Given that these two classes rarely had contact about academic matters, and that even among themselves, these boys and girls most often asked questions of friends of their own gender, these responses were somewhat surprising. After receiving eight helpful messages, Renee replied to her own question, saying:

> Stop answering this question. #1, I have too many answers, and #2, I have solved my problem and am using something else. Thank-you very much.

Two children replied to that message with additional information.

I believe that children can learn through both asking and answering authentic questions—questions which are of personal importance to them. When asking a question, a child needs to articulate what he or she wants to learn or obtain. If the response is not what was desired, the child has the opportunity to observe a different perspective on the question. The child may also realize that a single statement of a question may provoke different reactions in different people. Similarly, answering a question requires articulation of thoughts; in addition, it implies some interpretation of the question and what kind of answer was desired. Although these might not be conscious processes or those in which people choose to engage, they are possible in a question–answer scenario, particularly when the participants really want to communicate.

To research these issues, I am designing a computer-based environment and activities in which children can communicate easily and feedback is valued. In this chapter, I describe the first few weeks of a project in which over 100 students were given access to the initial version of this environment. The next section provides the context of my work. In the two following sections, I discuss the type of environment desired and the specific tool that was used. After that I describe how frequently the system was used and what types of messages were exchanged. Then follows a section that describes several patterns of interactions between the children. The final section briefly overviews the range of issues that arose during this project.

A CONTEXT FOR COMMUNICATION

Constructionism is based on the idea that people learn particularly well when making things—especially things which can be shared with others. A strong emphasis is placed on created objects being external to their creator, as things "in the world" can be "shown, discussed, examined, probed, and admired" (Papert, 1980, 1991, 1993). Sharing a creation can result not only in its refinement, but also in the learner obtaining a deeper understanding of other people's perspectives on the object and on the ideas to which it is related.

Although my primary interest is in people learning through communication with other people irrespective of the particular topic, I believe that the nature of the topic, as well as the environment and community of the participants, strongly impacts the development of communication. I have chosen to focus this chapter on fifth-grade students' discussions around one particular project on educational video game design in a constructionist environment.

Building on the work of Idit Harel (1991), Yasmin Kafai (1995) developed an environment in which, over the course of several months, children design and implement educational video games for younger students. The designers not only discuss their projects with the others in the class, but they also have the younger children test their games and give them feedback. These demonstrations, and the discussions that surround them, are critical to the process of creating objects for others; they provide the designers with new perspectives on their games.

These discussions have generally been ephemeral; the children rarely have even taken notes on what their classmates or play-testers said. Although the articulation of their ideas about their projects is an important step, I believe that it is important to think not only about what is said, but how it is said. Many of the designers have recognized this when writing text to be displayed after the game player did something wrong. Their verbal questions or explanations, on the other hand, have not been recorded in any way that would allow them to examine their own words.

The designers write in their Designer's Notebooks every day to form a permanent record of their goals, problems, and ideas. There is no sense of an audience for these writings; the notebooks are introduced as a private place. I believe this type of space is necessary, but although it is an external creation, the fact that it is not meant to be shared means that the children do not gain other perspectives on their writing.

I believe that the addition of a public communication space to the Game Design Project could provide designers with the ability not only to share their questions and ideas with more students, but to reflect on their own words. Kafai and Harel (1991a, 1991b) included a consulting component to one of their software design projects. In that situation, the consulting occurred on two specific occasions, in assigned pairs. Kafai suggested replacing these assignments by use of the on-line communication environment I was designing for in-school use. This would allow the designers to ask questions whenever they wished, and any of the previous designers, who would now be consultants, could answer them.

PROVIDING A TOOL FOR COMMUNICATION

Children in a traditional school setting may be allowed to talk with others in their own classroom, but the amount of time and the range of topics is often strictly limited by their teachers. Lunch periods and recesses are less constrained than class periods, but even if children find time then to talk about their own interests (Renninger, Hidi, & Krapp, 1992) with their peers, it may be hard to identify other children who share those interests. These problems are magnified when children who wish to communicate are in different classrooms.

In addition to the physical space between rooms, the logistics of a school day make it difficult for teachers to arrange regular times for their students to meet. A shared environment on the local-area computer network in which participants could leave messages by topic would provide students with a means of communicating with each other whenever they and their teachers deem appropriate. It would also allow each student to participate legitimately at a level with which he or she feels comfortable (Lave & Wenger, 1991). Reading messages without posting may seem to be a minimal form of engagement, but it would be one way for students to be part of the community; children would have the opportunity to increase their participation whenever they desire. Although private E-mail would be fairly simple to enable on most local-area networks, I do not believe that it is the ideal environment for a communication environment such as the one I envisioned for these students. Private E-mail is sent directly from one person to another; this limits the communication to people who are already known to share an interest in whatever topic a child would wish to discuss. Furthermore, it limits the conversation to a fixed number of people, and does not allow for other people to view the discussion and decide to join it.

A broadcast environment in which all messages are public, on the other hand, would allow for children to locate people who share their interests (assuming that those people also post messages), and also to learn about others' interests. As demonstrated by a study that I conducted about children's viewpoints on news, children have particular interests but can be entirely unaware that other children in their own classroom share their interests (Evard, 1994).

Several on-line systems have been created to support learning about particular topics, such as science (e.g., Barowy & Newman, 1994), social studies (e.g., Borovoy, Cooper, & Bellamy, 1994; Kass, Dooley, & Luksa, 1993), and use of language (e.g., Bruce, Peyton, & Batson, 1993; Bruce & Rubin, 1993). This type of focus allows for more tailored software. As I wanted to provide a means for children to encounter the interests of their peers, however, I chose to design an environment that would be of more general use.

A netnews type of broadcast environment seemed to be particularly well suited to discussion of the Game Design Project between the two classrooms of students. The students who had already created their own games possessed a certain amount of expertise in the domain of game design, and as such could answer many of the questions the novices would have. The games they had created were often very different from each other, however, so students had varying amounts of experience at particular aspects of game design. The new designers usually did not know which of the consultants had done things similar to what they designed, so asking their questions in a broadcast environment was the most efficient way of locating someone who had the knowledge that was needed. Both groups of children would access the messages while working on programming projects, which helped situate the activity appropriately (Suchman, 1987).

One final benefit of the broadcast environment is that everyone would be able to read all the different statements, questions, and answers. Some of the designers might have similar problems; reading each others' questions could help them locate students doing related things as well as eliminate redundancy of topics. By reading various answers to one question, students could view disparate viewpoints or problem-solving strategies. Children would also have the opportunity to share their expertise in particular areas, gaining a measure of appreciation in the community.

Other researchers have noticed the importance to children of publishing their work in an on-line environment (e.g., Bruce, et al., 1993). It is unclear if the children view posting of single messages as "publishing" them. Although student-generated messages may remain on the system as long as there is sufficient disk space, they are still individual messages rather than portions of a database such as the ones CSILE students create (Scardamalia & Bereiter, 1991). I chose not to provide an archival structure to this discussion environment; one goal of this research is to see if students see a need for such an addition to the environment, and what form they wish it to take.

INTRODUCTION OF THE SYSTEM

Mark Kortekaas of the MIT Media Lab developed a network-based news server entitled NewsMaker; his initial goal was to provide an environment in which students could write and edit articles to produce a printed newspaper. External news articles were to be transmitted daily for the children to use and possibly edit (Kortekaas, 1994). This initial framework was similar to what I wanted to build, and because we would be working at the same site, we decided to use the same software for both projects. I was able to participate in certain design decisions related to the environment I wanted to build, and because I have access to the source code, I will be able to modify the software according to the children's preferences when possible.

The class of "consultants" were able to use NewsMaker twice a week for the last 10 minutes of their computer time as long as they made progress on their own projects. The designers were free to use the system whenever they were working on their games, which was a minimum of four 45-minute periods per week. Each child had a personalized disk with which to boot any of the computers. This brought up the Microsoft Windows environment and allowed access to News-Maker. When a child entered NewsMaker, the main menu bar was present. The choices included the standard Windows options: File, Edit, Search, and Help. There were two additional menu items unique to NewsMaker entitled "Newspaper" and "Groups." The Newspaper menu items allowed the user to indicate which messages to include in a paper and then print. The Groups menu was where all of the discussion groups' names were listed; selecting one of these names displayed the list of messages in that group.

I created a group called "Game Design" for the designers and consultants to use in discussing their projects. NewsMaker itself was introduced to these two classrooms as a way for them to ask and answer questions about game design in particular. The other groups on other topics were not formally mentioned to them, although many of them did become interested in other groups, such as the external news feeds, and used them on a regular basis.

The designers were not given their NewsMaker disks on the first day of their Game Design Project because most of them were involved with setting up their designer notebooks and starting their games. One girl, Whitney, asked if she could learn to use NewsMaker so that she could ask a particular question. She successfully sent her message and then went to her next class. The next day, Whitney showed two other students how to post questions; instructions were given to the entire class on the third day of the project.

The consultants first used NewsMaker the afternoon of the day when Whitney sent her question about creating an extra shapes page. As there was only one question for them to answer, some of them answered it and then asked what they should do. These students did not seem able to determine what kinds of information would be helpful to the new game designers until they read the question messages. One boy, Ken, told me explicitly that he did not know what to write about. I said that he could give advice that would have helped him when he was just starting with his game. He thought about this, and said maybe he could tell them about a particular command that he had used, then stated, "but they probably already know it." He tried (unsuccessfully, due to network problems) to answer Whitney's question, and on the following day answered three more questions. As of this writing, none of the consultants has posted a message with advice unless it was in response to a question.

USAGE PATTERNS

During the first 3 weeks of the Game Design Project, 14 of the 20 game designers posted questions to the game design group. Of the other 6, 2 answered questions but did not post any of their own, and 4 read messages but did not write any. All but 1 of the 18 students in the consulting class posted answers to questions; the one boy who did not post at all was relatively new to the school and Logo programming. As could be expected, the largest number of messages were exchanged when the system was first introduced; although Fig. 10.1 displays a steady decrease, it does not reflect the quality of the messages nor the subsequent increase in "useful" communication (as categorized by the children).

To identify usage patterns, I categorized each of the 235 messages that the students posted to the Game Design group.[1] As expected, most of the messages were either questions or answers; those messages that did not fit either of those types were categorized by their primary content. These included agreements (e.g., with a person's posted message), "I don't know" statements (those without other information), thank-you's, evaluative remarks (including requests for clarification, unprompted clarifications, and comments on the tone of messages), replies made up of random characters, and blank replies. Over half of the mes-

[1]A total of 262 messages were posted in the Game Design group during this time; I wrote 10; the designers' teacher sent 2; the consultants' teacher answered 3 questions; and students from a fourth-grade class posted 12. These messages were also categorized, but are not included in these figures.

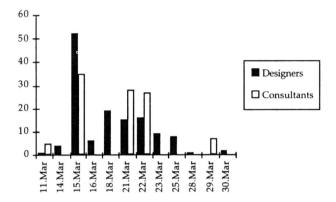

FIG. 10.1.   Number of posts in Game Design per day of usage.

sages were primarily questions or answers. Figures 10.2 and 10.3 break these categories down by the roles of the students in the two classrooms.

Somewhat surprisingly, the designers answered almost as many questions as the consultants did. This is likely due in part to the amount of time each classroom had to access NewsMaker, but it may also be because the designers had a greater investment in seeing their classmates' questions answered. In any case, the children did not seem to divide their community into two separate classrooms (designers and consultants) when writing messages. Very few students from the consulting class asked questions, but this was most likely because they were doing short-term projects for which they already had the knowledge they required.

Students in both classrooms made remarks about how "useful" various types

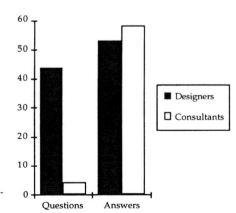

FIG. 10.2.   Questions and answers.

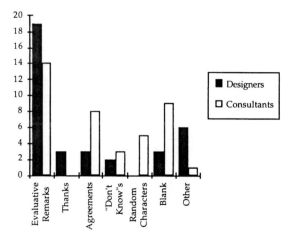

FIG. 10.3.   Other message categories.

of nonanswer messages were. The evaluative remarks were generally considered helpful, and messages of thanks were appreciated. Some messages consisted primarily of agreement with another person; although these were not considered useful, they were not labeled as harmful either. Posts that simply said "I don't know" were judged to be a waste of time by some of the children; responses that were blank or consisted of random characters were considered much worse, although some of the children allowed that the blank messages may have been due to interface problems.

The designers made more posts that were considered "useful" than the consultants did, as Fig. 10.3 shows. In some ways, this is not surprising, because they were answering their own classmates questions, and had a greater investment in the usage of the NewsMaker system than did children who only answered questions. When I talked with several of the consultants, they made it clear that part of the reason they did not spend much time answering questions was because they had their own work to do.

INTERACTIONS

There were many different types of exchanges between students. In this section, I discuss the most striking ones in the first 3 weeks of the project. Even within this short time, it was clear that there were developments on both the individual level and the community level.

Unknown Answers

Some of the students considered certain questions to be unanswerable. Most of the time when a child responded saying "you can't," he or she also included an alternate solution that avoided the problem. Whitney's first question[2] was one such problem:

Title: shapes page

how do you make a new shapes page?

I want to have more space on my shapes page .

Whitney X.

Although this is possible, it is nontrivial, and was not anything the children or their teachers had previously heard of or done. Even though they did not know how to make a new shapes page, several of the students answered Whitney, explaining what they would do.[3] For example, Simon suggested an alternative solution:

Title: Simon March 11, 1994

Dear Whitney,
    I don't know how to make a new shapes page but I do know how to erase shapes. All you have to do is go to the shape you want to erase and press F4. Bye!

Of the seven children who answered Whitney's question, five gave this type of alternative. In this case, their alternatives were not used because Whitney wanted to know the exact answer; she blamed these unhelpful answers on her statement of the question because, as she said, if she had told them she knew how to erase shapes but that she did not want to, they would not have told her that was the solution. In other cases, however, alternative answers were more useful.

Although many children began their replies with "I don't know" and went on to give an alternate solution, there were also five replies to various questions that simply stated "I don't know" without offering any advice. One such post was in response to Whitney's question.

Title: Whitney"s Answer

Dear Whitney,

    I don't know the answer to your question. I never had this problem. I hope I will be able to answer in the future!

Kim X

---

[2]All messages contained a title and a body; the date of posting and the author's name were also associated with them. Pseudonyms were substituted for names in the quoted messages.

[3]The children were uncertain how to title their responses to Whitney, and a couple of them commented that it would be better to have a reference to the question in the answer. For this reason, a reply command was implemented. It puts "RE:" in front of the message title and includes the message being replied to in the body of the reply, preceding each line by a >.

Many of the children were apologetic when they did not know an answer to give. Even so, several of the designers reacted negatively to these messages. Stephen asked a question and ended it with the words, "Don't answer I don't know!" Albert wrote a pointed message about certain types of messages that he considered unhelpful, in the middle of which he included the statement:

> . . . Answers like "I don't know" don't make a lot of sense, either. I think that when a person asks a question, they are trying to find out what people know, not what they don't know! . . .

Whitney made a similar statement. There were no more simple "I don't know" responses after these three messages were sent. This demonstrates the growth of a community sense of what was appropriate and helpful in this context.

Researching Answers

The children did not limit themselves to answering only those questions to which they already knew a solution. Some of them asked other people, searched in books, or even wrote test programs in their search for answers for other students. For example, Jorge posted the following question:

> Title: How many mammals live in the ocean?
>
> --Jorge X

A few minutes later, Emilie came up to me and asked, "How many mammals are there in the ocean?" When I asked her if she meant how many kinds or how many of each kind, she did not seem to know. We talked about it for a while. Then she went and looked up some things in one of the reference books. She spent at least 5 minutes of the 45-minute class period trying to answer this question, and finally returned to her computer to send this message:

> Title: RE: How many mammals live in the ocean?
>
> >--Jorge X
>
> I DON"T KNOW THE ANSWER BUT THERE ARE 20 SPEICIES OF WHALES+DOLPHINS
>
> EMILIE

Another designer, Jaques, also spent some of his time searching for the answer to Jorge's question. He found a poster in the classroom that listed several types of seals, whales, and dolphins, and typed them all into NewsMaker. He was quite persistent, and went back the next day to finish typing in the list. Jaques and Emilie could have simply spoken to Jorge, giving him the information they had found, but both of them chose to share what they learned with the entire community.

Several children stated that they tried various solutions in their attempts to answer messages. Deanna was unsuccessful in her attempt to find a solution to Emilie's question, "HOW DO YOU GET RID OF THE BOX IN THE CORNER OF THE SCREEN?" and explained the process as follows:

```
I think I know what you are talking about maybe if you try to
delete the screen it would erase but I tried that and it would
not work so I guess you are stuck (Deanna B.)
```

Although this may not seem helpful at first glance, Deanna did explain a method that would not solve the problem so that Emilie would not try the same things she had. Each of these children willingly did research to help their classmates, going beyond simply reporting what they already knew. The teachers were glad to see children voluntarily doing research, but were concerned that some of the students would take advantage of the others; this did not happen over the course of this project.

Appropriateness of Questions

Two types of questions were considered inappropriate by the students of this community: those that the questioner could or should have looked up without help, and those for which the NewsMaker environment was not suited. These limits to the children's communication were not formally dictated by the classroom rules or the technology, but were informally discussed and agreed on by the students.

Jorge's query about mammals in the ocean initiated a discussion about questions among the designers. The two students who did some research and posted responses clearly did not think the question was inappropriate, but others disagreed. Most of those who considered the question inappropriate were students in the design class, who stated in a classroom discussion that ocean questions were things for which they should search out answers on their own. One of the consultants, Isabel, posted this response:

```
Dear Jorge,
        Why don't you go and see if you can look up your ques-
tion somewhere in a book or ask someone else okay.
```

It is unclear if Isabel thought Jorge should not have asked his question on NewsMaker because she added that he could ask "someone else," but her tone seems to imply that he should have known to try looking it up in a book. The designers' teacher was quite clear in her message:

```
Dear Jorge,
    Is this question about how to design your game? Or is this a
question about information you need to know to create your
```

```
game? Who is responsible for doing the research about your
topic? Your classmates or you?
     I suggest that to answer this question, you leave the com-
puters and go into the classroom to consult the many books
about the ocean which are there. If the answer is not in one of
these books, I suggest you continue your research at the li-
brary.
                         Sincerely,
                         Ms. M.
```

This distinction between the science content of their games and the questions related to Logo programming was the first line drawn by the students, many of whom mentioned the question before the teacher posted the preceding message.

Several students went beyond the ocean–Logo distinction to say that there were some kinds of questions, such as those about the appearance of an image, for which the NewsMaker environment was not conducive. This topic went beyond a one-time classroom discussion to be incorporated in the children's discussions, and also in later posts. In his post entitled "False Answers" as well as in conversation, Albert stated that questions such as those about graphic design "don't make sense" in NewsMaker.

Some students included short code segments in their messages to demonstrate certain techniques, but because there was no connection between Logo and NewsMaker, the sender needed to retype the code. To avoid this problem, several of the students answered a question with a proposed meeting time, generally at lunch or on the bus. For example, Cheryl replied to Emilie's question with this message:

```
I can't write out the whole procedure right here because it's
too long, but maybe I can print it out and give it to you on
the bus.
```

I believe that it was important for these children to be able to recognize the limits of the technology that they were using and work out other means of communication when necessary.

Through exchanges such as these, the quality of questions became part of the discourse in the game designers' classroom. Several times a student mentioned to me or to another student that some of the answers received were not helpful because the question was not worded clearly, or because the question simply was not appropriate in the NewsMaker context. These children began to be aware of other students' perspectives of their messages, and to recognize that they were responsible for communicating clearly to their audience. They also developed a greater sense of what was helpful to ask about in the given context.

Evaluating Questions and Answers

As time went on, more of the messages included some kind of evaluative content. Many times students used phrases such as "it depends" or "I don't understand,"

and then explained the ambiguity they saw. For example, a consultant named Rachel replied to Jorge's mammal question by saying:

```
Dear Jorge,
It depends on if you mean how many kinds or how many of each
kind.
```

Students in the consulting class were concerned about what the other children should know; several messages included statements like Ursula's comment:

```
P.S. Do you already know this? because I think you do.
```

Sometimes misunderstandings or ambiguities would be identified when the initial message (generally a question) was read; these then would result in a conversation between two or more students. In the following example, one of the designers was trying to understand what another was asking:

```
Title: RE: RE: RE: RE: Reverse shapes

>>>> Does anyone know how to reverse a shape: make the black
>>>> part white, and the white part black?
>>>>
>>>> Albert
>>> no⁴
>>>
>> What do you mean? Do you mean on the shapes page? Or on
>> the screen?
>> Renee
>>
> The shapes page.
>
> Albert
>
Can't you just click space on all of the blocks in the square
and then make the picture by clicking again? Then the black or
background would be white and the picture or the white would
be black?
Renee
```

At other times, students who responded would not realize that they had misunderstood the question they were answering, but the questioner would see that the answer was not the one desired. In several of these cases, I heard the designer who had asked the question tell another student that the question had not ex-

---

⁴This reply by Lisa, who did not sign her name, seemed to be ignored by both Albert and Renee.

plained the situation in enough detail. Increasingly, the students who asked questions would clarify their own words after reading the responses.

```
Title: RE: RE: Following Shapes

>> How do you make one shape fallow another? One shape moving
>> by the arrow or letter keys, the other moving by computer,
>> following the other shape?
>> Renee
>
> WELL YOU COULD USE YOUR FOUR TURTLES, THEN SEE WHAT HAPPENS.
> TINA H.-307

I could use four turtles, but that doesn't answer my ques-
tion. How do you make a shape follow another shape that a per-
son is controlling? How do you make the shape that is follow-
ing, follow by computer?
Renee
```

I believe these exchanges demonstrate how the children were learning to clarify their written messages for each other, as well as to identify misunderstandings. The quality of original questions also increased with the children's experience. Students who did not participate in evaluative or clarifying remarks did not disparage these exchanges; rather, a community sense that such interactions were helpful began to develop.

DISCUSSION

There are a number of issues that I intend to study throughout this and subsequent projects. Here I introduce several of the topics that arose during the beginning of this project. To treat these issues more in depth, however, a longer time frame would need to be analyzed.

The students' usage of NewsMaker changed over time in at least two dimensions: the types of topics discussed and the characteristics of the messages. Three main types of issues were discussed electronically by the students in the designing and consulting classes during the first 3 weeks of their projects: programming issues, issues of the content of their games, and social etiquette. Later in the project, the students discussed educational issues as well; questions such as those about how things should look disappeared. There were fewer questions later in the project than there were in the first few days, but the posted questions were posted were increasingly detailed and descriptive. More of the questions in the later weeks of the project requested opinions rather than simply how to do something. For example, there were discussions on topics such as whether or not trick questions in a game would teach the user anything and how to make losing "funner" than just halting the game. The quality of discussion, both of topics and of discourse, increased over time.

When introducing this system to the children, I made no mention of any kind of social standards, as I preferred to see if the children would construct a self-governing community. This hope has been fulfilled; children have posted comments about what types of messages they consider helpful, and these opinions seem to have been heeded by the group. For example, several of the boys ended some of their answer messages with "DUH!" during the first few days of this project. Several of the students responded negatively to this, and some of them posted their opinions. Carrie responded to an unclear answer ending in "DUH!!!" by concluding her message similarly. Whitney was more explicit. In her message titled "Rude!" she stated:

```
I think that some of the answers that are given are rude and
impolite. . . . They should also not end the question writing
something like "Duh!" they should answer it with something
like "And that is how you do it.". So please stop thank you.
```

After that, none of the children included "DUH!" in their messages, and the tone in general was more positive.

Many people have observed the gender split in Usenet newsgroups. They have seen that the vast majority of people posting messages are male; it has been estimated that less than 10% of the messages are written by women. Many women with whom I have spoken say that although they do not post in the public forum, they often send private E-mail responses to questions posed in public. One of the reasons I preferred to provide public broadcast but not private E-mail in this system was that I wanted a community to develop and for all of the children to be able to take part in it. This has occurred, and I believe that the broadcast-only nature of the environment aided participation.

Girls and boys answered about the same number of questions in both classrooms; the girls were more likely to qualify their answers, however, whereas the boys were more direct. Female designers asked twice as many questions as their male counterparts did, and although the female consultants asked a total of four questions, none of the male consultants asked a question.

The children occasionally addressed a particular person in the title line of a message, but most posts were unaddressed. Those addressed to someone in particular were generally regarding something about which the questioner already had talked to the addressee, or about which the addressee was the one known expert. Although these messages were all answered by their addressees, occasionally another student would respond as well. These additional responses were welcomed by the questioners.

Occasionally a question similar to a previously asked one would be posted. Generally these were answered as if they had not been asked before, but a few times a respondent would refer to another answer by repeating it. For example, when Jaques asked a question similar to another, Stephan replied:

```
Jaques, just like I replied to somebody else, "Make 'em on you
shapes page!"
```

Only one student referred to a previous post by title during the first weeks of this project.

Frequently asked questions are considered a problem on many electronic bulletin boards, partly because they cause the entire group to revisit a topic that they have previously discussed. Such questions are most often asked by people who are new to the group and who have not seen the old discussions, so collections of such questions and their answers are commonly made to be supplied to new people. The students who used NewsMaker did not discuss creating any device for collecting information or for dealing with repeated questions. There are at least three possible reasons for this: all messages remained on the system throughout the project; all of the children started using the system at about the same time; and the duration of the entire project was only 4 months.

Each of these issues—changes in topic and presentation, sense of community, gender-related issues, establishment of connections, and common themes or questions—is something strongly affected by time. In this preliminary discussion, I have presented the first 3 weeks of a 4-month project; in future work, I plan to develop issues such as the ones I have mentioned here more fully. Even during the first 3 weeks of the project, however, a community began to develop. There was a growth in the students' ability to post their questions in ways that would help others understand them, and the quality of questions became something that the students discussed among themselves. I believe that posting questions in this public environment has helped the students' own words to become objects for them to think with and about.

ACKNOWLEDGMENTS

I would like to thank the children and their teachers for participating in this project and discussing their perspectives with me. Mark Kortekaas not only encouraged this use of his software, but allowed me to participate in its design and supported my work with it; his aid was invaluable to me. Yasmin Kafai has been my mentor during my first 2 years at Project Headlight. Without her support, this work would not have been possible. I also thank Edith Ackermann, Seymour Papert, and Mitchel Resnick for discussions about this project. The preparation of this chapter was supported by the National Science Foundation (Grant 9153719-MDR), the LEGO Group, Nintendo Inc., IBM Corporation, and the MIT Media Laboratory's News in the Future Consortium. The ideas expressed here do not necessarily reflect the positions of the supporting agencies.

REFERENCES

Barowy, W., & Newman, D. (1994). Community of explorers: Building a new kind of computer network for school science. Second Annual Report, Bolt, Beranek and Newman, Inc. Cambridge, MA.

Borovoy, R. D., Cooper, E. B. W., & Bellamy, R. K. E. (1994). Media fusion: An application of model-based communication. In the Proceedings of CHI'94, Boston.

Bruce, B., & Rubin, A. (1993). *Electronic quills: A situated evaluation of using computers for teaching writing in classrooms.* Hillsdale, NJ: Lawrence Erlbaum Associates.

Bruce, B., Peyton, J. K., & Batson, T. (1993). *Network-based classrooms: Promises and realities.* Cambridge, UK: Cambridge University Press.

Evard, M. (1994). What is "news"?: Children's conceptions and uses of news. Annual Meeting of the American Educational Research Association, New Orleans.

Harel, I. (1991). *Children designers.* Norwood, NJ: Ablex.

Kafai, Y. B. (1995). *Minds in play: Computer game design as a context for children's learning.* Hillsdale, NJ: Lawrence Erlbaum Associates.

Kafai, Y. B., & Harel, I. (1991a). Children's learning through consulting: When mathematical ideas, software design, and playful discourse are intertwined. In I. Harel & S. Papert (Eds.), *Constructionism* (pp. 111–140). Norwood, NJ: Ablex.

Kafai, Y. B., & Harel, I. (1991b). Learning through design and teaching: Exploring social and collaborative aspects of constructionism. In I. Harel & S. Papert (Eds.), *Constructionism* (pp. 85–106). Norwood, NJ: Ablex.

Kass, A., Dooley, S., & Luksa, F. (1993). *The broadcast news project: Using broadcast journalism as a vehicle for teaching social studies.* Evanston, IL: The Institute for the Learning Sciences, Northwestern University.

Kortekaas, M. (1994). News and education: Creation of "The Classroom Chronicle." Master's Thesis, Cambridge, MA: MIT Media Arts and Sciences Program.

Lave, J., & Wenger, E. (1991). *Situated learning: Legitimate peripheral participation.* Cambridge, UK: Cambridge University Press.

Papert, S. (1980). *Mindstorms.* New York: Basic Books.

Papert, S. (1991). Situating constructionism. In I. Harel & S. Papert (Eds.), *Constructionism* (pp. 1–11). Norwood, NJ: Ablex.

Papert, S. (1993). *The children's machine.* New York: Basic Books.

Renninger, K. A., Hidi, S., & Krapp, A. (Eds.) (1992). *The role of interest in learning and development.* Hillsdale, NJ: Lawrence Erlbaum Associates.

Scardamalia, M., & Bereiter, C. (1991). Higher levels of agency for children in knowledge building: A challenge for the design of new knowledge media. *The Journal of the Learning Sciences, 1*(1), 37–68.

Suchman, L. (1987). *Plans and situated actions: The problem of human-machine communication.* Cambridge, UK: Cambridge University Press.

"They Have Their Own Thoughts"[1]
A Story of Constructionist Learning in an Alternative African-Centered Community School

Paula K. Hooper

INTRODUCTION

Many children of color learn from an early age that there are doubts concerning their capacity to develop intellectually. Messages communicated from school (low ability placements in the primary grade), from peers (pervasive anti-intellectualism in their peer group), and the media (expectations of inferiority) all serve to impress upon them that they may not be up to the task of advanced studies. The lack of confidence engendered by the internalization of these messages shapes the meaning of any failure ("I guess this proves I'm not that smart") and undermines the capacity to work ("Why bang my head against the wall if I'm unable to learn the stuff anyway?") (Moses, 1989, p. 437).

Constructionism . . . has as its main feature the fact that it looks more closely than other educational -isms at the idea of mental construction. It attaches special importance to the role of constructions in the world as a support for those in the head, thereby becoming less of a purely mentalist doctrine. It also takes the idea of constructing in the head more seriously by recognizing more than one kind of construction and by asking questions about the materials used (Papert, 1993 p. 143).

In the passage quoted at the beginning of this chapter, Bob Moses describes how many school experiences convey messages of intellectual inability to children of color. He creates a very different type of school environment in order to counteract these messages, one that engenders confidence in children of color. His

---

[1]The title is taken from the song, *On Children*, as sung by "Sweet Honey in the Rock" with lyrics from *The Prophet* by Kahlil Gibran (*Good News*, 1981. Chicago: Flying Fish Records, Inc.).

Algebra Project aims to help African-American children make personal connections to algebraic ideas and thinking in ways that resonate with their sociocultural experiences (Moses, 1989).

Seymour Papert, as part of his constructionist approach to learning, emphasizes the importance of children making things. He sees computers as a new construction material, allowing children to explore new ideas in the process of making their own projects—and to explore those ideas in very different ways than they would in traditional school activities. The Logo programming language, created by Papert and his colleagues, has spawned a great deal of research into ways that programming provides children with new ways to relate to mathematical ideas. Very little of this research however, gives significant attention to the particular experiences of children of color working with Logo.

This chapter aims to weave together ideas that Moses and Papert describe through analyzing an experience from a school where constructionist tools are being used to help children of color develop new confidence in themselves as learners. In particular, I present a "learning story" of a child working on a Logo project within a school environment that nurtures her sense of herself as a learner.

The pivotal moments in this story have important implications for constructionism in practice. The story represents how children, in the process of making new computational artifacts, can take control of their own learning, developing and extending their own ideas. Moreover, it highlights the need for school environments to support and legitimize children's own personal ways of thinking about mental and physical constructs.

The learning story presented here takes place at Paige Academy (hereafter referred to as Paige), an alternative, African-centered school where the philosophy of education is rooted in the Nguzo Saba, The Seven Principles of Kwanza.[2] There the learning environment is developed within traditions of belonging to an African-American family. Learning and teaching at Paige are designed to provide education that encourages all children as learners within a culture rooted in African-American values, interactions, and ways of knowing. Classrooms are described as "organized to support a problem-solving approach to learning, with extensive reliance on the arts as a natural form of expression and exploration" (Paige-Cook, 1991, p. 2). The story presented here portrays how the African-centered ideology that defines Paige is put into practice through pedagogy that integrates children's interests, desires, and valuing of their cultural identities with addressing their academic needs.

---

[2]The Nguzo Saba, The Seven Principles of Kwanza are Umoja (Unity), Kujichagulia (Self-Determination), Ujimaa (Cooperative Economics), Ujamaa (Collective Work and Responsibiltiy), Nia (Purpose), Kuumba (Creativity), and Imani (Faith). For more information about the Nguzo Saba or the construction of Kwanza as an African-American celebration of cultural identity, you can refer to *The African American Holiday of Kwanzaa* by Maulana Karenga (Los Angeles: University of Sankore Press, 1988) or *Kwanzaa: A Family Affair* by Mildred Pitts Walter (New York: Lothrop, Lee, & Shepard Books, 1995).

The location of a culture of computing within this African-centered school culture creates a unique setting for exploring the influence of interactions between sociocultural context and uses of constructionist technologies on children developing new ideas. Most children at Paige have had extensive experience programming in several versions of Logo over the past three years. The children in Group 3 (children ages 8 to 11) at Paige usually have "Computer Class" for anywhere from 45 minutes to 2 hours, three times per week. All but one of the six children in this group have attended Paige since they were toddlers. Classes are supported by one or two teachers.

The following story is from the work of Shamia, an 8-year-old girl in Group 3. Prior to the time of this story, Shamia had done very little work writing her own procedures, although she was comfortable with modifying procedures that were provided as tools. She worked on this project during several class sessions over a 4-week period, often even after other students had left class.

Shamia's rainbow story is an example of a constructionist tool (LogoWriter) supporting a pedagogy that allows students to express themselves in their own ways. It offers a way of seeing children's self-expression as pivotal in their construction of new ideas. This story reveals that during her project, Shamia developed an understanding of mathematical ideas considered to be advanced for a child her age according to most elementary math curricula. Her story could emerge as it did because the culture of learning at Paige includes encouragement for her to assert her independence in discovering how to solve her problem in her own way.

LEARNING STORY: SHAMIA AND HER RAINBOW

Earlier in the school year, Shamia's class created a character called an Elephantbird. Once it became clear that the Elephantbird had captured children's interests, each child was asked to create his or her own project that included this unique character. Shamia created a LogoWriter animation for her Elephantbird to fly. For the background scenery of the animation, she planned a bench, a tree, and a rainbow in the sky. Her efforts to create each part led her to generate her own ways of thinking about mathematics or programming ideas (or both) that were new to her. For instance, when she made her bench, she learned a new strategy that she could use to build her procedures. Creating her tree led her to a new idea about sizes of turns and lengths for creating branches with equal parts.

This story is a description of pivotal moments within her process of making a rainbow for the sky in her scene. Creating her rainbow was a particularly rich part of her work because the process carried her into posing her own questions concerning several mathematical ideas, including decimals, the geometry of circles, relationships between division and multiplication, and linear relationships. She became invested in thinking about these ideas in order to fashion a procedure to draw her rainbow. This story describes some of the development of her thinking and how her work provided a context for her to assert her sense of independence and competence about figuring out computational ideas.

Defining the Problem and Asserting Her Way of Thinking

When Shamia began making her rainbow, she asked me to help her think about how to draw it. I asked her to use a marker to draw how she thought the first part of her rainbow might look on a card. She drew a picture of a half-circle. Next, I thought that the strategy of walking in the path of a half-circle could help her to reason out an instruction for drawing her half-circle. I asked her to "play turtle" and walk in the way the turtle would need to move. Reluctantly, Shamia started to walk and talk about the turtle going forward and turning to the right several times. From her movements, we decided that she would need to use the command `repeat`.

Under the picture she had drawn, I then wrote the frame of the `repeat` statement for her to use to fill in the commands she decided she would need to complete the statement. She stopped in the middle of her writing and asked to get one of her old disks, remembering that it had procedures to make circles. She remembered a page with procedures for circles of different sizes that her group had been given the previous year. The page contained three procedures: `bigc`, `midc`, and `smc`. It originally had provided tools for students to use in creating pictures with circles and to encourage their thinking about writing procedures. From the moment that Shamia decided to get her old disk, she began to show a much more assertive and independent attitude and was in hot pursuit of her own strategies for making her rainbow.

Solving the Initial Problem and Facing the "Bigger" One

Shamia copied the old page onto her new disk. She then examined the procedures and decided to modify the procedure called `bigc` that made a circle with the following `repeat` statement:

```
repeat 360 [fd 1 rt 1]
```

She was comfortable with changing numbers in `repeat` statements as a way of achieving various turtle graphics designs—although to my knowledge, she had never written her own procedure to make a circle or arc. She assumed that she needed to change the number 360 in order to figure out how to make the arc she envisioned. A method of trial and error in decreasing 360 led her to discover that the number of times to repeat for a half-circle was 180. She was satisfied when the procedure contained the following statement, which she said made "the

FIG. 11.1. The first arc of Shamia's rainbow.

line that makes a rainbow."[3] Her new `bigc` drew the semicircle shown in Fig.
11.1.

```
to bigc
repeat 180 [fd 1 rt 1]
end
```

When she looked at the single arc on the screen made by her `bigc` procedure,
Shamia realized that she was faced with the problem of how to make six more
arcs of different sizes to form a whole rainbow. Faced with this problem, she
wanted to settle for one line to show her rainbow, because she felt that it would
be "too hard" to make the other lines. Her classroom teacher, Brother Joe,[4]
stepped in at this point and told her that it was not too hard for her; she could
figure it out, and he was going to sit and work with her until they figured it out
together.

As Shamia worked with Brother Joe, she described her task as figuring out
how to use the `repeat` statement to make "the different lines in a rainbow." She
worked with Brother Joe for quite a while during this initial session. One of the
first ideas they established was that changing the number for the amount of turn
was the way to change the size of the curve. Using this idea, they began to
investigate a curve with a left turn of 2 using the following statement that draws
the circle shown in Fig. 11.2:

```
repeat 180 [fd 1 lt 2]
```

While Shamia and Brother Joe looked at the circle made by this statement, the
following dialogue occurred:

Brother Joe: Okay, that's good, but it's not right. We dou-
bled the turns and—
Shamia: Brother Joe, what's half of 180?

FIG. 11.2. Shamia's first attempt at the second arc created
this circle.

Brother Joe: Uh . . . 90.
Shamia: Did you see what it did? It made a whole circle. We're
going to have to use half of that.
Brother Joe: All right!

In this dialogue, Shamia expressed her way to view the relationship between the repetitions and the turns. She assertively cut off Brother Joe to ask for information she needed. Given this key piece of information along with a few other details,[5] Shamia modified bigc again to make Fig. 11.3. They figured out the direction the turtle would need to turn for each curve based on whether it was on the left or right side of the rainbow.

Shamia decided that there was too much space between the first curve that used 1 for the turn and the second one that used 2 for the turn. This problem caused her to think that the number for the turn would need to be between 1 and 2. Brother Joe told Shamia that the numbers in between 1 and 2 were decimals. He gave examples such as 1.3 and 1.6, explaining that the decimal part could be any number from 1 to 9. This situation was one of Shamia's first encounters with using decimal numbers. None of her work in math had included operations with decimals, although she had seen the older students in her group working with them. After discussing the spacing she wanted the curve to have between her first and second curves, Shamia decided to try 1.5.

At this point, Brother Joe drew upon Shamia's idea for dividing 180 by 2 in order to make a smaller half-circle. He explained that they would need to do the same thing to find 90 for the smaller half-circle. He continued to explain that this connection meant that she would need to divide 180 by the decimal number she chose for the turns in order to find the number of times to repeat. Brother Joe suggested finding a calculator to make the calculation they had identified, but Shamia told him that they could use LogoWriter as a calculator to show the division of 180. Their first calculation of 180 divided by 1.5 produced 120. Shamia thought about modifying bigc to make this curve fit between the two they already had. As she thought, she figured out that this curve needed to be

---

[5]There are a few other details that they had to think about that are not elaborated in this chapter. For example, one detail involved estimating how much to have the turtle move for spacing between the arcs.

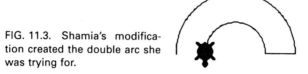

FIG. 11.3. Shamia's modification created the double arc she was trying for.

drawn to the left because the turtle was on the right side of the rainbow. She wrote the `repeat` statement for this curve and inserted it into the `bigc` procedure. To see what the procedure and picture for `bigc` looked like after these modifications, see Fig. 11.4.

```
to bigc
repeat 180 [fd 1 rt 1]
rt 90 fd 19 rt 90 repeat 120 [fd 1 lt 1.5]
rt 90 fd 19
rt 180 fd 29
lt 90
repeat 90 [fd 1 rt 2]
end
```

It seemed as though Shamia began to internalize the idea Brother Joe had helped her to examine about dividing 180 by the size of the turn. Her comprehension was initiated by her own invention of using 90 repetitions with turns of `rt 2`. Soon after they made this third semicircle, she began to say that they needed to divide 180 by "that number" (which to her meant turning angle) in order to "find the number for the number of times to repeat."

Becoming the Rainbow Maker

After awhile, Brother Joe had to leave class. As he left, he told Shamia that he felt she "knew how to do it, so she could work by herself." Working on her own, she asked for a "real" calculator. She said she did not like typing out the expressions in the command center of LogoWriter, and apparently she did not consider

FIG. 11.4. Further modifications allowed Shamia to repeat the curve, to the left or right, as needed.

this process to serve as a "real" calculator. She chose to find a calculator without mention of the fact that Brother Joe had originally suggested using one. Her choice of this tool seemed to be an assertion of her independence in beginning to generate the rest of her rainbow on her own.

With calculator in hand, she began to do the division of 180 by numbers such as 1.2, 3, 3.4, and 4.5 in order to get the information she needed to create the smaller arcs. She tried several different calculations and drawings to work out numbers for arcs of sizes that fit in a way that she liked. Each time she constructed a statement she needed, she added it to the bigc procedure along with the commands to move the turtle into an appropriate position. Her work showed her thinking about decimal numbers as subdivisions between whole numbers. She seemed to have a sense that 3.4 was between 3 and 4, yet a little closer to 3, and that 4.5 was halfway between 4 and 5.

Shamia began to work as though she were aware that she had developed her own new technique. At one point, she described what she was doing to make her rainbow by saying, "I'm trying to figure out repeat 60 [fd 1 rt 3] on the calculator. I did 180 divided by 3 and that gave me 60." It was clear from the way that Shamia worked out her calculations and developed her procedure that she was confident in her newfound talent to make half-circles of different sizes. Making her rainbow was a great source of pride and accomplishment for her in a personally meaningful way.

The final version of Shamia's procedure to draw a rainbow, in the way that she wrote it, follows. The picture it creates is shown in Fig. 11.5.

```
to bigc
repeat 180 [fd 1 rt 1]
rt 90 fd 19 rt 90 repeat 120 [fd 1 lt 1.5]
rt 90 fd 19
rt 180 fd 29
lt 90
repeat 90 [fd 1 rt 2]
lt 90
fd 29
pd
bk 10
lt 90
```

FIG. 11.5. Self-determination allowed Shamia to develop the technique that would finally accomplish her rainbow goal.

```
repeat 150 [fd 1 lt 1.2]
lt 90
fd 30
lt 90
repeat 60 [fd 1 rt 3]
lt 90
fd 30
lt 90
lt 90
fd 36
rt 90
repeat 40 [fd 1 lt 4.5]
rt 90
fd 20
rt 90
rt 90
fd 24
lt 90
repeat 30 [fd 1 rt 6.5]
lt 9
lt 90
fd 30
rt 90
rt 90
fd 30
fd 30
end
```

DISCUSSION

This story allows several observations to be made about Shamia's learning with Logo within the learning environment at Paige. Her work in this context indicates the significance of constructionism in practice as a way to assist children in having their own thoughts.

A Note on Shamia's Mathematical Thinking

During a class discussion of the ways students were figuring out how to make parts of their projects, Shamia described what she called her "rainbow maker" procedure in the following way: "The bigger the number, the smaller it gets. The number at the end, the bigger it gets, the smaller the circle gets." This statement reflected her understanding of part of the process she had developed for forming her rainbow. The way that she worked showed that she also recognized that the number of times to repeat would decrease as the number for the turns increased. The creation of "lines" for her rainbow seemed to become a method that she began to own.

Developing this method carried her into an informal experience with algebraic thinking. Her discovery reveals an informal understanding of an inverse relationship between the number of times to `repeat` and the turning angle for each arc. Her comment and her process of working make it seem that, even though she did not create the arcs in order, she knew that she could have drawn them in order from largest to smallest. Holding this possibility in her mind suggests that she was thinking about the relationship in a way similar to that shown here:

Turn	Repetitions
1	180
1.2	150
1.5	120
2	90
3	60
4.5	40
6.5	30

The method that Shamia created also involved her in making sense of decimal numbers. As described earlier, finding the appropriate sizes for the arcs made it necessary for her to use numbers that fell between the whole numbers familiar to her. When she was ready for a sense of completion on her rainbow, she actually overextended her use of decimals a bit. Her final calculation of 6.5 * 30 actually left the turtle at a heading that slightly overshot 180. No one noticed this error until much later because of her focus on 6.5 creating exactly the size of arc that she wanted.

Pursuing a Personal Path

Shamia's mathematical ideas about decimals and about the relationship between turns and repetitions emerged in the process of making a personally meaningful programming project. The emergence of her ideas raises issues about how teachers use Logo to create contexts for children's learning. Some teachers might have designed other activities for Shamia when it became clear that she was struggling to figure out factors of 180 or relationships between shapes of different sizes. They might have interpreted her struggle as an opportunity to pose tasks for her such as describing patterns in tables of numbers or comparing perimeters of the same shape in different sizes. The motivation behind these strategies could have been to help Shamia learn what she needs to know in order to be able to figure out the answer to her question. This kind of teaching, however, would have required Shamia to suspend the path of thinking that she had formed on her own. This pedagogical choice would have taken her away from the path of learning that she had constructed for herself, requiring her instead to engage in a teacher's path requiring her trust that it lead her to the answers she wanted.

Brother Joe recognized that her independence in thinking about the mathematical ideas was intertwined with creating her rainbow in her own way, so he pushed her to think about the ideas in the context of making her rainbow. His choice is consistent with his teaching practice, reflecting the values system of the school, rooted in the principles of Kwanza, by choosing to respect her determination to solve the problem in her own way. His choice to work collaboratively with her to stay engaged in figuring out her solution reflects the value of collective work that is also prevalent in both the values system and the practices of the school. Consistent with constructionist theory, her initiative to think about mathematical ideas that were sophisticated for her was directly connected to her project of making a rainbow. Logo acted as a tool for her use to construct her rainbow and create mental constructions that grew out of making her rainbow. The ownership of her strategies was closely connected to her engagement with the ideas.

Logo and Knowledge Construction

LogoWriter acted as both a palette upon which Shamia's idea to create a rainbow emerged and a drawing tool that required her to think about several mathematical ideas in order to create her rainbow. Her ideas about the relationships between the numbers for the turns and repetitions was elicited by her need to direct the turtle to draw with `repeat` statements. Logo acted as a tool for her knowledge construction because it was the context enabling her to generate her ideas, visualize her problems, and investigate solutions. The ownership of her programming project became a good backdrop for the interactions she had with Brother Joe so that they could discuss changes to make, why to make them, and ways to test them. It seemed as though doing this project on the computer helped her to assert her confidence in the way she wanted to think about the problem and find solutions.

CONCLUSION

This story is a glimpse into the life of a child whose developing ideas are meaningful to her and who has taken ownership of the process of understanding and applying complex mathematical ideas. Shamia worked on figuring out a way to understand the relationship between the numbers for the turning angle and the numbers for repetition because this understanding was going to help her make her rainbow. The ways that she asserted herself in calculating the statements for the arcs in her rainbow seemed similar to the kind of ownership a child can take in drawing a picture on paper. Her actions were like those of a young child taking a crayon out of her mother's hand and saying, "I want to draw it myself." Interestingly though, Shamia took ownership over defining and applying computational ideas in a way that is not typical of many children in school, particularly children of color.

As described earlier, Bob Moses points out the need to provide children of color with mathematics learning experiences that support rather than undermine their confidence in their abilities to work on challenging math problems. Shamia's "rainbow learning" experience presents a clear example of a child rising to the challenge of working to understand computational ideas that are new to her. There are also indications from this story that the espoused African-centered nature of the learning culture at Paige was involved in supporting Shamia's confident approach to solving her problems.

Reflecting Papert's views of constructionism, Logo was a successful tool for fostering Shamia's engagement and allowing her to find her own way to think about the rainbow. Turtle graphics provided her with a way to assert her own way of thinking about how to make her rainbow and to understand new ideas in the process of constructing all the parts of her rainbow.

The fact that Shamia is learning in a school environment where her interests and cultural heritage are recognized and respected is congruent with Moses' message and presents a unique opportunity for learning research. With the intention of supporting her learning needs as an African-American child, her teacher creates a learning environment filled with expectations that she can figure out a complex problem (like the rainbow), support for her work on her problem, and respect for her assertion of ownership of her strategy. Her story shows how this environment offers opportunities to explore resonances between the ways that mathematical ideas are embedded in work with Logo and the ways that mathematics learning is emergent from the pedagogy within an African-centered school. Her story is one of many from this school that help to make a case for including analysis of cultural diversity and sociocultural context within both research and practice of constructionism.

ACKNOWLEDGMENTS

This chapter is part of an ongoing thesis research study of children's learning at Paige Academy with constructionist technologies from a perspective that includes sociocultural context as an element of knowledge construction. This chapter would not have come together without the help of Mitchel Resnick. I thank Joe Cook, Seymour Papert, and Eleanor Duckworth for their constant encouragement and support for telling the stories of children at Paige. Special thanks to the students in Group 3 for their hard work and inspiration. I also thank the National Science Foundation (Grant 9153719-MDR), the LEGO Group, and Nintendo Inc., for their support of this research.

REFERENCES

Moses, R. (1989). The algebra project: Organizing in the spirit of Ella. *Harvard Educational Review, 59,* 423–443.

Paige-Cook, A. (1991). *Excellent early education, Paige Academy has it.* Unpublished manuscript. Boston, MA: Paige Academy.

Papert, S. (1993). *The children's machine*: *Rethinking school in the computer age.* New York: Basic Books.

PART IV ―――――――――――

LEARNING
ABOUT SYSTEMS

12

New Paradigms for Computing, New Paradigms for Thinking

Mitchel Resnick

INTRODUCTION

Educators are increasingly interested in providing students with computational tools that support exploration and experimentation. But designing such tools (and designing contexts for using such tools) is easier said than done. Doing it well requires intertwining many different threads of thought.

One thread involves an understanding of the learner: What are the learner's preconceptions and expectations? How will the learner integrate new experiences into existing frameworks? In what ways can learners construct new concepts and new meanings—and in what ways can new computational media provide scaffolding to support this process?

A second thread in the design fabric involves an understanding of domain knowledge. If a new computational tool or activity is intended to help students learn about a particular area of mathematics or science, the designer had better know something about that area of mathematics or science. Yet there is a deeper point. The best computational tools do not simply offer the same content in new clothing; rather, they aim to recast areas of knowledge, suggesting fundamentally new ways of thinking about the concepts in that domain, allowing learners to explore concepts that were previously inaccessible. A classic example is Logo's turtle geometry, which opens up new ways of thinking about geometry and makes possible new types of geometry explorations (Abelson & diSessa 1980; Papert 1980). The design of such tools requires a deep understanding of a particular domain.

A third thread involves an understanding of computational ideas and paradigms. Just as sculptors need to understand the qualities of clay (or whatever material they are using), designers of computational tools need to understand their chosen medium. The point is not simply for computational designers to make nicely crafted artifacts (although that, of course, is important). Computation is not just a medium for designers; it is a set of powerful ideas for students to learn and explore. Well-designed computational tools and activities can provide students with new ways of thinking about computational ideas. Again, Logo provides a classic example. Because Logo is a procedural programming language, it introduces students to ideas about procedural abstraction—ideas that are important not just in the world of computer science, but in many other disciplines (Harvey, 1985).

In this chapter, I focus especially on this third thread (though recognizing that it must be intertwined with the first two). In recent years, computer scientists have developed and experimented with a wide range of new programming paradigms: object orientation, logic, constraints, and parallelism. Each of these paradigms offers new design possibilities, new ways to create things with computers. Furthermore, each also offers new epistemological possibilities, new ways to think about computation and other phenomena in the world. An old saying goes something like this: If a person has only a hammer, the whole world looks like a nail. Adding new tools to the carpenter's toolkit changes the way the carpenter looks at the world. So, too, with computational paradigms: New paradigms can change the way computer users think about the world.

Here, I focus particularly on one new computational paradigm: parallelism. I describe a new parallel programming language, called StarLogo, that I designed explicitly as an environment for exploratory learning. I discuss how StarLogo can expand the space of design possibilities for students while also offering students new ways of looking at the world.

PARALLELISM

During the past two decades, there has been ever-increasing interest in parallel computation and parallel programming languages. Some researchers have added "parallel constructs" to existing programming languages, yielding new language dialects like Concurrent Pascal (Brinch Hansen, 1975) and MultiLisp (Halstead, 1985). Other researchers have created entirely new programming models, designed explicitly with parallelism in mind (e.g., Sabot, 1988).

In most of this research, the primary goal is to improve the speed of computation. A recent article in a major computer-science journal quotes a user saying, "Nobody wants parallelism. What we want is performance" (Pancake, 1991). In other words, many people see parallelism as a "necessary evil" in order to improve the speed at which programs execute. If they could, many language developers would hide parallelism from the user. Indeed, some researchers have developed "parallelizing compilers," which allow programmers to continue writing programs in traditional sequential style, putting the burden on the compiler to "parallelize" the code to improve performance.

In adding parallelism to Logo, I had a very different set of goals. I was not particularly concerned with performance or speed. Rather, I was interested in providing new ways for programmers to model, control, and think about actions that actually happen in parallel. Many things in the natural world (such as ants in a colony) and the manufactured world (such as rides in an amusement park) really do act in parallel. The most natural way to model and control such situations is with a parallel programming language. In these cases, parallelism isn't a trick to improve performance; it is the most natural way of expressing the desired behavior.

My interest in parallelism was motivated, in part, by my research on LEGO/Logo, a computer-controlled construction kit for children (Resnick 1993; Resnick, Ocko, & Papert 1988). When children build and program LEGO machines, they often want different machines to run different programs at the same time. For example, after building an amusement park with a LEGO Ferris wheel and a LEGO merry-go-round, a child might want the two rides to run different programs at the same time. That is a very natural thing to want. In fact, many children are surprised that traditional versions of Logo cannot do such a simple thing. Running simultaneous programs is a simple thing to think about, should it not be a simple thing to do in Logo?

To address this problem, I developed a parallel version of Logo called Multi-Logo (Resnick 1990). To enable users to create and execute multiple processes at the same time, MultiLogo adds one new programming construct: the "agent." Each agent is like a separate version of Logo—that is, each agent can control a computational process. By using multiple agents, users can control multiple processes. In this way, MultiLogo users can control the simultaneous actions of multiple LEGO machines in the world, or multiple Logo turtles on the screen. (A commercial version of Logo, called Microworlds, developed by Logo Computer Systems Inc., now offers many of the same capabilities as MultiLogo.)

BEYOND THE CENTRALIZED MINDSET

MultiLogo works well for situations with a few objects (LEGO machines or graphic turtles) acting in parallel. But what if you want to simulate a large flock of birds? Or a highway full of cars at rush hour? In these cases, you need hundreds (or even thousands) of objects acting in parallel and interacting with one another. For situations like these, I created a new version of Logo, called StarLogo (Resnick 1994).

One reason for my interest in these "massively parallel" situations is that people seem to have great difficulty thinking about and understanding such situations. When people see patterns in the world, they tend to assume some type of centralized control. For example, when people see a flock of birds, they typically assume that the bird in the front is leading and the others are following. That, however, is not the case. Most bird flocks do not have leaders at all. Rather, each bird follows a set of simple rules, reacting to the movements of the birds nearby. Orderly flock patterns arise from these simple, local interactions. The flock is organized without an organizer, coordinated without a coordinator (Heppner & Grenander, 1990).

Many other systems work the same way, with patterns determined not by some central authority, but by local interactions among decentralized components. As ants forage for food, their trail patterns are determined not by the dictates of the queen ant, but by local interactions among thousands of worker ants. Macroeconomic patterns arise from local interactions among millions of buyers and sellers. In immune systems, armies of antibodies seek out bacteria in a systematic, coordinated attack—without any "generals" organizing the overall battle plan.

StarLogo is intended to help people model such systems—and, in the process, develop new ways of thinking about such systems. Too often, when people observe systems in the world, they assume centralized control where it does not exist. The continuing resistance to evolutionary theories is an example: Many people still insist that someone or something must have explicitly designed the orderly structures that we call Life. Similarly, when people construct new systems (whether it is managers creating new organizational structures or engineers creating new technological structures), they often impose centralized control when it is not needed or is counterproductive.

The thesis underlying StarLogo is that people, by designing and playing with decentralized systems in StarLogo, will move beyond this centralized mindset, developing new ways of thinking about and understanding systems. Toward that end, StarLogo extends Logo in three major ways.

First, *StarLogo has many more turtles.* Although commercial versions of Logo typically have only a few turtles, StarLogo has *thousands* of turtles—and all of the turtles can perform their actions at the same time, in parallel. For many colony-type explorations, having hundreds of turtles is not just a nicety; it is a necessity. In many cases, the behavior of a colony changes qualitatively when the number of turtles is increased. An ant colony with 10 ants might not be able to make a stable pheromone trail to a food source, whereas a colony with 100 ants (following the exact same rules) might.

Second, *StarLogo turtles have better "senses."* The traditional Logo turtle was designed primarily as a drawing turtle, for creating geometric shapes and exploring geometric ideas. The StarLogo turtle, however, is more of a behavioral turtle. StarLogo turtles come equipped with "senses." They can detect and distinguish other turtles nearby, and they can "sniff" scents in the world. There is even a built-in primitive to make turtles follow the gradient of a scent—that is, to make turtles turn in the direction where the scent is strongest. Such turtle–turtle and turtle–world interactions are essential for creating and experimenting with self-organizing phenomena. Parallelism alone is not enough. If each turtle just acts on its own, without any interactions, interesting colony-level behaviors will never arise.

Third, *StarLogo reifies the turtles' world*. In traditional versions of Logo, the turtles' world does not have many distinguishing features. The world is simply a place where turtles draw with their pens. Each pixel of the world has a single piece of state information—its color. StarLogo attaches a much higher status to the turtles' world. The world is divided into small square sections called *patches*. The patches have many of the same capabilities as turtles—except that they cannot move. Each patch can hold an arbitrary variety of information. For example, if the turtles are programmed to release a "chemical" as they move, each patch can keep track of the amount of chemical that has been released within its borders. Patches can execute StarLogo commands, just as turtles do. For example, each patch could diffuse some of its "chemical" into neighboring patches, or it could grow "food" based on the level of chemical within its borders. Thus, the environment is given a status equal to that of the creatures inhabiting it.

In some ways, the ideas underlying StarLogo parallel the ideas underlying the early versions of Logo itself. In the late 1960s, Logo aimed to make then-new ideas from the computer-science community (such as procedural abstraction and recursion) accessible to a larger number of users. Similarly, StarLogo aims to make 1990s ideas from computer science (such massive parallelism) accessible to a larger audience. And, whereas Logo introduced a new object (the turtle) to facilitate explorations of particular mathematical-scientific ideas (such as differential geometry), StarLogo introduces another new object (the patch) to facilitate explorations of other mathematical-scientific ideas (such as self-organization).

The next three sections present three examples of StarLogo explorations. These examples aim to illustrate how new approaches to programming can encourage and facilitate new approaches to thinking.

NEW TURTLE GEOMETRY

While I was designing StarLogo, my primary goal was to develop a language for exploring biological phenomena, like ant-colony foraging. Once StarLogo was up and running, though, I stumbled upon some unexpected ways to use the new abundance of turtles.

At one point, I created 5,000 turtles, then typed the command setxy 0 0, making all of the turtles move to the middle of the screen, to the Cartesian point (0,0). Only a single turtle was visible on the screen, but in fact, that single turtle was at the top of a very tall "pile" of turtles, with 4,999 turtles underneath it—somewhat like the pile of turtles in Dr. Seuss's *Yertle the Turtle*.

The pile of turtles seemed like a neat trick. Then, suddenly, I realized an even better trick. I typed the command `forward 50`. The 5,000 turtles exploded outward from the center of the screen. Because the turtles had random headings, they all moved in random directions. But their overall pattern was anything but random. After the turtles had each moved forward five steps, they formed a circle of radius 5, centered on the point (0,0). After the turtles had moved another five steps, they formed a circle of radius 10. So the overall effect was an expanding circle. The circle grew until it reached a radius of 50.

This approach to drawing a circle represents a new form of "turtle geometry." In traditional turtle geometry, the Logo turtle uses a "pen" to draw various geometric shapes and patterns. For example, the command `repeat 360 [forward 1 right 1]` makes the Logo turtle draw a circle. The turtle takes a step forward, then turns a degree to the right, then takes another step forward, and so on. After 360 steps, the turtle returns to its starting point, having completed a circle. (Actually, it draws a regular polygon with 360 sides. If, however, you increase the number of steps, and decrease the turning angle, the polygon gets closer and closer to a circle, approaching a circle as its limit.) The StarLogo form of turtle geometry is quite different. Rather than a single turtle drawing geometric shapes and patterns, a collection of turtles use their own "bodies" to form geometric shapes and patterns. The turtles do not *draw* circles, the turtles *are* the circle.

The StarLogo approach works only if there are a large number of turtles. If there were only 50 turtles (instead of 5,000), the "circle of turtles" would have many "holes" in it. All of the turtles would lie on the same circle, but they would not appear as a "complete" circle. To give the appearance of a complete circle, turtles must be distributed around the entire circumference of the circle. The approach with 5,000 turtles relies on the statistical properties of a random distribution. Each of the 5,000 turtles has a random heading. There is a chance, of course, that all 5,000 turtles could have headings between 0 and 90, so they would form only a quartercircle. Statistically, though, the 5,000 turtles are almost certain to arrange themselves around the entire circumference (with gaps that are no more than a few thousandths of the circumference).

In this way, StarLogo serves as a type of microworld for exploring ideas about statistics and randomness (Wilensky, 1993). Indeed, the circle example forced some high-school students to rethink their notions of randomness. I asked some students to predict what would happen when 5,000 turtles (all starting at the center, with random headings) moved forward 50 steps, and one student responded: "Each turtle has a random heading, so they'll go all over the place." In his mind, randomness was clearly associated with disorder ("all over the place"). Even after seeing the turtles move outward in an expanding circle, one of the students remained bothered: "If the turtles have random headings, why are they always forming a circle?"

This "expanding-from-the-center" strategy is just one way to create a circle in

StarLogo. An alternative approach (connected to a different set of mathematical ideas) is the "constraint-plus-noise" strategy. In this approach, you create several dozen turtles, and you assign two "buddies" to each turtle. For example, turtle number 14 could have turtle 13 and turtle 15 as its two buddies. You then write a program so that each turtle tries to keep a "desired distance" away from each of its two buddies. If it gets too close to one of its buddies, it moves away a bit. If it gets too far from one of its buddies, it moves towards it a bit. The StarLogo code looks like this:

```
to constraint-rule
setheading toward :buddy1
forward 0.1 * ((distance :buddy1) - :desired-distance)
setheading toward :buddy2
forward 0.1 * ((distance :buddy2) - :desired-distance)
end
```

The turtles start scattered randomly on the screen (see Fig. 12.1a). Then, using the parallelism of StarLogo, all of the turtles run the constraint-rule at the same time. The turtles quickly settle into a stable state, with each turtle the same distance from each of its two buddies (see Fig. 12.1b). The collection of turtles

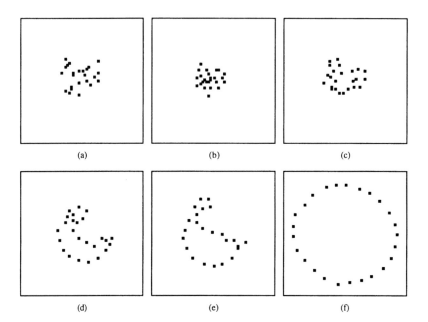

FIG. 12.1. When the constraint-rule is turned on, the turtles keep a uniform distance from their "buddies" (b). When the noise-rule is turned on, the turtles expand into a circle (c–f).

looks like a jumbled mess, with no clear pattern. Then you add one more rule (run in parallel with the `constraint-rule`): Each turtle should try to move away from all of the other turtles (not just its buddies).

```
to noise-rule
setheading toward pick-random-turtle
back 1
end
```

Once this new rule is added, the turtles begin to push away from one another. The overall movement has a distinctly organic feel, as if the group of turtles is trying to spring to life. At first, the turtles seem to be tied in knots, but they gradually push out the kinks and knots, expanding to a full circle (see Fig. 12.1c–12.1f).

This constraint-plus-noise approach is a general-purpose strategy that can be used in many problem-solving and design situations. Yet most people are unfamiliar with this strategy and this way of thinking; they have never had the appropriate tools to try it out and play with it.

Are the StarLogo approaches to turtle geometry better than traditional turtle geometry? That is the wrong question to ask. The point is not to provide *better* ways of doing geometry, but to provide *more* ways of doing and thinking about geometry. Each way of thinking about something strengthens and deepens each of the other ways of thinking about it. Understanding something in several different ways produces an overall understanding that is richer and of a different nature than any one way of understanding. Thus, the new StarLogo turtle geometry has the potential to supplement and reinforce other ways of thinking about geometry.

RUGBY TURTLES

At a recent workshop on computers and learning, the workshop organizers proposed three mathematical "challenge problems." Many different computational tools (Microworlds Logo, Boxer, StarLogo, Cabri, etc.) were available for use. The idea was to see whether different people approached these problems differently. In particular, would the choice of computational tools significantly affect the problem-solving strategies?

Workshop participants worked on the problems in the evenings (sometimes late into the night!). One of the problems captured my interest. It came from a British math textbook and involved the game of rugby:

After a try has been scored, the scoring team has the opportunity to gain further points by "kicking a conversion." The kick can be taken from anywhere on an imaginary line that is perpendicular to the try line and goes through the point that

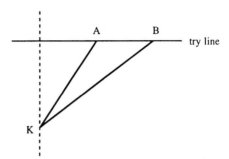

FIG. 12.2. How do you maximize the angle AKB?

the try was scored (see Fig. 12.2). Where should the kick be taken from to maximize
the angle AKB?

People at the workshop approached this problem in many different ways.
Some started with paper and pencil—sketching diagrams, writing equations,
taking derivatives. Other participants went right to the computer. Perhaps the
most common response was to use one of the "new geometry construction kits"
such as Cabri.

As soon as I read the problem, a very different approach sprang to my
StarLogo-biased mind. I immediately recognized a massively parallel approach
to the problem. Uri Wilensky was also interested in this approach, and we
decided to work on the problem together using StarLogo. Rather than seeing the
problem as a geometry problem, we viewed it as a probability and statistics
problem.

We imagined hundreds of rugby players standing at different points along the
line perpendicular to the try line, and we imagined each player kicking hundreds
of balls in random directions. To find the point K that maximizes the angle AKB,
we simply needed to figure out which of my hundreds of rugby players scored the
most conversions (by successfully kicking balls between the goalposts A and B).
The reason is clear: If each player is kicking balls in random directions, the
player with the largest AKB angle will score the most conversions. This strategy
is an example of what is sometimes called a Monte Carlo approach.

It was quite easy to write the StarLogo program to implement this strategy. We
used turtles to represent the rugby balls. To start, the program put thousands of
turtles/balls with random headings at random positions along the perpendicular
line. Then, the program "kicked" all of these turtles/balls, moving them forward
in straight lines. Finally, the program took all of the turtles that successfully went
through the goalposts and moved them back to their starting points on the
perpendicular line. The point with the most surviving turtles is the point that
maximizes the angle AKB.

This example illustrates how new computational tools can suggest and make
possible new problem-solving approaches to traditional problems. This approach

even has some advantages over more traditional strategies. If extra constraints were added to the problem, such as a wind blowing across the field, or a limitation on the distance a rugby player can kick a ball, it would be quite easy to adjust the StarLogo program to take the new constraints into account. It would be more difficult to adjust traditional geometric analyses.

TRAFFIC JAMS

Ari and Fadhil were students at a public high school in the Boston area. Both enjoyed working with computers, but neither had a very strong mathematical or scientific background. At the time Ari and Fadhil started working with StarLogo, they were also taking a driver's education class. Each had turned 16 years old a short time before, and they were excited about getting their driver's licenses. Much of their conversation focused on cars, so when I gave Ari and Fadhil a collection of articles to read, it is not surprising that a *Scientific American* article titled "Vehicular Traffic Flow" (Herman & Gardels, 1963) captured their attention.

Traditional studies of traffic flow rely on sophisticated analytic techniques from fields like queuing theory, but many of the same traffic phenomena can be explored with simple StarLogo programs. To get started, Ari and Fadhil decided to create a one-lane highway. (Later, they experimented with multiple lanes.) Ari suggested adding a police radar trap somewhere along the road to catch cars going above the speed limit. However, he also wanted each car to have its own radar detector, so cars would know to slow down when they approached the radar trap.

After some discussion, Ari and Fadhil programmed each driver to follow three simple rules: (a) If you see another car close ahead of you, slow down; (b) If there are no cars close ahead of you, speed up (unless you are already at the speed limit); (c) If you detect a radar trap, slow down.

Both students expected that a traffic jam would form behind the radar trap, and indeed it did. As the cars slowed down for the trap, the cars behind them were forced to slow down, as so on, creating a queue with roughly equal distances between the cars. When the cars moved beyond the trap, they accelerated smoothly until they reached the speed limit.

I asked the students what would happen if they ran the same program without the radar trap. The cars would be controlled by just two rules: If you see another car close ahead, slow down; if not, speed up. They predicted that the traffic flow would become uniform; cars would be evenly spaced, traveling at a constant speed. After all, without the radar trap, what could cause a jam? When we ran the program, however, a traffic jam formed. Along parts of the road, the cars were tightly packed and moving slowly. Elsewhere, they were spread out and moving at the speed limit (see Fig. 12.3).

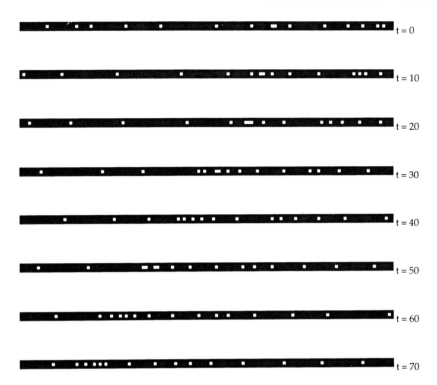

FIG. 12.3.   Traffic jam without radar trap (Cars move left to right, but jam moves right to left).

At first, the students were shocked. Their comments revealed the workings of a centralized mindset: They argued that traffic jams need some sort of centralized "seed" (like a radar trap or accident) in order to form. They couldn't believe that simple interactions among cars could create a jam. Yet that's what was happening in their simulation. If a few cars, by chance, happened to get near one another, they slowed down. This, in turn, made it likely that even more cars behind them would have to slow down, leading to a jam. By continuing to modify and play with their StarLogo program (adjusting initial speeds and positions, changing acceleration rates), Ari and Fadhil eventually developed better intuitions about traffic jams, recognizing how decentralized interactions can indeed cause the formation of larger-scale traffic patterns.

NEW WAYS OF THINKING

The centralized mindset is not just a misconception of scientifically naive high school students. It seems to affect the thinking of nearly everyone. For many years, even scientists assumed that bird flocks must have leaders. It is only recently that scientists have revised their theories, asserting that bird flocks are leaderless and self-organized. A similar bias toward centralized theories can be seen throughout the history of science, with scientists remaining committed to centralized explanations, even in the face of discrediting evidence.

The history of research on slime mold cells, as told by Evelyn Fox Keller (1985), provides a striking example of centralized thinking. At certain stages of their life cycle, slime mold cells gather together into clusters. For many years, scientists believed that the aggregation process was coordinated by specialized slime mold cells, known as "founder" or "pacemaker" cells. According to this theory, each pacemaker cell sends out a chemical signal, telling other slime mold cells to gather around it, resulting in a cluster.

In 1970, Keller and a colleague proposed an alternative model (Keller & Segel, 1970), showing how slime mold clusters can form if every individual cell follows the same set of simple rules, involving the emission and sensing of chemicals. Nevertheless, for the following decade, other researchers continued to assume that special pacemaker cells were required to initiate the aggregation process. As Keller and Segel (1970) wrote, with an air of disbelief: "The pacemaker view was embraced with a degree of enthusiasm that suggests that this question was in some sense foreclosed" (pp. 152–153). By the early 1980s, researchers had begun to accept the idea of aggregation among homogeneous cells, without any pacemaker, but the decade-long resistance serves as some indication of the strength of the centralized mindset.

For many years, there has been a self-reinforcing spiral. People saw the world in centralized ways, so they constructed centralized tools and models, which further encouraged a centralized view of the world. Until recently, there was little pressure against this centralization spiral. Even if someone wanted to experiment with decentralized approaches, there were few tools or opportunities to do so.

The centralization spiral is now starting to unwind. New computational tools based on the paradigm of massive parallelism are supporting and encouraging new ways of thinking. In some cases (as seen in the turtles-in-a-circle and rugby examples), these new tools can encourage new approaches to mathematical problems and new ways of conceptualizing mathematical ideas. In other cases (such as the traffic example), the tools can support explorations into the workings of real-world systems. Overall, these new tools provide an opportunity for students (and others) to move beyond the centralized mindset, suggesting an expanded set of models and metaphors for making sense of the world.

ACKNOWLEDGMENTS

This chapter was originally prepared for the NATO Advanced Workshop on "The Design of Computational Media to Support Exploratory Learning" (diSessa,

Hoyles, & Noss, 1995). Hal Abelson, Seymour Papert, Brian Silverman, Randy Sargent, Uri Wilensky, Ryan Evans, and Andy Begel have provided encouragement, inspiration, and ideas for the StarLogo project. Thanks to Andy diSessa, Celia Hoyles, Richard Noss, and Laurie Edwards for organizing the NATO workshop for which I wrote this chapter, and thanks to Andy diSessa, Yasmin Kafai, and Greg Kimberly for comments on an earlier draft of it. The LEGO Group and the National Science Foundation (Grants 9153719-MDR and 9358519-RED) have provided financial support for this research.

REFERENCES

Abelson, H., & diSessa, A. (1980). *Turtle geometry: The computer as a medium for exploring mathematics.* Cambridge, MA: MIT Press.

Brinch Hansen, P. (1975). The programming language Concurrent Pascal. *IEEE Trans. Software Eng., 1*(2), 199–207.

diSessa, A., Holyes, C., & Noss, R., (Eds.). (1995). *Computers and exploratory learning.* Heidelberg: Springer-Verlag.

Halstead, R. (1985). Multilisp: A language for concurrent symbolic computation. *ACM Trans. of Prog. Languages and Systems, 7*(4), 501–538.

Harvey, B. (1985). *Computer science Logo style.* Cambridge, MA: MIT Press.

Heppner, F., & Grenander, U. (1990). A stochastic nonlinear model for coordinated bird flocks. In S. Krasner (Ed.), *The ubiquity of chaos* (pp. 233–238). Washington, D.C.: AAAS Publications.

Herman, R., & Gardels, K. (1963). Vehicular traffic flow. *Scientific American, 209*(6), 35–43.

Keller, E. F. (1985). *Reflections on gender and science.* New Haven, CT: Yale University Press.

Keller, E. F., & Segel, L. (1970). Initiation of slime mold aggregation viewed as an instability. *Journal of Theoretical Biology, 26,* 399–415.

Pancake, C. (1991). Software support for parallel computing: Where are we headed? *Communications of the ACM, 34*(11), 53–64.

Papert, S. (1980). *Mindstorms: Children, computers, and powerful ideas.* New York: Basic Books.

Resnick, M. (1990). MultiLogo: A study of children and concurrent programming. *Interactive Learning Environments, 1*(3), 153–170.

Resnick, M. (1993). Behavior construction kits. *Communications of the ACM, 36*(7), 64–71.

Resnick, M. (1994). *Turtles, termites and traffic jams: Explorations in massively parallel microworlds.* Cambridge, MA: MIT Press.

Resnick, M., Ocko, S., & Papert, S. (1988). LEGO, Logo, and design. *Children's Environments Quarterly, 5*(4), 14–18.

Sabot, G. (1988). *The paralation model.* Cambridge, MA: MIT Press.

Wilensky, U. (1993). *Connected mathematics: Building concrete relationships with mathematical knowledge.* Unpublished doctoral dissertation, MIT Media Lab, Cambridge, MA.

13

Making Sense of Probability Through Paradox and Programming
A Case Study in a Connected Mathematics Framework

Uri Wilensky

INTRODUCTION

Many scholars have argued (e.g., Cohen, 1987; Gigerenzer, 1987; Hacking, 1987) that a probabilistic revolution has occurred in our century. In this short period, the use of statistical methods has exploded from nonexistence to relative rarity to virtual ubiquity in the scientific literature. In the university, courses in probability and statistics are required for virtually all students in the natural and social sciences. Our daily newspapers are full of statistics about such matters as lung cancer risks, divorce rates, birth control failure rates, variation in temperature, the purity of soap, and so on. Beyond ubiquity, the disciplines of probability and statistics have fundamentally changed the way we think about science and the way we think about our world. Notions of randomness and uncertainty have opened up whole new areas of mathematics and science. This has released a ground swell of interest in subjects such as complexity, chaos, and artificial life.

Yet, despite the rapid infiltration of probability and statistics into our science and media, there is substantial documentation of the widespread lack of understanding of the meaning of the statistics we encounter (Gould, 1991; Konold, 1991; Phillips, 1988; Piaget, 1975; Tversky & Kahneman, 1974). Even highly educated professionals who use probability and statistics in their daily work have great difficulty interpreting the statistics they produce (Kahneman & Tversky, 1982).

Besides a lack of competence and understanding, students express a great deal of dislike towards courses in probability and statistics—an antipathy well captured by the oft-quoted line attributed to both Mark Twain and Benjamin Disraeli: "There are three kinds of lies: lies, damn lies and statistics" (cited in Tripp, 1970, p. 612).

269

Most students first encounter the subject of probability in the form of school exercises that involve calculating ratios of frequencies and binomial coefficients. As a result, the subject matter of probability and statistics is seen as an assemblage of formulae to be committed to memory. When students fail to master the techniques taught to them, better methods are sought to improve their ability to calculate and apply the formulae. The educational establishment has expended considerable effort toward these performance goals. Very little effort, however, has been devoted to exploring and deepening the understanding of basic probabilistic concepts or to answering such questions as: "What is a normal distribution and what makes it useful?" or "How can something be both random and structured?" Whereas this focus on formalism and avoidance of meaning exploration may be seen as endemic to traditional school mathematics, this tendency is more pronounced in the case of probability and statistics. Partially because the meanings of core probabilistic notions are still being debated by philosophers of mathematics and science (e.g., Chaitin, 1987; Kolmogorov, 1950; Savage, 1954; Suppes, 1984; von Mises, 1957), it is assumed that these meanings are too hard for students to access. "Safe probability" is best practiced through formal exercises without too much attention to the meanings of underlying concepts.

There is a substantial literature concerning the topic of decision making under uncertainty (e.g., Cohen, 1979; Edwards & von Winterfeldt, 1986; Evans, 1993; Kahneman & Tversky, 1973, 1982; Nisbett, 1980; Nisbett, Krontz, Jepson, & Kunda, 1983; Tversky & Kahneman, 1974, 1980, 1983). Much of this literature documents the systematic errors and biases people display when attempting to make judgments under uncertainty. A common conclusion drawn by educators and researchers from this research is that "people just aren't built for doing probability"; our intuitions are faulty and not to be trusted. Again, therefore, the safe practice for educators wishing their students to master the material is to instill in them a mistrust of their intuitive responses and a healthy respect for the formulae.[1]

The cost of this highly formal instruction in probability and statistics is high. Although the "best and brightest" do manage to learn to use the right statistical tests in the appropriate contexts, even they do not really understand what they are doing. They experience a kind of "epistemological anxiety" (Wilensky, 1993; in preparation-a)—anxiety about the nature of the knowledge they are producing and what justifies it. This anxiety leads to skepticism about the validity of statistical knowledge. Add to this mix the unscrupulous use of statistical arguments to mislead voters and consumers, and we begin to understand why the subject stimulates so much distaste. The cost of this educational approach is to deprive learners from accessing core probabilistic and statistical notions, which are powerful means of making sense of the world.

---

[1]In a graduate probability course at MIT, the professor explicitly admonished the class members not to try to do inverse probabilities in their heads because their intuitions were not reliable. Instead, he told them to always use the Bayes formula to calculate inverse probabilities.

In this chapter, I present a case study of a learner engaged in a classical probability paradox. The learner was one of 17 interviewees studied in depth as part of the Connected Probability project. I start by briefly describing the Connected Probability project and its theoretical framework—the Connected Mathematics research program. Part of the learning environment provided in the Connected Probability project is a computer modeling language suitable for probability investigations—a version of the language StarLogo (Resnick, 1992; Wilensky, 1993). I then present the probability paradox with which the subject is engaged and an account of her investigation. The paradox was selected because of its potential for engaging learners in a deeper investigation into the meaning of the concept of "random"—a fundamental concept of probability theory. I conclude by arguing three points illustrated in the case study: (a) that providing support for seriously engaging such paradoxes is an important avenue to relieving epistemological anxiety about the nature of probabilistic concepts, (b) that programming can be an effective tool for resolving mathematical paradoxes (by making their hidden assumptions[2] explicit and concrete), and (c) that through programming their own computational models (and thus making their own mathematics), learners gain a much deeper understanding of probabilistic concepts than through the use of simulations or prebuilt computational models.

THEORETICAL FRAMEWORK

The Connected Mathematics Research Program

The name "Connected Mathematics" comes from two seemingly disparate sources, the literature of emergent artificial intelligence (AI) and the literature of feminist critique. From emergent AI, and in particular from the Society of Mind theory (Minsky, 1987; Papert, 1980), Connected Mathematics takes the idea that concepts cannot have only one meaning.[3] Only through their multiple connections do concepts gain meaning. From the feminist literature (e.g., Belenky, Clinchy, Goldberger, & Tarule, 1986; Gilligan, 1977; Keller, 1983; Surrey, 1991), it takes the idea of "connected knowing": knowing that is intimate and contextual as opposed to an alienated, disconnected, and formalistic knowing. In this section, I only briefly sketch the Connected Mathematics approach. A more comprehensive description can be found in (Wilensky, 1993; in preparation-a, in preparation-c).

The Connected Mathematics approach is rooted in the constructionist (Papert, 1991, 1993) learning paradigm. As such, it holds that the character of mathematical knowledge is inextricably interwoven with its genesis—both its historical genesis and its development in the mathematical learner. A conception of mathe-

---

[2]Assumptions implicit in the formulation of the paradox or in the preconceptions of the learner.
[3]A nice example of the many meanings of "derivative" can be found in a recent paper by Thurston (1994).

matics as disconnected from its development leads to the misguided pedagogy of the traditional mathematics curriculum—a "litany" of defintion-theorem-proof and its attendant concepts stipulated by formal definition.[4] In contrast to approaches that attempt to explain failures of mathematical understanding in technical or information processing terms, Connected Mathematics seeks to explain these obstacles in epistemological terms. Obstacles to understanding are failures of meaning making, and because meaning is made through building connections, Connected Mathematics sees these as fundamental failures of connection.

Paradox can be an important tool of a Connected Mathematics learning environment. The recognition of paradox is the recognition that (at least) two conceptual structures have not been integrated. This explicit recognition is the first step in making the connections between the two structures that will resolve the paradox and, most often, thereby, generate new mathematics.

The vision of mathematics as being made and not simply received leads naturally to a role for technology. Technology is not there simply to animate received truth; it is an expressive medium—a medium for the making of new mathematics. It follows that we can make better use of computational technologies than simply running black-box simulations—we can make mathematics by constructing computational embodiments of mathematical models. The true power of the computer will be seen, not in assisting the teaching of the old topics, but in transforming ideas about what can be learned.

Technology here is to be construed in a broad sense—the notations in which we express mathematics, and the mathematical concepts themselves are artifacts of the technology of the period of their creation. The emergence of new powerful computational technologies, therefore, implies a radical change in both the concepts and semiotic activities of a newly contextualized mathematics.

Connected Mathematics and Current Standards of Mathematics Reform. Connected mathematics moves beyond reform documents such as the Standards of the National Council of Teachers of Mathematics (NCTM Standards, 1991a, 1991b) in its serious reexamination of the warrant for the current mathematical curriculum (see also Confrey, 1993a, 1993b). In so doing, it proposes new standards for the curriculum in terms of content, process, beliefs, and context. It expands mathematics *content* beyond the boundaries circumscribed by school and outdated technology. New technologies are used imaginatively to make abstract mathematical concepts concrete, to explore areas of mathematics previ-

---

[4]Formal proof and definition is an after-the-fact reconstruction of the processes of coming to know in mathematics. The justification of such reconstruction for the purposes of communication within expert culture is certainly allowed. What is unfortunate and damaging pedagogoically is that this re-presentation becomes an active conception of what mathematics is and what it is to know mathematics.

ously inaccessible, and to create new mathematics (e.g., Abelson & diSessa, 1980; Abelson & Goldenberg, 1977; Cuoco & Goldenberg, 1992; Edwards, 1992; Feurzeig, 1989; Harel, 1992; Harel & Papert, 1991; Leron & Zazkis, 1992; Noss & Hoyles, 1991; Papert, 1972, 1980; Resnick, 1991; Schwartz & Yerushalmy, 1987; Wilensky, 1993).

In contrast to the NCTM Standards, which portray an "image" of mathematics (see Brandes, chapter 3, this volume) as essentially a problem solving activity, the vision of Connected Mathematics is more generative—the central activity being *making* new mathematics. In so doing, it fosters a culture of design and exploration—designing new representations of mathematics and encouraging critique of those designs.

Connected Mathematics acknowledges and attends to the affective side of learning mathematics. It looks critically at the role of *shame* in the mathematical community. Listening to learners and fostering an environment in which it becomes safe for mathematical learners to express their partial understandings[5] results in a dismantling of the culture of shame that paralyzes learners, preventing them from proposing the tentative conjectures and representations necessary to make mathematical progress. In doing so, it parts company with the literature on misconceptions, which highlights the gulf between expert and novice. Instead, Connected Mathematics stresses the continuity between expert and novice understanding,[6] noticing that even expert mathematicians have had to laboriously carve out small areas of well-connected clarity from the generally messy terrain[7] (see, e.g., Smith, diSessa, & Roschelle, 1994).

Connected Probability

The Connected Probability project is one major branch of the Connected Mathematics program. In the Connected Probability project, we are engaged in building Connected Mathematics environments for learning probability. As a first step

---

[5]The taboo against expressing partial understandings is endemic to school discourse. To break it, teachers must explictly model expressing their own confusions and groping for clarity. One reason this is hard to do is that it is very difficult to remember what it was like not to grasp a mathematical concept that is now self-evident. There are many striking parallels between the development of conservation in children (Piaget, 1952) and the acquistion of new mathematical concepts. One feature they share is the inconceivability of one's previous understanding—what is it like to think that there is more water in a tall glass than there was in the shorter glass that you emptied into the taller container? (For further discussion of this point, see Wilensky, 1993).

[6]Because it suggests that *making* is central to mathematical activity, the Connected Mathematics view is that learners make connections; they do not cross intellectual ravines. Thus, the process of becoming expert in mathematics is one of adding connections and not removing or replacing novice knowledge.

[7]Reflecting on the intellectual struggles of mathematical figures in history can be very encouraging to learners as they see that their own struggles are not so different from those of great mathematicians of the past.

toward this goal, 17 in-depth interviews[8] about probability were conducted with learners ages 14 to 64. Interviews were open-ended and most often experienced by the interviewees as extended conversations. The interviewer guided these conversations so that the majority of a list of 23 topics was addressed. The interview topics ranged from attitudes toward situations of uncertainty to interpretation of newspaper statistics to the design of studies for collecting desired statistics to formal probability problems.

These topics were valuable for gaining insight into people's ideas about probability, and for encouraging them to think through probabilistic issues. In one sense probability is ubiquitous in our everyday lives. Yet, because probability is fundamentally about large numbers of instances, these singular everyday experiences may not be useful for building our probabilistic intuition.[9] Rarely, in our everyday lives, do we have direct and controlled access to large numbers of experimental trials, measurements of large populations, or repeated assessments of likelihood with feedback. We do regularly assess the probability of specific events occurring. However, when the event either does or does not occur, we do not know how to feed this result back into our original assessment. After all, if we assess the probability of some event occurring as, say, 30%, and the event occurs, we have not gotten much information about the adequacy of our original judgment. Only by repeated trials can we get the feedback we need to evaluate our judgments. Without the necessary feedback, it is difficult to develop our probabilistic intuitions and make probabilistic concepts concrete.

A powerful way to bridge this gap between singular experiences and probabilistic reasoning is through the use of exploratory computational environments. The processing power of the computer can give learners immediate access to large amounts of data usually distributed widely over space or time. This can provide the necessary feedback needed to develop concrete understandings of probabilistic concepts. In creating an environment for learning probability, it is therefore natural to consider computational tools.

One of the investigatory tools made available to the learners in this study was a programming language, StarLogo, specially adapted for modeling probabilistic phenomena. StarLogo is a massively parallel version of the computer language Logo. It allows the user to control thousands of "turtles" on a computer screen. Each of the turtles (or agents) has its own local state and can be given its own local procedures and rules of interaction.[10] Thus, the user can model the emergent effects of the behavior of many distributed agents, each following its own

---

[8]The shortest interview was 2 hours long, the longest 18 hours, and the median 7 hours. These figures refer to the face-to-face interview time. Some interviews continued over electronic mail for up to 2 months following face-to-face interactions.

[9]Part of what makes an event singular is that we do not interpret it as a member of a class of events. It is only when we can stand at a distance from the event and see it in the context of many other events that we can begin to make the reference classes needed to make probabilistic judgments.

[10]These "object-oriented" features of the language make StarLogo a more accessible environment

local rules. In particular, the key probabilistic notion of distribution can be seen to arise from the actions of many independent agents (see Wilensky, 1995, in preparation-a). StarLogo facilitates the design of probability experiments that allow learners to test their conjectures. They can use the feedback to modify their conjectures and clarify their underlying structures via successive refinement (Leron, 1994). The use of StarLogo to design probability experiments is in keeping with the constructionist (Papert, 1991) model of learning—that a particularly felicitous way to build strong mental models is to produce physical or computational constructs that can be manipulated and debugged. As we shall see in the case that follows, being able to articulate a model of a probabilistic concept (through programming) can lead to rich insights into the nature of probabilistic concepts such as randomness and distribution. In contrast to consumers of ready made models, learners who construct computational models are afforded the opportunity to refine their models through debugging. Through debugging their programs, they can debug their probabilistic concepts and make them concrete (Wilensky, 1991).

THE CASE STUDY

Overview

In this chapter, I present a case study of a student engaged in exploring the meaning of randomness in the context of a particular mathematical problem. This problem, first proposed by Bertrand over a century ago (Bertrand, 1889) has led a fascinating mathematical life. Over the last hundred years, mathematicians have given many different solutions (e.g., Borel, 1909; Keynes, 1921; Poincaré, 1912; Uspensky, 1937; von Mises, 1964), and they continue to propose new solutions and reject old arguments to this day (e.g., Marinoff, 1994). This problem, which became known as "Bertrand's paradox,"[11] engaged leading mathematicians in a debate over the range of applicability of the principle of non-sufficient reason (also called the principle of indifference—i.e., the assignment of uniform probability distributions in situations of ignorance) that was a keystone of the evolving notion of randomness. Given the attention of Connected Mathematics to the genesis of mathematical knowledge both historically and developmentally, Bertrand's paradox was a natural candidate for inclusion in this study. It was hoped that the role of Bertrand's paradox in the historical development of the notion of random would be mirrored in the development of the interviewee's

---

for modeling. In contrast to other modeling environments, such as STELLA (Richmond & Peterson, 1990), which model with aggregate quantities and flows, StarLogo is "object" based, thus facilitating concrete interactions with the basic units of the model.

[11]The name "Bertrand's paradox" was given by Poincaré.

thinking. Interviewees were capable of calculating more than one numerical answer to the problem. The contradiction between two or more numerical answers to a seemingly well-specified probability question might then be experienced by the interviewee as a paradox. The resolution of this contradiction could then lead to a deeper and richer understanding of the notion of randomness.

In the case reported on later in this chapter, the paradoxical element was introduced by the interviewer. Once that intervention occurred, no further support was needed for the interviewee to recognize it as a paradox.[12] The resolution of the paradox, however, was greatly facilitated by use of the programming language.

Some researchers and educators have recently argued that students cannot make practical use of general purpose programming languages in their subject domain learning (e.g., Soloway, 1993; Steinberger, 1994).[13] It is my hope that the case study that follows will help dispel this claim and show the interesting and productive interactions that can occur between programming and learning mathematics. Indeed, it is through programming that the interviewee first "thickens" (Geertz, 1973) her understanding of "random"—by seeing the need for a process, be it computational or physical, to generate randomness. Thus, a computational idea leads to a mathematical idea, resulting in the recognition of the intimate tie between a random process and a probability distribution.[14] This thickening of the notion of random and embedding it in a web of related concepts and activities leads to a Connected Mathematics understanding of randomness.[15]

The Paradoxical Question

From a given circle, choose a random chord. What's the probability that the chord is longer than a radius?

This question was, in one sense, the most formally presented question in the interview. On the surface, it most mirrored the kinds of questions that students

---

[12]This was true in roughly half of the interviews in this study. The later in the interview the paradox occurred, the more likely that it was recognized and owned.

[13]A weaker form of this claim is that programming requires so much "overhead" that it distracts learners from the mathematics at hand. This paper does not respond directly to this weaker claim. Let me note briefly that (a) Logo and StarLogo are conceived here as lifelong tools and powerful expressive media across many domains, not just probability: (b) In contrast to languages such as Fortran or Basic, meaningful StarLogo programs are usually quite short, and StarLogo has "low threshold" (i.e., easy for novices to write meaningful programs) as a primary language design criterion (Papert, 1980; Resnick, 1991).

[14]Or, as some interviewees saw it, each process leads to a different "meaning" of random.

[15]A positivist or strict formalist critic might object that, in fact, the notion of randomness has been replaced by a more precise and technical notion. In practice, however, the old ideas do not die or even fade away. The new ideas coexist with the old and take much of their sustenance from their connections to prior conceptions and other contexts for recognizing randomness.

get in school. But, because of its hidden ambiguity, many rich interviews arose from it. It was particularly rich in evoking epistemological questioning and investigations into the meaning of the word random and how "randomness" connects to both mathematical distribution functions and the physical world.

The question was selected because it had many possible "reasonable" answers. Among the answers (backed up by solid reasonable arguments) that interviewees gave for the requested probability were ½, ⅔, ¾, $\sqrt[7]{3}$½. The language of the question, "choose a random chord," implies that the meaning of "random chord" is well specified—there should only be one way to choose chords that are truly random. All of the interviewees shared this assumption. When they encountered two different seemingly correct solutions to the question that led to different values for the probabilities, they were therefore confronted with a paradox.

Each of the answers listed in the preceding paragraph is in fact the correct answer for a particular probability experiment. Depending on the physical experiment conducted, or, in the corresponding mathematical language, the initial distribution that is assigned to the chord lengths, different answers will be obtained. By exploring the paradox, learners came to see that there was no unique way to specify a "random chord" (in one interviewee's language, "there's no such thing as a random chord"). Different ways of choosing chords are appropriate for different occasions. Different physical experiments lead to different probabilities and correspond to different ways of choosing chords. Depending on which method is used to select chords, different distributions of chord lengths will ensue. This leads to seeing the deep and powerful connections between randomness, distributions, and physical experiments. It lays the intuitive substrate needed to create probabilistic models and to make sense of more advanced probability concepts such as probability measures.

Case Study: Ellie

Of the 17 participants in the Connected Probability project, 15 got engaged with the random chord problem. The 15 interview fragments include many different themes and investigation paths. Each case is different. Nonetheless, the case that follows can be described as typical, if not in its specific details, then in the general outline of the investigation.

First Encounter. Ellie is a computer professional who has a solid undergraduate math background. Like many of the other interviewees, Ellie gets into trouble trying to understand the meaning of random. We could have resolved her difficulty by specifying a particular distribution of chords, or by describing a specific experiment to generate the chords. But had we done that, Ellie would not have developed her insights into the meaning of randomness. As teachers, it is often difficult for us to watch learners struggle with foundational questions and not "clear up the misunderstanding." However, the temptation to intervene is

FIG. 13.1.   Ellie's first drawing.

more easily resisted if we keep in mind that it is only by negotiating the meaning of the fundamental concepts, by following unproductive, semiproductive and multiple paths to this meaning, that learners can make these concepts concrete.

Many interviewees answered this question fairly quickly using the following argument. Chords range in size from 0 to 2r. Because we are picking chords at random, they are just as likely to be shorter than "r" as they are to be longer than "r." Hence the probability is equal to ½.

Ellie engaged herself with this question but approached it differently. She began thinking about the problem by drawing a circle and a chord on it that she knew had length equal to the circle's radius, as shown in Fig. 13.1.

After contemplating this drawing for a while, she then drew Fig. 13.2.

With the drawing of this picture came an insight. She pointed at the triangle in the figure and responded as follows:

Ellie: It has to be equilateral because all the sides are equal to a radius. So that means 6 of them fit around a circle. That's right, 6 * 60 = 360 degrees. So, that means if you pick a point on a circle and label it P, then to get a chord that's smaller than a radius you have to pick the second point on either this section of the circle [labeled A in Fig. 13.2] or this one [labeled B in Fig.13.2]. So since each of those are a sixth of the circle, you get a one third chance of getting a chord smaller than a radius and a two thirds chance of a chord larger than a radius.[16]

Ellie was quite satisfied with this answer and I believe would not have pursued the question any more if it had not been for my prodding.

Introducing the Paradox

U: I have another way of looking at this problem that gives a different answer.

E: Really? I don't see how that could be.

U: Can I show you?

---

[16]The transcripts have been "cleaned up" some (removing pauses, "umms," and many interjections) for clarity of the exposition. Bracketed comments are the author's clarifying remarks.

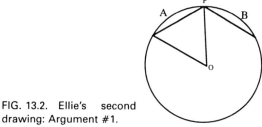

FIG. 13.2. Ellie's second drawing: Argument #1.

E: Sure. But I bet it's got a mistake in it and you're trying to trick me.
U: OK. Let me show you and you tell me.

I, then, drew Fig. 13.3.

U: Consider a circle, C1, of radius r. Draw a chord, AB, of length r. Then drop a perpendicular onto AB from the center of the circle, O, intersecting AB in a point, P. Then P is a mid-point of AB. Now we calculate the length of OP. We have OA = r and AP = r/2. By Pythagoras, we have OP = $\sqrt{3/2}$ * r. Now draw a circle, C2, of radius OP centered at O. If we pick any point on C2 and draw a tangent to the circle at that point, then the resultant chord of C1 has length r. If we pick a point, P′, inside C2 and draw the chord of circle C1, which has P′ as mid-point, then that chord must be longer than r. Similarly, if we pick a point inside C1 but outside C2 and draw the chord which has that point as mid-point, then that chord must be shorter than r. Now pick any point, Q, inside C1. Draw a chord, EF, which has Q as mid-point. EF will be bigger than a radius if and only if Q is inside C2. It follows that the probability of choosing a chord larger than a radius is the ratio of the areas of C1 and C2. The area of C1 = p * r². The area of C2 = p * OP² = p * ¾ * r². So the ratio of their areas is ¾ and therefore the probability of a chord being larger than a radius is also ¾, not ⅔ as you said.

This explanation had a disquieting effect on Ellie. She went over it many times, but was not able to find a "bug" in the argument. After repeatedly struggling to resolve the conflict, she let out her frustration:

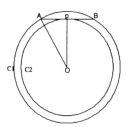

FIG. 13.3. Argument #2.

E: I don't get it. One of these arguments must be wrong! The probability of choosing a random chord bigger than a radius is either ⅔ or ¾. It can't be both. I'm still pretty sure that it's really ⅔ but I can't find a hole in the other argument.

U: Can both of the arguments be right?

E: No. Of course not.

U: Why not?

E: It's obvious! Call the probability of choosing a chord larger than a radius, p. Then my argument [henceforward, argument #1] says p = ⅔ and your argument [henceforward, argument #2] says p = ¾. If both arguments are correct then ⅔ = ¾, which is absurd.[17]

Here Ellie is quite sure that there is a definite and unique meaning to the concept "probability of choosing a random chord larger than a radius," even though she admits that she is not completely certain what that meaning is.

Programming

U: Would writing a computer program help to resolve this dilemma?

E: Good idea. I can program up a simulation of this experiment and compute which value for the probability is correct! I should have thought of that earlier.

Ellie then spent some time writing a StarLogo program. As she worked to code this up, she soon began to feel uneasy with her formulation. A few times she protested: "But I have to generate the chords somehow. Which of the two methods shall I use to generate them?" Nevertheless, she continued writing her program, using an approach based on argument #1. Basically, she made each turtle turn randomly and move forward a distance equal to the circle's radius to pick a point on the circle. Then she made the turtle return to the center, turn randomly again, and move forward to pick a second point on the circle, thus defining a chord. At various points, she was unsure how to model the situation. She experimented with using the same radius for each turtle as well as giving each turtle its own radius. She experimented with calculating the statistics over all trials of each turtle as opposed to calculating it over all the trials of all the turtles. Finally, she decided that both were interesting and printed out the "probability" over all trials as well as the minimum and maximum probability of any turtle.

Following are the main procedures of Ellie's program. Comments (preceded by semicolons) have been added by the author for clarity of the exposition.

---

[17]At this point, Ellie actually wrote down a formal mathematical proof by contradiction. The last line of the proof was ∴ ⅔ = ¾. Contradiction.

TURTLE PROCEDURES[18]
```
;; this turtle procedure sets up the turtles[19]
to setup
setxy 0 0               ;; place myself at the origin
make "radius 10         ;; make my radius 10 units
make "p1x 0             ;; make my radius 10 units initialize temporary variables
make "p1y 0
make "p2x 0
make "p2y 0
make "chord-length 0
make "trials 0
make "big 0
make "prob 0
end
```

```
;; This is a turtle procedure which generates a random chord.
to gen-random-chord
fd :radius              ;; go to the circumference of the circle
make "p1x xpos          ;; remember where I am
make "p1y ypos
bk :radius              ;; go back to the center of the circle (the origin)
rt random 360           ;; turn randomly
fd :radius              ;; go to a new point on the circumference of the circle
make "chord-length distance :p1x :p1y    ;; the chord length is the distance from where
                                            I was before to where I am now
bk :radius              ;; go back to the center of the circle (the origin)
end
```

```
;; this turtle-procedure gets executed by each turtle at each tick of the clock
to turtle-demon
gen-random-chord                    ;; choose a new chord by the procedure above
make "trials :trials + 1            ;; increment the number of chords chosen
if bigger? [make "big :big + 1]     ;; if the new chord is bigger than the radius, increment
                                       the number of chords chosen so far which are bigger
                                       than the radius
make "prob :big / :trials    ;; the probability (so far) of choosing a chord bigger than the radius is
                                the proportion of chords chosen so far which are bigger than the
                                radius
end
```

```
;; is the turtle's chord bigger than a radius?
to bigger?
:chord-length > :radius    ;; return "true" if chord chosen is bigger than the radius
end
```

OBSERVER PROCEDURES
```
;; observer-demon summarizes the results of all the turtles
;; it gets executed at every clock tick.
to observer-demon
```

---

[18]The StarLogo procedures are divided into turtle procedures and observer procedures. Turtle procedures are executed by each turtle in parallel. Observer procedures set up the general environment and summarize the behavior of turtles.

[19]In this case, each turtle sets itself up at the origin on the circumference of a circle of radius 10.

```
make "total-trials turtle-sum [:trials]    ;; get the total number of chords chosen by all
                                              the turtles
make "total-big turtle-sum [:big]          ;; get the total number of chords chosen by
                                              all the turtles bigger than a radius
make "total-prob :total-big / :total-trials  ;; the final probability of choosing a
                                              chord bigger than a radius is the
                                              ratio of the above two totals
every 10    ;; print some statistics including the probabilities of the turtles with the smallest
  [type :total-big    and largest probabilities
  type :total-trials
  print :total-prob
  type turtle-min [prob]
  print turtle-max [prob]]
end
```

Ellie ran her program, and it indeed confirmed her original analysis. On ⅔ of the total trials the chord was larger than a radius. For a while she worried about the fact that her extreme turtles had probabilities quite far away from ⅔, but eventually convinced herself that this was OK and that it was the average turtle "that mattered."

But Ellie was still bothered by the way the chords were generated.

E: OK, so we got ⅔ as we should have. But what's bothering me is that if I generate the chords using the idea you had, then I'll probably get ¾.[20] *Which is the real way to generate random chords?* (emphasis added)

The need to explicitly program the generation of the chords precipitated an epistemological shift. The focus was no longer on determining the probability. It now moved to finding the "true" way to generate random chords. This takes Ellie immediately into an investigation of what "random" means. At this stage she is still convinced, as she was before, about the probability, that there can be only one set of random chords. She assumes that the problem is to discover this unique set.

U: That's an interesting question.
E: Oh, I see. We have two methods for generating random chords. What we have to do is figure out which produces really random chords and which produces nonrandom chords. Only one of these would produce really random chords, and that's the one that would work in the real world.
U: The real world? Do you mean you could perform a physical experiment?
E: Yes. I suppose I could. . . . Say we have a circle drawn on the floor, and I throw a stick on it, and it lands on the circle. Then the stick makes a chord on the circle. We can throw sticks and see how many times we get a chord larger than a radius.
U: And what do you expect the answer to be in the physical experiment?

---

[20]Ellie did go on and write the code to do this experiment just as a check of her insight. Her new code is the same as the old code except for a rewrite of the procedure "gen-random-chord."

E: Egads. (*very excitedly*) We have the same problem in the real world! We could instead do the experiment by letting a pin drop on the circle, and wherever the pin dropped we could draw a chord with the pin as midpoint. Depending on which experiment we try, we will get either answer #1[21] or #2. Whoa, this is crazy. So which is a random chord? Both correspond to reality?. . . .

This was a breakthrough moment for Ellie, but she was not done yet. Although her insight suggests that both answers are physically realizable, Ellie was still worried on the "mathematics side" that one of the methods for generating chords might be "missing some chords" or "counting chords twice." Ellie needed to connect her insight about the physical experiment to her knowledge about randomness and distribution. She spent quite a bit of time looking over the two methods for generating chords to see if they were counting "all the chords once and only once." She determined that in her method, once she fixed a point P, there was a one-to-one correspondence between the points on the circle and the chords having P as an end point. She concluded, therefore, that there "are as many chords passing through P as there are points in the circle." However, there will be more chords of a large size than chords of a small size. As could be seen from her original argument, there will be twice as many chords of length between r and 2r as there are of chords of length between 0 and r. Now, for the first time, Ellie advanced the argument that many interviewees had given first.

Reflection

E: I never thought of the obvious. I've been sort of assuming all along that every chord of a given size is equally likely. But if that were true, then I could have solved this problem simply. Each chord would have an equal chance of being of a length between 0 and the diameter. So half the chords would be bigger than a radius and half smaller.

Ellie went on to see that, in argument #2, large chords are more probable than small chords. She reasoned that for every chord of a given size (or more accurately a small size interval), there was a thin annulus of points that would generate chords of that size by method #2. Annuli closer to the center of the circle would correspond to large chords, and annuli near the circumference would correspond to small chords. She went on to demonstrate that annuli close to the center would have larger areas than annuli close to the circumference. Thus large chords become increasingly more probable.[22]

---

[21]I chose not to intervene at this juncture and point out that the first experiment Ellie proposed did not correspond exactly to her first analysis and method of generating chords.

[22]Here is her argument: Choose a circle of radius "R" and a chord size interval, α, small relative to R. For calculating convenience, let us say R is large and α is 2. Then the annulus corresponding to

The preceding case illustrates how *programming* a StarLogo model helped Ellie make new connections between different representations of randomness. There was another way, however, that the StarLogo environment catalyzed her making new connections. The program that Ellie wrote placed all of the turtles at the origin and because Ellie, as a professional programmer, wrote state transparent code[23] they stayed at the origin. Initially, she had placed the turtles at the origin of the screen's coordinate system because she recognized a potential bug in her program. If she had created the turtles in random positions, as is typical in StarLogo, the turtles might have "wrapped"[24] around the screen when drawing their circles and thus incorrectly calculated their chord lengths. But, because the turtles remained centered at the origin, the program was not very visually appealing. While we were engaged in the interview, a student came by and watched. He asked us why nothing was happening on the screen. Ellie explained what she was investigating, and then had an idea of how to make the program more interesting. She decided to spread the turtles out a bit so that each could be seen tracing its circle, turning yellow if its chord was longer than a radius and green if it was shorter. To spread the turtles out without getting too close to the screen edge, Ellie told each turtle to execute the command fd random (60 - radius) telling each turtle to move a random amount out from the origin. In doing this, the result was not quite what Ellie had hoped for. Near the origin there was a splotch of color (mostly yellow) as all the turtles were squeezed together very tightly, whereas near the edges, the turtles were spaced out more sparsely as in Fig. 13.4.

What had happened here quite fortuitously was a mirroring of the original dilemma. Ellie had used a linear random function to move points into a circular planar area. There were an equal number of turtles in each equally thick disk around the origin, but the outer disks had greater area than the inner disks, and therefore appeared to be less crowded.

Ellie's function, therefore, which successfully spread turtles out evenly (and what she then called randomly) along a line, did not spread them out evenly on the planar screen. This experience was an important component of her subsequent "aha" moment—exposing her, as it did, to a crack in her solid and fixed notion of "random."

---

very small chords (length nearly zero) has area equal to π. However, the disk corresponding to large chords (length near 2R) has area equal to $\pi*(2R -1)$ which is substantially larger.

[23]In StarLogo, a procedure is "state transparent" if, after its execution, the state of the turtles (and the patches) is unaltered.

[24]In a typical Logo or StarLogo screen, when a turtle goes off the screen to the right or at the top, it reappears at the left or bottom.

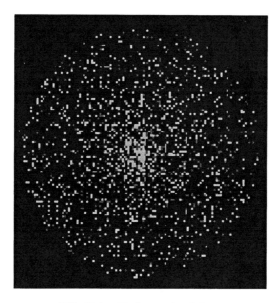

FIG. 13.4.   StarLogo simulation.

DISCUSSION

As can be seen from the preceding interview fragment, the primary obstacles to
Ellie's resolving the paradox are epistemological in nature. She faced such questions as: Can a definitive probability problem allow two different numerical
answers? Is the notion of a random chord well defined? What is the relationship
between a physical experiment and a mathematical calculation? How do you put
into correspondence an infinite number of chords and an infinite number of
points? When can you say you have selected a reference set for which it is
justified to say that all chords in it are equally likely to be selected?[25] As Ellie's
interview suggests, an important finding of the Connected Probability research is
that the primary obstacles to the interviewees' facility with probability are epistemological in nature. Their difficulties stem from fundamental confusion about
such notions as randomness, distribution, and expectation. The epistemological
status of these concepts was in doubt (What kinds of things are they? What
makes them work? Are they "natural" or constructed?). As a result, many interviewees reported an inability to resolve the competing claims of conflicting

---

[25]As was mentioned earlier, this is Ellie's version of the question debated by mathematicians as to
the applicability of the principle of insufficient reason.

probabilistic or statistical arguments. Faced with two equally compelling arguments, they are in the position of Buridan's ass: paralyzed between two equally appealing bales of hay. They cannot choose either one, and so never "get" any probability.

Paradox as a Learning Tool

Responses of the interviewees to this paralyzing situation included: (a) blaming themselves ("I just can't see why one of these is better than the other") and, in their discouragement, abandoning the domain to experts; (b) blaming the subject ("You can say anything with statistics and there's no way of proving you wrong"); (c) rejecting the importance of the conflict ("So, no big deal, they're both right.")[26] No amount of purely formal instruction in the use of probabilistic and statistical formulae can begin to address the "epistemological anxiety" that engenders these responses. What is needed is a therapeutic intervention—the valuation of both sides of a contradictory argument together with validation of the learner's competence to resolve these competing claims. In contrast to the literature on misconceptions, it is important to emphasize the continuity between the learner's confused and messy understanding of the domain and that of the experts.[27][28] Essentially, the gist of the intervention concerning paradox is creating an environment in which learners are encouraged to pay attention to a situation in which there are conflicting probabilistic arguments and to replace the experience of helplessness or anxiety in the face of this conflict with the feeling of excitement associated with a meaningful learning opportunity.

By the time Ellie had gotten to the circle chords question, she had already spent 5½ hours during 3 separate days over a 3-week period in a Connected Mathematics interview. During this time, she had encountered and constructed many paradoxes and, along the way, gained confidence in her ability to resolve them to her satisfaction. She, therefore, did not need much support on this occasion in accepting the paradox as an opportunity for learning. She took both arguments (her own and the interviewer's) seriously. Even though she suspected that the interviewer's argument was a clever trick, she felt a need to find a flaw in that argument. This need to find a flaw in one side of the paradox (as opposed to

---

[26]These three responses are equivalent to (a) giving up on the paradox, (b) asserting that the paradox is in fact a contradiction in the domain and thus invalidating the domain, or (c) refusing the paradox.

[27]Reflecting on the intellectual development of historical figures in the origins of probability can be very encouraging because they are often seen to be confused about the very same things. As was noted earlier, Ellie's concerns and confusions paralleled those of leading mathematicians over the last 100 years.

[28]The paradox will not be resolved through getting the received solution of experts. The expert solution relies on intermediate mental constructs that must be built by the learner. If instead, learners "dive in" to the paradox (as the experts did long ago), they will construct a richer intuitive conception of the key ideas in the domain.

just embracing the argument that seemed good to her) is a powerful avenue for learning. Less sophisticated learners are content to find an argument they can believe and do not feel a need to refute any counterarguments.[29] Seizing on the plausible argument without refuting the counterargument was a common phenomenon in the interviews and was particularly salient in discussions of the Monty Hall family of problems (Gilman, 1992; Wilensky, 1993).[30]

Programming—Making Probability Concrete

It was not until Ellie *programmed* a simulation of the problem that she began to resolve the paradox. Note that she had already begun to see the direction of resolution before she ran her simulation, even before she completed writing the program.[31] This was a common phenomenon across interviewees. Explicitly representing the situation in which the probability problem was embedded, thus making it concrete, was frequent enough to resolve the present difficulty and move to the next level of subtlety.[32] Writing the code to generate the chords forced Ellie to embody the randomness of the chords in a computational process. This led her to see that different computational processes generate different sets of chords (or distributions of chord lengths). Still clinging to the idea that there was only one truly random set of chords, she moved to the level of physical simulation where surely, she thought, she could see which set of chords would really be picked out. At that point came the "aha" that there was no unique set of real and truly random chords—different physical experiments would lead to different sets of "random" chords. She had made the connections between the physical experiments, the computational processes, and the mathematics of randomness and distribution. Equipped with this connected web of relations, Ellie

---

[29]Indeed, this is not surprising, because traditional "school mathematics" can be seen as a program that inculcates the belief that mathematics is about knowing correct procedures, not about debugging incorrect ones. This failure to connect old and new conceptions is critical from a "Connected Mathematics" perspective.

[30]One of these "Monty Hall" probability paradoxes made newspaper headlines (Tierney, 1991) after appearing in a column in *Parade* magazine (Vos Savant, 1991).

[31]As is elaborated on later in the chapter, the fact of Ellie's getting her insight before running her program further emphasizes the value of building a model over exploring the outputs of a model.

[32]Again, this was the norm in the Monty Hall family of problems. As soon as the interviewee started to write down a program for simulating the problem, what was going on became apparent. Often, they did not even bother to finish the programs. In contrast, in another paradox discussed in the interviews, the "envelope paradox," writing a program most often served to instantiate an already held theory and, therefore, running it "confirmed" the theory, often prematurely. In effect, the authority of the program sanctioned the solution. However, in that particular case, a community formed spontaneously to resolve the dilemma. Interviewees in the study got together and compared their different solutions. Because the interviewees wrote different programs with different results, the conflict created an opportunity for them to talk about how their programs encapsulated their theories. This led to more sophisticated critiques of the theories. (For a discussion of how programs and microworlds can encapsulate theories (see Edwards, 1995).

was able to make mathematical arguments about chord distributions reminiscent of measure-theoretic argumentation. We might venture to say that Ellie would now be ready to deal with the formalisms of measure theory and probability measures without getting lost. The concrete foundation built up during the interview would provide support in navigating through the formalism, guiding its use, and preventing its abuse.

Using Models Versus Building Models

Some researchers have argued (e.g., Soloway, 1993; Steinberger, 1994) that using specialized applications, domain-specific models, and exploratory simulations can provide the benefit of programming without the "overhead" associated with learning the language. An illuminating comparison can be made between the experience of programming random chords and that of using specialized probability courseware.

One such package, ConStats (Cohen, Smith, Chechile, & Cock, 1994), was designed with the objective of helping students gain "a deep conceptual understanding of introductory probability and statistics" through an "active experimental style of learning" (Cohen, Chechile, Smith, Tsai, & Burns, 1994). As such, it is based on constructivist principles. However, the experiments that students can conduct with ConStats consist of manipulating the parameters of a preconceived model. Students cannot program in ConStats or build models to pursue questions that arise.

The software is impressive, with well implemented graphics, an easy-to-learn user interface, extensive contextual help facilities, and a large selection of features. A principal emphasis of the software package is on distributions. The package contains many different distributions, both continuous and discrete, each with its own name and associated text describing its characteristics. In addition, for each kind of distribution, users have a host of parameters, which they can manipulate and view the resultant change in the graph of the "random variable."

ConStats has both the strengths and weaknesses of the broader class of what can be called "black-box" simulations (i.e., simulations in which the user does not have explicit access to the modeling algorithm). These strengths include the ability of users to engage quickly with high level models, the availability of specialized domain-specific tools, engaging user interfaces, and broad coverage of the subject domain. The chief weakness is the lack of "read-write" access to the model. As a result, learners cannot explore what processes govern the way the parameters change the model. More importantly, they cannot explore the consequences of changing the structure of these processes themselves. As a result, they do not develop a solid understanding of these underlying processes.

The ConStats software was used extensively by students in a number of university-level courses. After each course was completed, the students were given a posttest designed to measure their comprehension of concepts "covered" by the software. The researchers conducting the evaluation (Cohen, Chechile, et al., 1994) report that conceptual comprehension was significantly greater for those students using the software than for the control group. One of the questions on the posttest was "What is it about a variable that makes it a random variable?" The first author of the evaluation study reported (Cohen, personal communication, 1993) that in all the exams he has seen, not a single student had "given the correct answer," nor had a single one mentioned the concept of distribution in his or her answer.[33] Most students just left it blank. The most frequent nonblank answer was "a variable that has equal probability of taking on any of its possible values." Despite the fact that they had spent hours manipulating distributions and had plotted and histogrammed their "random variables," they missed the connection between these activities and the concept of random variable. The connection between distribution and randomness was perhaps too obvious to the software designers. They did not recognize the necessity of the learners constructing that connection for themselves if they were to explore it further through the software.

The ConStats software encourages exploration through changing parameters, which may explain its success in improving conceptual understanding in courseware subject matter. However, ConStats users' understanding of randomness is seemingly impoverished. They have not made connections between the distributions they manipulated and observed and the concept of random variable. It is unlikely that they have developed a widely connected and intuitive sense of the concept of randomness. In contrast, most of the interviewees in the Connected Probability project developed a deeper understanding of randomness. By explicitly confronting the question of the meaning of randomness, and by explicitly representing it in a program, the interviewees developed strong intuitions that were not developed by the users of the courseware.

Leaving aside the differences in conceptual understanding promoted by the two approaches, there is also an important issue of educational goals. Particularly in the area of statistics, the educational goal should emphasize interpreting and designing statistics from science and life rather than mastery of curricular materials. In order to make sense of scientific studies, it is not sufficient to be able to verify the stated model; one needs to see why those models are superior to alternative models. In order to understand a newspaper statistic, one must be able to reason about the underlying model used to create that statistic[34] and evaluate its plausibility. For these purposes, building probabilistic and statistical models is essential.

Computer-based exploratory environments for learning probability can facili-

---

[33]More recently, Cohen (personal communication, 1995) has replicated these posttests and has found a "very small number" of students who refer to distributions in their answers.

[34]A case study of two students trying to make sense of a divorce-rate statistic reported in the newspaper is presented in Wilensky (1993). In order to make sense of the statistic, they designed and critiqued many different models.

tate greater conceptual understanding. The computer's capacity to repeat and vary large numbers of trials, as well as its ability to show the results of these trials in compressed time (and often in visual form), makes it possible to encapsulate events that are usually distributed over time and space. This can provide learners with the kinds of concrete experiences they need to build solid probabilistic intuitions.

A central issue, then, is between learners using prebuilt models and learners making their own models. The ability to run prebuilt models interactively is an improvement over static textbook based approaches. By manipulating parameters of the model, users can make useful distinctions and test out some conjectures. The results of the Connected Probability project suggest that for learners to make use of these prebuilt models, they must first build their own models and design their own investigations.

It is possible to combine the two approaches (e.g., Eisenberg, 1991; Wilensky, 1995, in preparation-b) by providing prebuilt models that are embedded in programming environments, creating so-called "extensible applications" (Eisenberg, 1991). This combined approach has the advantages of both prebuilt and buildable models. The challenge of such an approach is to design the right middle level of primitives so that they are neither (a) too low-level so that the application becomes identical to its programming language, nor (b) too high-level so that the application turns into an exercise of running preconceived experiments. The metric by which the optimal level can be judged is in the usefulness to learners. This requires an extensive research program. The findings from this research must inform the development of modeling languages and their embedded extensible applications.

CONCLUDING REMARKS

In the Connected Probability project, learners such as Ellie succeeded in making deep probabilistic arguments that probed at the foundations of the discipline. Having understood the foundational concepts in this deep way, they developed a strong intuitive understanding of such concepts as randomness, distribution, and expectation. Solid intuitions about probability and statistics were clearly developed by learners in this study. This shows that we are not, by our natures, as some have argued, unable to reason intuitively about probability.

The Connected Probability project is an instantiation of the Connected Mathematics approach. The key elements of the Connected Mathematics approach that enabled these changes are

- The explorations of multiple meanings of concepts and making connections between these different representations.
  Like Ellie, they saw the connections between representations of randomness

in different domains including physical experiments, probability distributions, and computational processes.

- A focus on epistemological issues (as they specifically relate to how learners construct understandings).
  Ellie focused on what it means for something (a process) to be random? Is there only one way of choosing chords randomly or can there be multiple ways?

- The use of paradox.
  The paradox reinforced the focus on epistemological issues—it placed her epistemology of mathematics in doubt. Ellie wondered: What kind of discipline is mathematics if a "unique" probability can be equal to both ⅔ and ¾?

- Conducting a learner-owned investigation (as opposed to problem solving) as the central activity of mathematical learning.
  Even though the random chord problem started out as a classic formal problem, Ellie engaged herself with it to see it as her own.

- Acknowledgment of and attention to the affective side of learning mathematics.
  Ellie would not have engaged herself with the paradox had she not been encouraged to believe in the pursuit enough to overcome the epistemological anxiety that usually prevents learners from getting so engaged. Crucial to this self-confidence is a "cognitive-emotive" therapy for the sense of shame produced by a mathematical culture that prevents learners from expressing the epistemological anxiety and tentative understandings that are at its root.

- Making mathematics (and articulating it in a concrete form).
  Ellie is encouraged to create alternate representations of the problem and work out definitions of randomness that make sense to her. This enables her to see mathematics as a personal odyssey of meaning making, not an externally given corpus to be absorbed but not affected by her.

- The use of technology as a medium for making and articulating mathematics.
  Ellie was able to design her own experiment to explore the different sides of the paradox. This ability to express her partial understandings of "random chord" in a computational model was key to the refinement of her mental model and provided a powerful semiotic context for her articulation of her mathematical thought.

The availability of the programming environment facilitated many of these goals. The programming environment facilitated Ellie's conducting her own investigation. It provided a language, a different notation in which Ellie could express her mathematical ideas. It provided a signing environment, a placeholder for these ideas to exist outside of Ellie. Moreover, because this language is dynamic—it can be "run"—it provided feedback to Ellie's ideas. This trialogue between Ellie's mental model, the expression of her mental model in encapsulated code and the running of that code, allowed Ellie to successfully refine the creative structure of her thought. Although one might concede that it is theoretically possible for Ellie to have resolved her problem with a prebuilt model in which a randomizing parameter was modified, the learner-modeling approach is clearly significant in its outcome and arguably more practical in its implementation. This is because, for Ellie to have come to a similar set of insights, a model designer would have had to anticipate all of Ellie's concerns and built them into the model. Clearly, this is impossible to do in general—educational software designers cannot anticipate all the directions that a learner might want to investigate and incorporate them into a parameter model. Moreover, users of "parameter-twiddling" software realize that they are pursuing someone else's investigation. This realization decreases the motivation of discovery. Lastly, such closed environments reinforce a view of mathematics learning as a process of verifying already known mathematics, as opposed to seeing it as a personal odyssey of mathematics making. In designing computer-based environments for learning probability, we must remember that allowing users to create their own models is necessary for truly learner-owned investigations.

For many learners in the Connected Probability project, this experience of doing Connected Mathematics was so different from their experience in regular mathematics classrooms that they did not recognize their activity as being mathematics. Learners who had "always hated mathematics" and had been told that they were not "good at mathematics" were excitedly engaged in doing mathematics that could be easily recognized by mathematicians as "good mathematics." Having created a strong intuitive foundation for the conceptual domain, learners could also go on to engage the formal approaches and techniques with an appreciation for how they connect to core ideas of probability and statistics. Even more importantly, they now understood that mathematics is a living growing entity which they could literally make their own.

ACKNOWLEDGMENTS

A version of this chapter appeared in 1995 in the *Journal of Mathematical Behavior*, *14* (2). The preparation of this chapter was supported by the National Science Foundation (Grant 9153719-MDR), the LEGO Group, and Nintendo Inc. The ideas expressed here do not necessarily reflect the positions of the supporting agencies. I would like to thank Seymour Papert, Mitchel Resnick, and David Chen for extensive feedback about this research. I also thank Donna Woods, Paul Whitmore, Ken Ruthven, Walter Stroup, David Rosenthal, Richard Noss, Yasmin

Kafai, Wally Feurzeig, Laurie Edwards, Barbara Brizuela, and Aaron Brandes for helpful comments on drafts of this chapter. Finally, I thank Ellie and all the participants in the Connected Probability project. I have learned a lot from (and with) you.

REFERENCES

Abelson, H., & diSessa, A. (1980). *Turtle geometry: The computer as a medium for exploring mathematics*. Cambridge, MA: MIT Press.

Abelson, H., & Goldenberg, P. (1977). *Teacher's guide for computational model of animal behavior.* (LOGO Memo No. 46). Cambridge, MA: MIT Media Laboratory.

Belenky, M., Clinchy, B., Goldberger, N., & Tarule, J. (1986). *Women's ways of knowing*. New York: Basic Books.

Bertrand, J. (1889). *Calcul des probabilités*. Paris: Gauthier-Villars.

Borel, E. (1909). *Eléments de la théorie des probabilitiés*. Paris: Hermann et Fils.

Chaitin, G. (1987). *Information, randomness and incompleteness: Papers on algorithmic information theory*. Teaneck, NJ: World Scientific.

Cohen, B. (1987). Scientific revolutions, revolutions in science, and a probabilistic revolution 1800–1930. In Kruger, L., Daston, L., & Heidelberger, M. (Eds.), *The probabilistic revolution* (Vol. 1, pp. 23–44). Cambridge, MA: MIT Press.

Cohen, J. (1979). On the psychology of prediction whose is the fallacy? *Cognition, 7*, 385–407.

Cohen, S., Chechile, R. Smith, G., Tsai, F., & Burns, G. (1994). A method for evaluating the effectiveness of educational software. *Behavior Research Methods, Instruments and Computers, 26*(2), 236–241.

Cohen, S., Smith, G., Chechile, R., & Cock, R. (1994). Designing curricular software for conceptualizing statistics. In L. Brunelli & G. Cicchitelli (Eds.), *Proceedings of the first Conference of the International Association for Statistics Education* (pp. 237–245).

Collins, A., & Brown, J. S. (1988). The computer as a tool for learning through reflection. In H. Mandl & A. Lesgold (Eds.), *Learning issues for intelligent tutoring systems* (pp. 1–18). New York: Springer-Verlag.

Confrey, J. (1993a, April). *A constructivist research programme towards the reform of mathematics education*. Paper presented at the annual meeting of the American Educational Research Association, Atlanta, GA.

Confrey, J. (1993b). Learning to see children's mathematics: Crucial challenges in constructivist reform. In K. Tobin (Ed.), *The practice of constructivism in science education* (pp. 299–321). Washington, DC: American Association for the Advancement of Science.

Cuoco, A., & Goldenberg, E. P. (1992, June). Reconnecting geometry: A role for technology. In *Proceedings of Computers in the Geometry Classroom conference*, Northfield, MN: St. Olaf College.

Edwards, L. (1992). A LOGO microworld for transformational geometry. In C. Hoyles, & R. Noss (Eds.), *Learning mathematics and logo* (pp. 127–155). London: MIT Press.

Edwards, L. (1995). Microworlds as representations. In R. Noss, C. Hoyles, A. diSessa & L. Edwards (Eds.), *Proceedings of the NATO Advanced Technology Workshop on Computer Based Exploratory Learning Environments* (pp. 127–154). Asilomar, CA.

Edwards, W., & von Winterfeldt, D. (1986). On cognitive illusions and their implications. *Southern California Law Review, 59*(2), 401–451.

Eisenberg, M. (1991). *Programmable applications: Interpreter meets interface* (MIT AI Memo No. 1325). Cambridge, MA: MIT Artificial Intelligence Lab.

Evans, J. (1993). Bias and rationality. In K. I. Mantkelow & D. E. Over (Eds.), *Rationality: Psychological and Philosophical Perspectives* (pp. 6–30). London: Routledge.

Feurzeig, W. (1989). *A visual programming environment for mathematics education.* Paper presented at the Fourth International Conference for Logo and Mathematics Education, Jerusalem, Israel.

Geertz, C. (1973). *The interpretation of cultures.* New York: Basic Books.

Gigerenzer, G. (1987). The probabilistic revolution in psychology—An overview. In L. Kruger, L. Daston, & M. Heidelberger (Eds.), *The probabilistic revolution* (Vol. 2, pp. 7–11). Cambridge, MA: MIT Press.

Gilligan, C. (1977). *In a different voice: Psychological theory and women's development.* Cambridge, MA: Harvard University Press.

Gilman, L., (1992, January). The car and the goats. *American Mathematical Monthly, 99*(1), 3–7.

Gould, S. J. (1991). The streak of streaks. In S. J. Gould, *Bully for brontosaurus* (pp. 463–472). Cambridge, MA: W. W. Norton.

Hacking, I. (1987). Was there a probabilistic revolution 1800–1930? In L. Kruger, L. Daston, & M. Heidelberger (Eds.), *The probabilistic revolution* (Vol. 1, pp. 45–55). Cambridge, MA: MIT Press.

Harel, I. (1992). *Children designers.* Norwood, NJ: Ablex.

Harel, I. & Papert, S. (1990). Software design as a learning environment. *Interactive Learning Environments Journal, 1*(1), 41–84.

Kafai, Y., & Harel, I. (1991). Learning through design and teaching: Exploring social and collaborative aspects of constructionism. In I. Harel & S. Papert (Eds.) *Constructionism* (pp. 85–110). Norwood, NJ: Ablex.

Kahneman, D., & Tversky, A. (1973). On the psychology of prediction. *Psychological Review, 80*(4), 237–251.

Kahneman, D., & Tversky, A. (1982). On the study of statistical intuitions. In D. Kahneman, A. Tversky, & D. Slovic (Eds.), *Judgment under uncertainty: Heuristics and biases* (pp. 493–508). Cambridge, UK: Cambridge University Press.

Kaput, J. (1989). Notations and representations. In E. von Glaserfeld (Ed.), *Radical constructivism in mathematics education* (pp. 55–74). Netherlands: Kluwer Academic Press.

Keller, E. F. (1983). *A feeling for the organism: The life and work of Barbara McClintock.* San Francisco, CA: W. H. Freeman.

Keynes, J. M. (1921). *A treatise on probability.* London: MacMillan.

Kolmogorov, A. N. (1950). *Foundations of the theory of probability.* New York: Chelsea.

Konold, C. (1991). Understanding students' beliefs about probability. In E. von Glaserfeld (Ed.), *Radical constructivism in mathematics education* (pp. 139–156). Netherlands: Kluwer Academic Press.

Lakatos, I. (1976). *Proofs and refutations.* Cambridge, UK: Cambridge University Press.

Lampert, M. (1990). When the problem is not the question and the solution is not the answer: Mathematical knowing and teaching. *American Education Research Journal 27*, 29–63.

Leron, U. (1994). *Can we follow what we preach: Teaching according to constructivist principles.* CMESG Proceedings, Regina, Sask, Canada.

Leron, U., & Zazkis, R. (1992). Of geometry, turtles, and groups. In C. Hoyles, & R. Noss (Eds.), *Learning mathematics and LOGO* (pp. 319–352). London: MIT Press.

Marinoff, L. (1994). A resolution of Bertrand's Paradox. *Philosophy of Science, 61*, 1–24.

Minsky, M. (1987). *The society of mind.* New York: Simon & Schuster.

National Council of Teachers of Mathematics (1991a). *Curriculum and evaluation standards for school mathematics.* Reston, VA: Author.

National Council of Teachers of Mathematics (1991b). *Professional standards for teaching mathematics*. Reston, VA: Author.

Nisbett, R. (1980). *Human inference: Strategies and shortcoming of social judgment*. Englewood Cliffs, NJ: Prentice-Hall.

Nisbett, R., Krantz, D., Jepson, C., & Kunda, Z. (1983). The use of statistical heuristics in everyday inductive reasoning. *Psychological Review, 90*(4), 339–363.

Noss, R., & Hoyles, C. (1991). Logo and the learning of mathematics: Looking back and looking forward. In C. Hoyles, & R. Noss (Eds.), *Learning mathematics and Logo* (pp. 431–468). London: MIT Press.

Papert, S. (1972). Teaching children to be mathematicians vs. teaching about mathematics. *International Journal of Mathematics Education in Science and Technology, 3*, 249–262.

Papert, S. (1980). *Mindstorms: Children, computers, and powerful ideas*. New York: Basic Books.

Papert, S. (1991). Situating constructionism. In I. Harel & S. Papert (Eds.), *Constructionism* (pp. 1–12). Norwood, NJ: Ablex.

Papert, S. (1993). *The children's machine*. New York: Basic Books.

Phillips, J. (1988) *How to think about statistics*. New York: W. H. Freeman.

Piaget, J. (1952). *The Origins of intelligence in children*. New York: International University Press.

Piaget, J. (1975). *The origin of the idea of chance in children*. New York: Norton.

Poincaré, H. (1912). *Calcul des probabilités* Paris: Gauthier-Villars.

Resnick, M. (1991). Animal simulations with *Logo: Massive parallelism for the masses. In J. Meyer & S. Wilson (Eds.), *From animals to animats* (pp. 534–539). Cambridge, MA: MIT Press.

Resnick, M. (1992). *Beyond the centralized mindset: Explorations in massively parallel microworlds*. Unpublished doctoral dissertation, MIT Media Laboratory, Cambridge, MA.

Richmond, B., & Peterson, S. (1990). *STELLA II*. Hanover, NH: High Performance Systems, Inc.

Savage, L. (1954). *The foundations of statistics*. New York: Wiley.

Schwartz, J., & Yerushalmy, M. (1987). The geometric supposer: An intellectual prosthesis for making conjectures. *The College Mathematics Journal, 18*(1), 58–65.

Smith, J. P., diSessa, A. A., & Roschelle, J. (1994). Reconceiving misconceptions: A constructivist analysis of knowledge in transition. *Journal of the Learning Science, 3*, 115–163.

Soloway, E. (1993, October). Should we teach students to program? *CACM, 36*(1), 21–24.

Steinberger, M. (1994). Where does programming fit in? *Logo Update. 2*(3), 8.

Suppes, P. (1984). *Probabilistic metaphysics*. Oxford, UK: Blackwell.

Surrey, J. (1991). Relationship and empowerment. In J. Jordan, A. Kaplan, J. B. Miller, I. Stiver, & J. Surrey (Eds.), *Women's growth in connection: Writing from the stone center* (pp. 162–180). New York: Guilford.

Thurston, W. (1994, April). On proof and progress in mathematics. *Bulletin of the American Mathematical Society, 30*(2), 161–177.

Tierney, J. (1991, July 21). Behind Monty Hall's doors: Puzzle, debate and answer? *The New York Times National*, p. 1.

Tripp, R. T. (1970). *International thesaurus of quotations*. New York: Harper & Row.

Turkle S., & Papert, S. (1991). Epistemological pluralism and revaluation of the concrete. In I. Harel & S. Papert (Eds.), *Constructionism* (pp. 161–192). Norwood NJ: Ablex Publishing Corp.

Tversky, A., & Kahneman, D. (1974). Judgment under uncertainty: Heuristics and biases. *Science, 185*, 1124–1131.

Tversky, A. & Kahneman, D. (1980). Causal schemas in judgments under uncertainty. In M. Fischbein (Ed.), *Progress in social psychology* (pp. 49–72). Hillsdale, NJ: Lawrence Erlbaum Associates.

Tversky, A. & Kahneman, D. (1983). Extensional vs. intuitive reasoning: The conjunction fallacy in probability judgment. *Psychological Review, 90*(4), 293–315.

von Mises, R. (1964). *Mathematical theory of probability and statistics.* New York: Academic.

Vos Savant, M. (1991). "Ask Marilyn" column. *Parade Magazine,* September 9, 1990; December 2, 1990, February 17, 1991.

Wilensky, U. (1991). Abstract meditations on the concrete and concrete implications for mathematics education. In I. Harel & S. Papert (Eds.), *Constructionism* (pp. 193–204). Norwood NJ: Ablex.

Wilensky, U. (1993). *Connected mathematics: building concrete relationships with mathematical knowledge.* Unpublished doctoral dissertation, MIT Media Laboratory, Cambridge, MA.

Wilensky, U. (1995, July). *Learning probability through building computational models.* Paper presented at the 19th International Conference on the Psychology of Mathematics Education, Recife, Brazil.

Wilensky, U. (in preparation-a). *What is normal anyway? Therapy for epistemological anxiety.*

Wilensky, U. (in preparation-b). *GPCEE—An extensible microworld for exploring micro- and macro- views of gases.*

Wilensky, U. (in preparation-c). *Mathematics as a way of connecting.*

Ideal and Real Systems
A Study of Notions of Control in Undergraduates Who Design Robots

Fred G. Martin

INTRODUCTION

This chapter presents a study of Massachusetts Institute of Technology (MIT) undergraduate students' notions of control as embodied in the task of designing autonomous robots that perform in a competitive event. These robots were built by students who participated in the LEGO Robot Design Competition, a hands-on, workshop-like course that takes place every January at MIT.[1]

In the course, students are given a kit of parts with which to build their robots. The kits include a custom microprocessor board for control of the robot; LEGO Technic gears, beams, axles, and bricks for the structural work; and assorted electronic components for building sensors and other related parts. In addition to this specially designed robot-building kit, students are given the specifications for a competitive task to be performed by their robot. The job of the students, then, is to learn how to use the materials in their kits through the process of designing, constructing, and debugging a robot of their own conception. At the end of the 4-week course, the students' robots compete in a public event that draws an audience of several hundred people, including MIT students and faculty, local parents and their children—who all become excited robotic enthusiasts for the event.

The pedagogy of the Robot Design Project is based on the educational theory of *constructionism* espoused by Seymour Papert (Papert, 1986). According to

---

[1] The LEGO Robot Design project was created by this author in collaboration with Pankaj Oberoi and Randy Sargent, two fellow MIT students.

constructionist learning theory, people learn most effectively when they are involved in the creation of an external artifact in the world. This artifact becomes an "object to think with," which is used by the learner to explore and embody ideas related to the topic of inquiry.

For the purposes of the Robot Design Project, constructionism is reflected in the centrality of the students' robot design task. The entire course revolves around this challenge. Traditional academic mechanisms of lectures and recitation are used, but are subordinated to the practical work of getting the robots built and debugged. The most valuable interventions made by the course organizers on behalf of its students occur not in the classroom, but in the ever-present laboratory sessions. Additionally, students use each other as resources; they work in teams of two or three.

This chapter has three sections. The first section presents a case study of a pair of students who formed a team to build robots for two consecutive years of the robot design class. These students believed that control could best be achieved by having the robot keep track of its global position on the playing field at all times. Even in the face of failure, these two students held their views with conviction; only after repeated problems did one of them revise his beliefs.

The second section presents an overview of the task of designing a control system for a contest robot, and the sorts of ideas that students generate when devising their own solutions. This section presents a composite set of results from a number of different students' work; this composite portrait is representative of the sorts of issues encountered by most of the students in the class.

The methodologies chosen by the student robot designers in this study are in many ways a product of the modern engineering university curriculum. The final section analyzes the content of this curriculum, suggesting possible explanations for students' choices and why their intuitions about control were often misleading. In doing so, I point toward a direction for revising the curriculum to encompass a broader range of ideas about systems and control—one that would be more effective in preparing students for demands of modern technological systems.

CASE STUDY: POSITIONING AS A CONTROL PRINCIPLE

In this section, I present an in-depth case study of one particular team of students. This case study serves both to introduce the Robot Design Project and to illustrate the strong personal convictions brought to the project by the particular students in question. Even after their approach proved unsuccessful, these two students remained quite attached to their ideas about what type of control system would be best for operating their robot—an indication of the strength of their beliefs. In the subsequent section, I examine ways that students negotiate issues of control in a broader sense.

The students, whom I call "Stan" and "Dave," participated in robot-building teams for 2 consecutive years of the contest (1990 and 1991). Although all members of the team collaborated on the implementation of each robot, Stan and Dave's strategic ideas dominated the designs. (Their team had other members as well during each of the 2 years.)

Stan was a master LEGO Technic builder, having been an avid fan and collector of the materials from his childhood through his teenage years. His ability to design with the materials was quite impressive in both artistic and functional senses. He also was driven to create spectacular and elaborate designs that would have great audience appeal.

Dave, on the other hand, was an accomplished computer programmer who reveled in building sophisticated and elegant computer programs. Both Stan and Dave were pleased to defer to each other's strengths during implementation of their ideas but collaborated during the conceptual design stages.

In the first of these contests, entitled *Robo-Pong*, the goal was to transport ping-pong balls onto the other robot's side of the table. Stan and Dave chose to build a shooter robot. The task of building an effective shooting mechanism was a genuine challenge even for the experienced LEGO designer; there were a number of teams who gave up on building shooting robots after unsuccessful attempts to develop firing mechanisms that worked satisfactorily. Stan was undaunted and built a firing mechanism that was far better than any of the others, shooting the balls farther and recocking quicker.

The ball-firing mechanism, however, is only half of a shooter robot; the other half is a mechanism to feed the balls into the barrel of the shooter. For this, Stan ended up adopting a mechanism suggested to him by another team developing a shooter robot. (He obtained their permission before developing his own version of their idea.) The result was a robot that was quite competent at scooping up and firing balls—or so it seemed—when the robot operated under direct human control.

When Stan and Dave approached the control problem, they assessed the feedback control methods we were proposing for overall robot guidance and judged them as too error-prone and ambiguous. According to them, robots that used local feedback from the environment were inclined to wander and make missteps on their way to the feedback goal. Stan and Dave did not trust local feedback as the most effective or reliable way to accomplish the task.

Instead, their approach was based on two unusual sensor applications. The first was a method to ascertain the robot's initial orientation on the playing table. (*Robo-Pong* used a randomized angle of initial robot orientation.) The second was a mechanism intended to keep track of the robot's position on the playing table in terms of a displacement from its initial position. Thus, by knowing the initial orientation, and by recording all changes from it, they expected their robot to be able to navigate about the table at will, knowing its exact location at all times. Surely, they believed, this would be a more effective approach than relying on erratic data sampled as the robot wandered about the playing surface.

The primary sensor provided in the *Robo-Pong* robot-building kit for detecting inclination was the mercury switch. However, the kit included an alternate inclination sensor, which we had not tested but could potentially operate more effectively than the mercury switches. The device was a small metal can, larger than a pencil eraser but smaller than a thimble, which contained a tiny metal ball. The can's base was flat, and four wires protruded down from it. Inside the can, the four wires terminated in distinct contact areas. In operation, the ball rolled around inside the can and created an electrical contact between the inner wall of the can and one (or two) of the four contact areas.

We did not rely on the metal can sensor as the primary inclination-sensing device because we were unsure of how pronounced a contact bounce problem would be owing to vibration. Because the sensors were quite cheap, though, we decided to provide them anyway, buying enough to give two to each *Robo-Pong* team in addition to four mercury switches. We left the testing and evaluation of the device to the participants.

It turned out that the bounce problem with the metal can was indeed troublesome compared to the mercury sensors, so most participants used the mercury switches. Stan and Dave, however, thought of an unusual use for the metal can sensors. Because the robots were to start the contest on the inclined surface, the robots could use inclination sensors to determine their initial angle of approach up the slant of the incline. The bounce problem would be eliminated because the robot would be at rest at the start of the round.

Because the initial orientation was specified in 30-degree increments, there were, in principle, 12 discrete initial orientations. Stan and Dave realized that by using three metal can sensors (each of which gave an inclination reading accurate to one of four quadrants) rotated by 30 degrees with respect to one another, their robot could *precisely determine* its initial orientation. This precision would be necessary for combination with the other component of their strategy, a movement controller.

The movement controller was a method to enable the robot to keep precise track of its position as it navigated across the playing surface (finding its way from the starting position to the trough, for example). For this, Stan and Dave employed *shaft encoders*, sensor technology for measuring the angular rotation of a shaft.

Shaft encoders are typically employed in mechanical devices in which angular travel or displacement is confined within limits and hence can be repeatably measured. For example, a shaft encoder on a joint of a revolute robot arm (an arm with elbow-like joints) can measure the angle of the arm. Usually such encoders are used in conjunction with limit switches; to calibrate the joint for sensing, the controller will drive the joint until it triggers the limit switch, thereby determining the zero position of the joint. All subsequent readings are then made with respect to the zero position, which can be reliably reestablished at a later time.

For mobile applications, shaft encoders have questionable value in determining position because of the problem of a vehicle's wheels slipping with respect to the surface on which it is moving. This slippage causes errors in estimations of where the vehicle has moved on the surface. In mobile applications, shaft encoders are best suited for velocity and approximate distance measures; the speed-ometer-odometer of an automobile is an example of this usage.

Stan and Dave were cognizant of the slippage problem, but believed they had a workaround solution that would yield acceptable results. Rather than attaching the shaft encoders to the drive wheels, which they did realize would be quite prone to slippage, they added free-spinning *trailer wheels* that would rotate when dragged along the driving surface by the robot's movement from the drive mechanism. They attached the shaft encoders to the trailer wheels, which presumably were much less prone to slippage than the drive wheels.

Stan described the plan to me during early stages of his implementation. I argued with him that the approach was dubious; mobile robotics researchers had built various robots that attempted to perform global positioning based on shaft encoding, and they all had shortcomings that forced the robots to frequently recalibrate their estimates of position based on local environmental references. He was undeterred. Because I did not perceive my role as preventing him from exploring an idea that interested him, and as there was no harm in his trying it, I backed off.

Stan and Dave proceeded with the concept with Dave doing much of the programming. At various points during the development of the robot, they were able to make remarkable demonstrations of the robot's ability to respond to control commands and measure and correct for its motion. The robot could drive to specific commanded positions, or, if the robot were dragged along a table to a position 8 or 10 inches away and then released, the position controller would drive the robot back to within an inch of its original position. Of course this only worked when the robot was dragged with considerable downward pressure so that the trailer wheels tracked the movement (i.e., if they did not slip). I tried to argue with Stan that as impressive as this demonstration was, the approach was still futile because displacements in game play would be of the sort that *would* cause slippage. I think at this point Stan was so pleased with his apparent success that he was not listening to me.

The overall strategy was for the robot to drive down into the bottom of its side of the table and sweep back and forth along the trough, firing balls over to the opponent's side. If the robot's initial orientation were such that it was aimed upward, it would drive forward to knock one of the three top balls over the edge, as an "insurance" measure, before retreating into its main activity in the trough.

During the testing, Stan and Dave maintained confidence in their design. Indeed, the robot seemed largely to work; often it would only require minor hand-administered nudges during practice rounds to be successful. In the actual contest, however, the design failed badly. The slightest deviation from ideal circumstances caused the robot to fail without possibility for recovery. In ignoring feedback from the specific features of the playing field, the robot really had no hope if any number of things were to go wrong: a slight miscalculation as to the amount of rotation needed to orient properly, a bump from the opponent robot, or a even an irregularity in the surface of the playing field. Stan and Dave had fooled themselves during the robot testing—when the safety net of their prodding corrections was gone, the robot could not reliably perform the sequence of steps needed to work, and it was a competitive failure.

Stan and Dave teamed up again to design a robot for the subsequent *Robo-Cup* contest. In his first written report for that project, Stan reflected on his experiences in building the *Robo-Pong* robot.[2]

> *Lessons Learned.* Last year we spent a lot of time and resources on non-essentials. Our mechanical design was not stabilized until the night before the second contest. The majority of the time spent on software was in building a sophisticated object-oriented system. Our strategy was stable early enough, but it relied too heavily on unproven sensors and the accuracy of shaft encoders. This year we are focusing our energy on creating a robot that works well, even if we don't have time to make it look good.

> *Design Goals.* In the past, robots have often failed because one particular sensor is critical and the software doesn't handle exceptions and breakdowns very well. Our goal is to build a robot that can check for errors and compensate before the errors escalate. Reliability and robustness are the targets for our project. Given enough time for testing, most unexpected conditions can be accounted for.

It seemed as if Stan had learned his lesson. Yet, remarkably, Stan and Dave proceeded to repeat exactly the same mistakes in their *Robo-Cup* robot design.

Although Dave did not attempt to build as sophisticated a global positioning system, as he had in his Robo-Pong design, Stan and Dave did again employ shaft encoders as the primary sensor for their *Robo-Cup* design. In *Robo-Cup*, the contest task involved driving from the starting position to a ball dispenser, actuating the ball dispenser's control button (causing balls to drop from above), and delivering the balls to a soccer-like goal. Not surprisingly, Stan and Dave chose to shoot the balls in, reducing their robot's task to the job of successfully moving from the starting position to a location beneath the ball dispenser, from where balls could be shot directly into the goal area.

Stan and Dave's insistence on using the shaft encoders to guide their robot's movement from the starting position to the ball dispenser caused them to ignore an obvious alternative solution: a reflectivity coding on the playing surface which

---

[2]This and other student quotations are taken from students' weekly written design reports.

could have been used to indicate to the robot the position of the ball dispenser. They claimed that their robot moved too fast to be able to stop in time after detecting this feature.

For this contest, one of their troubles was gone: Rather than robots being subject to a random orientation at the start of the contest, they could be placed within the designated starting circle at any orientation by the robot's own designers. Knowing that an exact measure of initial position was critical to his robot's success, Stan requested permission to allow the use of a template that he could employ to help position his robot repeatably at the same location! We consented.

The performance of Stan and Dave's robot in the actual contest was disappointing. They were not able to tune the performance of the shaft encoders to be consistent. The night of the contest, the robot would stop its journey to the ball dispenser just about an inch short of the desired position, lock itself to the wall, and proceed to fire balls that would miss their target for the rest of the round. The location at which it would anchor itself was just at the threshold of its being able to trigger the ball dispenser at all; in one round it was not even able to do so, and spent the bulk of the round in futile attempts to strike the panel that would dispense the balls.

There is a short coda to this story. Beginning with the earlier *Robo-Puck* contest, we ran rematch competitions at the Boston Computer Museum each year, taking place several months after the date of the MIT contest. Stan rebuilt his robot from the ground up for the *Robo-Cup* rematch, this time using a strategy based on feedback from the playing field features rather than from shaft encoders. His efforts were rewarded: Although Stan's robot did not win the overall competition, it did win one round—Stan's first competitive victory in 2 years of robot building. In rebuilding his robot with the design principle of reacting directly with environmental features, Stan achieved success.

ROBOTIC CONTROL

The data for the issues discussed in this section are taken primarily from the students' work in the *Robo-Pong* contest, which took place in 1991, and the *Robo-Cup* contest, which took place in 1992. As mentioned, the task in the *Robo-Pong* contest was to transport ping-pong balls onto the other robot's side of a rectangular playing field. The field was inclined so that once balls were pushed over a center plateau, they would roll onto the opponent's side.

In the *Robo-Cup* contest, robots were required to draw balls from a vertically mounted ball dispenser, and then transport the balls into a soccer-like goal. The goal was divided horizontally into two halves; a ball delivered into the upper half of a goal would score three points, whereas a ball delivered into the lower half would score two points. (This point differential was created to encourage the design of robots that placed or fired balls into the upper portion of the goal rather than roll them into the lower portion.)

The Omniscient Robot Fallacy

Students' beliefs in how a robotic system should be understood and controlled were revealed by their approach to the central task of developing their robot's strategy. Some students approached the design of the robot strategy from what might be called an egocentric perspective, as if they were thinking, "What would I do if I were the robot?" These students imagined themselves at the helm of their robot, driving it around the table and performing tasks. This approach led to ideas such as the ones in the following narrative:

> Our strategy at present seems fairly well developed. First, [our robot] will imme-diately locate the other robot, roll over to it while lowering the forklift, and try to flip the other robot over. If it can knock it over, or even over the playing field wall, [our] robot has essentially won, as it can now freely place balls in the goal without interference. If this attempt fails after ten seconds or so, our robot will disengage, roll over to the ball dispenser, park, and get balls and shoot them at our goal with a cannon mechanism. Should the cannon prove unreliable, we may have to collect balls and deliver them manually, but having a cannon would be much more nifty, and would avoid a lot of line- or wall-following difficulty. (Martin, 1994, p. 127)

It is apparent in this discussion that the student did not think through, at a mechanistic level, the question of how the robot might actually perform these tasks; he imagined that it was simply a question of navigation as one might drive a car. Such students used their human senses and mental faculties for thinking about the robot control problem. The difficulty arose because robot sensors are extremely primitive, and robots do not have a bird's-eye view of their situation.

Many students initially generated fantastic ideas about what sorts of activities their robot might be able to perform. Here is another student's ideas about how to solve problems for a contest:

> I played around with a structure that was to be the "Goal Emulation Unit," which was an idea of mine. We had decided it would be a neat strategy to have something on our robot that looked like a goal, so that it could stand in front of the opponent's goal, and hopefully the opponent would place its balls into our robot's unit. . . . We had decided in the beginning that we wanted a fast robot. I thought it might be neat to chase after our opponent as soon as the round started and either steal his ball (assuming that it goes to the dispenser first) by pushing him out of the way, or having some sort of long arm that reached above the other robot to get the ball. (Martin, 1994, p. 127)

Written at the end of the second week of the project, this and the previous scenario represents the ideas of students who had difficulty imagining what sort of information the robot would be working with, and hence what sort of strategies or algorithms would yield realistic performance results.

Quite a large number of students initially generated ideas like these. If an idea required a complex mechanical structure, such as the "goal emulation unit" described in the previous passage, students discarded their ideas as soon as they were unable to build the mechanisms required to accomplish them (which was typically early in the project). If the complexity resided in the software design, however, many students continued to imagine their robot to be capable, in principle, of very sophisticated behaviors—until they attempted to implement those behaviors in actual code. For example, in the following comment, a student believed his robot to be all but completed, even though he had not begun to write its control program:

> As my team's robot stands now, it is 99% near completion. Only a few structural changes (might) have to be made and one or two sensors have to be attached; otherwise all that is left to do is program the baby. (Martin, 1994, p. 128)

Evidently, this student was not including the programming task in his estimate of the robot's percentage of completion. This attitude is typical; not only do students consistently underestimate the time-consuming nature of the programming task, but until they attempt the programming task, they do not realize what sort of robot behaviors are feasible to implement.

Other students more readily acknowledge the unknown nature of the programming task. Most fall back on previously learned approaches for dealing with complexity, as one student explained:

> In addition to assembling part of the robot base, I have been working with Interactive C, writing some code but mostly pseudocode, and relying heavily on abstraction and wishful thinking. (Martin, 1994, p. 128)

With only one week left before the contest, this student had not gotten into the hard work of getting his robot to perform real behaviors. Although the design techniques of abstraction and the use of pseudocode are often quite valuable, this student and the many others like him used these techniques in the place of experimentation. This led them into trouble because they assumed that their approaches would work, when often the problems of robot programming were of a different nature than the programming familiar to them. Their abstractions then became a hindrance when they tried to get the robot to actually perform a task.

Other students were more cognizant of the practicalities of the issue, realizing from the start that they needed to get a firm grasp on their robot's potential capabilities. After describing a number of different strategic possibilities, one student wrote this statement after the first week of work:

However, [my teammates] and I realize that the only way to find out what strategy works best is to build hardware that is robust and is powerful enough to implement a lot of different strategies and then implement the actual strategies in software. Our immediate goal is to construct powerful hardware both electrical and mechanical and then write the software to control it and implement the different strategies. (Martin, 1994, p. 128)

This experimental approach to developing a robot's program was initially favored by fewer of the students, although all of the students in the project overcame their expectations that their robots would perform "omniscient" acts.

Understanding Sensing

Few participants in the class had prior experience working with electronic sensors. When they were first introduced to sensors, either through the lecture-style presentation or in the course notes, many students expected that sensors would provide clear and unambiguous information about the world. As one student explained:

We plan to build the sensors and motors first, so that I can start playing with the control software and writing subroutines so that we can abstract away the working of the sensors as much as possible. (Martin, 1994, p. 129)

This student spoke for many when he proposed the use of modular abstraction to deliver clean information about the robot's state to some higher level control program. However, there are many reasons why sensors do not work as straightforwardly as the students would like, including problems with noise and other failure modes. Students are then surprised when they attempt to program a functional behavior into their robots. As one explained:

I decided to write the wall-following function which was the example in the text. It turned out to be much more difficult than the text had led me to believe. First of all, I needed to figure out how much power went to the inside motor in a turn. This took more than a few hours to finally debug and figure out what kind of radius each power differential would give. Another thing I had to figure out was the thresholding and logic statements needed for two sensors, one at the front and one at the back. This thresholding problem took me more than a while to figure out, and in the process, I found errors in my logic statements. . . . This method has not proved anything, because in its first incarnation, the robot was low on batteries . . . [the] present program hasn't been tested yet, because . . . we took the robot apart to strengthen each subsection, as in the wheel assemblies, and the subframe to connect them. (Martin, 1994, p. 129)

In the end, this student concluded that the results of his tests were moot, since the robot had a low battery level when the tests were being done. Even though he did not solve the particular problem at hand, it is clear from his narrative that he learned a great deal about the nature of the problem situation.

Here is another account of sensor troubles written by a participant who began systematic sensor experiments before the "crunch time" of the end of the project (and hence had time to write about it):

> The sensors have plagued me with problems from the start. The photoresistor sensors work great and I think that we can rely on them for the polarized light sensors. However, I think that the polarized light filters are not very reliable in tests that we have been using. It seems that the photoresistor in the polarized light sensor can't tell the difference between facing the opposite goal and being far away from its own goal. I think the problem lies in ambient light reaching the photoresistor. I think the only way to solve this problem is better shielding, but I think that the ambient light problem is unsolvable unless the contest is [held] in a pitch black room.
>
> The reflector sensors seem to work all right, but when we try to shield them from ambient light, we get random reflectance and therefore detection when we aren't supposed to. The problem seems to be solved when we place the sensor inside my sweater which is very "bumpy" and keeps light from randomly reflecting off of things. We are going to try to fix this problem this week because our strategy really depends on them. (Martin, 1994, p. 130)

These two cases are unusual only in that the respective work took place early in the course of the design project. They are quite typical, however, of what nearly all of the students encountered when they engaged in the actual programming task. Students then discovered all sorts of interrelations and complexities that arose, aside from implementation issues, that made it difficult to abstract sensor data into clean information upon which control strategies could be based. They realized that sensor data were erratic, that there were dependencies on hard-to-quantify properties of the mechanical system, and that the ultimate reliability of the sensor data depended on how one solved the control problem. For example, here a student found that the solution to achieving a good edge-following behavior lay in accomplishing several changes:

> When we first tested the robot's ability to detect a green/white boundary, the robot had difficulties. After some software changes (by [my partner]) and mechanical changes by me of placing the sensors even closer to the ground and also placing shields around the sensors, we have no problems detecting the boundary. (Martin, 1994, p. 130)

When building their control algorithms, students had a tendency to establish hard-coded thresholds for interpreting the meaning of sensor data. In *Robo-Pong*, two sensor varieties were particularly problematic in this regard: motor current sensing, which determined if a robot's movement was impeded (causing its motors to stall and hence draw more current) and light sensing (for determining on which side of the playing table the robot was located).

The trouble with motor current sensing was that the numerical value indicating a stalled motor would change as a function of the voltage of the motor's battery. When the battery voltage fell, as the battery gradually discharged with use, the current sensor would return higher values—and students' programs would interpret the higher values as an indication of a stalled motor, even though it was not.

Several teams of students failed adequately to deal with this problem and created robots that acted as if they were stuck when, in fact, they were just driving uphill. This occurred because uphill driving would necessarily cause additional load on the motors, which the robots' programs would interpret as the case when the robots were indeed stuck. In the main contest performance, one robot in particular suffered an amusing yet incapacitating failure mode of this type. It would repeatedly drive forward, stop, and back up as its program interpreted the motor current sensors as indicating that the robot was stuck. The robot seemed to be battling an invisible enemy as it tried again and again to collect the balls in its trough, each time backing up after advancing a few steps.

Students in *Robo-Cup* were warned of this problem and some concluded that the motor current sensing was simply too unreliable to be a part of their design. As one student explained:

> I wrote servo-like routines to monitor the clamp's position, and attach or release it as required. The original plan was to use the motor force sensing to determine if the motor was stalled, and control its motion like that. The force sensing, it turns out, is very unreliable, so we chose to install a potentiometer [a rotational position sensor] on the axle instead, and use that to keep track of position. (Martin, 1994, p. 131)

This student performed an analysis that this sensor was too erratic to be trusted, but most did not discover the sensor's failure mode. Students simply did not anticipate the sensor's fundamental unreliability.

The light sensors used by students in *Robo-Pong* to detect on which side of the playing field the robot was located were problematic in that they relied on room lighting to illuminate the table playing surface. Hence the values registered by sensors—of the amount light reflecting off of the playing surface—were dependent on the amount of ambient light in the room.

We as organizers were aware of this situation when we designed the contest and chose sensors for the robot-building kits, but we underestimated the impact on students' robots that resulted from changing the light levels for the contest performance. Anticipating that the lighting conditions would be different on the eve of the contest than they were in the development laboratory (since we intended to use camera lights), we had informed students that they should either shield their sensors from ambient light and provide a local source of illumination (e.g., a light-emitting diode or flashlight bulb), or write calibration software that would take into account the level of ambient lighting.

However, we failed to provide a readily accessible way for students to try different lighting conditions during robot development, and the camera lights we used were particularly harsh, causing wide fluctuations in light levels even from one side of the table to the other. It was an unfortunate situation because a number of otherwise competent robots became unreliable in the face of the extreme lighting conditions.

Even after making changes to ameliorate the problem in the subsequent contest year, students continued to have similar difficulties dealing with the sensor calibration issue.[3] Its implications were underestimated, and the concept seemed unfamiliar to them.

Models of Control

The overall strategies that students used to control their robots lay in a spectrum between two categories, which I shall call *reactive* strategies and *algorithmic* strategies. In addition, each of these strategies is built from two lower-level methods, *negative feedback* and *open-loop* approaches. Analysis of the various approaches that students took toward implementing an overall strategy to control their robots revealed interesting biases, as was the case in the analysis of students' approaches to understanding and deploying sensors.

These descriptions that categorize the students' robots were created in an analysis after the fact of the students' work on them; students were not aware of these categories during the course of their projects. I believe that students would recognize these distinctions, however, if asked.

The Higher Level: Algorithmic and Reactive Control.   The issue of control manifested itself in at least two aspects of the Robot Design Project: in the development of the robot's higher-level strategy from a conceptual standpoint, and in the actual programming of that strategy into the machine through the process of writing computer code. In the conceptual area, the *algorithmic* control method is dominant by far over the *reactive*.

The *algorithmic method* is characterized by a program that dictates a series of actions to be taken. (This is in contrast to the reactive approach, discussed later, in which a program chooses a path of action based on situated sensory input.)

---

[3]This situation led us to propose to a number of changes in the next year, *Robo-Cup*. First, we provided a light sensor that incorporated its own light transmitter, so that it would be substantially easier for students to deploy light sensors that were well-shielded from ambient light. Second, we incorporated a diffuse lighting fixture into the contest playing field itself, so that lighting conditions would not change drastically from development to performance situations. Also, we modified the programming environment to make it easier for students to construct sensor calibration routines: We made it possible for calibration settings to be "remembered" throughout multiple performance runs.

For example, here is an algorithmic main program loop from a student's solution to *Robo-Pong*.[4]

```
main()
{
    start_machine();   /*starts the machine up when*/
                       /*the light is on*/
    rotate_down();
    grab_balls();      /*go into our grab balls routine*/
    sleep(2.0);        /*wait two seconds*/
    other_side();
    finish();          /*block other machine or */
                       /*knock more balls over?*/

}
```

The code waits for the starting lamp to turn on (start_machine), then executes a routine to turn the robot downward (rotate_down), executes a routine to sweep across the ball trough (grab_balls), waits for two seconds, and then drives to the other robot's side of the table (other_side). This program solves the *Robo-Pong* contest by executing a specific series of actions.

Here is another example of the same approach, albeit slightly more complex, also for solving *Robo-Pong*. The names that the student has given to the sub-routines of his program are fairly self-explanatory of the action each subroutine performs:

```
game()
{
    start();
    Turn_to_Uphill();
    Go_Up_and_Orient_Plateau();
    DoorOpen();
    WalkPlateau();
    DoorClose();
    JiggleLeft();
    DoorOpen();
    FollowRightWall();
    DoorClose();
    JiggleLeft();
    DoorOpen();
    FollowRightWall();
    DoorClose();
    JiggleLeft();
    FollowRightWall();
```

---

[4]In this example and the other code samples presented in this chapter, the code comments are the students' original work.

```
AllOff();
}
```

Code written using the same algorithmic method can be found for *Robo-Cup* robots. Here is an example of such a main routine:

```
starting_routine()
  {
    /* drive forward full speed */
    drive(7);

    /* wait until sense edge */
    while(abs(ana(reflectance0)-white0)<40) {}

    /* drive a little further */
    sleep(distance(2.0));
    alloff();

    /* turn a little */
    pivot_on(7);
    msleep(80L);
    pivot_off();

    /* drive until front bumper triggers */
    while(!(digital(front_bumper)))
    drive(7);msleep(20L);
    drive(0);

    collect_balls(3);
    goto_goal();
    goto_button();

    collect_balls(3);
    goto_goal();
    goto_button();

    catch_ball();
    goto_goal();
    goto_button();
    return;
  }
```

As illustrated, the algorithmic control methodology consists of a list of instructions to be followed in order to accomplish the intended task. Each instruction may consist of a set of subactions, but the overall principle is to decompose the task into a sequence of activities to be followed, much like one might construct an algorithm to sort items in an array or compute a statistical quantity.

The trouble with the algorithmic approach is that there is no recovery path if things do not proceed according to the plan. Not only is there no way to recover from unexpected circumstances, but there simply is no provision for detecting that something out of the ordinary has occurred. These solutions have a problem reminiscent of comical factory scenes in which the machinery continues to plug away at an assembly process that has gone completely awry.

Students often deceive themselves as to the reliability of their algorithmic solutions. Suppose each component of an algorithmic solution has a 90% likelihood of working properly on any given occasion. One might think that the overall solution would have a similarly high probability, but this is not the case, because the probabilities multiply together with the overall result decreasing in likelihood with each step. If the algorithm has six independent steps, then the overall probability of proper functioning is only 53% (0.9 raised to the sixth power is approximately 0.53)—not nearly as good as the 90% chance that each individual step has of working properly. During testing, an algorithmic solution might require a gentle prod or correction here and there, and students do not realize that their machine actually needs this sort of help a significant portion of the time.

The *reactive methodology*, on the other hand, is characterized by actions that are triggered through constant reevaluations of external conditions (i.e., sensor readings) or internal conditions (i.e., program execution status). Although the algorithmic method does make use of external stimuli, the reactive method is more *driven* by this data, rather than by using it as part of a predetermined activity sequence.

There were no purely reactive robots in any of the contests; instead, some students combined elements of a reactive strategy into an overall algorithmic framework. An example is the robot *Crazy Train*, which was the champion of the *Robo-Pong* contest. The robot was a collector-style machine that scooped balls into its body.

Crazy Train worked as follows. As the round began, it took a reading from its inclination sensors to determine its initial bearing. It if determined that it was pointed toward the top of the hill, it would drive forward until it crossed the center plateau; in the process, it was likely to knock a center ball onto the opponent's territory (thus gaining an early advantage—insurance in case something went wrong later in the round). If not aimed uphill, or if it had completed the initial upward movement, *Crazy Train* would drive to its own ball trough and collect balls into its body. After making one sweep of the trough, it would drive onto its opponent's side of the table, delivering the balls it was carrying onto the opponent's side. In addition, when 10 seconds remained in the round, *Crazy Train* checked to see on which side of the table it presently stood. If for some reason it was still on its own side of the table, it would execute a "panic" routine, attempting to drive onto the opponent's side before the round ended.

There are two aspects of *Crazy Train's* program that characterize the reactive method. Firstly, *Crazy Train* had an unusual response to sensing its orientation at the start of each round. Depending on the orientation, the robot chose either to immediately knock a ball over the top—a potentially risky maneuver since the robot might get "lost" or entangled with the opponent—or the safer maneuver of traveling to its trough to collect balls. It chose to go for the early lead by knocking over a center ball only if it was an efficient maneuver: the case when the robot was already aimed toward the center plateau. In this fashion *Crazy Train* reacted to an external condition and chose an appropriate response.

The other reactive feature of *Crazy Train's* program was its panic behavior when the contest round was about to end. Here the main program, albeit an algorithmic one, was interrupted by another behavior which was triggered by a change in internal condition—a timer keeping track of remaining contest time. If necessary, the panic behavior attempts to drive onto the opponent's side. (If the sensor registers that the robot is already on the opponent's side, which should be the case if the algorithmic task has been completed successfully, then no additional action is needed.) The students who created *Crazy Train* implemented the panic behavior by exploiting Interactive C's multitasking capability. Their program had both the algorithmic behavior and the panic behavior as independent program tasks; at the appropriate time, the algorithmic task was terminated and the panic task was initiated. (A third program task was used to coordinate this activity.)

Crazy Train is perhaps the most dramatic example showing the usefulness of reactive program strategy, and, not too surprisingly, it was an overall contest winner. Its success can be attributed to a combination of its reliable and effective ball-gathering algorithmic strategy bolstered by useful reactive behaviors. There were a few game rounds in which the algorithmic strategy failed, but the reactive behaviors delivered a winning performance. *Crazy Train* also is representative of the extent to which reactive behaviors were used at all; that is, where reactive methods were used, they were simplistic, though sometimes effective, responses to a limited number of potential situations.

The Lower Level: Negative Feedback and Open-Loop Methods. The issue of reactive versus algorithmic control as it applies to the macro level of overall robot strategy has an analog at the micro level (the mechanism by which the strategy is actually carried out). The micro level consists of the low-level methods for driving the robot's motors to accomplish an intended action.

For example, the macro tasks of collecting and delivering balls in both *Robo-Pong* and *Robo-Cup* can be decomposed into micro- or sub-tasks such as climbing uphill or downhill, driving along the retaining wall of the playing field, or driving along a light-dark boundary painted on the playing field floor. The contests were specifically designed to be decomposable into subtasks such as these—ones that are feasible to be solved with the technology provided in the robot kit.

I distinguish two low-level control methods that were implemented in the robots: *negative feedback* and *open-loop control*. Most robots used a mixture of these two methods rather than one or the other exclusively.

In the negative feedback method, a robot responds to a situation with a small corrective action intended to reduce the difference between the current state and a goal state. This small maneuver is repeated; through repetitive application, the robot achieves the overall action desired by its designer. For example, a robot might follow along the edge of a wall with the use of a sensor that measures the distance to the wall, repeatedly turning to move toward the wall if it senses that it is too far away, or turning to move away from the wall if it is too close.

In the open-loop method, the robot responds to a situation with a single action that the designers presume will bring it to a new state with respect to its surroundings. A typical action would be a predetermined, timed motor movement, usually lasting one or more seconds. For example, the robot might turn its motors on for a period of two seconds (this value would be experimentally determined) in order to pivot 90° and thereby negotiate out of a corner.

Few of the robots' activities can be considered open loop in the formal sense because the open-loop-like maneuvers are part of a larger robot strategy that generally involves sensor input and hence is not truly open loop. However, if a robot takes an action that does not accomplish the desired result, and the control algorithm cannot recover gracefully from this circumstance (nor make any effort to detect it), the action is likely to be representative of open-loop thinking.

An example will help make these ideas more clear. *Groucho*, a *Robo-Pong* robot, employed the following strategy. It would drive into its trough at the beginning of the round and then execute a series of motions that would make it drive in a rectangular pattern, scooping balls from its trough and depositing them onto the opponent's territory. *Groucho* used an overall algorithmic strategy, repetitively performing the sequence of these steps, as illustrated in Fig. 14.1.

In implementing this strategy, however, the students who built *Groucho* used mixed techniques of feedback loops and open-loop control. At points 2 and 7, when *Groucho* is negotiating corners, they used feedback from the playing field walls to make it do so: The robot would hit the wall, back up, make a small rotation, drive forward, hit the wall, and try again. Typically the robot would strike the wall three to five times until it rotated sufficiently.

At points 3 and 5, however, the robot executed timed movements to accomplish the rotations. The designers had experimentally determined how great a rotational movement, measured in fractions of a second, would be required to perform the desired turn, and then hard-coded these timing constants into their program structure.

The question arises as to why the designers of this particular robot chose to implement a feedback-controlled turn during some points of their robot's path and open-loop-controlled turns at others. There is a clue to the explanation contained in the source code written for the robot. As mentioned, in the trough

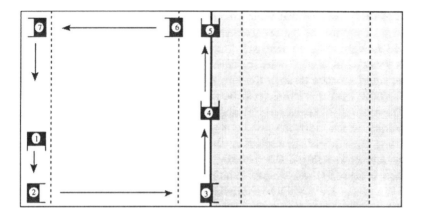

1. Robot drives along trough, scooping balls into its grasp.

2. Robot negotiates corner and turns uphill.

3. Robot stops at dividing edge, allowing balls to fall onto opponent's side.

4. Robot drives along edge to opposite side of the table.

5. Robot hits opposite side; turns to drive downhill.

6. Robot drives downhill.

7. Robot hits bottom wall and negotiates corner; continues pattern in step 1.

FIG. 14.1.   *Groucho's* strategy as played in *Robo-Pong* contest.

area, the students used feedback from touch contact to negotiate turns, but in the plateau area, they used timed turns rather than feedback from the center dividing line. It turns out, however, that the students attempted to base the plateau turns on feedback from the dividing line, but at some point commented out the code to do this, replacing it with a simple timed turn. Here is the relevant code excerpt from their program. The line bracketed with "/ *" and "* /" is the one that the students commented out; the subsequent line `left(100,1.);` implements the timed turn that replaced it.

```
printf("Crossed the border.}");
beep();beep();
time=seconds()+1.1;
/* while ((left_reflectance!=side)&&(seconds()<time))
  {bk(0);bk(1);fd(2);fd(3);} */
left(100,1.);
ao();
printf("On the Line . . . }");
```

It can be presumed that some kind of difficulty or unreliability was encountered with the use of the reflectance sensor to determine when the robot had turned enough, so the students substituted the open-loop turn movement instead. This robot's mechanics were sufficiently well-designed and reliable for the robot's performance through the turn to remain consistent through the contest performance, but this is not typically the case.

The example of *Groucho* brings out a tension between the negative feedback technique, which ultimately can be more reliable, and the open-loop technique, which is often quicker to implement and can result in faster performances but is more subject to failures. Often students consider the open-loop methods more reliable because they are simpler to implement and seem to work adequately, but many students are unaware of problems that would result from hard-coding timing constants into their movement programs. In the following two excerpts, students commented explicitly on this matter:

> We decided to simplify our strategy, making our robot more reliable and easier to build. We now plan to have our robot aimed at the dispenser at the outset of the contest. The robot will then move forward until it senses that it has crossed the white/green boundary, using an infrared reflectance sensor. The robot will then turn and press the button repeatedly, catching and shooting each ball into the net. *This strategy involves much open loop control, but greatly simplifies our control system,* making the robot more reliable. (Emphasis added.)

> I discussed with my teammates that if we're going to be a fast machine, then we'll have to implement a lot of open-loop [controls] interleaved with closed-loop feedback. Otherwise if we used mostly closed-loop [methods] to "feel" our way around the playing field, we'd be as slow as our opponents. (Martin, 1994, p. 141)

These students were conscious of the trade-offs involved, but others were not. Many students used open-loop movements based on timed actions; robots built from these constructs faced problems from a number of sources. Most important was the level of charge in the battery powering the motors. Because the durations of the open-loop movements were experimentally determined, they were highly dependent upon battery performance.

The robots were powered with lead acid rechargeable batteries, which have a characteristic discharge curve as shown in Fig. 14.2. As the battery is used, its voltage (which determines the amount of power delivered to the motors) gradually decreases. Often this deterioration was not immediately noticeable, so students were not necessarily aware of the situation as they were developing their programs. Finally, the battery would reach a point, the end of its usable life, when the voltage would drop off rapidly and the battery would be obviously "dead." However, during the usable period there would be a significant difference between the initial voltage and final voltage levels. (Some other types of batteries, such as nickel cadmium, have discharge curves in which the voltage level remains nearly constant for the bulk of the batteries' usage, until the level drops off

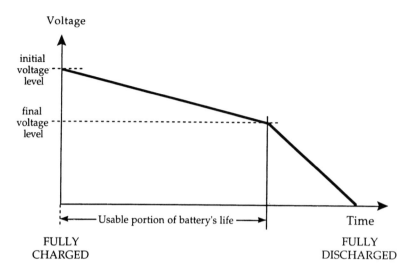

FIG. 14.2.   Idealized lead-acid cell discharge curve.

sharply, rendering the battery suddenly useless. Use of these batteries would have made the discharge effect less pronounced.)

Most students did not realize that the algorithms they had created to solve the contest were dependent upon battery level until they swapped a partially discharged battery for a fully charged one and discovered that their program no longer worked correctly. As mentioned earlier, this realization often did not occur until quite late in the robot's development—when there were only a few days or even hours left before the contest—and hence it was too late to make a substantive change in the robot's strategy (that is, substituting feedback-based movements for open-loop ones). Students would deal with the situation by doing final program development (i.e., tweaking of timing constants) with batteries as fully charged as possible.

The degree to which this problem would manifest itself in the students' designs was largely a function of the gear ratio (that is, ratio between motor rotational speed and final drive-wheel rotational speed) used in the robots' mechanics. If the gear ratio was such that the motor was driven in a "comfortable" portion of its power range, a slight change in battery level would not have a drastic effect on the performance of the motor. On the other hand, if the gear ratio caused a high amount of drag on the motor, slight changes in battery level would have a large effect on motor performance.

We as organizers only recognized this situation in retrospect, and hence were as confused as the students as to why some robots seemed to have little difficulty in performing reliably, at least in this regard, whereas others were quite troublesome. We were more savvy of these control issues when running *Robo-Cup* than we had been with *Robo-Pong*. In an attempt to encourage students to use feedback-based control rather than open-loop control, I wrote an additional chapter of the course notes for the *Robo-Cup* students that explained the differences and trade-offs between open-loop and feedback-based control. I also discussed the need for calibration of sensor values to local conditions.

A number of students became fixated on using feedback control in surprising ways, however, spending a considerable portion of development time creating a feedback controller to make their robot able to drive in a straight line. Here is how one student explained his system:

> The robot is now able to drive in a straight line thanks to its optical shaft encoders. The software continually samples both left and right sensors and adjusts the exact power level to the motors to compensate for any fluctuations in the motion of the robot. The algorithm itself is a combination of differential analysis and Newton's method, along with an "adjustable window" of correction. Simply stated, analyzing differentials gives a reasonable algorithm for adjusting the power levels of the motors, and the adjustable window minimizes excessive wobbling. This algorithm gives us as much accuracy as the resolution of the shaft encoders permits, while keeping wobbling reasonably low. (Martin, 1994, p. 143)

The ability to drive perfectly straight, however, often does little to help a robot in its overall ability to solve the contest task. Although the activity of driving straight is based on negative feedback control, a strategy that employs this ability in a central way should be considered open-loop at the next higher level, as the robot would be performing a task with little feedback from the crucial environmental features! Therefore, these students' belief that they were using the preferable feedback control was misguided.

Taken as a whole, the collection of biases revealed in students' thinking suggests important misconceptions and misunderstandings about what are effective ways to build reliable real-world systems.

ANALYSIS AND CONCLUSIONS

The examples in this chapter illustrate that students who participate in the robot design course have a variety of preconceptions about systems and control. These ideas are formed by experiences in the traditional academic curriculum and warrant examination specifically because they are not particularly effective when applied to the robot design task.

In the section entitled *Robotic Control*, we saw how many students have trouble seeing the contest task from a robot-centric perspective, and instead imagine the task from their own omniscient perspective. This naiveté is tempered when they try to put their ideas into being and realize that the robot's point of view is very different from their own.

With few exceptions, all of the robots created for *Robo-Pong* and *Robo-Cup* used fundamentally algorithmic solutions. This fact is not surprising; there are at least two factors that would strongly encourage the formulation of algorithmic solutions. One of these is the nature of the contests themselves, which require a series of activities to take place in a short period of time. A robot that wandered about as it waited to be guided into action by sensory stimuli would not be efficient; the typical winning robot employs a fast, reliable, and effective algorithmic strategy. If they are not interfered with, these robots successfully perform their tasks on nearly every run.

The other factor encouraging algorithmic solutions is the Interactive C programming language, which is fundamentally procedural. Although it is a general-purpose programming language and can in principle support the construction of a variety of control methodologies, as a procedural language it encourages students to create procedural control structures. Other language approaches, such as rule-based languages or control architectures like Brooks' *subsumption language* (Brooks, 1986), would facilitate reactive control strategies.

One feature of Interactive C, however, did encourage reactive control: the multitasking capability. Indeed, this feature was used by students to implement reactive controls, as was discussed in the *Crazy Train* robot design. This evidence points to the effect that the programming language has on students' control ideas; extensions or revisions of the programming language could encourage students to think differently about control.

Although it is then not unexpected that students create largely algorithmic robots, what remains surprising is how poorly these systems perform with respect to the students' own expectations. Nearly all of the students who participate in the class are genuinely surprised by the difficulty of getting their robot to work reliably. They blame performance problems on failures of particular components of their systems rather than reevaluating their overall approach to control.

The students' control ideas come from those presented in their university courses. At MIT, examples are found in the introductory computer science course, *Structure and Interpretation of Computer Programs* (course number 6.001), and the *Software Engineering Laboratory* course (course number 6.170). Among the central ideas developed in 6.001 is the concept of *abstraction*: that by encapsulating messy implementation detail into conceptual "black boxes," complex systems can be built from components with relatively clear functionality. Abstraction is a way of managing complexity—a way of keeping minutia in check and creating large systems with clearly understood parts. As stated in the text of the course (Abelson & Sussman, 1985):

> In our study of program design, we have seen that expert programmers control the complexity of their designs by using the same general techniques used by designers of all complex systems. They combine primitive elements to form compound objects, they abstract compound objects to form higher-level building blocks, and they

preserve modularity by adopting appropriate large-scale views of system structure. (p. 293)

The software engineering course expands and fleshes out this principle, teaching programming techniques such as procedural and data abstraction through extended programming projects. The course makes a point of teaching how to write programs in a modular fashion, test code modules independently, and then integrate them into a complete system. Typical final projects are the design and implementation of a text editor or a computerized Othello game.

Although these projects are ideal for the goals of the course—teaching abstraction and modularity in the architecture of large computer programs—they promulgate the mindset that large systems are made from parts that are completely understandable and formally specifiable. In both of these examples, as in many others, the computer program consists of precisely formalizable data structures and algorithms that operate upon this known data to generate known results. Indeed, a large portion of the software engineering course is dedicated to methodology of testing with the intent of proving that a given program module will yield correct results when presented with data that satisfies particular conditions.

Much of the engineering curriculum is based on modern system theory: mathematical methods for understanding algorithms and systems that take particular inputs and yield particular outputs. Dynamical systems analysis, in which system state is represented by a state vector, and signal-processing theory based on transfer functions are leading examples. These domains of theory deal with systems that are perfectly represented in the mathematical models that students learn to manipulate.

Of course the value of such engineering knowledge is precisely that it allows us to construct systems that are indeed controlled to extreme degrees of precision. The great engineering successes are based on our ability to understand, model, analyze, and precisely control the world around us. However, not all large systems are controllable by these means. As discussed by Ferguson (1992), recent work on chaotic systems has challenged the assumptions of those working on automated traffic control systems:

> For engineers, a central discovery in the formal study of chaos is that a tiny change in the initial conditions of a dynamic system can result in a major unexpected departure from the calculated final conditions. It was long believed that a highly complex system, such as all automobile traffic in the United States, is in principle fully predictable and thus controllable. "Chaos" has proved this belief wrong. The idea that roads will be safe only when all cars are guided automatically by a control system is a typical but dangerous conceit of engineers who believe that full control of the physical world is possible. (p. 172)

Students often believe that sensors and the control problem in general are simple enough to be solved in a closed-form manner. Some have attempted to build environments for simulating the performance of their robot as if it were a character in a videogame system. This raises the issue of the role of simulation in understanding and representing complex systems. For some domains (e.g., VLSI design) simulation is a powerful and accurate technique for developing and testing complex systems. For others (e.g., structural engineering), difficult issues of determining the applicability of a simulated model to the actual artifact affect the reliability of the simulation in profound ways. An additional complicating factor is that many simulation packages are developed by theoretical rather than practicing engineers, raising the question that the practicing engineer must trust the output of the simulation without necessarily knowing the founding assumptions upon which it is based. Henry Petroski (1992) quoted a Canadian structural engineer on this point:

> Because structural analysis and detailing programs are complex, the profession as a whole will use programs written by a few. These few will come from the ranks of the structural "analysts" . . . and not from the structural "designers." Generally speaking, it is difficult to envision a mechanism for ensuring that the products of such a person will display the experience and intuition of a competent designer. (p. 201)

The reliance on simulation as an engineering technique is a consequence of the assumption that complete control of the physical world can be attained. Although simulations can reveal problems before they develop into serious engineering failures, overreliance on the trustworthiness of simulations can lead to disasters. Contemporary examples of failures due to inadequacies in simulation abound; here are two striking ones from Peter Neumann's column in the *Communications of the Association for Computing Machinery* periodical (Neumann, 1993):

> On April 1, 1991, a Titan 4 upgraded rocket booster (SRB) blew up on the test-stand at Edwards Air Force Base. The program director noted that extensive 3-D computer simulations of the motor's firing dynamics did not reveal subtle factors that apparently contributed to failure. He added that full-scale testing was essential precisely because computer analyses cannot accurately predict all nuances of the rocket motor dynamics. (See *Aviation Week*, May 27, 1991, and Henry Spencer, 1991, *Software Engineering Notes, 16*[4], 14–15.)
>
> The collapse of the Hartford Civic Center Coliseum 2.4-acre roof under heavy ice and snow on January 18, 1978 apparently resulted from the wrong model being selected for beam connection in the simulation program. *After* the collapse, the program was rerun with the correct model—and the results were precisely what occurred. (Noted by Richard S. D'Ippolito in *SEN 11*, 5, Oct. 1986, p. 10.)

If engineering students gain early hands-on experience with the complexity of electrical, mechanical, structural, and software systems, they will have more respect for the sorts of pitfalls that can be expected later when working on real projects, as in the case of the Civic Center cited earlier. With project experience like that acquired in the robot design course, students have the chance to learn the limitations of traditional control and analysis and gain the experience that is needed to be an engineer with a mindset grounded in reality.

ACKNOWLEDGMENTS

This chapter is based on a chapter of my recently completed doctoral dissertation, "Circuits to Control: Learning Engineering by Designing LEGO Robots." My thesis advisor, Edith Ackermann, and the members of my doctoral committee, Seymour Papert, Donald Schön, and Pattie Maes, provided much-welcomed advice, counterpoint, and support during the process of developing these ideas. I collaborated closely with Randy Sargent and Pankaj Oberoi when developing the MIT 6.270 LEGO Robot Design Competition. Mitchel Resnick, Yasmin Kafai, and Michele Evard provided helpful and timely feedback on earlier drafts of this chapter. The work described in the chapter was done at the MIT Media Laboratory and was supported by grants from the National Science Foundation (Grant 9153719-MDR), the LEGO Group, and Nintendo Inc. The ideas presented herein do not necessarily represent the views of these funding agencies.

REFERENCES

Abelson, H. & Sussman, G. J. (1985). *Structure and interpretation of computer programs.* Cambridge, MA: MIT Press.
Brooks, R. A. (1986). A robust layered control system for a mobile robot. *IEEE Journal of Robotics and Automation, RA-2*(1), 14–23.
Ferguson, E. S. (1992). *Engineering and the mind's eye.* Cambridge, MA: MIT Press.
Martin, F. G. (1994). *Circuits to control: Learning engineering by designing LEGO robots.* Unpublished doctoral dissertation, MIT Media Lab, Cambridge, MA.
Neumann, P. G. (1993). Inside risks: Modeling and simulation. *Communications of the ACM, 36*(4), 124.
Papert, S. (1986). *Constructionism: A new opportunity for elementary science education.* (Proposal to the National Science Foundation.) Cambridge, MA: MIT Media Laboratory.
Petroski, H. (1992). *To engineer is human: The role of failure in successful design.* New York: Vintage Books.

Author Index

Subject Index

Lightning Source UK Ltd.
Milton Keynes UK
27 October 2010

161971UK00001B/116/P